**REALITY SHOCK**

*why nurses leave nursing*

# REALITY SHOCK
## *why nurses leave nursing*

**MARLENE KRAMER, R.N., Ph.D.**

Professor, School of Nursing,
University of California,
San Francisco Medical Center,
San Francisco, California

Illustrated

## THE C. V. MOSBY COMPANY

SAINT LOUIS   1974

**Library of Congress Cataloging in Publication Data**

Kramer, Marlene.
   Reality shock.

    1. Nurses and nursing. 2. Nursing as a profession.
I. Title. [DNLM: 1. Conflict (Psychology).
2. Nursing. 3. Social adjustment. WY87 K89r 1974]
RT42.K7  610.73′0692    73-22243
ISBN 0-8016-2741-9

W/M/M  9  8  7

To HELEN NAHM and to the nurses
in the medical center and class samples
*without their support and cooperation,
this study and book would not have
become a reality.*

# PREFACE

Probable-Possible, my black hen,
She lays eggs in the Relative When
She doesn't lay eggs in the Positive Now
Because she's unable to postulate How.

WINSOR, 1956

Many young graduate nurses of today, upon beginning their first work experience, are confronted with the same kind of dilemma as the black hen. Prepared by teachers who are visionary, the neophyte nurse often possesses some skills and knowledge that at present are unmarketable, and lacks skills and knowledge needed to function in today's health care scene. As is often heard, "new graduates can analyze and synthesize, but can't catheterize."

Preparing for the future by equipping the nurses of tomorrow with visions of how things can and should be, and with the prerequisite skills to function autonomously and collaboratively with others in the health care system, is not wrong or misguided. The Relative When will be upon us before the ink on this page is dry. Inability to function in the Positive Now will constitute a problem for awhile, but before long the sheer demands of the work scene correct those deficiencies. No, the real problem is the lack of ability and knowledge to postulate How. The new graduate of today, steeped in the visions and skills of the future, must be taught to postulate how to make those visions a reality.

That is what this book is all about. It is a report of eight years of study and research into the problem of "reality shock" as man-

ifested and dealt with by young graduate nurses, and a test of the effectiveness of one program designed to do something about it.

As a scientist writing the story of what happens to new graduate nurses upon employment and delineating the underlying theory based upon many years of systematic observation and research, I had a strong desire to report in detail peripheral issues related to the theory, analytical procedures, and statistical data and computations. Doing this, however, would markedly decrease the readability and usefulness of the book for the general reader. For the reader who is interested in more detail, the above information, including lists of articles used in the Anticipatory Socialization program, is available from me upon request.

The Anticipatory Socialization program, the experiment in this study, is designed to acquaint (or shock) nursing students with the realities of the Positive Now; to share with them the ways in which selected nurse practitioners of today are postulating how to solve conflicts and make their visions of the future a reality. Through this means, it was anticipated that these neophyte nurses would be better able to function in the Positive Now without losing their vision and ability to function in the Relative When, and also without the numbing and shattering effects of reality shock.

Reality shock is a term used to describe the phenomenon and the specific shocklike reactions of new workers when they find themselves in a work situation for which they have spent several years preparing and for which they thought they were going to be prepared, and then suddenly find that they are not. The concept as used in this book will focus mainly on the discrepancy and the shocklike reactions that follow when the aspirant professional perceives that many professional ideals and values are not operational and go unrewarded in the work setting.

As a phenomenon, reality shock has several cousins. One that we are hearing more and more about is "culture shock," the shocked surprise and reactions to it when one discovers that his own culture is not necessarily the only or best way of organizing societal life and interacting with one's fellow men. The culture shock phenomenon has been particularly noted in anthropologists, missionaries, Peace Corps workers, Americans living abroad for any length of time, and to a lesser degree in tourists. "Acculturation shock" is another cousin, very closely related to culture shock. Acculturation refers to changes in the culture or cultural traits of groups or individuals as adaptation to a culture different from one's own takes place. This kind of shock has been seen most often in people who suddenly leave a controlled environment, wherein variant cultural patterns predominated, for active involvement in the dominant cultural scene. Examples of this are Indians who leave the reservations, Amish leaving a specific community, religious leaving the cloistered life, and inmates released after a long prison term.

Recently, Toffler has added to our understanding of social shock phenomena by describing the cause, signs, and symptoms of "future shock," a malady defined as the shattering stress and disorientation induced in individuals by subjecting them to too much change in too short a period of time. Modern men, but particularly those living in urban areas, are highly susceptible to future shock.

In general, all of these shocklike phenomena have two things in common. The dynamic of causation is some kind of discrepancy between cultures, between now and the future, or between what one was schooled for and what one is expected to do in the work world.

The signs and symptoms—or how the human organism responds to the perceived discrepancy—is another area of high similarity. If an individual is not equipped for the discrepancy, the impact produces various stressful emotional reactions—fear, anger, hate, self-pity, outrage, withdrawal—which often take control of one's behavior toward clients and co-workers. There are also areas of differences—specifically, the cause of the particular kind of shock, and whether or not the shock-prone individual is prepared to resolve the shock-producing conflict. These two factors are closely related because it is the cause that generates the possible avenues of solution—either prevention or at least reduction in severity.

The nature, signs and symptoms, and cause of reality shock, particularly as it is produced and fostered by the value and expectation discrepancy between the school and work settings, are presented in the early part of Chapter 1. A detailed look at the culprit constitutes the latter part of this chapter. In Chapter 2, the search is on for a way to do something about the problem. Is there a way of lessening it or helping new graduates deal with it more effectively? The other three of the four planks of the theoretical framework guiding this research (the first was professional-bureaucratic conflict theory presented in Chapter 1) are presented, along with their implications for guiding the development of the intervention and prevention program that is discussed in Chapter 3. Also contained in the third chapter is a series of composites describing the status and attitudinal and behavioral characteristics of four groups of graduate nurses practicing in work settings all over the United States.

Did the prevention program reduce reality shock? Did the nurses who had it hold their jobs longer? Did it effect more changes? The answers to these questions are detailed in Chapter 4. A further understanding of the process of adjustment that young nurse graduates go through in adapting to the working world is presented in Chapter 5 as an emerging theory of postgraduate professional socialization. A vivid and sensitive account of one young woman's "becoming" is presented as further illustration of the effects of reality shock and the various strategies and struggles used to resolve it.

Chapter 6 presents some additional insights into the process of reality shock, both from the perspective of the new graduate nurse and from the viewpoint of a socialization agent dealing with this tension-laden situation. Reporting on a trial of a reality shock program in an in-service setting, this presentation is both poignant and informative.

In the last chapter of the book, an attempt has been made to sort out and bring order and pattern to the problem of reality shock in young graduate nurses by posing the specific question: What can and should be done about it?

Different groups of nurses will be reading this book for different reasons, from different perspectives, and in different ways. Faculty in undergraduate and graduate programs in nursing, as well as students in graduate programs, hopefully will read the book with the idea of what they might possibly do about preventing reality shock or better equipping the new graduate to deal with it. Perhaps it will also be a stimulus to them to reexamine their own adjustment to the school-work conflict and determine whether their resolution was growth producing. It is to the faculty, but even more so to graduate students—the nursing leaders of tomorrow—that we must look for eventual solution and amelioration of the problem of reality shock. Unfortunately, these graduate students may be suffering most acutely from unresolved shock themselves. Perhaps an exposé and analysis of experiences, feelings, and perspectives of others that are closely akin to what they are feeling and perceiving will do much to help them work through the conflict in a growth-producing manner, rather than to withdraw or substitute teaching as a nonviable alternative.

This book may also be valuable to graduate students as a supplemental methodology reader. Throughout the course of this project, a variety of research methods, tools, and techniques were used—some correctly, others incorrectly. In the writing of this book, an attempt has been made to share with the reader the many decisions that must be made in the conduct of research. Perhaps in seeing the arbitrariness of some decisions and the consequences of others, the neophyte researcher may come to understand research as the exciting, fulfilling, but difficult venture that it is.

A major readership group is expected to be nursing students—probably at the senior level—and new graduate nurses. The book might well serve as a textbook for courses in leadership, change agent theory, and professional adjustments. There are many examples throughout the book of conflict situations reported by nurse practitioners. If these are worked through, individually or in groups, and then solutions shared, increased knowledge and understanding—the foundation upon which strategies of conflict resolution are built—of the possible wide range of alternatives should result. For new practitioners in the throes of reality shock, it is a big help to know that they are not alone. Hopefully, the book will provide insights that will assist them in working out satisfactory solutions to their own conflicts.

The last major readership group will be nurses in the work setting. This includes staff nurses, head nurses and supervisors, administrators, and in-service nurse educators, who are the formal and informal socialization agents in the work scene. Much of what can and should be done about reality shock is up to them, whether they graduated two or twenty-two years ago. Many have already encountered reality shock and dealt with it in their own way. For some, this adjustment was probably maladaptive and not growth producing. For those who have experienced the intense frustration of working with new graduates in the throes of reality shock—new graduates who find it difficult to stay longer than a few months in their first job—hopefully this book will offer insight into the source of their dilemmas and offer strategies for smoothing the transition from school to work. It may well come as close to being a textbook for in-service education as anything on the market today. It is suggested that such educators may wish to begin with Chapter 6, which describes a trial run of the reality shock program, and then look at the postgraduate socialization process as described by a group of young nurses in their diaries and extensively by one other nurse (Chapter 5).

Although the study reported in this book was done on baccalaureate students and nurses, in whom reality shock is most often observed, contacts and observations with students, nurses, nurse educators, and administrators all over the country have provided ample evidence that reality shock is widespread. It is found also in graduates of diploma and associate degree programs. Notice how frequently the designation Dip (meaning diploma) or ADN (meaning Associate Degree Nurse) follows the tape-recorded excerpts used to illustrate various points in this book. Reality shock differs in intensity rather than kind. The farther away a program gets from an apprenticeship system, and the more an educational program attempts to prepare nurses who can deal effectively with the knowledge and technological explosions now and in the future, the greater will be the likelihood of producing school-work conflict and reality shock. Conflict is not bad; it is stimulating and healthy. What is unhealthy is producing graduates who do not expect the conflict and who do not have strategies developed for handling it in a growth-producing manner.

The extensive research that forms the basis of this book would not have been possible without the support of two grants (NU00273 and NU00435) from the Division of Nursing, Bureau of Health Manpower, USPHS, Washington, D. C. I gratefully acknowledge this support. The tremendous cooperation of the many nurses who participated in this study, both as subjects and as validity testers, must also be acknowledged. They gave generously of their time and of themselves, exerting considerable effort to keep me informed of events and reactions to events, job changes, address changes, and so on, for more than four years. Two other people, Gerry Miller and Mary Bodamer, merit a warm note of appreciation for assisting with the monumental analytical and tabulative work.

**Marlene Kramer**

# CONTENTS

1 The seeds of discontent, 1

2 A search for a way out, 27

3 The anticipatory socialization program, 67

4 Effects of the anticipatory socialization program, 104

5 Postgraduation nurse socialization: an emergent theory, 137

6 Reality testing a reality shock program, 191
   PATRICIA BENNER

7 The end of the journey—or the beginning? 216

## Appendixes

A Summary of role value orientations, 234

B Comparison of various groups of nurses on Corwin Role Conception and Role Deprivation Scales, 236

C Data analysis tables, 238

D Multivariate analysis on operationalization of professional behavior, 245

## CHAPTER ONE

# THE SEEDS OF DISCONTENT

## TYPICAL SITUATIONS

The setting is a 20-bed postcardiac surgical ward of a large county hospital. It's the evening shift—about 4:30 P.M.—and you are alone because the one aide who works with you has gone to dinner. The day shift report indicates that the ward is fairly quiet and that most of the patients are status quo. All the patients on this ward are pre- or postcardiac surgery, many having been just recently transferred out of the cardiac ICU which is adjacent to the ward. You are in the process of making rounds to see all the patients. Halfway down the large open-ward is Mrs. Swape, a 52-year-old postpump patient who also works as one of the volunteers on the ward. She seems very sad and lonely, and you remember that the day nurse had remarked that Mrs. Swape had not been her usual cheerful self that day. You pause in your flurry of activity, approach Mrs. Swape, and gently cover her hand with yours. As she looks up at you, you think you detect tears welling up in her eyes. This is most unusual. During all of her past surgery, she has been very highly controlled: never crying or complaining, always saying "thank you" to the nurses, even when you had to do painful procedures like suctioning and turning her. You've been concerned about her and this "super" control.

Reflecting to yourself that maybe Mrs. Swape is ready to open up and talk, you gently pull the curtains around the bed and seat yourself on the edge. After a few minutes, Mrs. Swape begins to talk. She is in the middle of telling you how afraid she is—not about the operation and the surgery, but afraid the nurses on the ward won't like her anymore. It seems that a few years ago she had had surgery and had had a postsurgical psychosis that resulted in her really "flipping-out" for a few days: pulling our IV's, NG tubes, throwing things, and screaming at the nurse and everything. She remembered this after she came out of it and was so fearful that she might do it again with this surgery, and then the nurses wouldn't like her anymore or let her come back to work on the ward as a volunteer. Mrs. Swape is in the middle of telling you this. Her face is pinched and anxious and she looks as though she will "let go" any minute now.

Suddenly you hear the food cart clanging through the doors of the ward. At this hospital the trays do not come up from the kitchen prepared; there are just pots of food, and the staff has to serve it on plates, construct the special low-salt diets, etc. Furthermore, the cart has to be returned to the kitchen for use on the other floors. Most of your patients are fairly recent open-heart surgery patients. They need their food, particularly the potassium. If you stay with Mrs. Swape, there's no one there to serve them the food; if you don't serve them the food and return the cart, the supervisor will call or come to the ward, and you know from past experiences that she takes a dim view of this kind of "inefficiency." If you leave, even for a minute, your intuition and judgment tell you that the climate will be broken and Mrs. Swape will clam up again. (NG: BS/12[729]12/71)°

· · ·

You still have the same kinds of problems in public health. I'm a little freer because I'm in the home and I can do what I want when I want; but

°All interview excerpts in this book are coded and identified in the following manner. The first letters designate the kind of worker, that is, NG(new graduate):BS, Dip, or AD; Med Ctr:BS; LVN; Aide; Orderly. The set of numbers following the / refers to the number of months of employment if the worker was a new graduate. The series of numbers in [] is the code number of the individual, known only to the investigators. Following the [] is the month and year of the interview or diary data.

at the same time, the county sets priorities. Communicable diseases are high on the list; TB and VD followup also. A woman with a prenatal problem is very low on the list. When you get into a home and you find you really get to know the patient— no, person, not a patient—you find out where they are at, what's happening; and if you are sensitive you really want to do something about it. This woman had three young children already and was pregnant with the fourth. I was trying to get her into prenatal clinic. She really needed to come: she was beginning to fill with fluid, and I could tell from taking her pulse that her blood pressure was up. She'd missed a couple of appointments already because she couldn't get any transportation in. I said I'd see what I could do. You go back and you find out that this patient doesn't fit into the right classification. They don't have transportation services for those classified as prenatal. The poor woman just couldn't get transportation. Buses cost a lot and they live a long ways away. We have a driver at the Health Department who drives TB patients, so I thought I would get this driver to go out and pick up this prenatal woman. Oftentimes I would see the driver just sitting on the bench with nothing to do. I made all arrangements and filled out all the forms and went and talked to the community worker who drives patients back and forth; and she said. "Sorry, I can't do it; I can only transport [a particular classification of] patients." The driver was sitting there knitting, not doing a thing; but still she couldn't go out and pick up this woman. I explained that she really needs the transportation and "if you aren't busy"...."I'm sorry; they have to be in a certain category." I talked to everybody to see if I could get some help for this woman. The woman didn't wear the right label, so her need was just pushed aside and ignored. (NG:BS/12[729]12/71)

What would you have done in these situations? Take the first one. Would you have continued talking with Mrs. Swape, letting the food for the other patients get cold, and incurring the wrath of the supervisor and nurses on the other wards because the patients there couldn't get their food? Would you have ignored Mrs. Swape and served the food? Or would you have tried to effect some sort of compromise, perhaps asking one of the ambulatory patients to round up the other ambulatory patients and serve the food for all the patients? These are some possible short-range solutions. Would you have started there, or

would you have ignored these completely and focused only on long-range cause-and-effect solutions, or both?

Would your long-range approach have been to try and get the whole system of food service changed; to get it improved for your ward, and possibly make it worse for some other ward; or perhaps work with the supervisor, attempting to change her attitude to acceptance of your "peculiar" ideas a little more, and helping you by serving the trays instead of creating a fuss? Or maybe you could try to get the nurse's aide to bring a bag supper that could be eaten at any time during the evening. But would that solve the basic issue or problem? In this instance it was food service for many that interferred with individualized care for a single patient. Later in the evening, when the aide might be eating her bag supper, it could very well be some other need of the majority, or routine of the ward, that would interrupt or impede individualized care. What would you do then?

Perhaps there is an even more basic question that must be asked: "Is there a problem?" Serving the food to the large majority of patients is what is important. Maybe you are thinking: "I'd serve the food; all she's doing is sitting and chatting with the patient and that's not really nursing. Many nurses do too much talking and not enough work." While it is true that this will accomplish the task, it is only necessary to be a patient, or to listen carefully to some patient tell you about his hospital experiences and what helped him and what did not, to realize that this kind of value system does not promote individualized, quality patient care.

Perhaps you are thinking: "There's no problem. Definitely I'd stay and listen to Mrs. Swape. That's really the most important thing. It's too bad about the other patients, but they'll eventually get their food." If this reflects your perception, then your goal is probably to enact a professional dogma in a narrow, circumscribed area, rather than to achieve long-range goals of improved health care and maintenance for many people. It can be assumed that you do not really have a serious commitment to your profession, that you are not willing to pay the price of enough awareness of the system to do anything about it. This attitude often is expressed by nurses who are deep in the throes of "reality shock" and cannot adapt to it. A new graduate told the interviewer:

I know just how she feels. I've been in that situation a lot of times myself, and I know how she's torn. I know what my instructor would tell me to do! Stay with Mrs. Swape. Obviously! Your concern at this moment is about her and her total needs, so stay with her and do a good job of listening to her and seeing what you can do to get her to air how she's feeling and perhaps begin to relax and mend. That would be how my instructor would see it, and me too. That's how I was when I graduated, and really how I'd like to be able to do it now. But the fact is, I am responsible for those 19 others, and they do need their food too. You can't just ignore them. The thing that really burns me up is that when you take a problem like this to your supervisor, or even once I took it to the Director of Nursing, they just shrug. They don't see it; they can't seem to understand why I'm so upset about it. They see this just as something that happens only every once in awhile, and that on those occasions you just have to say: "Sorry, Mrs. Swape, I'll try to get back to you later." Then they pat you on the head and send you on your way; and the worst thing is, they think they've really helped you.They don't seem to realize that these are things that don't happen just once in awhile; they happen over and over again every day. But these little things are what's really nursing, and the constant frustration over them really eats at me. What would I do? I hate to say it, but I've been worn down. When I graduated, I would have stayed and listened to Mrs. Swape. Now? I'd probably go ahead and serve the trays. That's what's important in terms of keeping your job and getting good performance ratings. Those are really the only two choices I see. (NG:AD/13[8]2/72)

The above response aptly points out one of the major causes of reality shock in the new graduate: the discrepancy between what she learned was good and valued in the prework socialization period, and what she now finds out is the way things are done. This kind of discrepancy, which will be labeled professional-bureaucratic work conflict (explained later in this chapter), is the primary problem that gives rise to many of the other contributory causes of reality shock, such as interpersonal incompetency, inability to bargain for identity, and lack of role negotiation.

A discussion of reality shock (particularly as it compares and contrasts with culture shock) —its signs, symptoms, and resolution—will be presented now. This will be followed by consideration of two conflicting systems of work organization: the professional, into which many nurses are socialized; and the bureaucratic, under which most professionals must work. In the preceding examples, the bureaucratic system is manifested in values such as efficient food service to the majority, and classification and treatment of patients by categories. The professional work system is exemplified by concern for the needs of the individual patient, a view of exceptions as routine and based on individual consideration and judgment. This professional-bureaucratic role conflict problem will be explored as evidenced in nursing and in other professions.

## REALITY SHOCK—WHAT IS IT?

The kind of "reality" of importance in the phenomenon "reality shock" is the work situation as perceived, experienced, and shared by groups of nurses. It's true that no two people experience reality in the same way; so how can we talk about reality shock when the realities that might go into this construct are so varied? If taken from the psychological perspective of exploring the uniqueness of each person's experiences, we would find more differences than similarities. Yet, because we are social beings living, working, and being socialized into systems that have more commonalities than differences, shared perceptions and realities occur. For example, the reality—the value system and corresponding desired behavior—for student nurses in Texas is more like the reality for student nurses in New York or Iowa than is the degree of correspondence between reality perception of student nurses and staff nurses in an adjacent hospital in the same community. It is from this sociological perspective of looking at common perceptions of the school and work worlds that this book is written.

Shock, as used in the construct of reality shock, means the total social, physical, and emotional response of a person to the unexpected, unwanted, or undesired, and in the most severe degree to the intolerable. It is the startling discovery and reaction to the discovery that school-bred values conflict with work-world values. In some instances, reaction to the disparity between expectations and reality is so strong that the individual literally cannot persevere in the situation.

The shock is manifested in a variety of ways but, not surprisingly, has been found to follow a fairly discernible pattern, generally consisting of several phases: honeymoon, shock or rejection, recovery, and resolution. In this book the term "reality shock" will be used to designate the overall process or a phase within the process; the meaning will be clear from the context.

## REALITY AND CULTURE SHOCK: SIMILARITIES

Culture shock is the social shock phenomenon that conceptually comes closest to reality shock. An intensive study of its properties and processes suggests areas of similarities and differences. By definition, culture shock is a state of anxiety precipitated by the loss of familiar signs and symbols of social intercourse when one is suddenly immersed into a cultural system markedly different from his home or familiar culture. Nostrand goes so far as to define it as a "somewhat psychotic state that people get into when they are in a cultural situation whose cues are misleading because they have learned either responses that are wrong for the cues or no response at all."[°] If the nursing school and the work situation are viewed as separate subcultures with their own systems of values, signs and symbols of social intercourse, and common cues and responses, then it can be anticipated that going from one subculture into another has many parallels with moving from America to India. The mental states induced by the discrepant value systems can be expected to be similar.

When a person enters a strange culture, be it foreign or the subculture of the work world,

°From Nostrand, H.: Describing and teaching the sociocultural context of a foreign language and literature. In Valdman, A., editor: Trends in language teaching, New York, © 1966, McGraw-Hill Book Co., p. 6. Used with permission of McGraw-Hill Book Co.

Everything is WONDERFUL!

his first reaction is frequently one of fascination. With friends and colleagues acting as buffers and interceders, the newcomer has no real contact with the host country. (Is it possible that in-service educators buffer the reality world for the new graduate?) In this cocoon the new world of nursing looks rosy. The honeymoon phase is in full swing when the new graduate picks and chooses the parts of the new culture that are fascinating to her.

I can't believe how content I was compared with everybody else. They were so frustrated and I was so contented—I thought something was wrong with me. (NG:BS/2[12]9/71)

. . .

Oh, it's just super. I love it; I really do. It's all so perfect. Everything. Better than I ever thought it would be. (NG:Dip/1[3]3/69)

Soon however, familiar cues such as rewards, sanctions, and role behaviors are lost. The honeymoon phase is over. Shock and rejection sets in as the new graduate comes into daily contact with conflicting values and ways of doing things, things for which appropriate skills, interpersonal cues, and responses are lacking. This is a crucial phase; conflict resolution may well be maladaptive at this point, and progress toward self-discovery and growth arrested.

In the shock and rejection phase, reactions vary, but there is usually some form of rejection.

The newcomer may lash out bitterly toward the strange culture and reject all parts of it. Coupled with rejection is regression: the home environment suddenly assumes enormous proportions; there is excessive fear and mistrust, and a great concern over minor pains and illness.[1] This same kind of rejection and regression is manifested in the new graduate's desire for school-culture symbols (such as bath blankets, nursing care plans, or nursing histories) without corresponding regard for possible adaptation of these into the work situation. Preoccupation with the past and daydreaming have been observed. Contact and reassurance from former nursing instructors, usually through frequent letters, phone calls, or visits, are often sought.

A person in this phase may go to the opposite extreme and completely reject his home country or home values (those associated with the school subculture). In the context of culture shock, this reaction is termed "going native" and is characterized by a process in which the adopted nationality and culture is embraced wholeheartedly and unreservedly as a means of overcoming the shock. In terms of reality shock, this phenomenon of rejection

can be seen in the young graduate who totally rejects her school-bred idealism and professional values, and becomes a superefficient bureaucratic technician.

Another form of rejection is against oneself. The person in this phase of culture or reality shock may feel he is a failure, that he cannot possibly make good, that all the money spent on him was wasted. He blames himself for every mistake, and feels utterly defeated when he is not an instantaneous success in everything.

Also prevalent in reality shock is a rejection of the sponsoring or sending agency that "got me into this in the first place." This can be seen in the bitterness and feelings of betrayal expressed by neophyte nurses when they speak of their formal professional education.

I feel let down and betrayed by my school. They should have known what I needed to know to be a good nurse, and have put it into the curriculum. My education was worthless. (NG:BS/3[96]9/69)

Another major symptom of this shock rejection phase is protective isolationism: a withdrawal, banding together and dependence on people who hold the same values (for example, residents of one's same nationality). Although not as prevalent in reality shock, probably because it is more difficult to withdraw in this fashion, it is seen nonetheless.

I went on nights so I could be by myself and do my own thing—the way I was taught to do it, not the way they do things here. Working by myself protected me from having to get involved in what I considered to be the wrong way of doing things. (Med Ctr:BS[2213]4/68)

Closely intermingled with the shock symptoms of rejection and protective isolationism are other signs of coping with difficulty, such as hostile or aggressive attitudes toward the host culture, moral outrage, vocal criticism, and excessive fatigue. The hostility and aggression may well grow out of honest difficulties in getting along, be it finding a place to do your laundry in India, or suddenly being assigned to care for six patients in X hospital.

The people in the host culture or subculture may try to help, but just do not seem to understand your great concern, or they might be-

little the newcomer's difficulties in adjustment and offer no help whatsoever. The result, either way, is a feeling of "I just don't like them," and the next reaction is often criticism of the new culture. This criticism is not an objective appraisal, but superficial and hypercritical. Instead of trying to see things as they really are, and accounting for what seems like illogical or irrational patterns through honest analysis of the conditions and historical circumstances that have created them, the tendency is to perceive them as being directed against you personally, and to negate and derogate them universally and unilaterally. This paranoid criticism is often accompanied by expressions of moralistic outrage against the people associated with the school subculture: "How could they do this to me! I thought I would be prepared, but I wasn't." This moral outrage aspect of rejection is very upsetting and devastating for both the new graduate and the people with whom she is working. Not infrequently the feelings of anger and hostility are accompanied by evangelistic messages of "how things should be," "how we were taught to do things in school," or "the right way of doing things." Such message activity not only alienates the people in the new subculture,

but also so preoccupies the newcomer that she is unable to hear and perceive cues and messages sent her way.

The physical responses to the shock, anger, hostility, and frustration of this rejection phase of reality shock, as well as the tremendous amount of energy needed to propagate one's own message, leads to another common symptom of this phase: excessive fatigue and illness. Although anger may be expressed through overt aggression, depression and withdrawal to one's bed appears to be the more prevalent behavior in both culture and reality shock.

I went home from work and slept the clock around; I just can't seem to get enough sleep. (NG:AD/1[34] 6/68)

Other reactions to reality shock reflect various combinations of the signs and symptoms just described.

Like wow! It's awful. I can't believe it; I never thought it would be like this. I knew it wouldn't be a picnic, but this is ridiculous. The stupid way they do things, sometimes I wonder if any of these gals have ever been to nursing school. They know nothing at all about care plans or histories or discharge summaries. And the aides are so mean to the patients. Boy, I hope I never get like that. (NG:BS/3 [711]3/72)

. . .

Now, here you are an RN; but that doesn't mean anything, because you're slow. And sometimes I'm slow on purpose because I don't see any value . . . you know, a bed needs changing. I don't see any value in sticking the patient in a chair and changing the bed in three seconds and walking out. I like to take my time and talk to the patient and see if there's something I can find out—if he's having difficulties or something like that. So when I'm at the bed, it's not just making the bed; it's including the patient. But *they're* looking just at the speed and the technical things which are important. But the patient is why everybody is here. (NG:BS/3[11] 8/71)

. . .

I had been on the floor six weeks, and suddenly one day I was told that a meeting was set up: the girl from in-service, and supervisor, and one of the nurses, and myself. We're in this meeting, and there were many charges and accusations made against me. This really bothered me because that was the

first I had *heard* of it. I was amazed and dumbfounded to think I had been on the floor for six weeks and no one had bothered to tell me. (NG: AD/3[9]8/71)

. . .

I'm somewhat disappointed because they don't care as much about patients as I had been led to believe. And nurses don't make the decisions my instructors always said they would . . . no feedback, positive or negative . . . it's hard to know what's expected of you. (NG:BS/12[918]6/70)

. . .

I'd just started, but immediately I thought the care was so bad that I didn't want to be a part of it. I was not able to effectively change the work in that environment [after two weeks] to the degree that I had pride in what I was doing. I would go home every night really upset, and cry and cry, and then be so exhausted that I'd have to go to bed. (NG:BS/6[750]11/70)

. . .

I talked with Jean the other day. I told her that I was in a slump. I felt my first slump! I had never been in such a slump before in my life. You know, apathy. I didn't care about any of this junk. One hour I'll be excessively a go-getter; then the next hour, ugh—I'll just be down. I have never been this way in my life. It's so weird. I don't understand it. (NG:Dip/5[21]1/72)

. . .

And then there's the sleep syndrome: when you go home all you want to do is sleep so you can get up and go to work the next day. Pretty soon all you are doing is sleeping and working. (NG:AD/1[30]1/72)

. . .

I can see myself now looking at things that I was very angry about before (you know, like Susie, the ward clerk). I can remember just being so absolutely angry that I would just go home with an ulcer every day; and now . . . I don't know when it happened—I can't put my finger on it—but now I go home and nothing, nobody on that ward really bothers me anymore, even Susie. I say: "Heck with it, lady!" (NG:Dip/5[21]1/72)

A beginning sense of humor is the first sign of the recovery phase. There is a lessening of tension and an ability to see the amusing side of things, coupled with a beginning capacity to weigh, assess, and objectively evaluate aspects of the host culture. There is an increasing competence to accurately predict the actions and reactions of others in a situation.

With these developing abilities, the final stage of biculturalism might be reached. This is a degree of understanding of the new culture to the extent that the individual can begin to react in appropriate ways. The home culture is not abdicated, nor is the new culture fused. As new cues are learned and assimilated, the bases of tension are little by little removed, as well as blinders that prevented clear and open perception. The shock of self-discovery as the beginning of healing in culture shock not only enables the individual to grow more fully as a person, it also permits him to meet the work expectations of the new culture to a greater degree. Oberg (1960) asserts that as long as someone is suffering from culture shock he cannot effectively fulfill job expectations. That this reaction to the unexpected and undesired is displeasing and uncomfortable is self-evident. That it is also unproductive has not been scientifically proved, although there is considerable empirical data to point to reality shock as one of the major reasons why new graduate nurses "don't carry their weight for at least six months," "have no idea of what goes on in a hospital because they coddle them too much in school," "aren't worth their salt," and

"have done very little if anything to improve or better patient care."

A comparison between the final phases of culture shock and reality shock cannot be made yet. Although the shock phase and symptoms have been alluded to or described many times by both graduates and employers, there has been no work done in respect to the resolution phase of reality shock. A beginning description of possible resolutions will be considered in Chapters 5 and 6.

## REALITY AND CULTURE SHOCK: DIFFERENCES

Culture shock is universalistic and applies to some degree to all aspects of living. That is, an individual going into a totally foreign culture is affected by it in all areas of living—working, shopping, eating, and so forth. As such, it is much harder to run away from, to escape, to isolate oneself. One is almost forced to make some kind of adjustment, and to make it relatively fast. Unless there is a fairly extensive "home" community available, it is almost impossible to be productive in a foreign culture for long periods of time without resolution of culture shock.

Such is not the case with reality shock. Particular to the work situation, the symptoms of reality shock invade but are not further gen-

erated by one's living patterns. Since working hours do not make up the whole of one's existence, it is much easier to run away from the shock-producing conflict, thus making it possible to postpone resolution at work for a long time. Furthermore, with every job change there is at least the possibility that reality shock may recur.

For much the same reasons as outlined above, culture shock is viewed as something more fatalistic than reality shock. Most people going into a foreign culture do so with the knowledge that they are not going to change the culture of their host country; they know that they have to make some adjustment or adaptation. This is not so with reality shock. Largely unanticipated and unrecognized by the neophyte, there is continual hope that "things will change for the better" or that somewhere the perfect work situation exists. Unequipped with the knowledge, skills, and social power to bring about change on the new job, the neophyte's unfulfilled hope generates continued frustration and despair. Reality shock is more gradual, may last longer, and generates cumulative anxiety; culture shock is usually more total, more acute, and calls for a quicker resolution.

There is also some difference in the adaptation goal for each of the shock phenomena. In culture shock (unless one is changing his place of residence permanently), the adaptation goal is temporary. The goal of adaptation in a reality shock situation is the creation of a viable habitat in which one can be productive, effective, and content for a longer and probably indefinite period of time. The level of commitment is therefore different. The possibility of change, and the extent to which one will put forth effort to change, is dependent upon how permanent a person views himself in the situation. One potential way of handling the frustration of reality shock is to deliberately view a job as only temporary, which psychologically justifies less involvement, commitment, and need for change.

Not only is the adaptation goal different in the two shock conditions, available resources may also differ. Often the individual in culture shock can find someone in the community from his home culture with whom he can relate, with whom he can isolate himself, or who might serve as a role model of culture shock adaptation. Such may not be the case for the nurse in reality shock. All too often there is no one around who still has similar school-bred ideals and has been successful in interpreting and implementing these values in the work environment.

Another noticeable difference between reality shock and culture shock is that the newcomer in the work world is less likely than a foreigner to elicit tolerance, understanding, and expectations of differences because his external appearances and qualifications are similar. In the reality shock situation, the newcomer arrives in uniform with nursing license in hand; she is expected to be competent. When the newcomer does not live up to expectations, disappointment and denigration occur. Coworkers and employers show these feelings, which in turn escalate the reality shock conditions. In culture shock, competence expectations are not nearly so high or open. There is much more likelihood of the individual being given a chance "till he learns our ways."

A last major difference is that in culture shock there tends to be a feeling that one's home culture is "better" than the foreign. (This feeling springs quite naturally from the fact that one is more comfortable and fluent in the home culture.) This works to mitigate against rejection of home culture values. In reality shock, the certitude and belief in home values (school-bred values) is much more of an unknown variable. The socialization process may have been less than complete, and not all nurses graduate with the conviction that they received a good nursing education. Therefore, it is likely that the rejection of school-bred values in the process of reality shock resolution will be much greater than in culture shock. This is quite unfortunate for the future upgrading of nursing care services. It is also an option that, regrettably, many baccalaureate nurses elect (Corwin, 1960, and Kramer, June 1966).

Hopefully it will not be long before we can develop in nursing individuals who have the ability to become bicultural, who can abstract the best parts of the two subcultures and from them create a third configuration. This desired third configuration is one that will mesh with their own identities, one that will fit them better and be more functional than either of the original two subcultures.

## SHOCK OR STRESS

Some authors distinguish between culture shock and culture stress. This distinction also may be useful in respect to reality shock. Guthrie hypothesized that the degree of culture *shock* experienced is directly related to the degree of difference between the home and foreign culture, while the degree of culture *stress* is inversely related to that same difference. A person going into a radically different culture is bombarded immediately with strangeness and uncertainty, and experiences a high degree of culture shock. On the other hand, a person who enters a culture that is quite similar to his home culture (for example, the neophyte nurse going from student to worker status in her home hospital) may experience very little shock because he thinks he can interpret life there as he did in his home culture. Gradually he finds that his interpretations of the interpersonal cues and value systems differ from those of the new cultural community. This conflict causes stress, particularly if the person is not able to recognize the overt differences between the two cultures, and insists on treating people in the new culture as he would in his home culture. This distinction between culture stress and culture shock may help to explain some of the individual differences and lack of fulfillment of expectations noted and reported by neophyte nurses.

I thought I'd work at [X Hospital] to begin with as I worked there often as a student and figured that being a new graduate would be enough of an adjustment without having to adjust to a new hospital as well. At first everything was OK; but then all of a sudden everything fell apart, and I sort of felt like I was in a strange world that I didn't recognize. Nothing seemed to work . . . I was treating people as I always had, but it didn't work anymore. NG:BS/3[42]9/67

It may well be that culture or reality stress is

even more of a problem than shock. Whereas shock might pass, stress lingers—gnawing and sapping one's strength and perhaps going unnoticed from one day to the next. At this point in the development of the theory and process of reality shock, it would seem wise to view shock and stress as different in degree rather than kind; hence they can be viewed as the same phenomenon at different places along a continuum.

## CAN ANYTHING BE DONE

Much work has been done on the effects of cross-cultural training as a means of allaying culture shock and improving situational effectiveness. The major tools developed to accomplish this are called "culture assimilators"—

programmed learning experiences designed to expose members of one culture to some of the basic concepts, attitudes, role perceptions, customs, and values of another culture . . . assimilators can be general or specific; that is, they may train an individual to behave effectively in a very narrow set of social situations, such as in a hospital or as a community development worker, or for a broad group of social situations.[*]

In the culture assimilator programs

the trainee is presented with episodes about problems related to common sources of cultural misunderstanding and conflict. He must assess the causes of misunderstanding in each episode and he is given immediate positive or negative feedback on the basis of his analysis. Thus, the trainee symbolically becomes a participant in cross-cultural situations rather than remaining a passive reader.[†]

A somewhat similar approach, but on a group basis, was used in the program to reduce reality shock reported in this book. A search was begun for identification of shock-producing conflicts in values and behaviors between the school and the work subcultures in nursing,

---

[*]Fielder, F., Mitchell, T., and Triandis, H.: The culture assimilator: an approach to cross-cultural training, J. Appl. Psychol. **55**(2)95-102, 1971. Copyright 1971 by the American Psychological Association. Reprinted by permission.

[†]Chemers, M.: Cross-cultural training as a means for improving situational favorableness, Human Relations **22** (6):531-546, 1969.

and causes for underlying conflicts in values were sought. It was not difficult to find shock-producing incidents. New graduates were asked to "describe themselves in specific situations that were particularly satisfying and/or dissatisfying to them." It was found that not only shock-producing situations but also some idea of the severity and the cause of the shock could be ascertained by analyzing the responses to these questions. By this method, it was discerned that one—perhaps the major—producer of reality shock in new graduate nurses is the discrepancy between the nature and method of organizing the work as they had been taught in school (hereafter labeled professional mode), and the nature of the dominant method of organizing nursing work as it is practiced and enforced in the work situation (hereafter labeled bureaucratic mode). Other shock-producing stimuli were identified and are described in detail in Chapter 6.

## DEVELOPMENT OF PROFESSIONAL–BUREAUCRATIC CONFLICT

Professional-bureaucratic conflict is not new, nor is the problem endemic to nurses or to this society. No profession has escaped the advancing tide of bureaucratization. With this tide has come increasing awareness and study of the conflict experienced by professionals employed in bureaucratic settings, and the adaptations of both man and organizations to the conflict. This conflict has been shown to exist in scientists in industry, intellectuals in labor unions, social workers in health agencies, teachers in schools, and physicians in industry and bureaucratized medicine. It has been studied in Egypt, Japan, Israel, and France, as well as in the United States. The dislike of petty and excessive rules or regulations by professional staff nurses was also found to be a paramount cause of dissatisfaction with nursing for British nurses. A 1971 study by Johnson provides some evidence that nursing supervisors are affected by professional-bureaucratic role conflict and that they do not present consistent conflict resolution behavior to their head nurses. An understanding of the historical evolution and development of differing methods of organizing work in response to technologi-

cal and human demands of society will help in comprehending the scope and magnitude of the professional-bureaucratic conflict.

### Evolution of systems of work organization

*Patrimonial organizations.* From a time and technological perspective, one of the earliest and simplest forms of organizing work was the patrimonial organization. While an organization is defined as a social unit consisting of a network of relations that orient and regulate behavior among people in the pursuit of special goals, patrimonial organizations were dominated by a single individual who determined all goals and functions. The functions performed were very diffuse, and there was no known calculability of functions by those outside the organization. The people within the social unit were dependent upon the central figure for their very existence and livelihood; if all went well with him, things were good for the worker also. Changes in the function or assignment of individuals in this kind of organization were on a basis of sociometric choice of the central figure rather than competence or length of tenure. However, as dependent and unfree as the labor market was, the other side of the coin was equally important. In medieval Europe, since "employees" were personally bound to the king and could not leave him, he was legally responsible for them and could not fire or fine them.

*Effects of industrialization.* The patrimonial system of work organization may have been effective in medieval Europe when travel was laborious at best, few highly specialized skills were needed to meet personal wants, and people were content to remain geographically stable. With the development of mercantilism, increased demands for goods and services, and the industrial revolution, a more effective system of work organization was rediscovered. Bureaucratic systems of work organization existed long ago, particularly in the military and civic enterprises of China and Prussia, but their application to the production of goods—apart from governmental or state control—was a post–industrial revolution phenomenon. Based on the precepts of replaceability and interchangeability of parts, division of labor, and standardization of components, the bureaucratic system of work organization was soon able to utilize the increasing manpower force and increasing technological knowledge to effect a marked upswing in productivity of goods and services. Demonstrable achievements, such as a decrease in car assembly time from 5½ man-hours in 1914 to 68 minutes in 1959, prompted many people to adopt the conviction that this was the only way to organize work. What was suitable for the production of goods was seen to be also applicable for the production of services—what works on nonhuman material will also work effectively on human beings. Therein lies the problem. Can the production of services be effectively organized on the same basis as the production of goods? Can goods and services effectively organized under a bureaucratic system of work during an age of limited technology be produced under the same system in an age when the technology is expanding more rapidly than man's ability to communicate and absorb the developments? (Imagine hospitals issuing recalls to 50,000 patients who were wrongly treated; at least Ford can correct its mistakes.)

A new variable in organizing work in the bureaucratic mode is a cultural value rejection of assemblylike, fragmented, meaningless tasks and routines; depersonalization; and the problem of boredom. If the worker rejects the bureaucratic work organization and responds with high absenteeism, turnover, and goldbricking, then, though the bureaucratic system may be an efficient means of work organization from a rational viewpoint, it may be inefficient from a human viewpoint.

*Human relations approach.* Concurrent with and paralleling the changes in systems of work organization that have occurred in past centuries has been an increasing awareness and concern for the welfare of the worker and the meaning of work for men. Most readers are quite familiar with the works of Dickens in this regard. During the first third of the present century, attempts were made through better "human engineering" to rationalize the way in which work was done, the way in which the work force was utilized to increase output.

With the considerable improved human conditions following World War II, emphasis shifted to a human relations approach. Working men began to demand that the work environment meet some of the social needs in addition to their needs for survival and security. Social needs were used to increase motivation and organizational productivity.

The late 1950's and early 1960's saw two themes emerging. One was the development of people for higher responsibilities. This was characterized by increasing the qualifications of management personnel, and a plethora of management development workshops sprang up. A second theme was an increased demand for more effective communication systems, occasioned to a large extent by large-scale decentralization of decision-making and the growth of sophisticated computers with a new language. In the mid-1960's a new theme, organization development, emerged. Organization development is the name attached to total-system, planned-change efforts for coping with the dilemma: how can human resources and energy be mobilized to achieve the organization's goals and, at the same time, maintain a viable, growing organization of people whose personal needs for self-worth, growth, and satisfaction are significantly met at work? System examination, which is characteristic of organizational development, focuses on the organization as a complex, human system with a unique character, its own culture, and a value system. These, as well as the information systems and work procedures must be continually examined, analyzed, and improved if optimum productivity and motivation are to result.

It is in this context that Bennis predicts the *Coming Death of Bureaucracy* and the rise of "adhocracy" as a potential method of work organization. In Bennis' system, workers would come together in small ad hoc work units to accomplish a specific task or goal for which they were highly specialized and competent, and then disband when the goal had been achieved. The goals of the organization would be achieved through a flexible, constantly shifting arrangement of these ad hoc units, composed of those workers with the capabilities and expertise to best achieve the task at hand.

It is quite likely that new forms of work organization will develop in the future, hopefully in response to the less predictable, less stable, more dynamic and fluid tasks and conditions that await us in the twenty-first century. However, it is also probable that these new organizational forms will emerge from and have their roots in the present bureaucratic system of work organization. So perhaps it would be well to take a close look at the characteristics of that which we call the bureaucratic system of work organization and see if, perhaps, we can get some leads on how to prepare ourselves and the nurses of tomorrow to function in an organizational work system in which form follows function, rather than the reverse.

Scott proposes that there are at least two different ways in which a task, such as assembling a car, might be organized. The whole task might be done by a single worker, such as the assembling of a Mercedes-Benz by a single mechanic; or workers may each do a part of the task, as is usually done on the Detroit assembly lines. What are the results of organizing work on a segmented or part-task basis as opposed to a whole-task principle?

### Part-task system

Because the task is segmented, only a few skills are needed in the part-task operation. These skills are usually learned on the job in a relatively short period of time; and it is worthwhile for the organization to teach the worker how to do them exactly the way in which they are to be done, that is, in a particularistic rather than a universalistic fashion. A byproduct of this factor is increased loyalty of the worker to that particular organization. Since the worker repeats the same task very frequently, he has the opportunity to develop tremendous skill and speed in the performance of the task, and his work output can easily be judged in terms of the units completed. When the total function of the operation has been segmented into component tasks, each performed by a different group of workers, it is mandatory that some kind of external controls and coordination, usually in the form of rules and supervisory officials, be set up to ensure

the success and efficiency of the total operation. The supervisory official who performs this coordinating function must necessarily have more knowledge, understanding, and authority than the worker who is doing only a component part of the whole. Therefore, there is the need for a hierarchical control and authority structure.

Other necessary byproducts also accrue. Since the worker is only going to be doing a limited segment of the task, for which he will be trained on the job, hiring standards for this kind of operation can be quite low. This work system is very vulnerable to breakdown, but because of the low hiring standards and rapid on-the-job training, the breakdown parts (people or machines) can be readily and fairly easily replaced. All of these facets would tend to make the system economically efficient.

### Whole-task system

A work system organized on the whole-task principle would require that the worker possess all of the immediately and potentially necessary knowledge and skills to do the total job. Since the scope of knowledge and skills needed is extensive and broad, it generally requires considerable time to acquire them, usually before employment, in an institution designed for educational purposes. Since the knowledge and skills are to be used in a variety of situations, they would be universal rather than particular to a specific organization. Because of the highly esoteric and individualistic combination and recombination of the subtasks that go to make up a whole task, evaluation of productivity is not necessarily made on the rapid and repetitive performance of any subtask, but on the skill and judgment used in the combination of the subtasks. Judgment of outcomes is best made in terms of correct procedure rather than units of successful outcome.

Since the individual worker executes the entire operation, coordination of tasks and external controls are not needed, rather internalized coordination and standards of performance, norms, or codes of ethics are employed. Evaluation and quality control are made on the basis of correct procedures; such judgment must be made by others who have equal knowledge and skill. There is no need for a hierarchical control or authority structure; a peer control structure is not only desirable but essential.

Other byproducts indicate that hiring standards must be fairly rigid and meet prescribed specifications. This work system is not particularly vulnerable to breakdown, because the worker controls all facets. He can make immediate and current adjustments to compensate for breakdown. When massive breakdown occurs, the worker is not easily replaced. Because of the longer training period, higher job standards and qualifications, this system is more costly than the part-task system, particularly when the nature of the task is routine.

Another variable that must be examined in respect to these differing modes of work organization is the resistance factor in accomplishing tasks.

### Active and inert tasks

To determine which system works best, the nature and characteristics of the task to be performed must be analyzed, as well as whether a single worker does the entire task or only part of it. If we define a task as a set of activities performed to achieve a *desired result,* and the end product of performing a task as an outcome or *actual result,* the goal is to decrease the margin of error between the desired and actual outcome. Carrying out a set of task activities, however, always entails overcoming some kind of resistance; for example, the inertia of an object that is to be moved, opposition to a competitor, or the complexity presented by a problem to be solved. The amount of resistance to be overcome is not the critical factor. Both people and machines can be trained or programmed to overcome given amounts of resistance. What is critical is the variability and predictability of resistance, because changes in these factors resist training or programming. On the basis of the above, Scott distinguishes two polar types of tasks. Inert tasks are those in which the resistance is constant, and therefore predictable. Active tasks are those in which the resistance is variable across performances, therefore less predictable.

The classification of tasks into inert and active has important implications for designing efficient work arrangements and for evaluating and controlling task performances. Because of the predictability and constancy in degree of resistance, inert tasks are those that are routine and standardized. They are known in advance, and performance programs for them can be devised; many can be computerized. Minimal decision-making is required; workers can be trained to do them with little training. Active tasks are nonroutine in nature because of their variable and less predictable resistance patterns. They require greater discretion and judgment on the part of the worker and greater individual competence. This necessitates more training, and is therefore more costly.

It can be seen that inert, routine tasks are quite suitable for the part-task system of organization, which results in or has the characteristics of that kind of organizational system generally called "bureaucratic." Note the high degree of correspondence between the usually accepted characteristics of a bureaucracy and those resulting from a part-task organizational system.

Active, nonroutine tasks can be seen to be suitable for the whole-task organizational systems, which has the major characteristics of what is generally labeled the professional system of work. Again note the almost exact correspondence between common descriptions of the characteristics of a profession and those that result from the whole-task analysis. (See opposite page.)

Throughout this book and the study reported herein, the term "professional" will be used to represent the whole-task work system, with its specified characteristics; "bureaucratic" will mean the part-task work system and its characteristics.

### Examples and clarifications

It is possible to process active tasks through the bureaucratic or part-task system; in fact, this is often done. In such cases, however, participants must behave as if the resistance offered by the objects being processed were constant. It is quite likely that standard approaches to active tasks will entail a high pro-

**Characteristics of a bureaucracy**

Specialization of roles and tasks

Autonomous rational rules

Overall orientation to rational, efficient implementation of specific goals

Organization of positions into a hierarchical authority structure

The impersonal orientation of contacts between officials and clients

**Characteristics of a profession**

Specialized competence having an intellectual component

Extensive autonomy in exercising this special competence

Strong commitment to a career based on a special competence

Influence and responsibility in the use of special competence

Development of training facilities that are controlled by the professional group

Decision-making governed by internalized standards

**Part-task analysis**

Few skills required, particularistic in nature

Specialized skills learned on the job

Loyalty to the organization

Evaluation through work output

Hierarchical control and authority structure

External standards through rules and regulations

Control and coordination by an official who is removed from the workers

Development of a layer in the organization whose major purpose is to maintain the organization

**Whole-task analysis**

Worker must possess total knowledge and skills

Skills learned in separate educational institutions

Loyalty to an occupation or discipline

Long training period

Evaluation through process rather than output

Internal standards and coordination

Peer control and authority structure

portion of errors or failures (instances in which the actual result is not consonant with the desired result).

As an example, assembling an automobile can be viewed as an inert task in which several workers or groups of workers are trained to perform various segmented tasks. The degree of resistance to each task is known and standardized (the amount of inertia that must be overcome to lift a fender and place it on a car, or the energy required to tighten the wheel lugs, and so forth), and constant over repeated performances. Since the resistance is predictable and known, and since workers can be efficiently programmed accordingly, the likelihood is very high that the job will be accomplished accurately (desired outcome will fit actual outcome) and inexpensively.

On the other hand, is getting a postoperative patient out of bed an active or inert task? Would a professional (whole-task) or bureaucratic (part-task) method of work organization have the least likelihood of error? With very little experience, it becomes clear that the task of getting a postoperative patient out of bed has a great degree of variable resistance. Is this a patient who has had open heart surgery or an appendectomy? Is the patient a child, a

middle-aged adult, or an octogenarian? Is it the first day after the operation or several days later? Is he a hypoglycemic patient on intravenous feeding or a well-nourished patient? If the work of getting this task organized and accomplished is done on a bureaucratic principle (assign a nurse's aide to get all the postoperative patients up and walking), we can readily see that the likelihood of accurate task performance (correspondence between actual and desired results) is in grave doubt, although this would probably be the least expensive way of accomplishing the task. If the professional method were used, the margin of error would undoubtedly be reduced, but the cost would increase. Summarily then, quality of outcome is high and cost is low when inert tasks are done by the bureaucratic mode of work organization and active tasks are done in the professional mode. When inert tasks are done in the professional mode (that is, professional workers doing routine, repetitive tasks such as filling in diet slips or making unoccupied beds), quality outcome will probably be high, at least initially. Segmenting of tasks makes it difficult to see relationships of the parts to the whole. However, assignment of such tasks to a worker who has the ability and has been prepared to see the whole, results in boredom, low morale, worker dissatisfaction, and decreased productivity. Costs will definitely be higher than need be when professional workers perform inert tasks.

Another factor that enters the picture, and one that is directly related to the potential development of adhocracy as a form of work organization, is the evolutionary nature of the variability of resistance. What is highly variable today may be highly standardized and routine in the future due to increased experience, knowledge, and techniques. An active task of today—for example, assessing a patient's reaction to a specific drug—may be an inert task tomorrow. It is quite possible that adhocracy as a form of work organization has as its essence the considered and everchanging assessment of the resistance of tasks, and the use of appropriate systems of work, to achieve error-free results within acceptable costs.

To summarize, tasks aimed at surmounting constant resistance can be effectively and efficiently organized by means of bureaucratic arrangements. Tasks aimed at overcoming variable resistance are usually better organized in a professional manner since skilled, nonroutine responses are better calculated to meet unpredictable resistance with a minimum of errors. The problem in respect to reality shock occurs because student nurses are socialized into performing and expecting others to perform according to the professional whole-task work system; yet as employees in the work world it becomes all too obvious that this is not the way in which work is organized. The majority of nursing care today is organized on a bureaucratic part-task basis: the RN passes medications (which can be one of the more inert of all the care tasks a nurse does); the LVN gives treatments; the nurse's aides give baths, take temperatures, and so on. It is rapid and efficient completion of part-tasks, or the successful putting together or coordination of the part-tasks of other workers, for which the nurse is recognized and organizationally promoted. Is any wonder that nurses educated into and expecting one form of work organization are shocked to find out that it just is not that way in the work world?

The dominant form of socialization taking place in our schools of nursing today is the professional (whole-task) system. Student nurses are taught to take care of the whole patient. They are taught that patients should receive comprehensive care and that they should attempt to satisfy or meet the needs of the total family. Seldom are they taught to look at all the tasks that go into the care of a patient and analyze them in terms of their degree of resistance, and then decide which worker is the best and most economically prepared to accomplish each task. This whole-task approach to the socialization of student nurses creates a marked problem for them in delegating tasks to others.

I never get through on time. My head nurse says I should delegate more, but I can't. I've just got to do everything myself. That's the way I was taught to do it, and that's the way I think it's best. (NG:Dip/3[88]8/68)

## SUPPORTING STUDIES

Organizations have become a dominating influence in the American occupational structure in the last several decades. They are no longer restricted to manual or semiskilled occupations, but now include those generally labeled professional. (It is not the purpose of this book to explore whether nursing is or is not a profession, or whether it is an emerging or developing profession.) With the exception of teachers, journalists, and clergymen, between 1900 and 1950 the personnel in the main salaried professions increased more than ten times. While the labor force only doubled, the total number of professionals quadrupled. With this influx of professionals into the ranks of organizational employees, there has been and must continue to be increasing attention devoted to incipient problems of both the professional employee and the employing organization.

### Conflict in social workers

An increasing amount of research has been done in this problem area, both with respect to nurses and in terms of other occupational groups. Scott (1969) studied the professional-bureaucratic problems of 90 social workers in a county agency. Using the task analysis framework presented earlier, he describes four areas of conflict that arise because of the different organizational principles of the professional and bureaucratic systems with respect to task.

1. Professionals' resistance to bureaucratic rules. Bureaucratic systems require rules in order to decrease the amount of time needed to coordinate and supervise the component tasks of individual employees. Professionals are trained to use individual judgment rather than established rules to coordinate and execute the component tasks in rendering service to clients. When professionals are employed by bureaucratic organizations, some degree of autonomy must be sacrificed because they do not possess the requisite skills for doing the entire task of the complex organization. Since this is contrary to the professional's orientation, it is likely that the professional employee will resist established rules, departing from them in favor of internalized professional norms.

2. Professionals' rejection of bureaucratic standards. The standards of the bureaucratic system are based on skill and precision in the execution of a defined and limited task. Emphasis is on the "concretely possible" and the proven way of doing things. Evaluation of the outcome of a task is partly in terms of adherence to the prescribed procedural steps. In the professional system, standards based on present knowledge are flexible and constantly subject to change. In the setting where these standards are learned, the emphasis is on the "potentially possible" and innovative way of doing things. There is frequently a time lag between the initiation of new ideas in the learning setting and the acceptance of these ideas in the practicing setting. When a professional transfers from the learning to the practicing setting, he is likely to experience a conflict in standards.

3. Professionals' resistance to bureaucratic supervision. The bureaucratic system exists and functions on authority of position, while in the professional system authority stems from knowledge and competence. When employed by a bureaucracy, professionals many times are supervised by individuals in authority positions who have little or no knowledge of the task they are supervising. Hughes identifies this problem of authority as the primary source of professional-bureaucratic conflict.

4. Professionals' conditional loyalty to the bureaucracy. The bureaucratic system thrives on and rewards its members for loyalty to a given institution. The professional system provides mobility opportunities and sanctions through internalization and loyalty to its behavioral expectations. Since the two loyalties are often opposed, professional workers may tend to view the organization as a short-term instrument of personal actualization, and hence render only conditional and temporary loyalty.

In addition to the four areas of conflict noted above, Blau and Scott identify the internalized ethical code and the peer control structure of the professional system as additional sources of conflict. The difficulties likely to be encountered by the professional (operating through an internalized ethical code) in a bureaucratic system (operating on explicit rules) have been covered in the preceding paragraphs. The conflict of peer control with the hierarchical control structure was implied in the section on bureaucratic supervision. Particularly significant, however, is this point: through its peer control structure, the professional system constantly supports its members in their resistance to bureaucratic rules, standards, and supervision. Therefore, even while working within a system that does not overtly reward the professional employee for enacting professional behavior, the professional employee may be reinforced by members of his professional system. This support would probably increase his role conflict and feelings of being deprived of enacting the role for which he was prepared.

### High school teachers

Corwin reported on a study of the relationship between professionalism and conflict resolution behavior of 1,500 public high school teachers. Rank ordering both the schools and individuals according to their professional and employee orientations (very similar to bureaucratic as used in the context of this book), Corwin notes that perhaps the most important result of the analysis was the finding that most measures of staff conflict increase with the average professional orientation of a faculty.° However, a marked exception to this finding was that major conflict incidents became less frequent as a faculty's professionalism rose. In other words, while it is true that conflict and militancy rise as an outcome of the clash between the two competing principles of work organization (professional and bureaucratic), as faculties become more professional they are more able to keep conflicts from assuming major proportions than when their professionalism is low. The results of this study have important implications for nursing. We in nursing must learn to view and accept conflict as potentially healthy and growth-producing. As we become more professionally oriented, we should be better able to police ourselves and prevent conflict from getting out of hand.

Corwin also found that the mean conflict scores of the 14 most professionally oriented faculties were higher in the more bureaucratized than in the less bureaucratized schools. This suggests that professionalization is most likely to provoke conflict when it is in a bureaucratic context. This finding is consistent with that of a study of a nationwide sample of collegiate nurses. Those nurses who attempted to hold simultaneously high loyalty to both the professional and bureaucratic work systems reported considerably more role conflict than did those with reverse loyalties. This conclusion, as well as Corwin's earlier study of nurses (1960) and his study of teachers (1970), substantiates one of the major premises of the theory that the professional and bureaucratic systems of work organization are inherently antithetical; that inter- and intra-personal role conflict will be an outcome of the combination of these two loyalties, either within the same individual or between the individual and the work setting (employment of a professional employee in a highly bureaucratized setting).

## Business school graduates

Reality shock of business school graduates was investigated by Schein in his followup study of randomly selected panels of students graduating from Massachusetts Institute of Technology, School of Business. Schein describes the reality shock of these college graduates as dissatisfaction "embedded in the psychological conflict between the graduate's expectations and values, and the company's attempt to indoctrinate him in its values." He found in his interviews with students about their attitudes and desires that they were really concerned with far deeper issues than salary, promotion, and company benefits.

The graduate needs to know:

1. Will the job give me an opportunity to *test myself*, to find out if I can do anything worthwhile, and make a meaningful contribution to the company's efforts?
2. Will the job give me the opportunity to *learn* and *grow*, and to make use of my present abilities and education?
3. Will I be able to retain my integrity and individuality, and not be forced to conform to a company pattern or be brainwashed into an organization-man mentality?
4. Will the company be dynamic and exciting, receptive to new ideas, and run according to rational business principles?°

It was noted that through his formal education the college graduate acquired knowledge of management principles and how to take the corporate point of view. His initial job experiences, however, were aimed at teaching him how to be a good subordinate, how to be influenced, and how to be a loyal and reliable member of the organization. The moral outrage produced by this kind of discrepancy is as evident in the business school graduate as it is in the neophyte nurse.

In my interviews with graduates after they had been on the job for six months to one year, almost every one stated in one way or another that he was shocked by the degree to which his "good ideas" were rejected, the way they were undermined, sidetracked, or even sabotaged.°

°Adapted from: Militant professionalism by Ronald Corwin, p. 295. Copyright © 1970 Meredith Corporation. By permission of Appleton-Century-Crofts, Educational Division, Meredith Corporation.

°Excerpted from "The First Job Dilemma" by Edgar Schein in *Psychology Today* Magazine, March 1968. Copyright © Communications/Research/Machines, Inc., pp. 29-31.

## PROFESSIONAL-BUREAUCRATIC CONFLICT IN NURSES

The composition of the nurse role and incipient conflict in role value systems has been the primary or secondary concern of many investigators studying nurses. (See Appendix A.)

### Diploma and baccalaureate students and nurses

Three of the major studies of this problem will be presented and discussed in some length, as they had major relevance to the development of the theory guiding this research. In 1960 Corwin began his work on the problem of professional-bureaucratic role conflict by studying the relationship between type of nurse socialization pattern and magnitude of conflict. He investigated this relationship in a sample of 296 graduate and student nurses from 7 hospitals and 4 schools of nursing in a midwestern metropolis. Maintaining that not only do professional conceptions interfere with bureaucratic values, and vice versa, he also conjectured that both the bureaucratic and professional conceptions interfered with traditional nursing or service values. The professional has shifted attention from the patient to technical activities, and the bureaucrat is rewarded for skill in administration.

An important perspective is the notion that any given individual can and does hold these potentially conflicting value orientations simultaneously. Corwin contends that any nurse must profess some loyalty to patients, some to the employing organization, and some loyalty to the profession. It is the relative emphasis and priority of loyalties that constitute the specific role organization and give rise to potential conflict. The particular conflict of concern here is one that Corwin labeled role deprivation. This is defined as the disparity between idealized role conception and that which is found operable and sanctioned in the work situation. In the context of the study reported in this book, role deprivation is one of the major sources of reality shock.

Graduation from a nursing school and induction into employment in a hospital is anticipated by Corwin as a period of great conflict. It is at this time that the professional ideals stressed in school confront the bureaucratic principles that operate in the hospital. In the training program the nurse's intellectual capacity as a decision maker, her responsibility for patient welfare, and her leadership potential are emphasized. Within the hospital much of the work is standardized and rules may be arbitrarily constraining. Corwin assumes that a difference between hospital and college nursing programs is in the direction of greater professionalism in the latter.

Corwin administered three Likert-type scales specifically designed to assess bureaucratic, professional, and service role conceptions, and the degree of role deprivation or conflict reported by nurses.[2]

There are six items on the bureaucratic scale and eight on both the professional and service scales. For each item, the respondent is asked to indicate the degree to which a given situation *should be* the practice in nursing, and also the extent to which it *actually is* practiced. The responses to the *should* question constitute the role conception scales. The role deprivation scores are obtained by the numerical differences between the way things *should be* and *are*. A five-point scale is used, running from strongly agree, agree, undecided, disagree, and strongly disagree. Examples of items from each of these scales follow.

Corwin found that his nurse subjects expressed discrepancies in roles: those holding

Professional item:

All graduate nurses in a hospital spend, on the average,
   at least six hours a week reading professional journals
   and taking refresher courses.
   A. Do you think this *should be* true of all nurses?
   B. *Is* this true of nurses at your hospital?

| Strongly agree | Agree | Undecided | Disagree | Strongly disagree |
|---|---|---|---|---|
|  |  |  |  |  |
|  |  |  |  |  |

**Bureaucratic item:**

When a supervisor at a hospital considers a graduate for promotion, one of the most important factors is the length of experience on the job.

A. Do you think this is what supervisors *should* regard as important?

B. *Is* this what supervisors at your hospital actually do regard as important?

| Strongly agree | Agree | Undecided | Disagree | Strongly disagree |
|---|---|---|---|---|
| | | | | |
| | | | | |

**Service item:**

At some hospitals, the graduate nurses who are most successful are the ones who are realistic and practical about their jobs, rather than the ones who attempt to live according to idealistic principles about serving humanity.

A. Do you think this *should be* true of all nurses?

B. *Is* this the way things are at your hospital?

| Strongly agree | Agree | Undecided | Disagree | Strongly disagree |
|---|---|---|---|---|
| | | | | |
| | | | | |

high bureaucratic combined with high professional orientations expressed greater discrepancies than did those who adopted other styles of role organization. The smallest discrepancies were among those who simultaneously held low bureaucratic and low professional role conceptions. Degree nurses maintained high professional role conceptions more frequently than did diploma nurses, combining them with either high or low bureaucratic conceptions. The result was a high intensity of conflict. Graduate diploma nurses lowered their professional conceptions after graduation. Among degree nurses the professional conception was maintained after employment, while at the same time they increased their allegiance to the bureaucracy.

Corwin and Taves used essentially the same frame of reference as the Corwin study described above. The major hypothesis supported by their findings is that the type of role conception held, the certainty with which it is held, and the amount of role deprivation will be experienced differently by nurses with different types of training and in different stages of their careers. Also, the type, clarity, and deprivation of role conceptions will influence career aspirations. Because the diploma program is controlled almost exclusively by the hospitals, it can be expected to instill loyalty to hospitals. On the other hand, degree programs are in a position to promote profession-

alization because of their relative autonomy with respect to hospitals. (It must be noted that Corwin's data was collected in 1959; much has happened in nursing since then. It is highly probable that diploma and collegiate schools of nursing are much closer in orientation now than they were 15 years ago.)

Degree students were found to develop relatively low identification with the hospital and to feel deprived in their bureaucratic role (more bureaucratic loyalty was demanded than what they held in their role conceptions) after graduation in spite of a rather high professional self-conception. Diploma nurses with strong bureaucratic orientations are less interested in teaching but more interested in promotion within the hospital.

### Head nurse and faculty evaluations

Smith, studying the discrepancy in value climate confronting student nurses in collegiate nursing programs, analyzed 13 head nurses' written evaluations for 42 staff nurses, and 14 teachers' evaluations for 56 student nurses, to ascertain the differences between head nurses and teachers in conceptions of valued nurse behaviors. A crucial assumption in this investigation was that these written evaluations reflected the nursing role values of the person who produced them and that these were among the crucial values communicated to students.

Smith found that discrepancies in nursing role values between head nurses and nursing faculty did exist: head nurses emphasized traits such as "leadership, group-orientation, conforming behavior, neatness, and helpfulness"; faculty emphasized traits such as "independence, empathy, team-orientedness, interest and skill in teaching patients, and cognitive skills." It seems then that head nurses and faculty do have different conceptions of nursing, and that

these create for the nursing student a climate in which she is continually exposed to two disparate and positively sanctioned sets of patterned behavior. She is taught to practice according to the teacher's dominant orientation to nursing, yet as she performs in the nursing unit the head nurse is upholding for her a different set of expectations, expectations oriented to administrative principles.[°]

It is these administrative expectations, more functional in the organizational setting, that may produce role deprivation in the professional aspirant or employee.

### Disparate reward systems

While differing expectations may produce conflict, the magnitude of such conflict is undoubtedly increased when disparate reward systems also exist. Benne and Bennis, studying 90 nurses working in outpatient departments of 7 hospitals in the Boston area, found differing reward systems between the nurse and her supervisor to be one of the three major areas of tension in nurses. The first area that they discuss is the nurse's "blurred self-image." They point out that "real" nursing is considered to be bedside care. Nurses bring this image into nursing school, and often the schools cannot dislodge it even when they try. In the work situation the nurse is actually required to perform four major types of duties: technical, administrative, organizational and educative. Consequently there is a sharp discontinuity between the job the nurse expects to perform and the actualities of her work.

The second major conflict described by these authors is the nurse-doctor conflict. They believe that this is one of the most pervasive tensions within nursing because of misunderstanding on both sides. In professionalizing, nurses have formed an alliance with the behavioral sciences, while doctors are still primarily oriented to the biological sciences. Therefore, while nurses base their relationships with patients primarily on communication principles and skills, physicians utilize a predominantly biological approach. The dilemma of a nurse is that while she may expect to function with professional independence of judgment in certain areas of work, many doctors will expect her to behave only as an obedient extension of their own professional judgment. The authors conclude that

on the one hand we find schools of nursing and professional nursing associations reinforcing the nurse's self-image of an autonomous professional person, sharing substantial equality in appropriate judgments about treatment processes. On the other hand we find doctors, perhaps reinforced by neglect of the study of nursing—if not by contrary indoctrination—with their professional education ignoring or controverting this self-image of professional person or colleague which many nurses hold.[°]

Particularly significant is that much of the reward system in the hospital is controlled by or through the physician. Evidence that this emphasis is still quite prevalent is noted by Gale in her study of the role coordination between nurses and nurse's aides. She found that the nurse placed considerably more emphasis on diagnostic procedures than on nursing procedures—the former, of course, always ordered by and under the supervision and reward (or punishment) of the physician.

The third area of conflict is that between nurse and supervisor, the supervisor being the most immediate personification of the organization. Based on the premise that the ability of supervisors to influence nurses' behavior effectively is proportional to the degree to

[°]Smith, K.: Discrepancies in the value climate of nursing students; a comparison of head nurses and nursing educators. Doctoral dissertation, Stanford University, 1964, p. 121.

Benne, K., and Bennis, W.: Role confusion and conflict within nursing, Am. J. Nurs. **59**(3)380-383, 1969, © American Journal of Nursing Co.

which they can reward the individual nurse, Benne and Bennis asked nurses what they would hope to get as a reward and what they realistically predicted to get in return for doing a good job. They found almost no correlation. Furthermore, they infer that supervisors may not be aware of the rewards that nurses genuinely desire.

### Baccalaureate nurses as seen over a period of time

Following up and extending the work of Corwin, I conducted a study to determine the effect of exposure to bureaucratic employment on the professional values of new collegiate graduate nurses.[3] With a 100% sample from three California State College nursing programs (N = 79), the group was divided randomly into a control group of 20 and an observed group of 59. All 79 graduates were tested one month before graduation, using the Corwin professional-bureaucratic role conception and role deprivation scales described on p. 19. These scales provide a measure of the respondent's professional and bureaucratic value orientation as well as a measure of role deprivation. Three months after employment, the observed group of 59 graduates were retested with the same instrument, and each had a tape-recorded interview designed to elicit feelings and attitudes relative to initial employment experience. Six months after employment, all 79 subjects were tested with the same instrument and interviewed for the same reasons. (The purpose of the control group was to aid in the assessment of repeated contacts with the investigator and repeated scale administration). In addition to the role value and role deprivation scale scores, information obtained through the interviews included data such as job and work history, degree of satisfaction with the job and nursing, difficulties encountered, satisfying and dissatisfying situations, and assessment of degree of success in the job. Results indicated that there is a significant increase in bureaucratic role conception after exposure to the employing organization. Most of this increase occurred during the first three months, but the continued increase during the second three months was

also significant. There was a continual drop in the professional role conception scale scores during the first six months after employment.

The magnitude of the subjects' role deprivation did appear to be related to role value configuration held, although not completely in the direction predicted. For the group as a whole there was a significant increase in role deprivation during the first three months of employment. Analysis of the significances of difference in mean role deprivation scores among nurses holding different role configurations indicated that (1) a high commitment to professional values is associated with greater role deprivation than is a low degree of loyalty to professional values; (2) high bureaucratic orientation decreases the probability of high role deprivation, but low bureaucratic orientation does not necessarily increase it; and (3) when a high bureaucratic orientation is combined with a high professional orientation, there is a greater degree of role deprivation than when both are low.

Professional role conception was the source of most significant variance in role deprivation scores, although service conception contributed meaningfully also. Bureaucratic orientation did not contribute importantly except at the six-month period, when there was a significant interaction between bureaucratic and professional. As predicted, subjects with both high bureaucratic and high professional orientations had higher role deprivation scores than subjects with high bureaucratic and low professional orientations. This supports the theory that the two systems are inherently antithetical and that simultaneous loyalty to both systems is associated with role value conflict. Low bureaucratic–high professional subjects had higher role deprivation scores than high bureaucratic–low professional nurses. The low bureaucratic–low professional subjects had the lowest role deprivation scores at graduation; after employment, however, they were replaced by the high bureaucratic–low professional subjects. There were no significant differences in career patterns or scale scores between the control and observed groups, indicating that, at least with this sample, the possible contamination effects of repeated exposure were not sufficient to distort the effects of bureaucratic employment.

A followup of this nurse sample was done two years later, at which time 80% of the original subjects (N = 63) responded to a mail questionnaire and retook the Corwin professional-bureaucratic role conception scales. Some of the trends suggested by the initial study became the hypothesis for this followup study. Specifically, it was predicted that prolonged exposure to employing organizations would result in stabilization of the bureaucratic role conception at a fairly high level and a continued significant decrease in the professional role conception. Results indicated that this hypothesis was tenable. There was a slight decrease in the mean bureaucratic scale score, but it was not statistically important; a highly significant decrease in professional role conception scores; and an increase in role deprivation among the subjects from the six-month to the two-year testing, but this was not significant.

The results of this followup study prompt several disturbing questions. How low will professional role conception drop? What can be done to keep it from falling, or better, to stabilize it? Are there factors or variables within the organization that would permit a retention of professional ideals? These questions must await further study. But the major implication of this two-year followup study is that with continued employment, nurses who initially held high professional role conceptions showed a significant decline in these values. This is akin to saying that *nurses become less professional with continued employment.*

### Eight different groups of nurses

A 1972 study by Hogan, approached from a theoretical perspective different from that of professional-bureaucratic role conflict, confirmed some of the findings from the Kramer and Corwin studies but reported differences in other areas. The Hogan study attempted to determine the effect of baccalaureate education on the attitudes of registered nurses toward the nursing profession. Utilizing a sample of 300 professional nurses subdivided into six categories of 50 subjects each, the investigator administered a questionnaire consisting of a semantic differential and a Likert-type professionalism scale. The six categories of nurses studied were (1) eight-year-plus professionals: nurses with a baccalaureate degree or higher who had been employed as nurses for at least eight years; (2) entering RN's: graduates from diploma or Associate Arts nursing programs who were enrolled in the first semester of their Baccalaureate degree nursing program; (3) graduating RN's: the same as number two, only they had just graduated or were within one month of graduation from the baccalaureate nursing program; (4) one-year RN's: the same as numbers 2 and 3 except that these were diploma or Associate Arts nurses who had earned a baccalaureate degree and had been employed in nursing for one year following graduation from the baccalaureate nursing program; (5) graduating basics: students who entered a baccalaureate nursing program as freshmen without any prior nursing education, and who had just graduated or were within one month of graduating from the baccalaureate nursing program; (6) one-year basics: the same as number 5, except these were basic students who had been employed as nurses for approximately one year since graduation from a basic baccalaureate nursing program.

Comparing the scores on the professionalism scale, the total factor scores (evaluation, potency, and activity) and item scores of the semantic differential for these six groups of nurses, Hogan found that the entering RN's, that is, registered nurses from nondegree programs, had lower professional attitudes than any of the other five groups studied. This is consistent with the findings of Corwin who found that in 1959 both diploma RN's and diploma students scored lower on his professional role conception scale than did degree students or RN's.

Hogan found that the highest professional attitudes were evidenced by graduating RN's, nondegree registered nurses who returned to school for a baccalaureate degree, followed closely by eight-year-plus professionals. Both of these findings are difficult to interpret because Hogan does not report the positions that the graduating RN's were aspiring to or the positions occupied by the eight-year-plus professionals. It has been found consistently that nurses with baccalaureate or higher degrees who aspire to, or who occupy, teaching positions evince markedly higher professional value scores on the Corwin scales than do their counterparts in nursing practice. Hogan's grouping together of nurse educators and nurse practitioners tends to cloud the issue.

Another of Hogan's findings, however is very similar to the process found in the post-graduation and two-year followup studies of California State College nursing graduates described earlier. Hogan found that the graduating basics considered nursing to be more positive, potent, and active than did any of the other groups studied, and that the one-year basics held significantly lower professional attitudes toward nursing than did the graduating basics. Although Hogan's sample was cross-sectional and the Kramer sample longitudinal, there are enough similarities here to make comparison worthwhile. The Hogan graduating basics are virtually the same as Kramer's 79 new baccalaureate graduates from three California State College nursing programs. Hogan's one-year basics might be equated to these same nurses one year later. In both studies, the findings were highly similar. There is a marked decrease in professionalism following one or two years of employment and a marked reduction in one's evaluation of nursing. The fact that the samples in these two studies came from different types of schools in two widely disparate geographical areas (Missouri and California), and that different, although similar, measurement and analytical tools were used, increases rather than decreases the power of this finding. Baccalaureate nurses who remain in nursing practice (as opposed to teaching) become less professional in their nursing attitudes than they were at graduation. Hogan also concludes that

the work environment did not sufficiently reward or, in fact, thwarted professional attitudes; hence, they were dropped or reduced.

## SUMMARY

The concept of professional-bureaucratic conflict as a major source of reality shock was introduced through excerpts from tape-recorded interviews with practicing nurses. Dimensions, symptoms, and phases of reality shock were presented and similarities and differences between culture and reality shock were discussed.

Theoretical dimensions of the professional-bureaucratic work organization problem were explored through an analysis of work tasks in a constantly changing technological society. A suggestion was made that such an approach would lead to development of organizational forms following function rather than the reverse. A review of some of the major research in this area indicates:

1. Professional-bureaucratic conflict is a relatively new phenomenon; it is an outgrowth of the combination of increased bureaucratization and professionalization, as well as the increased employment of professionals in organizations. This type of conflict situation can and does occur in a variety of settings and occupations.

2. Conflicting loyalties to the professional and bureaucratic systems of work organization leads to reality shock, a condition that is detrimental to the individual, the profession, and to society.

3. The severity of professional-bureaucratic conflict, and resultant reality shock, is related to type of educational preparation, role configuration, disparity in reward systems, and to structural features of the organization. With increased professionalism, there is often increased conflict. Organizational conflict is not necessarily deterimental; indeed, it is often the source of innovation. The question is whether the bureaucratic structure is flexible enough to accommodate the conflict associated with the professional mode.

The next chapter will focus on a study designed to ameliorate the degree of reality shock experienced by two classes of baccalaureate nurses and to equip them with growth-producing conflict resolution strategies. The eclectic theoretical framework that generated the remainder of the hypothesis for the study will be described, as well as the design, procedures, and methods of study.

## NOTES

1. This is not to be confused with the increased rate of illness resulting from exposure to strains or organisms to which one is unaccustomed. Example: a nurse just starting out in a pediatric ward being exposed to and coming down with "infant trots."
2. Validity studies on these scales were done by both Corwin and myself. Test-retest reliability studies done by the author on 52 senior student nurses before and after a three-week Christmas break indicated satisfactory reliabilities ranging from .86 to .89 for the role conception and role deprivation scales.
3. Corwin's study was cross-sectional, observing different groups of people representing points along a continuum; while the Kramer study was longitudinal and observed the same group of people as they moved through the steps or phases of the continuum.

## REFERENCES

Becker, H.: The teacher in the authority system of the public school, J. Educational Sociol. **27**:128-141, November 1953.

Beckhard, R.: Organization development; strategies and models, Reading, Mass., 1969, Addison-Wesley Publishing Co.

Ben-David, J.: The professional role of the physician in bureaucratized medicine; a study in role conflict, Human Relations **11**(1):255-274, 1958.

Benne, K., and Bennis, W.: Role confusion and conflict within nursing, Am. J. Nurs., part one, **59**(2):196-198, 1959; part two, **59**(3):380-383.

Bennis, W. G.: The coming death of bureaucracy: in Think Magazine, International Business Machines Corp. A notes and quotes reprint, Hartford, 1966, Connecticut General Life Insurance Co.

Bennis, W. G.: Post-bureaucratic leadership, Trans-Action **6**:44, July 1969.

Blau, P. M., and Scott, W. R.: Formal organization, San Francisco, 1962, Chandler Publishing Co.

Brewster, E. T., and Brewster, E. S.: Involvement as a means of second culture learning, Practical Anthropology **19**(1):27-44, 1972.

Chemers, M.: Cross-cultural training as a means for improving situational favorableness, Human Relations **22**(6):531-546, 1969.

Corwin, R.: Militant professionalism, New York, 1970, Appleton-Century-Crofts.

Corwin, R.: Role conception and mobility aspiration; a study in the formation and transformation of nursing identities, unpublished doctoral dissertation, University of Minnesota, 1960, Department of Sociology.

Corwin, R.: The professional employee; a study of conflict in nursing roles, Am. J. Sociol. **66**(6):604-615, 1961.

Corwin, R., and Taves, M.: Some concomitants of bureaucratic and professional conceptions of the nurse role, Nurs. Research **11**:223-225, 1962.

Fiedler, F., Mitchell, T., and Triandis, H.: The culture assimilator; an approach to cross-cultural training, J. Applied Psychol. **55**(2):95-102, 1971.

Gale, C.: The nurse's aide; a study of low role coordination, doctoral dissertation, 1969, Stanford University.

Goldstein, B., Northwood, L., and Goldstein, R.: Medicine in industry; problems of administrators and practitioners, J. Health Soc. **1**(4):259-268, 1960.

Goss, M.: Influence and authority among physicians in an outpatient clinic, Am. Sociol. Rev. **26**(1):39-50, 1961.

Guthrie, G. M.: Preparing Americans for participation in another culture, a paper presented to the Conferences on Peace Corps and the Behavioral Sciences, Washington, D. C., 1963, p. 15.

Hogan, C.: Registered nurses' completion of a Bachelor of Science degree in nursing—its effects on their attitude toward the nursing profession, doctoral dissertation, St. Louis, 1972, St. Louis University, Department of Education.

Hughes, E.: Profession, Daedalus, **92**, 1963.

Jablonsky, A., editor: Imperatives for change, Proceedings of the New York State Education Department Conference on College and University Programs for Teachers of the Disadvantaged, April 10-11, 1967, ERIC #EDO 012-734.

The job blahs; who wants to work?, Newsweek, March 26, 1973, pp. 79-89.

Johnson, N.: The professional-bureaucratic conflict, J. of Nurs. Administration **1**(3):31-39, 1971.

Kornhauser, W.: Scientists in industry, Berkeley, Calif., 1962, University of California Press.

Kramer, M.: Some effects of exposure to employing bureaucracies on the role conceptions and role deprivation of neophyte collegiate nurses, unpublished doctoral dissertation, 1966, Stanford University.

Kramer, M.: The new graduate speaks, Am. J. Nurs. **66**(11):2420-2424, 1966.

Kramer, M.: Comparative study of characteristics, attitudes and opinions of neophyte British and American nurses, Internat. J. Nurs. Studies **4**:281-294, 1967.

Kramer, M.: Collegiate graduate nurses in medical center hospitals; mutual challenge or duel, Nurs. Research **18**(3):196-210, 1969.

Kramer, M.: New graduate speaks—again, Am. J. Nurs. **69**(9):1903-07, 1969.

Kramer, M.: Role conception of baccalaureate nurses and success in hospital nursing, Nurs. Research **19**(5):428-439, 1970.

Lederer, W., and Burdick, E.: The ugly american, New York, 1958, W. W. Norton & Co., Inc.

Nostrand, H.: Describing and teaching the sociocultural context of a foreign language and literature. In Valdman, A., editor: Trends in language teaching, New York, 1966, McGraw-Hill Book Co., p. 6.

Oberg, K.: Cultural shock adjustment to new cultural environments, Practical Anthropology **7**(4):177-182, 1960.

Reyburn, W. D.: Crossing cultural frontiers, Practical Anthropology 15(6):249-257, 1968.

Schein, E.: The first job dilemma, Psychology Today 1(10):27-37, 1968.

Scott, W. R.: Some implications of organization theory for research on health services, Milbank Memorial Fund Quarterly, 44(4), 1966, part two.

Scott, W. R.: Professionals in bureaucracies—areas of conflict. In Vollmer, H. M., and Mills, D. L., editors: Professionalization, New Jersey, 1966, Prentice-Hall, Inc., pp. 265-275.

Scott, W. R.: Professional employees in a bureaucratic structure; social work. In Etzioni, A., editor: The semi-professions and their organization, New York, 1969, The Free Press, pp. 82-140.

Shinn, R.: The locus of authority; participatory democracy in the age of the expert. In Manschreck, C. L., editor: Erosion of authority, Nashville, 1971, Abingdon Press.

Smalley, W.: Culture shock, language shock, and the shock of self-discovery, Practical Anthropology 10(2): 49-56, 1963.

Smith, K.: Discrepancies in the value climate of nursing students; a comparison of head nurses and nursing educators, unpublished doctoral dissertation, 1964, Stanford University, Department of Education, pp. 11-23.

Szanton, D. L.: Cultural confrontation in the Philippines. In Taylor, R. B., editor: Cultural frontiers of the peace corps, Cambridge, 1966, The M. I. T. Press.

Toffler, A.: Future shock, New York, 1970, Random House, Inc., p. 2.

Triandis, H. C.: Interpersonal relations in international organizations, Organizational Behavior and Human Performance 2:26-55, 1967.

Wilensky, H.: Intellectuals in labor unions, New York, 1956, The Free Press.

Winsor, F.: The space-child's Mother Goose, Atlantic Monthly, December 1956, p. 41.

Work and enjoy it, inc., National Observer 12(11), 1973.

## CHAPTER TWO

# A SEARCH FOR A WAY OUT

The problem of community, which is the form of personal life, is the one of deciding on whose terms it shall be lived. Simply to impose my terms on the other person is to deny his freedom and responsibility; Simply to accept his terms without demur is to abandon my own. In either case, there is no community but a kind of fusion or absorption instead. For community implies a mutuality of distinct initiatives as an ongoing project.°

In the community of nursing, potential conflict can be expected between the idealistic, futuristic goals of nurse educators and their students, and the more immediately relevant, present-day, action-oriented concerns of the practitioner. This conflict can be growth-producing, a mutuality of distinct initiatives generating positive forward movement; or it can be a devastating, negative force engendering hostility, frustration, and exodus. Which shall it be for the community of nursing?

## THE POSITIVE NOW OR THE RELATIVE WHEN?

There are many who would reason as follows. If, in fact, new graduate nurses who have been socialized into a professional system of work organization encounter a great deal of difficulty and lose their professional value orientation fairly quickly upon employment, if they are unable to practice nursing in the Positive Now and leave nursing practice in disgust and disillusionment, why socialize them with Relative When values to begin with? Why not simply train neophyte nurses in such a way that they will be operational in present nursing practice? If educators would focus on

teaching nurse aspirants the role-specific behaviors (such as punctuality, organization, skilled performance of procedures) of the work subculture and the corresponding value system, then little role transformation would be required when the apprentice nurse changes her status from student to graduate. Conflict between nursing in the Positive Now and the Relative When and attendant deleterious results would be avoided.

This solution might work except for one factor that appears to be constant in our society and in the world: change—changing values, mores, technology, political theories, and the like. Our future is a world we cannot predict. If the goal of man is to actualize himself and to provide the opportunity for each person to maintain as positive a state of health as possible, then we as nurses must aspire to create a health care system in the future that is better than the present one. We must prepare nurses to practice not only in the Positive Now but also in the Relative When. It is not enough to teach nurse aspirants the specific behaviors and facts needed to nurse in the system of today; we must equip them with the tools needed to nurse in the future.

What tools will be useful in a future that we cannot even predict? The tools we fashion cannot be physical; technology is changing at a rapid pace. Nor can they be concepts or facts, for these change as new perceptions emerge. The tool then, that we offer is process—process to confront, relate to, modify the facts and the technology.°

Grappling with the realities of the knowl-

---

°Johann, R. O.: From Love is not enough, New York, © 1965, America Press, Inc. Reprinted with permission.

°Tools for change. In Strategy notebook, San Francisco, Interaction Associates, Inc., p. 5.

edge and medical technological explosions already upon us and still to come, nurse aspirants can no longer be taught all the facts and techniques needed to function in the variety of settings and situations in which nursing is practiced. Nor would this be desirable if it were possible. The nurses of tomorrow must be schooled in broad scientific principles that are applicable in a variety of situations, rather than specific facts and techniques that are highly useful in particular instances. The former is characteristic of the whole-task approach, while the latter emanates from a part-task bureaucratic view.

This is not to say that individual nurses who were trained in the bureaucratic mode can never accomplish or have never attained a more comprehensive whole-task view of the nature of the caring process. They may well have reached this goal through an inductive process of learning and perfecting specific knowledge and skills ("When Mrs. Jones gives me a tongue lashing, she will calm down if I do thus and so." Or, "I can prevent Mr. Baker from angrily refusing his Bird treatments if I do thus and so."). If internally motivated, this nurse might abstract and formulate some general guidelines or principles for handling hostile patients. The point is that, with the tremendous increase in knowledge and demand for economy of learning and performance, it is more efficient to utilize a whole-task principle type of learning than an education based on the learning of part-task techniques and skills. To be sure, the latter may have more immediate usefulness, but the former has more long-range dividends.

Another reason for utilizing a whole-task approach in the preparation of professional practitioners, even though it may cause conflict within the community of nursing, is the recognition of discontinuity in patient and client care. It is widely recognized among nurse educators, practitioners, and nursing service administrators that the present quality of nursing care can and should be improved. We are becoming increasingly aware of the fragmentation and spottiness of nursing care as it is usually delivered. From the early writings of Mauksch to later, more scientific approaches, the message is loud and consistent. At a time in their lives when people most need the tenderness, concern, and care of a constant person, they are burdened with the necessity of interacting with a host of caretakers ranging from the "dusting and polishing" aide to the medication nurse, the treatment nurse, the school nurse, the TB followup nurse, and so on. It was anticipated that preparing neophyte nurse practitioners to see the patient as a whole, to plan for continuity and comprehensiveness of patient care, would put the patient back together again, much like the proverbial Humpty Dumpty.

## WHY AREN'T NEW GRADUATES MORE EFFECTIVE?

Any community puts its hope and faith for the future on its educational products of today. The community of nursing expected and continues to expect that the graduate nurses of today, who are receiving a much sounder scientific and humanistic education than the nurses prepared several decades ago, will make some fundamental and positive improvements in patient care. The nurses prepared today are the leaders of tomorrow. They are expected to be actionary, not reactionary. Therein lies the future of the community of nursing.

Some new graduates have lived up to these expectations. Yet Reinkemeyer feels that collegiate graduates have not made the improvements expected because of status discrepancies in the nurse's preparation as a professional at the undergraduate rather than at the graduate level. Thomas argues that nursing service is not ready for these "products of excellence" from today's school, while other directors of nursing raise many questions regarding the effectiveness of today's neophyte nurse practitioner. A 1972 study by Waters and associates seems to indicate that if the baccalaureate practitioner is making fundamental improvements in patient care, the processes of bringing about these improvements are not observable from behavior or apparent through interviewing. It must be concluded that today's graduates are not having the impact on improvement of health care that was expected of them.

Why haven't the expected improvements

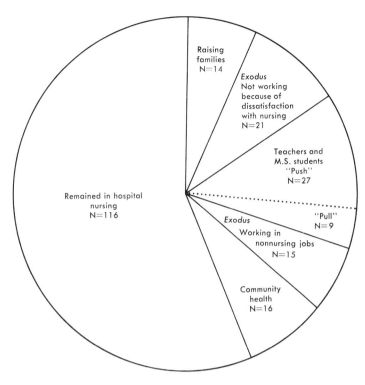

Raising
families
N=14

Exodus
Not working
because of
dissatisfaction
with nursing
N=21

Teachers and
M.S. students
"Push"
N=27

Remained in hospital
nursing
N=116

Exodus
Working in
nonnursing jobs
N=15

"Pull"
N=9

Community
health
N=16

N=218

come about? From research and empirical observations, it is conjectured that there are at least three possible reasons for this seeming impotence of the new graduate. One factor is the large *exodus* of nurses from the job scene for reasons other than marriage and family. It was found, for example, that in one group of 220 baccalaureate nurses, most of whom had been working for one or two years after graduation, 28.9% left nursing practice within the two-year period of the study because of job dissatisfaction. With this kind of attrition rate, it is understandable why health care improvements are not forthcoming.

The figure above shows the location of 218 of those nurses (one died; the other could not be located) at the time of the two-year followup. They all originally had been working in medical center hospitals.

Another potential reason why the new baccalaureate graduate may not be making the fundamental improvements in nursing care that were expected of her might be the problem of her *lack of self-confidence*. This may be true of diploma and ADN nurses as well.

As one director of nursing stated it, the new graduate has an "amazing lack of self-confidence . . . a fear of her own concept of her inadequacy."

One of their biggest difficulties is their limited self-assurance. They are intelligent young women, who are scared to death that they are going to fall flat on their face . . . Their utter lack of confidence [is evident]. They know how to nurse, but when they come onto the floors they are extremely hesitant . . . .[°]

The appellation "lack of self-confidence" may well be masking an underlying issue. The new graduate might be suffering from a lack of "interpersonal competency," which comes through to others and self as a lack of confidence. The process goes something like this. The neophyte nurse is socialized into a set of values that are different from those operative in the work situation. Values are commands or directives for action to which individuals

---

[°]Kramer, M.: Collegiate graduate nurses in medical center hospitals: mutual challenge or duel, Nurs. Res. **18**(3): 196-210, 1969, © American Journal of Nursing Co.

are committed. As such we operate on our values, using them not only to guide our own actions but also to interpret and predict the actions of others. When individuals are placed into a social system that is governed by a different set of values, they are no longer able to predict accurately their interpersonal impact upon others or others' impact upon themselves. They therefore are or become interpersonally incompetent.

Foote and Cottrell define interpersonal competence as the skill or set of abilities allowing an individual to shape the responses he gets from others. Weinstein describes three of these abilities. First, the individual must be able to correctly predict the impact that his actions will have on other persons' definitions of the situation. Others behave in terms of the way *they* define the situation, that is, according to their own value and perceptual systems. Secondly, the individual must possess a varied and large repertoire of potential lines of action. Thirdly, the individual must have the necessary intrapersonal resources to be able to employ effective tactics in situations where they are appropriate. In all likelihood, the neophyte nurse is not interpersonally competent in the work situation. Because she is operating in a value framework different from that of most of her co-workers, she is not able to correctly predict the impact her behavior will have on others' definitions of the situation. She possesses few strategies or lines of action that are appropriate to the work situation. Without these, she will not be interpersonally competent even if she does have the needed personal resources such as technical skill and professional judgment.

The manifestation of interpersonal incompetence as lack of self-confidence is undoubtedly due to the confusion and diffuse sense of failure that results from inability to understand and predict why things are happening as they are.

If individuals are in social systems where they are unable to predict accurately their interpersonal impact upon others, and others' impact upon themselves, they may begin to feel confused. "Why are people behaving that way toward me?" "Why do they interpret me incorrectly?" Since such ques-

tions are not sanctioned in a rationally dominated system, much less answered, the confusion will tend to turn to frustration and feelings of failure . . . .°

In an attempt to maintain her sense of esteem, the neophyte may react both by questioning the honesty and genuineness of the interpersonal behavior of the other nurses and by labeling her feelings of confusion and frustration as lack of self-confidence rather than failure of interpersonal competence in the new subculture.

There is also probably considerable justification for the neophyte's perceived lack of confidence in the area of skills, routines, and other job-specific behaviors. The new nurse does have a lack of technical knowledge and skill. Since these are the qualities most highly prized in the work setting, it is to be expected that she will lack confidence in her ability to perform them in the work setting. Many new graduates set up skill mastery as one test or ground upon which to prove themselves. Asking for feedback to determine how well they are performing in this test situation might well be interpreted as a lack of self-confidence. So the appellate "lack of self-confidence" is probably two-pronged. It consists of a genuine lack of confidence in one's ability to perform skills and routines that have not been practiced sufficiently, and it entails a probably unrecognized lack of interpersonal competence, both in predicting the behavior of others who are operating on a different value system and in possession of lines of action appropriate to influence others.

This two-pronged lack of self-confidence is not only antithetical to independence, autonomy, and self-directedness—traits usually ascribed to someone of professional status—it is also detrimental to the whole concept of influencing others, of making planned changes and of instigating distinct initiatives as an ongoing enterprise of a community. The confusion, frustration, sense of failure, and despair that results from it certainly contributes to

°Argyris, G.: Interpersonal competence and organizational effectiveness. In Bennis, W. G., and associates: Interpersonal dynamics, Homewood, Ill., 1968, Dorsey Press, p. 588.

the exodus of nurses from practice and does much to explain why innovative changes in nursing practice have not been forthcoming from these practitioners.

Some directors of nursing, as well as many young graduates who have been interviewed, agree that lack of confidence in performing clinical nursing skills is a major problem. In Paynich's study, this was listed by baccalaureate students as their primary reason for seeking summer work experience as nurses' aides. Some directors and new graduates feel that this lack of confidence in skill performance is transmitted to the nurse by her instructors, who themselves are "young, immature, unseasoned, and unsure of themselves in the clinical areas."[1]

It's no wonder that we lack confidence in what we know and what we can do. All but one of my instructors in school was fresh out of school, with very little practical know-how under her belt. One day we counted it up. For seven of the eight instructors I had, their combined work experience was less than one and a half years. They knew the theory well, but were of absolutely no help in using it to get the work done. If you ran into snags with the aides, or with bucking the system, or how to get something done that was a little difficult, the teacher was no help. (NG:BS/6[87]11/68)

One student in Paynich's survey stated that "clinical instructors should have two to four years of experience before being allowed to teach." It is also quite possible—indeed probable—that the young instructors about whom this student was speaking were themselves interpersonally incompetent in the work subculture. They lacked the strategies and the empathetic ability to predict how others in the work system, who were operating on a different set of values, defined the situation. Lacking this interpersonal competence, they were unable to transmit these skills to their students; and so the lack of confidence problem persists and grows.

The lack of self-confidence of the new graduate, particularly in the area of skills, and the lack of strategies to deal effectively with the feelings engendered by this lack of skill expertise is described in the following excerpts from tape-recorded interviews.

The nurses assume that if you are a nurse you should know this; and if you go up to them and ask them a very simple question, they kind of look at you funny, as if you should know this— you should have good judgment and all this. [Can you give me a specific example?] Medications, for example. I've never worked with medications too much. And whether or not you should mix a certain medication in an IV or a volutrol, or how much water you should put into the vial and things like that . . . they say; "Well, you should know this; it takes common sense." This sort of thing frustrates me; it hinders me from asking other questions that I have doubts about. And it hurts. It makes me feel dumb. (NG:BS/2[1]9/71)

. . .

I have talked with other girls, and I think we are pretty much the same. In school, we didn't do this, and we didn't learn that, and we should have learned this or that. And right now, we are on our own and we are supposed to know what action to take; but we just get stuck, and we don't know what to do. I think in this aspect we are almost the same. Sometimes we do something wrong and the staff nurses look at us as if to say, "Well, you are really dumb. You are so stupid, you don't know what to do." I think they expect us to know as much as they do. Sometimes I feel really frustrated because I do something wrong and they look at me just like I was a fool. (NG:AD/2[4]9/71)

This kind of socialization from staff nurses is not universal by any means, but it is frequent and general enough to be a marked contributory factor to the chronicity and persistence of the lack of self-confidence seen in new graduate nurses. As long as this problem persists, the neophyte nurse, the hope of the future, will be unable to effect needed improvements in nursing practice.

It is a major premise of this research that the main reason for the lack of new graduate effectiveness in changing nursing practice, and the reason that is at the heart of the exodus and lack of confidence, is the nurse's *inability to convert professional-bureaucratic work organizational conflict* into growth-producing initiatives for herself, for the nursing community, and for the health care system. Socialized into one kind of system by faculty who themselves lack experience and perhaps success in implementing professional ideals and stan-

# PROFESSIONAL-BUREAUCRATIC ROLE CONFLICT THEORY

dards into practice, the young graduate lacks both the strategies and confidence in her ability to do so. She flees the work scene, often into the ranks of education where she in turn teaches an idealized version of practice (untested in the reality situation) to other nurse aspirants. The process repeats itself. For the most part, nurse faculty do not model the process of operationalizing professional values. The tendency is for them to demonstrate either the imposition or the compartmentalization of one's professional values. They may recognize that there is a difference between their values and those in the work scene and attempt to impose their values on the service staff. Or faculty may assume that their value system and work values are highly similar. Students perceive this as compartmentalization— "When my instructor is on the floor, I do it her way; otherwise I do it the head nurse's way. But above all, don't let the instructor know there's a difference."

Experienced nurse practitioners of today are also not effective in utilizing conflict as potential growth-producing experiences, either for themselves or in helping the neophyte. Viewed from the perspective of the new graduate, the nurse practitioner is seen as someone who imposes her terms and values. The newcomer is considered to have adjusted when she has fused her values with those of the working community. Rather than growth, fusion or absorption as a method of conflict resolution produces stagnation, apathy, and perhaps most important, continued intolerance. If one elects the conformist route, that is, discards his professional values and wholeheartedly identifies with those of the organization, he will become more and more intolerant of the next deviant, such as another new graduate with a value system that is now different from the one that has been adopted. Again, it is possible for the process to repeat itself: new graduate arrives, experiences conflict between school and work values, sees other staff nurses modeling and being rewarded for enactment of work-oriented values, abdicates school values, and absorbs those of the work culture. She then models and reinforces these values for the next new graduate who comes along. The problem grows and magnifies. The work gets done, but does nursing practice and the health care system improve?

## CONSTRUCTIVE CONFLICT RESOLUTION—THE GOAL

What is meant by constructive or growth-producing conflict resolution? Begin with the posture that conflict in today's ever-changing world is inevitable and that it is not necessarily detrimental to productivity and job satisfaction. Assume that, if managed properly, conflict is the avenue to needed social change. Several perspectives are useful for viewing this change. Argyris sees growth-producing conflict management as maintenance of an open stance, a posture wherein the individual is open to process feedback. He can perceive, weigh, and assess various parameters of a problem and solve conflict situations so that they stay solved. Deutsch views conflict resolution from a dyadic perspective. Faced with a conflict situation in which activities for goal accomplishment of two or more persons are incompatible, an individual (or a group) can elect to move toward either constructive or destructive resolution. In constructive conflict resolution the participants move toward and enact the characteristics of cooperative groups. They attempt to highlight mutual interests, enhance mutual power, adopt trusting and friendly attitudes, have a positive and responsive attitude to the other's needs, minimize the salience of opposed interests, and have open, honest communications. Destructive conflict resolution is akin to the characteristics of competitive groups. Those involved attempt to decrease each other's power, have suspicious, hostile, and exploitive attitudes, magnify opposed interests, use threat and intimidation, and have devious communication patterns. From both an individual and an interactional perspective, growth-producing conflict resolution means behavioral strategies in which the individual weighs and assesses the values of both the school and work subcultural systems and consciously strives to evolve a cooperative stance in managing the conflict.

## CONSTRUCTING THE THEORETICAL FRAMEWORK

It is not enough to identify a problem (the potential conflict faced by professional employees) and to identify the effects of malresolution of the conflict (reality shock, exodus, ineffectual practice). Design and evaluation of potential solutions are mandatory. Operating on this premise, a study was designed to ascertain whether something could be done about

**PROFESSIONAL-BUREAUCRATIC FACTS**

PROFESSIONAL VALUES

BUREAUCRATIC VALUES

ROLE CONFLICT & ROLE DEPRIVATION

CONFLICT: PRACTICE → TEACHING

this professional-bureaucratic work discrepancy so that the conflict would be resolved in a constructive manner. It was anticipated that reality shock would be lessened and resultant withdrawal would not occur. Synthesizing from the theoretical notions and empirical facts on professional-bureaucratic conflict described in Chapter 1, it is possible to abstract a set of interrelated facts and assumptions that form the first cornerstone of an emerging, eclectic theory of professional-bureaucratic conflict resolution.

1. Collegiate graduate nurses have higher professional and lower bureaucratic values than do diploma nurses.
2. This makes them highly susceptible to role conflict and role deprivation.
3. With high conflict there is a great likelihood they will leave active nursing practice or flee into teaching.
4. It is undesirable to have nurse educators who are teaching as a means of escaping from practice or to have nurses fleeing from nursing altogether.

Although the early Corwin and Kramer studies provide convincing evidence of the effects of the bureaucratic social structure on the role organization of novice nurses, and of the major changes in role organization that tend to occur during initial experiences as a graduate nurse, empirically we know that some individuals still maintain a personal role definition that includes a high professional component. Some individuals do not flee the work scene even though they appear to be in conflict. Some nurses appear to be able to retain their professional loyalties and be personally and professionally competent, productive, and happy in the work scene. What factors aid in these kinds of adjustments?

In attempting to understand and explain

individual differences in role configuration,[2] role adaptation, and potential conflict resolution, two theories are particularly relevant and useful. Kelman's theory of social influence is helpful in understanding a possible reason why different neophytes develop different role configurations. Merton's idea of anticipatory socialization helps to explain both individual differences in role configuration and different modes of adaptation.

### Social influence: effects upon others

Kelman has defined three processes or steps that we go through in social influence: compliance, identification, and internalization. These processes are not mutually exclusive, nor do they occur in pure and distinct forms in real-life situations, but they are identifiable. *Compliance* occurs when an individual accepts influence from another person or group because he wants a favorable reaction from them. He does not adopt the induced behavior because he necessarily believes in its content, but because he sees it as instrumental in getting something he wants—social approval, a promotion, a raise, or perhaps just simply holding onto his job.

*Identification* occurs when a person adopts the behavior of another because this particular behavior is related to the way in which the person wants to be perceived by and to interact with the other. The efforts involved when an individual learns to imitate the behavior of a desired role model exemplify this process. There is a selectivity in what attitudes and actions are imitated from the chosen role model, rather than a complete parrotting of behavior. The basic sense of identity and stability of the individual's self-concept are not at stake in the identification process, because the values and behaviors are added onto or encapsulated rather than integrated into the individual's self-concept system.

*Internalization* occurs when an individual accepts influence because he believes in it. The induced behavior is congruent with his value system and is integrated into that value system. It becomes a part of the person's self-concept system. As such, the internalized behavior is intrinsically rewarding; both the

behavior and the rewards gradually become independent of any external source.

Just as there is a difference in the conditions under which the above three processes of social influence occur, so also is there a difference in conditions under which they can subsequently be changed. Compliant responses will be abandoned when the behavior is no longer seen as the best route for achieving desired social rewards. A response adopted through identification will be terminated if it is no longer seen as a path toward maintaining or establishing satisfying relationships with the desired role model. And last, identification responses will be dropped if they are no longer perceived as a way of maximizing the individual's value system.

Kelman's theory of social influence has relevance for the problem under consideration here. In compliance behavior, a role model is not needed. One needs only to perceive some person or group as the controller of desired rewards (for example, the head nurse or supervisor controls rewards such as desirable shifts, days off, assignment) and be aware of the behavior necessary to get these rewards. The role incumbent can then enact compliant behavior to obtain these rewards. Compliant behavior is probably the first step in the process of adaptation that confronts the new graduate. Some of these conformations might be cognitively expected, but there is considerable evidence that the emotional impact is a surprise.

I knew I'd be working for eight hours, but I had no idea how long that is . . . how tired I'd be. You have to plan everything around work—social activities, classes, washing, shopping, dental appointments—just everything. It's all just so different than when I was in school. (NG:BS/3[13]9/65)

Prepared or not, the young graduate learns very soon that she must comply with at least some of the fundamental parameters of a position (recording her time, completing proper forms, and so forth). She soon learns that she is rewarded for enacting this compliant behavior, and she may begin to conform even more to get further desired rewards. At this point it can be expected that she is raising her bureaucratic loyalty. Neophyte nurses expressed more bureaucratic loyalties as measured by the Corwin scales 3 months after employment than they had at graduation. Interviews with new graduates also verified this compliant process.

There are some things you just have to do if you like them or not—like getting to work on time, and taking your turn on weekends, and not calling in sick before or after a holiday, and stocking shelves with supplies, and putting cath trays in the same place as everyone else. At first I thought this was a real bore, but I realize now that you have to have some rules and order. I used to think the head nurse was nuts when she'd compliment someone on how nice the shelves in the treatment room looked. But lately I've gotten that, and it's kind of nice. I guess it's really important that you be able to find the equipment you need to do things. (Med Ctr:BS[2513]6/68)

Somewhere during this compliant process, a crucial point is reached. The individual may move into the identification phase wherein some model person or group is personally defined for aspiration. Desiring to be a member of this group or to be like them, the individual imitates selective attitudes and actions. To the extent that these promote a satisfying self-defining relationship, the identification process will continue, and the individual will profess beliefs and attitudes highly similar to those of the model person or group.

When the role-taking or identification phase is complete, internalization has occurred. In this state, the assumed values, beliefs, and ensuing behavior are so much a part of the individual that compliance or conformity to them is intrinsically rewarding and self-satisfying. In this phase, the person no longer needs the role model required during the identification phase.

Now, let's return to our neophyte nurse and hypothesize as to what might be happening to her as she enters her first postgraduate position. During the compliant phase she has undoubtedly raised her bureaucratic values. It is at this point that a crucial juncture is reached. Role models are not mandatory for compliance behavior, but they are imperative during the identification phase. If the available models to be selected and imitated by the neophyte are highly bureaucratic in orientation, the likelihood is very strong that the neophyte will continue to raise her bureaucratic loyalties and probably demur to a decrease in professional loyalties. Unless her chosen role models hold both high professional and high bureaucratic values and enact behavior that shows her how to resolve the potential conflict ensuing from these two different work systems, she will not learn to resolve conflict in a growth-producing manner. If the selected and imitated role models are highly profes-

**ANTICIPATORY SOCIALIZATION THEORY**

sional in orientation and do not demonstrate how professional behavior can be operationalized in the work setting, the resultant identification of the neophyte will probably be an increase in professional values and a lowering of bureaucratic loyalties. This unfortunately is a frequently untenable position which often leads to frustration and flight behavior.

The important point is that the identification phase of social influence is the critical juncture. Dependent as it is upon role models, it explains not only why different neophytes develop different role configurations, it also casts the die for the later internalization phase. In this internalization stage of social influence, models are not necessary. In all likelihood individuals in this phase present the most effective models for others who are in the identification phase, because it is the "internalized" who stabilize the system. It can be seen that to effectively produce nurses of high professional orientation, capable of enacting growth-producing conflict resolution behavior, appropriate role models must be available during the identification phase of social influence.

### Anticipatory socialization: preparing ahead

Studying the behavior and attitudinal changes of soldiers during World War II, Stouffer and associates noted that often those who successfully assumed new statuses began to acquire the necessary behavioral characteristics, attitudes, and role orientations prior to the time of formally making the change (for example, progressing from corporal to sargeant). This premature taking on or identification (in the sense of the preceding discussion of Kelman's theory) with the behavior and attitudes of an "aspired to" reference group Merton termed anticipatory socialization.

The idea of anticipatory socialization may be a missing link in resolving professional-bureaucratic conflict. In the status shift from student to graduate nurse, we are dealing with a system in which change in status is expected and readily possible. But there is a value and behavior difference between the two groups. This disparity between membership and reference groups can well explain individual differences in role configurations. For example, collegiate graduate nurses tend to express a high professional–low bureaucratic role configuration at graduation. This is the prevailing attitudinal composition of the student membership group to which the neophyte belongs and also of the faculty group with which many of them identify. However, there are some students who profess high bureaucratic–low professional orientations. These students are not infrequently perceived as deviants by their peers or by the faculty. It is not at all uncommon to find that these nurses have either work-oriented role models° or specific aspirations to some work-oriented position. In other words, they themselves have begun the process of anticipatory socialization to some work-oriented group while at the same time belonging, at least marginally, to the student membership group.

Perhaps most significant is the idea that if anticipatory socialization is functional for an individual in an open society, why not *make* it happen, rather than *letting* it happen? Why not equip neophytes with a thorough knowledge of the social system into which they will be going? Why not teach them the empathic behavior lines of action taken by a highly adaptive reference group of nurses? If this were done, it seems the chances would be greater that the neophyte would be interpersonally competent and effective in the work situation. More accurate role-taking would be highly instrumental in resolving conflict in a growth-producing way and eventually lead to improvements in nursing practice.

In the Army example cited earlier, the goal of anticipatory socialization and of subsequent success was conformity. The goal of the kind of program speculated here is modeling of a reference group of nurses who are highly adaptive, innovative opinion leaders and change agents, not successful conformists. It

---

°Many nurse faculty resist the idea of students working as nurse's aides during vacation periods. "They learn all the wrong ways of doing things, and they learn sloppy work habits, and then our job is twice as difficult when they come back to school. We have to beat all those notions out of their heads again." In the context of the discussion just presented, this faculty member is saying that the student had taken on the values and behaviors of a work membership group, and that these are in conflict with those of the faculty.

must be noted that the reason such a reference group is possible in the work system is that there is some support for the innovator with high professional values. For example, directors of nursing services as a group score much higher on the Corwin professional role conception scales than do supervisors in the same organization. (See Appendix B. Also note the kind of support for innovativeness and active professionalism provided by the director of nursing in the interview excerpts on p. 118 and in the Letters from Lynn, p. 185.)

More data in this regard is provided in the following excerpt of an interview between the investigator and a nursing service supervisor at one of the medical centers.

INVESTIGATOR: Now that the interviews with six nurses are all completed, I wonder if you could tell me a little something about each nurse from your perspective and from your contact with her.

SUPERVISOR: Well, Janie [one of the nurses with high professional–high bureaucratic values, listed as highly successful] is a "real trouble-maker," but she's a good nurse. She's always trying to get something going, institute something new, or upset the established routine in some way. I find her very difficult to work with and impossible to control. She manages her own unit okay though, or else I wouldn't have agreed with the others that she was "highly successful." Mrs. Adams [the DNS] gives her her head though, and she really thinks she's great. She says that Janie breathes life into the place and is the hope of the future. I think that's sort of strong. There are other nurses here who I think are much better in managing their units and getting the work done. (MedCtr:[19]5/68)

It seems clear from this excerpt that the director of nursing is instrumental in assisting this young baccalaureate nurse to be innovative and a change agent. This type of support, even if it is weak, is absolutely necessary if these kinds of values and behaviors are to root, flourish, and hopefully expand.

Since a group of highly adaptive nurses who have constructively resolved professional-bureaucratic role conflict were needed as role models, the problem became one of locating this rather unique reference group to which student nurses could be anticipatorily socialized. If the propositions are accepted that neophyte nurses identify their former instructors as role models, that neither nurse faculty nor nursing supervisors display the kind of adaptive professional values and behavior desired, and that many collegiate graduate nurses lose their professional loyalties soon after employment, then it is logical to conclude that none of these are suitable reference groups for anticipatory socialization.

Still another factor needs to be considered. Traditionally, when role socialization is conceptualized, the implicit assumption is that a consensus exists within society, and particularly among the agents of socialization, as to the legitimate content of the role expectations associated with anticipated statuses. Such is frequently not the case. As described in much greater detail in Chapter 6, many agents socialize the neophyte nurse. Although the faculty of the school, in-service educators, and head nurses might be designated as the formal socializers, there are many others in the informal system (physicians, aides, orderlies, staff nurses, and patients, to mention a few) who often have more influence over the role incumbent than the formal socializers. The point of particular emphasis, however, is that there is no consensus within the health care society, either among the formal or informal socializers, as to the legitimate content of the role expectations of the staff nurse. Virtually every socialization agent views her differently and has different expectations of her role.

The interrelated facts and assumptions that constitute the second cornerstone of the theoretical framework are:

1. Collegiate graduates usually identify instructors as role models.
2. Collegiate nurse faculty do not possess the same values as nurses in the work setting.

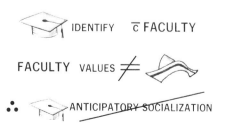

3. Student nurses do not have the opportunity for anticipatory socialization; that is, to imitate role models who enact growth-producing conflict resolution behavior.

## BRIDGE OVER TROUBLED WATERS

COLLEGIATE
NURSE
ANTICIPATORY
SOCIALIZATION
PROFESSIONAL
NURSE

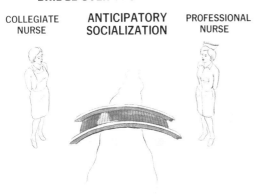

4. Planned anticipatory socialization will smooth the transition from student to effective and productive graduate nurse.

This brings us to the third cornerstone in the theory of professional-bureaucratic conflict resolution.

### Professional socialization: child or adult?

Learning to become a nurse is accomplished through a process called socialization during which new values and behaviors appropriate to adult positions and group memberships are inculcated into the aspirant. Of the many roles that the modern adult is called upon to perform, few exceed in importance the acquisition of requisite skills and attitudes for occupations. The behavior and attitudinal changes relative to occupations are usually internalized in the course of induction or training procedures such as those found in a school of nursing. These training procedures result in new images, expectations, skills, and norms as the person defines himself and as others view him. There are both internal and external changes: within the individual, in his role set, and in the interaction between them.

Any socialization may be totally congruent or partially incongruent. Congruent socialization is the ability and motivation to act or behave on the basis of a value or belief system that matches one's behavior. The internal changes—beliefs and values—are congruent with the external changes—specific behaviors through which beliefs are translated into action. Incongruent socialization is any omission or combination of omissions of either values or behavior. There are at least three possibilities. An individual can subscribe to the values of a particular culture or subculture, but not to the behavior; he can subscribe to the behavior but not the values; or he can adopt neither the values nor the behavior. You probably have known student and staff nurses whose socialization fits each of these categories: the fully congruent, committed in both thought and action; the dilettante who can mouth the words of value, the things one "ought" to do, but whose behavior or performance is well below par; or the chameleon who bends with the wind, appearing to be uncommitted to any kind of belief system, but behaviorally competent within the system he is presently in. His conformity is essentially adaptive without the corresponding value basis. And then, of course, we've all attempted to work with and develop the individual who adopts neither the desired values or behaviors. This individual is often so indifferent to the values, and may feel he has so little stake in the system, as not to warrant even behavioral conformity.

Nursing schools and nurse-employing organizations represent two different subcultures of the nursing world. The norms, values, and behavioral expectations are more different between school and work than they are between two different work settings. It is therefore quite possible for a person to be congruently socialized into one subculture but not into another. To the extent that the two subcultures propagate values, attitudes, and behaviors that are different, an individual who desires to move from one subculture to another will encounter difficulty. Moreover, congruent socialization in one subculture often results in a defensive stance that makes it difficult for the individual to change or be receptive to social changes demanded in another subculture of our highly technological society. For example, in the school subculture autonomy and independence of thought and behavior are valued and in some areas behaviorally expected. The student acquires experience in autonomy, particularly in relationship to being responsible for her own learning, in seeking out learning opportunities via attendance at rounds, off-the-ward conferences, and so on. In the work subculture, some aspects of autonomy are valued, but the new graduate soon learns that absenting herself from the unit to attend a conference is not one of these. This incongruence (from her perspective) engenders a defensive stand that is translated into: "There's no opportunity for learning here." This defensive attitude makes it difficult for her to perceive the other areas of informal learning that are open to her in the new subculture.

Probably more than in any other occupation, the goal of professional training institutions is to inculcate into their aspirants not only the behaviors but, more importantly, the norms and values deemed imperative for survival of the occupation. To achieve this, stringent methods are sometimes used. Moore advances the punishment-centered thesis that practices such as hazing or suffering have a definite function in the socialization into all occupations that emphasize attention to standards of competence and performance and to identification with an occupation as a collectivity. These are conditions that prevail most often in the professional occupations. Moore contends that such socialization means cognitive learning as well as at least minimum internalization of appropriate norms. To achieve this maximum socialization, professional schools frequently sequester their trainees in situations that almost amount to "total institutions" or else effect approximate social isolation by the sheer burden of work demanded and the close living conditions. The fact that the initiate is often put through a set of tasks and duties that are difficult and frequently unpleasant is further support of the punishment-centered theory. Some of these tasks are commonly ritualized and in that sense arbitrary. For all of these tasks, there is always the possibility of failure. Sharing the challenging and painful experiences with others results in a sort of fellowship of suffering that persists long after the experience is over.

Another aspect of the punishment-centered theory as a means of achieving maximum

congruent socialization is evidenced by the persistent possibility of failure following graduation—a characteristic of most professional occupations. Punishment does not stop after completion of the cognitive studies; the neophyte professional is usually required to do the dirty work or the scut work of his profession until such time as he has proved himself worthy, by both knowledge competence and appropiate norms, to enter into the community.

The learning of a technical language, while not central to the punishment-centered theory, is another feature of professional socialization that tends to identify and exclude, and thus to confirm occupational identity.

The person who successfully learns the language and skills of a trade, and survives the ordeals that punished him and his fellows will emerge, we are arguing, not only with an internalized occupational commitment but also with an identification with the collectivity, the brotherhood. Yet note that for professional and similar occupations subject to continuing internal specialization and to substantial differences in the style and setting of occupational activities, identification with the occupational collectivity must be increasingly nostalgic: shared suffering and success in the past. Note also that the shared experience need not be entirely simultaneous, as long as the socializing system endures. This circumstance undoubtedly accounts for resistance to major changes in occupational training, for such changes would destroy a bridge across age groups—a bridge increasingly difficult to maintain in technical occupations, where the young, distressingly, know more than their elders. And even if the young are punished no less, and perhaps more, suffering comes in new forms that the older worker did not experience.°

Thus, we see in the tenets of professional socialization not only the means to perpetuation and survival of the system, but also to effecting maximum internal and external socialization.

By way of summary, socialization consists of both internal and external changes in an

---

°Moore, W. E.: Occupational socialization. In Goslin, D. A., editor: Handbook of socialization theory and research, © 1969 by Rand McNally and Co., Chicago, pp. 880. Reprinted by permission of Rand McNally College Publishing Co.

individual. In congruent socialization, the attitudes and values instilled will match the behaviors taught, practiced, and rewarded. In professional socialization, the goal is toward both normative and behavioral changes, but it appears that more emphasis might be placed on inculcation of proper norms, values, and behaviors toward other members of the collectivity or brotherhood than on the behaviors that are specific to the occupational role for which one is preparing. This latter point is the main thesis of two investigators who studied professional socialization in medical schools.

Olmsted and Paget contend that professional socialization is a special kind of socialization containing elements of both child and adult socialization, although identical to neither. To understand this significant point, look at some of the similarities and differences between child and adult socialization and contrast these with medical education as Olmsted and Paget do, with professional nursing education as known by the reader empirically and also through the work of Olesen and Whittaker.

Brim notes that the purpose and function of childhood socialization is to develop the personality, to provide the child with a sense of identity: "Who am I?" Childhood socialization is basically additive and elaborative; it deals essentially with what people "should" or "ought" to do or think, not with what they in fact do and think. "Thus, childhood socialization is directed to the learning of values, in contrast to adult socialization, which focuses on the learning of behaviors."

Not only is the content of childhood socialization different from that of adult, but the structure also differs. Adult socialization typically does not require the individual to play the learner role, nor does it typically occur in settings in which the individual is acted upon by socializers with a great power differential over him. This can be contrasted with childhood socialization wherein the learner role is dominant and typical and the one being socialized is acted upon by individuals with considerable power and authority.

Olmsted and Paget contend that, viewed from this perspective, medical school (professional socialization) is an extension of child-

**PROFESSIONAL SOCIALIZATION THEORY**

THE PATIENT SHOULD HAVE ALL HIS NEEDS MET.

hood socialization. Analysis of the descriptive accounts of nursing school socialization provided by Olesen and Whittaker or Williams and Williams would lead to the same conclusion for nursing students. In both of these situations, typically, the student is provided with a core of "shoulds"—attitudes, values and norms that have as their content what the faculty believe doctors and nurses should and should not do and think in a variety of situations. These attitudes, values, and norms are *role general* rather than *role specific*—they pertain to the abstract role of nurse or doctor rather than to a specific role that the student will one day occupy. Another element of childhood socialization that is evident in professional health occupation socialization is playing the role of learner in a situation where there is considerable authority differential. In short, it seems that the socialization that takes place in medical and nursing schools prepares students to be medical and nursing students but not physicians and nurses. Although the conditions exist for maximum congruent socialization to take place, the emphasis is on the "shoulds" or values of practice and on role general rather than role specific knowledge and skills. The focus in nursing school is on the principles and skills required in the general assessment of health of preschool children (role general behavior) rather than on the specific and rapid assessment of two-year-old Johnny with raspy, stridorous respirations. It is likely that upon graduation the student will be incongruently socialized in the adult occupation sense (that is, having both values and corresponding role specific behaviors). Socialized into a world of "shoulds," and with corresponding role general behaviors, the new graduate is charged with the task of translating these "shoulds" into concrete role specific behaviors.

I believe better nursing students could be graduated if more time was spent in the clinical setting. We graduate with a good picture of how nurses *should* perform but there's a whale of a difference between knowing this and actually doing it°.

According to Olmsted and Paget, a major portion of professional socilization occurs after the completion of medical school in the context of internship and residency programs. It is here that the neophyte learns the role specific behaviors. Much of this socialization is provided by patients. This brings us to the crucial question relative to the professional socialization of nurses. Given the parallel in emphasis on shoulds in nursing education and the focus on role general nursing behaviors, is it not true that the initial work experience of the neophyte nurse must be viewed as a continuation of her professional socialization if adult socialization is ever to occur?

In comparison to school, work *demands* adult socialization. The work environment insists that the nurse produce role behaviors not in generalities but in specifics: the care of a given caseload of patients, with multiple unknowns and uncertainties, to be completed within a specific period of time. The neophyte very quickly perceives that the role specific behaviors demanded of her are predicated upon a value system somewhat different from the one promulgated in the school setting. She finds herself in a situation in which she not only lacks the necessary role specific behaviors, but the value system upon which her general nursing behavior is built seems to be in opposition to the prevailing value system of the work environment.

Clearly, some kind of role transformation will be necessary. Olmsted and Paget make the point that if students are placed in social-

izing contexts that perpetuate *preadult* socialization, role transformation must occur after school is completed and in contexts in which the appropriateness or desirability of the change, because it is left unexamined and many times is made under great pressure, are open to serious question. On the other hand, if alternative socialization routes are designed and planned, if some of this role transformation takes place during the school socialization, it is likely that given the opportunity to mediate conflicting demands the individual will learn behaviors and will reorder previously held values so that she becomes a somewhat different person.

This became one of the guiding principles in the development of an anticipatory socialization program designed to help student nurses deal constructively with professional-bureaucratic conflict and resultant reality shock. The purpose of the anticipatory socialization program was to offer an alternative adult socialization route during the nursing school period. By arranging for role transformation to occur while the student was still in school, the change would be subject to deliberative planning and evolution.

From an historical perspective, the above ideas may be viewed as follows. In the apprenticeship system of traditional diploma programs, there was little disparity between school and work. Located in and controlled by work organizations, role specific behaviors and values consonant with the work scene were deliberatively taught; little or no role transformation was needed upon employment. In associate degree and baccalaureate nursing programs (and increasingly in diploma programs), there is a separation between the employing and educational organizations. Emphasis is on role general behaviors and values—preparation for future roles. Although this lessens the likelihood of built-in obsolescence prevalent when role specific behaviors are emphasized, it increases the disparity between school-taught and work-needed values. Little or no role transformation is done while the student is in the educational institution; therefore, marked discontinuity occurs upon employment. In the proposed anticipatory social-

---

°Paynich, M. L.: Why do basic nursing students work in nursing? Nursing Outlook 19(4):145, 1971. © American Journal of Nursing Co.

ization program, emphasis on role general behaviors and values continues but there is also deliberative, planned socialization into role specific behaviors of adaptation, conflict management, and influencing. The student is "inoculated" with increasing resistance to persuasion; she is "inoculated" so that she will not opt out through overconformity during the role transformation phase.

Summarily, the following principles are abstracted from the foregoing theories of adult and professional socialization.

1. To become functional in the adult occupational world, one must be congruently socialized into the values and corresponding role-specific behaviors.

## TO STAY OR NOT TO STAY

2. Professional socialization contains many elements of childhood socialization, emphasizing "shoulds" and role-general behaviors.

3. Because there is little plan for guided role transformation in school, socialization into role-specific behaviors occurs after graduation. This role transformation, occurring concomitantly with adult socialization, is frequently unguided and unexamined.

## THE DILEMMA

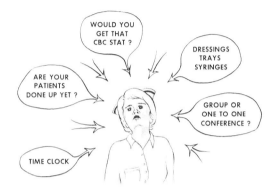

### Sociological immunization: a timely vaccination

With this mixture of adult and childhood socialization, it is clear that the new graduate is ill prepared attitudinally and behaviorally to enter the work scene. Equipped with a high professional and low bureaucratic orientation, a bushel basket of shoulds and a paper bag of skills, techniques, and role specific behaviors, and because of her lack of presocialization into work-related values, she is a prime candidate for massive role conflict. Is it any wonder that she is quick to abandon the work scene or abdicate cherished values of individualized, comprehensive patient care? Is it any wonder that the new graduates of today have been unable to make the fundamental improvements in patient care that were expected of them? Some way must be found to protect and safeguard professional values during the crucial phase of role transformation when, hopefully, the neophyte will have been able to operationalize them into her practice. McGuire's sociological immunization theory provides this needed dimension[3] and is the fourth cornerstone in the evolving theory of conflict resolution.

Concern over the vulnerability of people's convictions in situations of forced exposure led McGuire to explore the conditions under which beliefs could be immunized against persuasion. Hovland had demonstrated the relative ineffectiveness of persuasive techniques when persons could choose the situations to which they wished to expose themselves. People characteristically defend their beliefs and convictions by avoiding exposure to counter-arguments and by avoiding receipt of information that disagrees with opinions already formed. Probably one of the most dramatic examples of this high vulnerability of untried beliefs in a forced exposure situation was seen in prisoner-of-war camps, where those beliefs that are most culturally pervasive in our society, and against which little opposition had ever been heard, were the ones most amenable to influence. Defending one's belief by avoiding discrepant information may be highly effective in maintaining them so long as the person can adequately regulate his own exposure to arguments; it becomes ineffective and leaves him poorly prepared to resist counter-arguments when he is involuntarily exposed to counterbeliefs and agruments.

It is likely that a person living in an ideologically monolithic environment will underestimate the vulnerability of his beliefs and perhaps even refuse to entertain the idea that they may be attacked. Hence, he will have little motivation or practice in developing arguments to support his beliefs or refutations for attacks on them. McGuire and Papageorgis suggest that this deficiency in both practice and motivation for developing resistance to beliefs is

closely analogous to the health problem of the person who has been brought up in so aseptic an environment that he has failed to develop resistance to infection and, hence, although appearing in very good health, proves quite vulnerable when suddenly exposed to a massive dose of an infectious virus. The disease resistance of such a person might be raised by either of two procedures: he might be given supportive therapy—good diet, exercise, rest, etc.—designed to better his physical condition; or alternatively, he might be given an inoculation of the infectious virus itself (in a weakened form) such as would stimulate, without overcoming, his defenses. With respect to developing immunity to specific diseases, the inoculation procedure is generally more effective.[*]

Pursuing this medical analogy into the area of resistance to persuasion, McGuire and

[*]McGuire, W. J., and Papageorgis, D.: The relative efficacy of various types of prior belief-defense in producing immunity against persuasion, J. Abnorm. Psychol. **62**(2): 327-337, 1961. Copyright 1961 by the American Psychological Association. Reprinted by permission.

SOCIOLOGICAL
IMMUNIZATION
THEORY

Papageorgis conducted a series of experiments to ascertain whether "supportive therapy" has more or less immunizing effectiveness than the "inoculation" procedure. The supportive therapy approach consisted of arguments positively supporting a belief while ignoring possible counterarguments. The inoculation procedure consisted of refutational defenses that mentioned and disproved possible counterarguments against the belief while ignoring arguments positively supporting the belief.[4] To conduct this and other experiments it was necessary to first identify those widely held cultural beliefs, about which there is so little belief-dissonant information available that it is likely that most people would have built up no defensive arguments. Hence, they would be highly vulnerable to persuasion. These pervasive cultural beliefs are called cultural truisms. People were asked to rate on a 15-point scale the extent to which they concurred with statements such as: "We should brush our teeth after each meal if at all possible." When 75% of the subjects responded at the 15-point level of the scale, the item was considered a cultural truism.

The experiment was usually presented under some sort of deception to fairly large (N = 73 to N = 168) groups of college students. (Cultural truisms are rarer in college samples than had been expected.) The subjects were first pretested on the extent to which they concurred with the one or more cultural truisms under study (example: teeth brushing). They received either supportive or immunizing treatments, after which they were again tested to measure the direct effects of the treatments. In a followup experimental session, the subjects were exposed to strong counterarguments on both those beliefs for which they had been immunized (example: tooth brushing) and those for which they had not been immunized (example: effectiveness of penicillin). Another posttest assessing the present strength of beliefs in the cultural truism was administered to ascertain the relative effectiveness of the defensive treatments in conferring resistance to counterpersuasion. Both sets of beliefs were imbedded in whatever tool was being used for the experiment.

To return to our neophyte collegiate graduate, what might be happening to her and to her professional subcultural beliefs? Olesen and Whittaker (1968) note that during schooling the collegiate student nurse is assailed with a dominant belief system that is more or less homogeneously maintained and propagated by the faculty. In a study of the uses of laughter (1966), these same investigators show how it is made uncomfortable for students to express ideas and notions contrary to this dominant value system. When this occurs, it is reasonable to believe that the outcome is the transmission of nursing subcultural truisms that are untried and highly vulnerable.

What are some of these nursing subcultural truisms? A preliminary investigation, using procedures similar to those of McGuire, produced the following. On a 15-point scale, 92 of 103 (93%) collegiate senior student nurses responded at the affirmative extreme (14 or 15) to the belief that "For most doctors and nurses, the care and well-being of the patient is the most important consideration." Of these students 90% responded at 14 or 15 on a 15-point scale to this belief? "If at all possible, the professional nurse has the responsibility to see that her patients receive quality nursing care even if this means counteracting hospital routines or doctors orders." Another subcultural truism candidate (87%) is: "With few exceptions, all patients should have nursing care plans written for them."

With a group of 154 Master's degree students and using a 7-point scale, the following were found to be subcultural truisms (rated 6 or 7 in intensity of agreement or 1 or 2 in intensity of disagreement by 75% or better of the group).

> Nursing, as an occupation, ranks lower in status than medicine. (Agree)
> Physicians seldom make mistakes in prescribing patient care. (Disagree)
> For the most part, hospitals of today meet the needs of the majority of patients who are admitted to them. (Disagree)

The following beliefs approached subcultural truism status.

> Many nurses go into teaching because they have found in the work situation that

# IMMUNIZE OR
# THEY WILL BREAK

they can't give the kind of care they would like to give. (Agree, 68%)

Practicing physicians, almost without exception, are truly concerned about patients and patient care. (Disagree, 60.4%) Interestingly, when staff nurses were substituted for physicians in the preceding statement, the percentage dropped to 19.5%.

There is a suggestion of a subcultural truism by Kraegel and associates when they state:

When the staff of the project to be described here asked 100 senior nursing students if they felt patients' needs were being met in the various clinical settings, only one student answered in the affirmative.°

If there are such subcultural truisms, and if they are persuasively reinforced during the student socialization period, and if the student has little or no need to doubt them or to prepare refutations in their defense, what is the probable fate of these beliefs when she enters the work world, where surely they will be attacked or conflicting evidence will be presented? This is only the extreme of the problem. What about the myriad of beliefs and values that may not be so pervasive as to earn

°Kragel and associates: A system of patient care based on patient needs, Nursing Outlook **20**(4):257-264, 1972, © American Journal of Nursing Co.

the label subcultural truisms, but which for any given individual may function as untried, highly vulnerable beliefs? For example, 68% of the 103 collegiate senior students were in extreme affirmative agreement that "My knowledge, competence, and skill will be recognized and rewarded as a graduate staff nurse." It seems that one of the highly desirable functions of professional school socialization is to immunize the student against possible future attacks on her professional beliefs. In this way she can maintain and activate them in the work world, rather than let them fall and break through capitulation.

## Putting the theories together

The foregoing sections have presented the details of the eclectic theoretical framework that generated the hypotheses of this research study and guided the decision-making necessary at various junctures.

Based upon this theoretical framework, the following propositions were generated.

1. Some degree of professional-bureaucratic conflict is inevitable, but conflict is not necessarily bad.

2. Growth-producing conflict resolution behavior can be facilitated by exposing students to conflict situations early in their educational careers.

3. Skills of interpersonal competency can be enhanced through controlled and manageable exposure to conflicts while in school as opposed to the overwhelming confrontation after graduation.

4. Development of strategies or lines of action can be facilitated through exposure to an outside reference group to which student nurses can anticipatorily socialize themselves. In this way students would be stimulated to learn and model adaptive conflict resolution behavior.

5. Pre-exposure to the anticipated process of reality shock, its signs and symptoms, and possible resolution channels would help to decrease the discomfort of the ensuing shock situation and assist in making this a self-discovery and growth-producing experience.

6. Deliberate attacks on cherished profes-

sional values and provision of refutational defenses with opportunity for practice of same would help to safeguard these highly vulnerable beliefs. If beliefs are safeguarded for at least an initial period of the new work experience, the likelihood of their being operationalized will increase.

Behaviorally, the end result of all of this, should be new graduates who: (1) do not run away from nursing practice, particularly hospital nursing practice; (2) demonstrate in their nursing practice that they resolve the professional-bureaucratic conflict, through a deliberate intermeshing of the principles of both, without either abdication or fusion; and (3) report less role conflict and role deprivation, and who are judged by others as being happy in their work.

## INTEGRATIVE RESOLUTION

### RESEARCH DESIGN

In many ways, a research study can be viewed as a group of people going on a journey by car. Before one takes a trip, certain kinds of preparations and resources are needed. Certainly one would need a map to tell him where to go, what roads to take, when to turn off to get where he wants to go, and so on. The research design fulfills many of the same functions for a research study as does a road map for an automobile journey. The more complete, the more detailed, and the more thought-out the road map, the greater the likelihood that the travelers will get where they want to go and won't get hung up on detours or dead ends.

## Preliminary study

After a person gets the idea of where he wants to go on the trip (this idea is ordered and focused by the theoretical framework), the first step is to make necessary preparations. Does he have everything he needs? For the trip reported on here, a lot of preparation was needed before the journey could begin.

Given the previously described theoretical notions, assumptions, and the generated propositions, the initial step was to design an Anticipatory Socialization and sociological immunization program that would expose and hopefully reduce the professional-bureaucratic conflict and resultant reality shock while at the same time fostering the retention of professional ideals. Of paramount importance was the location of a reference group of nurses who would represent the desired outcome of integrated professional-bureaucratic values and growth-producing role conflict resolution behavior. It was conjectured that exposure to the values and behaviors of such a planned reference group would provide student nurses with the needed conditions for anticipatory socialization to occur. Needed was a reference group of nurses whose values and behavior could be inspected, analyzed, and hopefully incorporated into those of the aspirant professional nurses. Ideally this reference group could and should be culled from nurse practitioners in the various settings in which the student nurses went for clinical practice. But for various reasons the reference group desired was not available—either they didn't exist or student nurses did not see these nurses receiving rewards for the kinds of behaviors that they were being taught to value.

To locate the kind of reference group of nurses needed for the Anticipatory Socialization program, characteristics had to be thought through and specified carefully. Student nurses were being socialized into a professional work system. They had role models in the person of their instructors, but these models were seldom fully functional and operational within the work subculture. They were more like house guests who came in, visited (much like the students), and then left to return for later visits. It was known from previous research that the majority of staff nurses with whom students would have contact would be more likely to be bureaucratic role models. If nurses do not acquire at least a modicum of bureaucratic loyalty, they are usually perceived as troublemakers (not necessarily a derogatory label, as we shall see later on) or malcontents who express a great deal of dissatisfaction and disillusionment with their job and with nursing. This was not the kind of reference group desired for an anticipatory socialization program for student nurses. What was desired was a group of nurses who were reported as successful in their job situations (and therefore sufficiently loyal to the employing organization to "get along"), but who at the same time had retained their professional loyalties and were able to operationalize them in the work setting. Put another way, the reference group desired were nurses who were bicultural, who had learned how to be interpersonally competent in the work subculture without losing their school values framework or competency. It was assumed that nurses with these characteristics would have worked out some constructive conflict resolution and would be reasonably happy with nursing and with their jobs.

From an experiential viewpoint, it was known that this kind of nurse existed. In many clinical settings that were observed, staff or head nurses, supervisors, or directors of nursing could identify and describe some nurse who was "doing great things." They generally spoke of her with respect and stated that she was enthusiastic about nursing and her job. Observations of these staff nurses in the wards or in the field confirmed these reports. From previous work, it was known that nurses who stated they were "happy in their jobs" scored low on Corwin's Role Deprivation scale, which is considered to be a measure of degree of perceived intrarole conflict. Since retention of professional values was one of the major criteria for reference group selection, the end result was to find a group of nurses who reported both high bureaucratic and high professional loyalty, were considered to be successful nurses by their employers, and who had low role deprivation. Since the bureaucratic and professional work systems are basically antithetical, it was anticipated that it would be difficult to find nurses with this kind of role value configuration. It was therefore necessary to begin with a fairly large sample of nurses to find an appropriate subsample with the characteristics described for the reference group.

Since the primary focus of the overall study was to be generic baccalaureate nurses (as noted earlier, Corwin found that the professional-bureaucratic conflict problem was most acute in this group), it was desirable to draw a sample from as large a pool of the baccalaureate nurse population as possible. It was reasoned and subsequently checked out that hospitals associated with university medical centers attract more baccalaureate nurses than any other kind of hospital since these are the settings in which the college-prepared nurse frequently receives her clinical experience. Although it was known that public health departments employ large numbers of baccalaureate nurses, the pool there is not as large as in a single medical center hospital; furthermore, there are marked regional differences in hiring policies in public health departments. A second criterion governing selection of the sample was national representation, both in terms of states and in respect to generic collegiate nurse production.

Three major sources were used to locate medical centers that, for purposes of this study, were defined as health care facilities, associated with colleges or universities, providing diverse and comprehensive inpatient and outpatient services to clients, actively engaged in patient care research, and sponsoring training programs for physicians, nurses, and other health workers. The 1966-1967 guide issue of *Hospitals* was checked for all hospitals with over 200 beds and identifying themselves as medical centers. This list was then cross-checked with a list of approved medical schools obtained from the American Medical Association and with a list of collegiate schools

of nursing accredited by the National League for Nursing. Hospitals associated with these programs were added to the initial list of 272 hospitals. The directors of nursing of these 272 hospitals were then contacted by mail and asked to complete a postcard giving the total number of registered nurses on staff, the number of these classified as head nurses and supervisors, and the number of generic baccalaureate graduate nurses on staff. The 196 (72%) returns were then rank ordered by state on the basis of number and percentage of baccalaureate nurse staff. In 1966-1968 there was usually only 1, and seldom more than 2, medical centers per state having a collegiate nurse staff of greater than 15% or numbering more than 20 nurses. The third criteria used in selecting medical centers was the number of collegiate graduates produced in the state. Selecting only those states in which the production was in the upper third of rank ordering by states, a final sample of 37 medical centers was obtained. (See Kramer, 1969a, p. 199, for the listing of states and medical centers.)

The director of nursing service (DNS) of each of these 37 medical center hospitals was contacted by letter; the study was explained and her cooperation enlisted. All were very accommodating and, contrary to expectations, there were no refusals to participate. To obtain a sample in which there was a high probability of finding the subsample reference group desired, each DNS was requested to select six nurses from her staff according to the following criteria:

1. Two generic baccalaureate graduate nurses considered to be very successful.
2. Two generic baccalaureate graduate nurses considered average in success.
3. Two generic baccalaureate graduate nurses considered to be less successful than average.
4. All nurses selected must have been employed in nursing for at least nine months, and preferably for one year.

No criterion for success was given. It was reasoned that since all medical center organizations have similar goals the mechanisms for achievement of these goals and the concomitant participation behavior required would be similar. The factors constituting success were not of importance in this study. What was important was that the nurse be *perceived* as successful. The assumption was made that if she was perceived as being successful, she would be receiving cues to this effect from her employer. These cues and the subsequent rewards would be reinforcing to her and would tend to transmit the message that whatever she was doing—whatever nurse and employee behavior she was enacting—was appropriate, valued, and approved. Furthermore, it was assumed that this successful behavior would be reflective of some degree of bureaucratic loyalty.

One might question if there is not a great deal of room for error and potential ambiguity in the specifications for sample selection given to the DNS. Before initiating the study, a trial run was made of these and other directions with three DNSs to see what kinds of responses they evoked. Satisfaction that the directions as stated above did evoke similar responses was obtained. Clarity of direction was also checked at the end of the interviewing at each medical center by asking the DNS if there was any difficulty in selecting the nurses and what means had been used. Little difficulty was reported. Only one of the directors indicated difficulty in the selection area; that organization stated it had no nurses in the "less successful than average" category. The resultant subsample sizes were, therefore, 74 "more successful than average," 74 "average," and 72 "less successful than average."

It will be remembered that the goal in this sample selection was to find a reference group of nurse practitioners who were highly successful, who had a high bureaucratic–high professional role conception and low role deprivation. Being considered highly successful was a preliminary prediction that the nurse had a high bureaucratic role conception and was making a satisfying role transformation. It was now necessary to identify the role value configurations of the 74 highly successful nurses and then to observe them in clinical practice to ascertain how they were successfully blending together the bureaucratic and professional systems of work. It was therefore planned that all nurses would be interviewed and tested on the Corwin Role Conception and Role Deprivation scales (described on p. 19) and that, on the basis of these results, some of the nurses would be observed in practice.

All 220 of these nurses from medical center hospitals were interviewed and tested in 1968. Mail questionnaires were obtained in 1969; 209 were retested and 205 reinterviewed in 1970. Also in 1970, a small control group of 12 nurses from 8 medical centers who had not previously been associated with the study were interviewed. The purpose of interviewing these control group nurses was to assess the possible impact that repeated contact with me might be having on the reality shock experience and career decision-making patterns. There were no obvious differences noted; the control group nurses were also reporting reality shock symptoms, job-hopping, and conflict resolution patterns similar to those of the main group.

Eighteen nurses who fitted the preliminary specifications for the desired reference group were identified. These nurses had professional and bureaucratic role conceptions above the median for the total group of 220, role deprivation scores below the median, and were reported as being highly successful by their employers. All but two of these nurses were then observed in their respective clinical settings for periods of one week or more. The objective of this field observation was to observe and gather critical incident material on how these nurses handled typical professional-bureaucratic conflicts, how they operationalized their professional values, particularly in the face of resistance or obstruction, what resources in their environment they sought out or utilized, and where they received or how they mustered support for their ideals and goals. In short, what were the strategies they used in being interpersonally competent in the work subculture? Some of these nurses were observed at intervals over a three-year period. In most cases, co-workers, physicians, and supervisors of these nurses were also interviewed. In effect, data were collected by a variety of means to construct a picture of the norms, values, and operational behavior of this reference group of nurses. It was this data, and particularly that related to actual conflict resolution strategies, that was concurrently used in the development and implementation of the Anticipatory Socialization program.

To recapitulate, this preliminary four-year study of medical center nurses was designed to identify and locate a reference group of nurse practitioners who were successful in their work situation and who retained high professional values that were operative in the work subculture. Utilizing Merton's idea that a reference group to which one aspires and to which one gears oneself in prejoining value socialization will markedly expedite the process of moving from one group to another, an anticipatory socialization program based on the conflict resolution strategies, behaviors, and attitudes of this reference group would be developed and taught to two classes of generic baccalaureate student nurses. In this way it was anticipated that the reality shock resulting from professional-bureaucratic conflict would be reduced and the professional productivity of the nurses in the work subculture increased.

The theoretical notions of Merton and McGuire were used in selecting and pacing material from the reference group nurses. For example, McGuire's finding that pre-exposure to attack of one's untried beliefs, accompanied by possible counterarguments, is an effective way of maintaining one's beliefs was used in the following way. There existed among the group of student nurses in the "Anticipatory Socialization study the cultural truism that "everything possible must be done to save life —that human life is respected and dignified to the greatest possible degree." Very early in the Anticipatory Socialization seminars, a tape recording of an incident related by a new graduate nurse was played for the students. In this incident, the nurse described a situation in which an 80-year-old man who had had several previous heart attacks came into her ward for emergency treatment for another coronary. Extraordinary life-saving measures were instituted. The nurse, with a great deal of emotion, shock, and pathos in her voice, described what happened—how the

physician said he was going to do an open cardiac massage "just for practice," how undignified the whole procedure was, her conflict and emotional feelings about the whole thing, and so on. Following the tape recording, it was obvious from looking at the faces of these first-year students that they were shocked. Their first response was to deny that such a thing could happen; many completely withdrew. Several subsequently told their regular clinical instructors about the recording and were told: "Oh, don't worry about that; it seldom happens. When it does, you'll be able to handle it just fine." This incident was discussed pro and con in the Anticipatory Socialization seminars for several weeks. Students were given ample time to think about and evaluate the situation. Some of their most cherished values were attacked over and over again. Gradually solutions, attitudes, and reactions of the reference group of nurses from the medical centers were fed into the students' discussions as some possible defenses against the values being attacked. (In many instances when new situations would come up, I telephoned or wrote to one or several of the reference nurses to learn how she would have handled such a situation.)

**Plan and aims**

With the completion of the preliminary study, I began the major study, which was designed to assess the effects of an Anticipatory Socialization program on the value orientation, chosen work locale, and career pattern of a sample of two classes of generic baccalaureate nurses. The Anticipatory Socialization program consisted of a three-year series of formal classes, seminars, and teaching-learning activities. These were designed to expose and involve the nursing student early and consistently in the realities of the bureaucratic work scene and simultaneously to allow her the opportunity to develop integrative nurse role strategies that would permit her to survive and be successful within the bureaucratic setting while retaining professional values.

The specific aims of the Anticipatory Socialization program and of the major study were:

1. To increase the number of collegiate

nurses working in hospitals or correspondingly to decrease the number who flee from nursing practice, particularly hospital nursing practice.[5]

2. To increase retention of the professional role conception of collegiate nurses working in hospitals.
3. To decrease the role deprivation of collegiate nurses working in hospitals.

It is a well-known fact that the number of collegiate graduate nurses staffing general hospitals is disproportionately low. Most of them seek employment in public health, school nursing, or psychiatric nursing. Many nurses will agree with Davis and associates that the hospital is a chief work locale of nursing. In order to improve the quality of patient care, it is necessary to attract and retain in hospital nursing those nurses who hold strong professional role conceptions and who are able to work within the demands and constraints of the bureaucratically organized hospital. The same is also true for public health departments, which are also bureaucratically organized. It has been demonstrated that although collegiate graduate nurses profess high professional role conceptions, they do not remain long in hospital employ, probably because of low commitment to bureaucratic work principles. Therefore, in order to attract and retain collegiate nurses in the hospital work scene, some method of integrating the professional role conception with the needs of the bureaucratic work organization must be found. The Anticipatory Socialization program was designed to do this.

A time series design was used to investigate the effect of the Anticipatory Socialization program (independent variable) on the chosen work locale and role conceptions of collegiate graduate nurses (dependent variables). A group of 45 nursing students who entered the University of California School of Nursing in September 1965, and who graduated in June 1968, served as a control group. These students did not have the Anticipatory Socialization program. They were pretested, midtested, and posttested by nonproject staff under my supervision. Two experimental groups (the 57 students who entered the school in September 1966 and graduated in June 1969 and the 59

students entering in September 1967 and graduating in June 1970) had the Anticipatory Socialization program during their entire three years in the School of Nursing. Both the control and experimental groups were tested and interviewed one year after graduation and again two years after graduation. If arranged by the nurse, the supervisor and a co-worker of each nurse was also interviewed at the one-year anniversary. Selected field observations were done on 8 to 10 students in each class.

This is not an experimental research design. The control and experimental groups are not completely comparable; they are from similar but not identical populations. The major source of design error resides in the potential history and maturation of each group as well as some unequal exposure to the Anticipatory Socialization program. Every effort possible was made to control, or at least assess, the effect of this error. The general nursing curriculum, other than the Anticipatory Socialization program, remained the same for the three classes of students. Admission and graduation requirements were held constant. The effect of exposure to different faculty groups (occasioned by resignation and appointment of new faculty) was considered. Events external to the curriculum, such as the Free Speech Movement, San Francisco State turmoil, black student demands, and the People's Park Movement, were recorded and studied as possible contaminants of the findings. Unequal exposure to the Anticipatory Socialization program was handled through crossbreaks. By regrouping subjects according to their extent of participation in the Anticipatory Socialization program, the results could be analyzed according to these groupings.

A summary of the groups' exposure to the Anticipatory Socialization program, testing periods, and chronological schedule is contained in Table 2-1.

### Hypotheses

Based upon the eclectic theoretical framework described earlier, it was hypothesized that:

1. If collegiate student nurses are provided the exposure to and opportunity to work out professional-bureaucratic work con-

**Table 2-1.** Summary of the research design

| Class year | Pretest T1 | Treatment | T2 | T3 | Test or interview T4 | T5 | T6 |
|---|---|---|---|---|---|---|---|
| 1968 (Control) (N = 45) | S '65 | None | | S '66 | J '68 | J '69 | J '70 |
| 1969 (Experimental) (N = 57) | S '66 | A.S. program | J '67 | S '67 | J '69 | J '70 | J '71 |
| 1970 (Experimental) (N = 59) | S '67 | A.S. program | J '68 | S '68 | J '70 | J '71 | J '72 |

S = September, J = June.

flicts with guidance and support during the school socialization period (Anticipatory Socialization program), then reality shock and role deprivation will be experienced as part of the school period.

2. Collegiate student nurses who had the Anticipatory Socialization program will experience less role deprivation upon employment than will a comparable group of nurses who did not have this program.

3. A higher percentage of the collegiate student nurses who had the Anticipatory Socialization program will remain in hospital work two years after graduation than will a comparable group who did not have the program.

4. A higher percentage of collegiate student nurses who had the Anticipatory Socialization program will retain professional nurse role conceptions and behaviors upon employment than will a comparable group who did not have the program.

5. A higher percentage of collegiate nurses who had the Anticipatory Socialization program will report use of integrative role strategies than will a comparable group who did not have the program.

For a complete understanding of these hypotheses, it is necessary to make some of the concepts and terminology explicit. A *role* is a set of expectations about how a person in a given position in a particular social system should act and how the individual in a reciprocal position should act. These expectations include prescriptions of rights and duties. Role expectations have both an action and a cognitive component. *Role behavior*, the

action component, is the observable action or behavior of an individual functioning in a given position in a social system. *Role conception*, the cognitive component, is the internal representation of the role expectations held by an individual at a specified time, including cognitions, values, anticipated maneuvers, and responses.

Historically, the conceptions of the nurse role have emerged along three main dimensions and imply three main value systems. The *service role conception* is conceived of nursing as a "calling." It embodies the "angel of mercy" concept and is primarily altruistic and selfless in motivation. The *professional role conception* refers to the occupational principles, role expectations, and role behaviors that transcend the location of specific employment. These principles, expectations, and behaviors are inherent in and acceded to by all members of the group who earn the right to be a member of the particular occupational group. The *bureaucratic role conception* refers to the rules, regulations, and procedures that describe and govern the nurse's job and role expectations in a specific employing organization. All of these definitions are abstracted from the work of Corwin; they are operationalized as scores on the Likert-type scales that he developed.

*Role configuration* refers to a composite of the above role conceptions. Although service, bureaucratic, and professional role conceptions are somewhat disparate, it is assumed that nursing is patterned around these conceptions; hence, nurses must adopt some aspects of all three roles—*some* devotion to patients, *some* loyalty to the hospital administration, and *some* dedication to professional principles.

A nurse therefore may be said to hold a role configuration that is high bureaucratic and low professional, meaning that when compared with some specific cohort she is very high in her loyalty to the hospital administration and to the rules and regulations of the bureaucratic system of work organization; at the same time, she has a low degree of loyalty to the professional principles that govern the concept of nursing as a profession.

*Role deprivation* is a concept that has been alluded to earlier but never completely defined. Since a nurse's role concept consists of elements of all three of the above components, and since at least the professional and bureaucratic role conceptions are incompatible, a nurse is potentially confronted with dilemmas. The basic questions then concern the relative emphasis the nurse places on each conception (since the range of loyalties that can be expressed is probably limited) and her perception of situational determinants permitting her to enact the nurse role as she has conceptualized it.

Satisfactory enactment of a role is contingent upon a situation and climate that the actor perceives as being suitable or favorable to role execution. When the situation is perceived as containing limitations on enacting the role as conceived, presumably the individual feels deprived. In this study, the term perceived situational limitations to role enactment refers to this phenomenon as reported by the role actor. Role deprivation is the corresponding inferred, internal response of the role incumbent. Role deprivation is operationally defined as scores on the role deprivation scales derived from the Corwin Role Conception–Role Deprivation scales (p. 19).

At this time, there is no direct measurement of the social-psychological phenomenon of reality shock. It can be observed and described; characteristics such as moral outrage and polarization of positions are clearly identifiable. It is possible that in the future a tool can be developed to assess the stage and degree of reality shock. In the present study the concept of role deprivation, which measures the degree of professional-bureaucratic conflict (the underlying cause of reality shock) was used as an indirect measure of reality shock. Role deprivation is considered to be a subjective report of the degree of reality shock being perceived and registered by the individual at a point in time.

### Independent variable

An independent variable in a research study is like the vehicle for making a trip. To take an automobile journey, a car is needed to get us to the cities we've elected to see. In the research study being described here, we want to test a specific vehicle—the Anticipatory Socialization program—to see if it will help us reach our goals.

The Anticipatory Socialization program (the independent variable), developed from testing and observing the medical center reference group and utilizing some of the principles of sociological immunization in its delivery format, will be described in detail in Chapter 3, but at this point it is well to clarify for the reader the differential use of the terms anticipatory socialization program and reality shock program, as used in Chapter 6. The reality shock and anticipatory socialization programs are similar in that both deal with role transformation, with the phases of reality shock phenomenon, and with professional-bureaucratic conflict. They differ in two respects. The reality shock program is remedial; the anticipatory socialization program is preventative. Anticipatory socialization happens before the attack; the counterarguments are developed as part of the program. In the reality shock program, the attack occurs naturally; the victims learn to develop their counterarguments on the spot. The other difference between the two programs is in the nature of the conflicts discussed. The Anticipatory Socialization program was designed specifically to counteract and reduce the effects of professional-bureaucratic conflict. Although probably the major cause, professional-bureaucratic conflict is not the only contributor to reality shock. Other shock-producing conflicts include interpersonal incompetency, life role conflicts, generation gaps, patient-nurse conflicts, and so on. The Reality Shock program includes specific methods, approaches, and ways of dealing with these other conflicts as well as with the professional-bureaucratic conflict; the Anticipatory Socialization program includes mainly the latter.

### Dependent variables

If we drive a Chevy Nova at 60 miles an hour along Route 80, starting at San Francisco, we will know that our car is functioning satisfactorily if we reach Reno and go on to visit the Air Force Chapel in Denver and the stockyards in Chicago within two weeks. Other cars might make the trip, or other places can be visited. However, given the original planning of this trip, we decided to see if *this* vehicle could get us to *these* places under specified conditions. These places represent the dependent variables of a research study.

In addition to *bureaucratic* and *professional role conceptions* and *role deprivation*, which have been defined earlier, there are four other variables that function as dependent variables in this study. They will be discussed in terms of the potential effect which the independent variable, the Anticipatory Socialization program, had on them.

*Integrative role behaviors.* This is defined as the reported action choice that represents a compromise between behaviors that clearly support professional values and those that clearly reflect allegiance to bureaucratic values. They are the kinds of behaviors that a nurse who is attempting to operationalize professional values in a bureaucratic setting would choose. Inferentially, the choice of the integrative role behaviors means that some degree of growth-producing conflict resolution behavior is taking place, that biculturalism is occurring. Operationally, this concept is defined as scores on the integrative role behavior scales developed by me.

These scales consist of a series of seven

---

It is a hospital policy that all patients must be discharged in a wheelchair, accompanied by a member of the hospital staff. Mr. Smith, recovering from a stroke, has had a long and difficult period of rehabilitation and is now ready to go home. He has finally learned to walk with the aid of two canes and is proud of this accomplishment and wants to show his daughter how well he is doing when she picks him up at the hospital entrance. He objects to having to ride in a wheelchair to the hospital entrance. You, as the nurse, judge that Mr. Smith is quite capable of walking the distance required and that forcing him to ride in the wheelchair will threaten his slowly developing self-confidence. However, it is a hospital rule.

Indicate the extent to which you would choose each of the listed behaviors.

|  | Strongly agree | Agree | Undecided | Disagree | Strongly disagree |
|---|---|---|---|---|---|
| A. Let Mr. Smith walk down to the hospital entrance since it is very important not to threaten his slowly developing self-confidence by making him ride when he feels he is capable of walking. |  |  |  |  |  |
| B. Explain to Mr. Smith that he may become weak and tired and that it would be unsafe for him to walk that far. Have him use the wheelchair. |  |  |  |  |  |
| C. Have Mr. Smith ride to the hospital entrance in a wheelchair, explaining to him that it is a hospital rule made for the benefit of all patients. |  |  |  |  |  |
| D. Call the physician and ask him if it is all right for Mr. Smith to walk to the hospital entrance. |  |  |  |  |  |
| E. Call your supervisor and ask her if you might break the hospital rule so that Mr. Smith might walk to the entrance. |  |  |  |  |  |
| F. Let Mr. Smith walk to the hospital entrance, accompanied by an orderly wheeling an empty wheelchair in case Mr. Smith gets tired and wants to ride. |  |  |  |  |  |

conflict situations.[6] The respondent is asked to state the extent to which she would elect to enact certain behaviors. (See example on opposite page.)

Autonomous action such as deciding to protect the patient's self-esteem at all cost or asking a colleague such as a physician would be considered professional behavior choices. Following the letter of hospital rules or obtaining the permission of the supervisor for variance from the rule are examples of bureaucratic behavior. Compromise behaviors that represent an integration of professional and bureaucratic work systems, such as having the patient ride part way and then walk, are reflective of growth-producing conflict management. The integration role behavior score is composed of the arithmetic sum of the degree to which the respondent would choose these kinds of behaviors when presented with the conflict situations.

*Work locale and patterns.* Since most nurses start their nursing careers in hospital staff nursing, looking at the exodus from this locale of practice affords an opportunity for indirectly measuring flight behavior. Other aspects of this variable include:

1. The initial work locale and how long one was employed in this initial setting.
2. Reasons for leaving initial job.
3. Job transfers (in the same organization) within the first two working years after graduation.
4. Indices of flight behavior such as:
   a. Number of job changes in the same geographical area within the first two years after graduation.
   b. Leaving nursing practice for school or for a position in which RN licensure is not required.
5. Continuity of employment (remaining in initial work locale) during the entire first two working years after graduation.
6. Continuity of hospital employment (remaining in hospital work) during the first two working years after graduation.

*Change agent activity.* This variable was chosen because it represents the closest behavioral manifestation of operationalizing professional values in a bureaucratic setting

as could be identified. Nursing literature is replete with exhortations to the effect that professional nurses should be or are problem solvers and change agents.

Change agent theory is often taught in nursing programs; yet the extent to which students are allowed to apply theory to practice varies considerably. Even when they do have the opportunity, it is often in an artificial situation where the staff nurses or nursing personnel whom one is attempting to influence or change may go along with the student "so as not to give her a bad time." This does not mean that this kind of theory application activity should be terminated, but that it be recognized for what it is: a practice attempt at implementation in a frequently distorted and artificial situation and often under considerable time pressure. From the theoretical perspective of this study, the change agent variable was chosen because effectiveness in this area could well represent biculturalism.

The question upon entry into an organization is whether the entrant will be an innovator—one who makes an impact and has influence—or whether the entrant will conform to the prevailing norms and values of the organization to the extent that his "differentness" as a source of input and innovation is lost. Successful introduction of change into a social system indicates that the individual has gained influence and social power in the new system and can influence others to accept change. Therefore, we would not expect individuals who remain alienated, angry, and detached from the social system to be effective change agents. They might recommend many changes and be innovative or "different" in their own performance, but because of their attitude they will probably be considered outsiders and not as having a great deal of influence. Just as the angry or alienated entrant will probably not be able to accomplish planned change, so also will the overconformist be limited in making an impact toward innovative change to improve nursing practice. The overly conforming individual will see no need, nor be motivated to effect change, since she has been successful in reducing her conflict by reducing her differentness and therefore fusing herself with the system. Thus, successful change agent activity should be an indirect indication of whether the graduate is highly integrative and bicultural in her adjustment and, therefore, whether she has gained enough interpersonal competency in a social system to influence others. The level of change agent activity is viewed as an indication that an individual has attained enough personal insight and awareness and has dealt with role conflict successfully enough to engage in problem-solving and create change in his environment.

Rogers defines a change agent as "a professional who influences innovation decisions in a direction deemed desirable by a change agency." In this study, change agent activity was defined as any attempt to influence the behavior of others in a nursing subculturally desirable direction. The change activities had to be identifiable from the typescripts of the tape-recorded interviews with the nurses in the study and their supervisors and co-workers. There had to be evidence that the desired change was potentially beneficial to nursing or patient care (for example, an attempt to organize an agency-sponsored volley-ball team was not considered a change activity), that preplanning had been done, and that the activity of influence involved more than just the change initiator. Change activity as used in this research could not be spontaneous, nor could it involve only a single individual. An example of the latter might be an individual nurse who changed the way in which she gave intramuscular injections to a particular patient. This might be a planned activity, but if there was no attempt to influence others it was not considered to be a change activity. The dimensions of change agent activity that were included in this variable were the nature of the change as determined by the goal or objective of the change, the frequency of the change agent activity initiated, the effectiveness of the change agent activity, and the recipient or beneficiary of the attempted change agent activity.

*Index of professionalism.* One of the primary goals of both the content of the Anticipatory Socilization program and the immuni-

zation method by which it was taught was the retention of professional ideals and values. These could be inferentially measured through the change agent activity variable, or indirectly through subject self-report on the Corwin Professional Value scales. However, it was also desired to get some assessment of this concept of professionalism that might be comparable to the general notion of professionalism rather than specific to nurses alone.

An index does not define a concept; it is a substitute for something that cannot be measured directly. In this study, the Index of Professionalism was constructed from indicators abstracted from the general literature as indicative of the concept of professionalism in use in the general society. It does not measure adherence to the principles underlying the professional system of work organization as do the Corwin Role Conception and Kramer Behavior Strategy scales. It is intended to get at a differential assessment of how professional nurses are in terms of a comparison to some sort of professional criterion.

The index as developed consisted of the sum of weighted scores, from 0 to a maximum of 5, on each of the following nine indicators.

1. Professional courses since graduation: none = weight of 0; one = 1; two = 2; three = 3; four or more or fulltime graduate school = 4
2. Number of professional journals subscribed to: none; 1; 2 to 3; 4 or more
3. Professional books purchased since graduation: none; 1 to 2; 3 to 5; 6 or more
4. Hours per week spent in professional reading: none; 1 to 2; 3 to 4; 5 to 7; 8 or more
5. Activity and membership in professional organizations (this may include more than one organization, in which case the combined degree of activity was used): none; member only; some activity once a year; activities 2 to 5 times per year; 6 to 11 times per year; monthly or more
6. Publications in professional literature: none; 1; 2 or more
7. Professional speeches given: none; 1 to 2; 3 to 4; 5 or more

8. Offices held or leadership roles within professional organizations: none; member of committee; chairman of committee; officer in district or regional organization
9. Extent of professional activity within employing organization (Professional Performance Committee, Nursing Audit Committee, Nursing Care Plan Committee): none; member of committee; chairman of committee

## Time schedule

In all three classes of students, the Corwin role conception (BPS) scales were administered upon entrance to the School of Nursing (T1). Demographic data was also obtained at this time via a questionnaire; data on variables such as number of semester units completed and grade-point average were obtained from student records. During the nursing program, students in the classes of 1969 and 1970 were exposed to the Anticipatory Socialization program; students in the classes of 1968 were not. About one month before graduation (T4), the students in all three classes were retested on the BPS to measure the effects of the experimental program on role conceptions and role deprivation. Between 11 and 13 months after employment the nurses in all classes took the Kramer Role Behavior scales (T5) to ascertain the extent of their reported integrative role behavior choice. (This was usually equivalent to the same amount of time postgraduation, but not always. Some students took the summer off and began working later.) At this time they also completed a questionnaire designed to obtain the information needed for the dependent variables of chosen work locale and the Index of Professionalism. Data for the change agent activity variable was obtained from the tape-recorded interviews with the nurses, their supervisors, and co-workers, which were also done at T5. Between 23 to 26 months after working (T6), the nurses in all three classes were again tested on the BPS. They completed another questionnaire relative to their job histories and also took a psychological test at this time (the Personal Orientation Inventory). Between T5

and T6, two or three members of all three classes were observed in their clinical practice; a few were also interviewed again.

## Description of the sample

Three classes of student nurses in the generic program at the University of California School of Nursing, San Francisco, participated as subjects in this study. The 45 students in the class graduated in 1968 constituted the control group; they had the regular School of Nursing program. The classes of 1969 and 1970 formed the experimental groups and had the Anticipatory Socilization program plus the regular nursing program.

Upon entrance into the School of Nursing, most of these young women (there were no men in any of the classes) were 20 years old, single (about three or four in each class were married or divorced), Caucasian (about three or four in each class were Oriental; no other minorities were represented), and came from Protestant, middle-class backgrounds. Half (50%) of the students in the three classes reported that their fathers were in professional or managerial occupations; 30% of the fathers were in semiskilled occupations or minor clerical work.[7]

The three classes were very similar with respect to the amount of health-related job experience before and during their tenure in the School of Nursing. A little more than one fourth (29%) of the stdudents had health-related job experience (usually as a nurse's aide in a general hospital) before entrance into the school; over four fifths (82%) worked in similar capacities during the summer between their first and second year in the school. During the second summer, almost three fourths (71%) worked in the health field. Of the 161 students in the total sample, only 17 of them (10%) had never worked as a nurse's aide or in a job in the health field before graduation from the School of Nursing.

At the time of graduation, roughly two thirds of each class were single; one third was married or divorced. Within one year after graduation, the ratio of single to married was roughly 40:60; a year after that it was about 30:70. At the three-year postgraduation anniversary date, 75% of the Class of 1968, 84% of the Class of 1969, and 79% of the Class of 1970 were married or divorced. Compared with national figures, a larger percentage of the nurses in these three classes were married than for practicing registered nurses in general. (As of the 1966 Inventory [ANA], about 64% of the practicing registered nurses in the country were married.) As indicated by father's occupation or husband's actual or preparatory occupation, the nurses in this sample improved their social class status through marriage. At the time of the two-year followup, 112 of the 161 (70%) nurses were married. Of these 112 married nurses, 80% reported that their husbands were in professional or managerial occupations (as compared with 63% of the fathers); 6% reported that their husbands were in blue-collar jobs or minor clerical work.

All students in the control group had the option to participate or not in the testing and interview features of the research. The same was true for the experimental classes of 1969 and 1970. In addition, these students had the option of participating in the summer and evening aspects of the Anticipatory Socialization program. The remainder of the Anticipatory Socialization program was incorporated and integrated into the regular nursing curriculum for the students in the Classes of 1969 and 1970.

At the time of the first summer program, it was explained to the students that this was a five-year study covering their three years in the nursing program and a followup two years after graduation. They were told that tests, scales, and questionnaires would be administered at periodic intervals and that they would be followed up after graduation with interviews and observations. Students signed written consent forms stating that they wished to participate for the entire five-year period.

We see that we have three drivers making this automobile trip—the Classes of 1968, 1969, and 1970. One person—the Class of 1968—is going to make the trip in the regular Chevy Nova; the other two—the Classes of 1969 and 1970—are going to make it in sort of a "souped up" model. We want to know

whether all three drivers get to the places we've decided to visit. To be fair, all three people must be pretty much the same to begin with—for example, have equal driving ability, with no one taking along a family of children that would slow her down.

It was deemed very important that the resources of the three classes be equal on those variables that might have some relevance to the study variables. Such variables that were possible to measure with some degree of accuracy were intellectual ability, educational achievement, previous college experience, age, and entering professional, bureaucratic, and service role conception scores. Intellectual ability could be measured by the cooperative School and College Ability Tests (SCAT). These tests were administered routinely to all students entering this school of nursing. Best and most accurately described as academic aptitude tests, the SCAT measures two kinds of school-related abilities: verbal comprehension and manipulation and application of number concepts. According to Green, the two subscores (quantitative and verbal) are combined into a single score that can confidently be interpreted as a measure of general intelligence.

Educational achievement was measured by comparing the cumulative college grade-point average of the students in the three classes upon entrance into the School of Nursing. This particular nursing program accepts only transfer students who have completed at least two years (60 semester units) of college work.

Although 60 semester units of college work are required for entrance, increasing numbers of students are entering the nursing program with more extensive college experience. Because it was possible that additional college work might perhaps have increased a student's life experiences and made her more or less rejective of promulgated school values, this variable was checked by looking at the total number of college units earned prior to admission to the School of Nursing. Results of analysis of these variables (Appendix C, Table C-1) indicated that the three classes were quite homogeneous at the time of entrance into the School of Nursing. There were no significant differences among the three classes on SCAT scores, entering GPA, or number of semester units of college work. The median age of students in all classes was 20, with the three classes having all students between the ages of 19 and 26 upon admission to the School of Nursing. The students in the three classes were also highly similar in respect to their professional and bureaucratic role conception scores upon entrance into the School of Nursing (Appendix C, Table C-2). There was, however, a significant difference between the classes on the service role conception scale, with the Class of 1970 scoring much lower than the other two classes. No explanation can be offered. The faculty working with the students were unable to report any kind of subjective data that would substantiate or explain the less altruistic test posture of the Class of 1970.

There was one other variable that might have a marked effect on both the success of the independent variable as well as affecting the dependent variable. The Free Speech Movement on the Berkeley campus probably heralded the start of the more or less organized student revolt throughout the United States. At least superficially, the whole student rebellion movement is antiestablishment and hence antibureaucratic—or so it is frequently associated in the minds of students. It would be expected that students involved in or exposed to such a movement would be more adverse to subscribing to a bureaucratic role value orientation than students who were not involved. Conversely, they might be so disenchanted with the revolutionary movement that they would move in an opposite direction and quickly adopt the bureaucratic system. It is not known what, if any, effect the campus revolutionary movement had on this research study, but it is important to note the facts. The Free Speech Movement began in the fall of 1964. Although students can transfer into the School of Nursing from any accredited college or university, most of them come from some campus of the University of California system. In the Class of 1968, 40% (N = 18) of the students came from the Berke-

ley campus; 47.4% (N = 27) in the Class of 1969; 44.1% (N = 26) in the Class of 1970. In the fall of 1964, the students in the Class of 1968 would have been in their second year at Berkeley; the Class of 1969 in their first year. It is quite likely that there were students in all three classes who were very active in various kinds of activist movements.[8]

### Controlling sources of error

For the most part, our three drivers were pretty much the same in the resources they brought with them to make this trip. But that's not enough. To see if the "souped up" Chevy Nova is a better way of getting us to the places we want to visit than is the regular Chevy Nova, we've got to make sure that, as much as possible, traveling conditions are the same. Both cars must have equal access to service stations along the way, and there must be similar roadside diners and waitresses, and road and weather conditions, and so on.

To assess the effects of the Anticipatory Socialization program on the work locale and value orientation of the nurses in the experimental groups, it was necessary to control as much as possible the *curriculum* that both the control and experimental classes were exposed to. At the time of this study, the University of California, San Francisco, School of Nursing had an integrated, process-oriented nursing curriculum. Stressing the integrative rather than additive character of learning, the focus was on the student's learning how to learn and nurse (process), rather than on the accumulation of facts and knowledge. The goal of the program was to prepare a nurse who was capable of discovering and utilizing concepts and principles that were generalizable across age groups, settings, and clinical areas. Students were introduced immediately and continually to nursing care of patients of all ages and in a variety of settings and clinical areas. The emphasis was on maximum involvement rather than observation. The program was five years in length, with the first two years spent on a general liberal arts campus and the last three years on the medical center campus. During this three-year professional aspect of the program, the student took both liberal arts and nursing courses. All teaching of clinical nursing courses was on a team basis.

It is naive to think that any one student's curriculum is identically the same as any other's, but as nearly as could be determined, possible differences were identified and held constant. The only planned difference in the curricula for the Class of 1968 as opposed to the classes of 1969 and 1970 was the inclusion of the Anticipatory Socialization program for the latter groups. Students in all three classes had essentially the same program. With the exception of one psychiatric nursing facility, the same agencies were used for clinical experiences. The length, number, and sequencing of required courses, types of presentations, seminars, and so forth, were held constant, with one exception. Although the sequencing was not changed, approximately 20 students in the Class of 1970 had the option of accelerating their program by going to school during the summer quarter. This acceleration was based on student choice, not merit. Additionally, some of the students in the Class of 1969 led a total campus initiative to institute a campuswide interdisciplinary course. They were effective, so this one-unit course was added as a required course for the students in the Class of 1970.

The *faculty* is one of the most uncontrollable sources of potential differences. At best, only possible effects can be assessed. Only the characteristics of the nurse faculty were studied and analyzed. The required courses taught by nonnurse faculty remained the same and, with the exception of a statistics course, these courses were taught by the same people to all three classes.

There were three variables considered to be of importance in looking at faculty composition as it might affect the outcome of this study: faculty members' role conceptions and role deprivation as measured by the Corwin scales, the amount of nursing practice experience that the individuals had before employment on the faculty, and whether they were currently employed in practice. The first variable was considered to be important because the faculty was being counted upon to professionally socialize the students. If, for some

reason, they did not profess the high professional (and low bureaucratic) orientations usually found in other collegiate nurse faculty, the whole scheme of things would have been upset. By the same token, if they had high bureaucratic orientations, a confounding variable would have been introduced. Another possibility is that they may have had very low role deprivation scores, which again would have been highly unusual, and which may have indicated that, contrary to expectations, this nurse faculty had devised constructive ways of dealing with the professional-bureaucratic role conflict faced by practitioners.

Work experience was considered an important variable for two reasons. One, there is some evidence that the longer the nursing practice work experience, the greater the likelihood that the nurse faculty member will have learned some integrative role behaviors; that is, faced with the reality shock and professional-bureaucratic conflict herself, she will have resolved some conflict in this length of time.° Presumably if a faculty member has acquired integrative role behaviors, she will transmit these to her students. Ordinarily this is desirable, but in this instance such teaching would have confounded this study since this is what the Anticipatory Socialization program set out to do.

Current confrontation with work values (for example, as a paid employee on a part-time basis while employed on the faculty fulltime) was considered a crucial variable. Being away from the constant nursing service (patient care) demands allows faculty to idealize about how they should and would respond. It is the idealized version, rather than the version that is practical in the work situation, that is transmitted to students. It was hoped that faculty who were employed on a part-time basis would be evenly distributed among the faculty teaching the three classes of students.

In this particular nursing program, faculty taught in teams according to year groups: Team 1 taught all first-year students; Team 2,

---

°Kramer, M.: The new graduate speaks—again, Am. J. Nurs. 69(9):1903-1907, 1969.

second-year students, and so on. It was therefore probable that all students in a given year would be exposed to all members of the faculty team at some time during the academic year, although instructors would likely have more intensive contact with some students. It was impossible to weigh and assess this relative contact; therefore, the scores and work experience of all faculty who taught the students in the Class of 1968 during their three years in the program were compared with scores of faculty teaching the students in the Classes of 1969 and 1970. There was a group of 31 faculty members teaching the Class of 1968 during their three years in the school, 34 for the Class of 1969, and 30 for the Class of 1970. Eight of the faculty members taught the students in all three classes; 12 taught the students in both the classes of 1968 and 1969; 11 taught students in both the classes of 1969 and 1970. As a rough indication of the comparability of the faculty teaching the students in the three classes, an analysis was done on their role conception and role deprivation scores (Appendix C, Table C-3). Results indicated that there were no differences in role conceptions between the faculty groups who taught the three classes.

All faculty in this program held at least a Master's degree; two faculty members in the undergraduate program held doctoral degrees. Previous work experience is not a requirement for employment, but is highly desirable. Most of the faculty held dual clinical preparation at the Master's level. Previous work experience and career patterns of the faculty are presented in Table 2-2.

The similarity of the three faculty groups in respect to work experience and career patterns lends support to the belief that the students in the three classes were exposed not only to a highly similar curriculum, but also to faculty groups who held similar values and had similar amounts of prior and present exposure to work values and potential professional-bureaucratic conflict. Any changes appearing in the students in respect to these variables should, therefore, be due to the Anticipatory Socialization program to which the classes of 1969 and 1970 were exposed.

At the time of initiation of this study (1965), I was a faculty member at the University of California School of Nursing, teaching pediatric and obstetric nursing to second-year students. The Class of 1968 had just entered the first year of the professional portion of their program. I did not teach or have any contact with the students in the Class of 1968; a fellow faculty member administered all BPS tests at all time intervals to that class.

The following year, 1966, when the Class of 1968 was in the second year of the nursing program, I became coordinator of the first-year faculty team and began teaching the Anticipatory Socialization program to the students entering that year (Class of 1969). Shortly thereafter, I was appointed Assistant Dean of the undergraduate nursing program, and

**Table 2-2.** Comparison of specified characteristics of faculty teaching classes of 1968, 1969, and 1970

| | Number of months of teaching experience prior to present position | | Number of months of previous nursing practice work experience | | Median number of job changes prior to present position | Number who are currently employed in practice setting[*] |
|---|---|---|---|---|---|---|
| | RANGE | MEDIAN | RANGE | MEDIAN | | |
| Class of '68 (N = 31) | 0-207 | 12 | 0-228 | 24 | 4 | 6 |
| Class of '69 (N = 34) | 0-207 | None | 0-228 | 19 | 3 | 4 |
| Class of '70 (N = 30) | 0-120 | None | 0-120 | 24 | 3 | 5 |

[*]This number may be inaccurate since some faculty are reluctant to acknowledge moonlighting jobs.

therefore had access to teaching all three years of the curriculum. This made it possible to assign myself so that I could continue to teach the Anticipatory Socialization program in all three years to the students in the Classes of 1969 and 1970, but not teach in any way the students in the Class of 1968.

Since a good deal of the Anticipatory Socialization program was incorporated into the ongoing undergraduate nursing curriculum, it is important to review and explain how this was accomplished. In this undergraduate nursing curriculum, two hours every other week were allocated for leadership seminars with groups of approximately 16 students. The focus of these leadership seminars was to be threefold: organizational theory, the teaching-learning process, and group dynamics. It was reasoned that the Anticipatory Socialization program would fit very nicely into the focus of organization theory, so approximately one third of the seminars were thus apportioned for the classes of 1969 and 1970 and were taught by me. The Class of 1968 also had the same amount of time allocated to leadership seminars. As is typical in most programs, and most fortunately for this study, the faculty member responsible for teaching the leadership seminars to the Class of 1968 was schooled in psychiatric nursing. She was quite knowledgeable about group dynamics but knew little about organizational theory. A review of the course outlines and lecture notes for the year in which the Class of 1968 had their leadership seminars indicates that none of the time was spent in discussion of organizational theory or problems. The bulk of the time was devoted to consideration of group theory and psychodynamic skills.

The same pattern was found in subsequent years of the program. In the second and third years, again time was allocated for leadership and organizational theory but, lacking knowledge and theory in this area, none of the faculty felt comfortable to teach it. For the students in the Class of 1968, most of their leadership time was spent on studying the effects of different kinds of leadership in groups and on ecology. The classes of 1969 and 1970 had some of this material, but again I was

able to assign myself to teach these classes and used the opportunity to teach the Anticipatory Socialization program.

After the Class of 1968 had completed the third year of this nursing program, a somewhat unusual, albeit quite fortuitous for this research study, occurrence resulted in an almost complete turnover of the third-year faculty team for reasons unrelated to the research. This made it not only feasible, but quite mandatory to conduct a very thorough and complete orientation for the large number of new third-year faculty. During the summer, therefore, I conducted a two-week workshop for orientation of this new faculty group to the total program and to third-year content. It also provided a golden opportunity for very extensive indoctrination of the faculty into the content of the third-year Anticipatory Socialization program, thus building in greater likelihood of reinforcement of the concepts by the faculty to the students. The faculty turnover in the third year between the Classes of 1969 and 1970 was minimal.

What the students were told about the research program has been explained earlier; it must also be explained how this program was interpreted to faculty. The Dean of the School of Nursing at the time reviewed the research proposal extensively and considered it meritorious. It was considered very necessary that the faculty not be informed of the goals and hypotheses of the study, as this knowledge could very much have distorted the outcomes. As a result, the faculty were told only that a research study on the usefulness of students' summer work experience was being done and that I was volunteering to teach the leadership seminars. The program was fitted into the curricula specified by the faculty so that, except for the summer and evening programs, there was essentially nothing to explain.

Disregarding for a moment the expected and desired differences in the students in the control and experimental classes at graduation, look at a few other measures to see if there is evidence to warrant the conclusion that the three classes of nurses came from the same or very similar populations initially and, with exposure to the regular nursing program, came out somewhat the same at the end. Two variables were studied: the cumulative GPA upon graduation and the students' performance on state board examinations. These numbers do not mean a great deal in respect to what a student really got out of a nursing program, but are useful because they do show that, at least in the ways that are usually measured in our society, one group of students was not superior to another. An analysis of scores (Appendix C, Table C-4) indicates that the three classes were virtually the same in their state board performance. There was one failure on one section of the examination for one student in each of the Classes of 1968 and 1970. There was a significant difference in the cumulative GPA for the three classes, however. The students in the Class of 1968 were higher achievers during their tenure in the School of Nursing than either of the other two classes. It will be shown later that the role conception profile scores of the Class of 1968 were much closer to the faculty mean than were any of the other classes. This would lead one to speculate that, since the nurse role value orientations between this class and the faculty were more congruent, the faculty perceived the 1968 students as more successful and consequently rewarded them with higher grades.

## SUMMARY

In this chapter the theoretical framework generating the hypotheses and supporting the research decisions made in this study has been presented. Instead of just listing the theories, I have attempted to map out the basic notions, facts, ideas, and potential for action of concepts such as anticipatory socialization, sociological immunization, and adult socialization. This was done because many nurses—educators as well as practitioners—do not have the time or motivation to check primary sources. If this book is to be helpful in ameliorating reality shock, in developing interpersonal competency, and in defining lines of action for constructive conflict resolution, the material in the first two chapters must be well understood.

An encapsulated version of the theoretical framework forms a summary for this chapter. Differences in the way in which work is orga-

nized and tasks are approached constitute the professional and bureaucratic systems of work organization. The professional system is the usual approach in schools of nursing, whereas the bureaucratic system prevails in work organizations. This disparity leads to marked differences in the school and work subcultures and produces reality shock. Reality shock is not only uncomfortable, it causes nurses to flee the nursing practice scene, seriously deterring improvement of nursing and the health care system. The lack of interpersonal competency on the part of new graduates also contributes to reality shock and interferes with system improvement.

Many of the school-bred values transmitted to student nurses are untried and untested by the student while she is in school. Hence they are very vulnerable to capitulation upon graduation. Retention of these values can be augmented through a process of ideological immunization. Holding onto professional beliefs after graduation will increase the likelihood that neophyte nurses will eventually be able to put them into practice. This, coupled with exposure to knowledge and behaviors of a reference group of unique, highly adaptive nurse practitioners, will aid the student nurse in anticipatorily acquiring strategies or lines of action that will help her to become interpersonally competent in her future work role. This will decrease the effects of reality shock for the nurse and will move her along the road toward biculturalism, hopefully resulting in a happier and more productive professional nurse.

### NOTES

1. This is not a one-sided recognition of the problem. Many young instructors have confided that they feel "terribly insecure and lacking in self-confidence in clinical skills. I just never had a chance to practice them or to acquire skill and competence on my own. I should have worked for a couple of years before going on to graduate school."

2. Role configuration means a composite of the service, bureaucratic, and professional role conceptions as measured by the Corwin scales described on p. 19. Although these role conceptions are somewhat disparate, it is assumed that nursing is patterned around these conceptions and that nurses must adopt aspects of all three roles: *some* devotion to patients, *some* loyalty to the hospital administration, and *some* dedication to professional principles.

3. This theoretical aspect was initially included intuitively and empirically in the independent variable. It was only later in discussions of this research with a colleague, Dr. S. Dale McLemore of the University of Texas, Department of Sociology, that the similarity between what was actually being done and actions suggested by McGuire's theory was realized. Dr. McLemore's suggestion in this regard is gratefully acknowledged.

4. It is crucial to note that the pre-exposure to counterarguments had to be in a weakened form that stimulated, but did not overcome, the receiver's defenses. For an overview of the extensive work that has been done in this area, see Janis, I. L.: Effects of fear arousal on attitude change; recent developments in theory and experimental research. In Berkowitz, L., editor: Advances in experimental social psychology, vol. 3, New York, 1967, Academic Press, pp. 166-224.

5. It is perhaps wise that this point be explicated. I am not opposed to nurses working in settings other than hospitals. The bias that is operative in this study is opposition to flight behavior as a method of conflict resolution. Since it is empirically known that baccalaureate nurses often choose public health nursing as a flight from hospital nursing, it may appear that I think collegiate nurses should work only in hospitals. Such is not the case. It is the contention, however, that quality of nursing care will not be improved until professional nurses stop running away and learn how to operationalize their beliefs in all kinds of work settings, including the hospital.

6. For a description of the development and validation of these scales, see Kramer, M.: Professional-bureaucratic conflict and integrative role behavior. In Batey, M., editor: Communicating nursing research; is the gap being bridged? 1972, WICHE, pp. 57-71.

7. Hollingshead, A. B., and Redlich, F. C.: Social class and mental illness, New York, 1958, John Wiley & Sons, Inc., pp. 387-97, was used to classify occupations. Professional and managerial occupations correspond to Hollingshead's Groups I and II; semiskilled and minor clerical jobs are in Groups IV through VII.

The students in this sample are similar in respect to social class background of those entering the school 8 years earlier (Olesen, V. L., and Whittaker, E. W.: The silent dialogue, San Francisco, 1968, Jossey-Bass Inc., Publishers, pp. 83-87). Using the same Index of Social Position, Olesen and Whittaker report that 43% of the students' fathers worked in jobs that were professional or managerial, 20% were in a middle category, and 37% were in minor clerical work. When compared with a sample of 244 basic collegiate student nurses in the Western Region (Gortner, S.: Nursing majors in twelve western universities; a comparison of registered nurse students and basic senior students, unpublished doctoral dissertation, 1964, University of California, Berkeley, Department of Education, p. 288), the students in the present research sample have more fathers in managerial and professional occupations—38% in the Gortner sample and 50% in the present sample.

8. Lipset, S. M., and Wolin, S., editors: The Berkeley Student revolt: facts and interpretations, New York, 1965, Doubleday & Co., Inc. Page xi of Introduction is especially helpful for a possible interpretation of the effects of exposure to this movement on the attitudes of students.

## REFERENCES

American Nurses Association: Facts about nursing; a statistical summary, 1970-71 edition, New York, 1971, The Association, p. 7.

Anderson, L. R., and McGuire, W. J.: Prior reassurance of group consensus as a factor in producing resistance to persuasion, Sociometry 28(1):44-46, March 1965.

Argyris, C.: Interpersonal competence and organizational effectiveness. In Bennis, W. G., and associates: Interpersonal dynamics, Homewood, Ill., 1968, Dorsey Press.

Benne, K. D., and Bennis, W.: The role of the professional nurse, Am. J. Nurs. 59(2):196-198, 1959.

Benne, K. D., and Bennis, W.: What is real nursing?, Am. J. Nurs. 59(3):380-383, 1959.

Brim, O. G.: Socialization through the life cycle. In Brim, O. G., and Wheeler, S., editors: Socialization after childhood, New York, 1966, John Wiley & Sons, Inc., pp. 1-49.

Brim, O. G.: Adult socialization. In Clausen, J. A., and associates, editors: Socialization and society, Boston, 1968, Little, Brown & Co., pp. 184-226.

Cass, D. E.: Expectations of the staff nurse in nursing practice, Nurs. Clin. North Am. 3(1):111-115, 1968.

Clark, P. B., and Wilson, J. Q.: Incentive systems; a theory of organizations, Administrative Science Quarterly 6:129-166, 1961.

Cooper, S.: Symposium on nursing practice; expectations and reality, Nurs. Clin. North Am. 3(1):95-97, 1968.

Corwin, R. G.: Role conception and mobility aspiration; a study in the formation and transformation of nursing identities, unpublished doctoral dissertation, 1960, University of Minnesota.

Corwin, R. G., Taves, M., and Haas, E.: Professional disillusionment, Nurs. Res. 10:141-144, 1961.

Davis, Fred, and associates: The nursing profession, New York, 1966, John Wiley & Sons, Inc., pp. 138-175.

Deutsch, M.: Conflicts; productive and destructive, Journal of Social Issues 25(1):7-41, 1969.

Dornbusch, S. M.: The military academy as an assimilating institution, Social Forces 33:316-321, 1955.

Dunn, H.: Facing realities in nursing administration today, Am. J. Nurs. 68(5):1013-1018, 1968.

Festinger, L.: A theory of cognitive dissonance, New York, 1957, Harper & Row, Publishers.

Foote, N., and Cottrell, L. S., Jr.: Identity and interpersonal competence, Chicago, 1955, University of Chicago Press.

Glass, H. P.: Teaching behavior in the nursing laboratory in selected baccalaureate nursing programs in Canada, doctoral dissertation, New York, 1971, Columbia University, Teachers' College.

Goffman, E.: Asylums; essays on the social situation of mental patients and other inmates, New York, 1961, Doubleday & Co., Inc.

Green, R. A.: SCAT. In Buros, O. K., editor: The sixth

mental measurements yearbook, Highland Park, N. J., 1965, The Gryphon Press, pp. 716-718.

Hovland, C. I.: Reconciling conflicting results derived from experimental and survey studies of attitude change, Am. Psychol. 14:8-17, 1959.

Interaction Associates, Inc.: Tools for change, ed. 2, San Francisco, 1971, Interaction Associates, Inc.

Interaction Associates, Inc.: Tools for change, Strategy Notebook, San Francisco, 1972, Interaction Associates, Inc.

Janis, I. L.: Motivational effects of different sequential arrangements of conflicting arguments; a theoretical analysis. In Hovland, C. I., editor: The order of presentation in persuasion, Vol. 1, New Haven, 1957, Yale University Press, pp. 170-186.

Johann, R. O.: Conflicts and person. In Savary, L. M., S.J., and associates: Listen to love, New York, 1971, Regina Press, p. 211.

Johnson, D. E.: Competence in practice; technical and professional, Nurs. Outlook 14:30-33, 1966.

Johnson, D. E.: Professional practice in nursing: in The shifting scene; directions for practice, papers presented at the twenty-third conference of the Council of Member Agencies of the Department of Baccalaureate and Higher Degree Programs held in New York, May 5-7, 1967, New York, 1967, Department of Baccalaureate and Higher Degree Programs, National League for Nursing, pp. 26-34.

Johnson, D. E.: Definition of professional nursing practice. In Toward differentiation of baccalaureate and associate degree nursing education and practice, proceedings of a workshop held in August 1968, San Francisco, 1969, University of California, School of Nursing, Continuing Education in the Health Sciences, pp. 1-10.

Kelman, H.: Processes of opinion changes, Public Opinion Quarterly 25(1):57-78, 1961.

Kraegel, J. M., Schmidt, V., Shukla, R. K., and Goldsmith, C. E.: A system of patient care based on patient needs, Nurs. Outlook 20(4):257-264, 1972.

Kramer, M.: Some effects of exposure to employing bureaucracies on the role conceptions and role deprivation of neophyte collegiate nurses, unpublished dissertation, 1966, Stanford University.

Kramer, M.: Role models, role conceptions, and role deprivation, Nurs. Research 17(2):115-120, 1968.

Kramer, M.: Collegiate graduate nurses in medical center hospitals; mutual challenge or duel, Nurs. Research 18(3):196-210, 1969.

Kramer, M.: The new graduate speaks—again, Am. J. Nurs. 69(9):1903-1907, 1969.

Kramer, M.: Role conception of baccalaureate nurses and success in hospital nursing, Nurs. Research 19(5):428-439, 1970.

Kramer, M., and Baker, C.: The exodus; can nursing afford it? Journal of Nursing Administration 1(3):15-30, 1971.

Lewis, E.: Four nurses who wanted to make a difference, Am. J. Nurs. 69(4):777-782, 1969.

Logsdon, A.: Preparing for unexpected responsibilities, Nurs. Clin. North Am. 3(1):143-152, 1968.

Mauksch, H. O.: It defies all logic—but a hospital does function, The Modern Hospital, October 1960, pp. 67-70.

McGuire, W. J.: Resistance to persuasion conferred by active and passive prior refutation of the same and alternative counterarguments, J. Abnorm. Psychol. 63(2):326-332, 1961.

McGuire, W. J.: Persistence of the resistance to persuasion induced by various types of prior belief defenses, J. Abnorm. Psychol. 64(4):241-248, 1962.

McGuire, W. J., and Papageorgis, D.: The relative efficacy of various types of prior belief-defense in producing immunity against persuasion, J. Abnorm. Psychol. 62(2):327-337, 1961.

McGuire, W., and Papageorgis, D.: Effectiveness of forewarning in developing resistance to persuasion, Public Opinion Quarterly 26:24-34, 1962.

McGuire, W.: Inducing resistance to persuasion. In Jahoda, M., and Warren, N., editors: Attitudes, Baltimore, 1966, Penguin Books, pp. 163-186.

Merton, R. K.: Social theory and social structure, New York, 1968, The Free Press.

Moore, W.: Occupational socialization. In Goslin, D., editor: Handbook of socialization theory and research, Chicago, 1969, Rand McNally & Co., pp. 861-883.

Olesen, V. L., and Whittaker, E. W.: Adjudication of student awareness in professional socialization; the language of laughter and silences, The Sociological Quarterly, 1966, pp. 381-396.

Olesen, V. L., and Whittaker, E. W.: The silent dialogue, San Francisco, 1968, Jossey-Bass Inc., Publishers.

Olmsted, A. G., and Paget, M. A.: Some theoretical issues in professional socialization, J. Med. Educ. 44:663-669, August 1969.

Orne, M., and Wender, P.: Anticipatory socialization for psychotherapy, method and rationale, Am. J. Psychiatry 124(9):88-98, 1968.

Papageorgis, D., and McGuire, W. J.: The generality of immunity to persuasion produced by pre-exposure to weakened counterarguments, J. Abnorm. Psychol. 62(3):475-481, 1961.

Paynich, M. L.: Why do basic nursing students work in nursing? Nurs. Outlook 19(4):242-245, 1971.

Reinkemeyer, A.: New approaches to professional preparation, Nurs. Forum 9(1):27-40, 1970.

Rogers, E. M., and Svenning, L.: Change agents, clients, and change. In Modernization among peasants; the impact of communication, New York, 1969, Holt, Rinehart & Winston, Inc., pp. 169-231.

Rogers, M.: Educational revolution in nursing, New York, 1961, The MacMillan Co.

Rosow, I.: Forms and functions of adult socialization, Social Forces 44:35-45, 1965.

Schein, E. H.: The Chinese indoctrination program for prisoners of war, Psychiatry 19:149-172, 1956.

Smith, K. M.: Discrepancies in the role-specific values of head nurses and nursing educators, Nurs. Research 14:196-202, Summer 1965.

Stouffer, S., and associates: The American soldier; adjustment to army life, vol. I, Studies in the social psychology of World War II, Princeton, N. J., 1949, Princeton University Press.

Thomas, L.: Is nursing service administration prepared for the professional nurse? J. Nurs. Educ. 4(1):5-7, 1965.

Tschudin, M. S.: Education preparation needed by the nurse in the future, Nurs. Outlook 12:32-35, April 1964.

U. S. Senate Committee on Government Operations, Permanent Sub-Committee on Investigations: Communist interrogation, indoctrination and exploitation of American military and political prisoners, 84th Cong. 2d Sess. Washington, D. C., 1956, U. S. Government Printing Office.

Walker, B. B.: The postsurgery heart patient; amount of uninterrupted time for sleep and rest during the first, second, and third post-operative days in a teaching hospital, Nurs. Research 21(2):164-169, 1972.

Warnecke, R. B., and Riddle, D.: The lay image and the professional role; an exploration of discontinuity in the process of anticipatory socialization, 1968, ERIC Document Service, EDO 28971.

Waters, V., Chater, S., Vivier, M. L., Urrea, J., and Wilson, H.: Technical and professional nursing; an exploratory study, Nurs. Research 21(2):124-131, 1972.

Weinstein, E. A.: The development of interpersonal competence. In Goslin, D. A., editor: Handbook of socialization theory and research, Chicago, 1969, Rand McNally & Co.

Williams, T., and Williams, M.: The socialization of the student nurse, Nurs. Research 8:18-25, Winter 1959.

## CHAPTER THREE

# THE ANTICIPATORY SOCIALIZATION PROGRAM

All that is necessary for the forces of evil to win in the world is for enough good men to do nothing.

EDMUND BURKE

In the Valley and in the City, the projects grow and people get a new kind of care by those who care and who dare to change the system by working within it.

*(letter from a graduate of experimental class 1½ years after employment)*

The above two quotes aptly describe what the Anticipatory Socialization program was all about. Although the word evil is much too strong, the idea is that improvements in the quality of patient care and the health care system will be brought about by nurses who truly care enough to work within the system to do something. On the other hand, the status quo will be maintained and fostered, not by indolent, uncaring nurses but rather by good nurses who do nothing.

In this chapter this book departs substantively from a research report. It is customary for an investigator to describe, carefully and in considerable detail, the independent variable or the treatment of a research study. It is only in this way that the reader can judge the efficacy and logical relationship between the variables and that other investigators can ever hope to replicate the study. This will not be done here. The Anticipatory Socialization program, the independent variable, was a product of its times. It was a blend of the investigator as teacher as she was at that point in time and of a particular group of students as they were within a social system as it existed then (1966 to 1970). The times are different now; so also are the resources and constraints.

To fully describe the program as it was then lacks utility and purpose. What is more important and meaningful is to describe the overall goals, purposes, and strategies of the Anticipatory Socialization program. The substantive issues and plans are timeless. The utility of this chapter lies in the strategies presented, not in the specifics. To duplicate or model the idea of the program is fine; to replicate the independent variable is wasteful.

With this in mind, let's begin by taking a look at a vehicle that will provide the transportation to our desired goals. What was the substantive content and approach of the Anticipatory Socialization program? The major idea was to use methods suggested by the work on sociological immunization to anticipatorily socialize two classes of student nurses into the attitudes and role specific behaviors that were being used by nurses who were successful in operationalizing their professional values in the work setting and in handling conflict in a growth-producing manner. Two specific goals were made overt:

1. The students were to receive a mild reality shock with accompanying defenses so that their untried professional beliefs would be challenged, but so that they would have the opportunity to work out some of their own defenses to protect them.

2. The students would be presented with all possible dimensions of the expected problems so that they in turn would be free and responsible to choose viable alternatives for themselves. These "all possible dimensions" included specific information on the genesis and growth of professional-bureaucratic conflict, the

causes, signs, and symptoms of reality shock, and specific strategies used by a reference group of practicing nurses to resolve professional-bureaucratic conflict in a growth-producing manner.

To accomplish these goals a two-pronged curricular program, designed to overcome some of the work difficulties known to be encountered by many new graduates, was developed. One component was designed to sociologically immunize student nurses to the values of the work world. In this way the anticipated reality shock would be reduced or better managed. This goal would be implemented in three ways: (1) by exposing students early to some of the potential conflicts they would encounter as graduate nurses, (2) by attacking early some of the professional and idealized beliefs—cultural truisms such as "everybody really cares about the patients" —that nursing students generally receive from school of nursing faculty, and (3) by equipping the students with a knowledge base of the evolution, characteristics, and exigencies of the bureaucratic system of work. By doing these things it was thought that as new graduates they would be in a position to judge for themselves what works, what does not, and when it is more effective to go over, go through or bypass the established system.

At least for the present and immediate future, it will probably be necessary for most nurses to work in some kind of bureaucratic organization. To improve the patient care of the present and future, it is desirable that nurses view and care for patients from a whole-task (professional) perspective. With a combination of high professional and high bureaucratic loyalties, it is highly probable that role conflict will occur. Such role conflict is a leading determinant of reality shock. Through a program designed to confront the student with the facts of reality, the tools for change, strategies of constructive conflict resolution, understanding of the system in which change must take place, and role models to demonstrate innovative and successful practice, it was anticipated that reality shock would be encountered while in school and thereby substantially lessened upon graduation.

From the findings of McGuire and others, it could be anticipated that if a person encounters an attack to his cultural truisms, and if he is provided with some counterarguments to the attack, a process of immunization will occur whereby the person will be better able to retain and uphold the attacked values. One of the major problems in developing a program such as this was to obtain practical and realistic counterarguments to the professional values that baccalaureate nurses report are attacked in the work scene. Very little is published on this. Most of the professional writing is done by nurse educators who present an idealized, sometimes codified version of preferred behavior that usually has not been reality tested. It was therefore decided that, to find out what successful nurses in the real world were doing to amalgamate and articulate conflicting value systems, some of these nurses would have to be located and studied. This reference group would provide both role specific behaviors and attitudes to be modeled. This is what lead to the development and execution of the preliminary medical center study described in detail in Chapter 2.

It was through a study of these nurses that the second component of the two-pronged Anticipatory Socialization program was developed. The nurse subjects had to be equipped with tested counterarguments to their beliefs to be effectively immunized. Furthermore, passage from a reference group to a membership group is markedly hastened when the aspirant prematurely adopts the values and behavior standards of the reference group. This is anticipatory socialization. What was desired in this program was that the students learn to appreciate and adopt the values and attitudes of a select group of practicing nurses who had learned to operate professionally within a bureaucratic framework. Through this anticipatory socialization it was thought that the students would then be able to resist the deprofessionalization and flight pattern observed in earlier samples of baccalaureate nurses. In summary then, the outside reference group of nurses provided much of the material (content and process) for the Anticipatory Socialization program; results from McGuire's research provided the teaching strategies.

## A FOUR-PHASE VEHICLE

The original program was planned to include four phases. Decisions on the length of each phase were determined as much by intuition and natural breaks in the school calendar as by rationale. The content of each phase, however, was based on the findings of previous research, especially the study of the initial effect of exposure to employing organizations on the role values of new baccalaureate graduates. In this study, interviews were done with new baccalaureate graduates at three-month intervals after they had begun to work. From this data, four specific phases were inferred. The Anticipatory Socialization program put nursing students prematurely through these phases and attempted to equip them to handle the challenges to their professional value system that they would encounter at each phase.

### Phase 1: the encounter

The first phase covered the entire first year in the school of nursing. The program consisted of 10 seminars held twice a month with students in groups of 15 or 16. The major focus of these seminars was to produce a mild shock to the student through an attack on the professional values that were being flung at her from all directions. In respect to the degree of shock to be produced and anticipated effects, the work of Janis and others on the effects of fear arousal on attitude change was used extensively. Janis also provides a schematic summary that gives some guidance to the teacher in estimating, through observation of students' attitudes and emotional symptoms, the behavioral consequences of the degree of shock stimuli used. This guided my judgment in deciding when to back off and when to present more shock stimuli.

The source of the shock stimuli used during the encounter phase was tape-recorded incidents gathered as part of my previous research. These consisted of new graduates' responses to two questions in particular on the interview schedule that was used: "Describe yourself in some work situation that was par-

ticularly dissatisfying to you," and the reverse query. In responding to these questions, the interviewee usually sketched in the outlines of a conflict situation and then proceeded to tell what she had done about it. If the situation ended favorably or pleasantly or had high rewards, it was given in response to the "satisfying" question. If the results were negative, it was cited in response to the "dissatisfying" situation.

The taped incidents served as an attack upon untried beliefs and values. They also provided students with a frame of reference within which they could begin to develop counterarguments to the attack and lines of action that would be potentially useful in the situation. The usual procedure consisted of playing taped segments describing the outlines of a conflict situation. This would generally bring about a diffuse emotional reaction and response. As the student presented arguments, I did everything possible to present logical, realistic attacks. For example, in the tapes in which the nurse described the physician who did an open cardiac massage on an 80-year-old man "just for practice," the students reacted vehemently that "this just wasn't true; it couldn't be," or "that's impossible; the nurse just must stop it." The instructor took the role of strongly supporting the physician with questions such as: "Well, if he doesn't practice, how is he going to know how to do it?" or "Would withdrawing from helping the physician create more danger for the patient?" This generally led to spirited discussion during which the students were led to develop refutational defenses. The content for both the counterarguments and refutational defenses were obtained from the reference group of medical center nurses.

In the beginning, the seminars were deliberately terminated on an anxious, unsettled tone. The hope was that this would further stimulate the students to carry out what Janis calls the "work of worrying." Sometimes this was quite effective, but at other times it boomeranged.

What caused the boomerang effect? The students would invariably continue to mull over the dilemma after they left the seminar, so not uncommonly they would bring it up in other classes. The usual tendency was for other faculty to provide the student with support defenses ("You're absolutely right; the dignity of the patient must be maintained at all costs" or "No, physicians do not practice on patients.") These in turn would mightily tempt the student to turn off the challenge that the attack presented. It is often a tendency for people to ignore the unpleasant or block out their perceptions of things going on around them that do not fit into the dominant value system of self or of the environment. The student, enmeshed in an environment in which she observes high status people (the faculty) promulgating values and behavior that are not necessarily operational or valued by the reality scene (usually in the form of the head nurse), has a strong tendency to stop her recognition of practitioner values deviant to those promulgated by the faculty. This point can be illustrated in the following tape-recorded dialogue in a first-year nursing (junior year in college) seminar.

INSTRUCTOR: It's difficult to imagine how quality nursing care can be given without written nursing care plans. And you will find that on most of the units, each of the patients has a care plan and that the nurses follow them. You'll find that these plans will be very useful to you since you will only be on the wards two mornings a week. You'll get a good idea of the conditions of your patient and what needs to be done for him.

STUDENT NO. 1: But Miss J, I was up on the ward last week and I looked all over for a nursing care plan on my patient. When I asked the head nurse about it, she just looked at me kind of funny and said: "I guess we'll have to get one."

INSTRUCTOR: Oh, that's just *that* head nurse. I'll speak to her about it. I'm sure you will find them everywhere else, and of course you'll always see to it that you make out a plan for any patient that you care for.

The student dropped her protest at this point. In the next seminar, one of the students volunteered the information that her patient did not have a care plan and that when she asked the head nurse about it she was told that they just did not have time to make out care plans on everyone. The instructor responded that perhaps occasionally, in extreme emergencies, nurses might not have time to write them, but that would not happen to them on their assignments and they would surely make out plans for their patients.

For the rest of this semester, there were no further protests by the students regarding the presence or absence of nursing care plans. At the beginning of the next semester, I encountered the first student who had spoken about nursing care plans in the seminar on one of the wards. She was busily filling out a care plan on the patient she was caring for. I asked her how the care plans were going. She smiled and said enthusiastically: "They're really great. I don't think I could get along without them, and the patients get much better care." I asked her whether most of the patients had nursing care plans. She responded: "Oh, yes, the staff nurses do most of them but we students do them too."

After this conversation, I checked and found that 8 of the 32 patients on the unit had written nursing care plans. These 8 patients were presently or had been cared for the preceding week by the 5 student nurses assigned to that ward. None of the patients not cared for by student nurses had written care plans. It is improbable that this student deliberately lied. In all likelihood her perceptions had been dulled or distorted by the dominance and rewards of the value system of the instructor. There was simply no advantage or mileage to be gained by noticing and commenting on things that the instructor did not reward her for noticing.

The preceding is an example of the kinds of material discussed in the leadership seminars with the first-year students. The focus was not on the content of nursing care plans or whether or not they were helpful or should be done, but the reality of the situation: in general they aren't done, sometimes because of lack of time, but also because of lack of skill and motivation. The approach used was to openly acknowledge the disparity between what the students were learning in school and the realities of the work scene. Students were then encouraged to go out and interview staff and head nurses and nurse's aides to determine their views and ideas about the value of care plans. From this they then formulated several change agent plans, which they tried. Some of the students arrived at the conclusion that written plans were not needed for all patients. This kind of conclusion would then throw the student into conflict with her clinical laboratory instructor, who usually did not share the student's evaluation of the situation. This kind of conflict was also legitimate material for discussion in the Anticipatory Socialization seminars. What do you do when you find you are in conflict with an authority source who has power to reward or punish you?

In addition to providing some reality shocks, the conflict tape recordings, as well as the conflict situations the students themselves brought to the seminar, provided the opportunity for transmission of didactic and theoretical material on the emergence of bureaucratic organizations, their characteristics, advantages, disadvantages, and so on. Issues suggested by the conflict situations were explored and used as an entree to present the student with information regarding division of labor, degree of bureaucratization, and the bureaucratic system of work. For example, there are degrees of bureaucratization. Professionals can generally get along better in organizations that are less hierarchically structured and that have more decentralized authority. Students were taught how to assess an organization for these kinds of features, what kinds of things to look for when they went to visit a hospital or agency, and how to make inferences regarding degree of bureaucratization from a nursing assignment sheet.

The prevailing stance taken in the seminars was that conflicts and issues such as those brought by the students or exemplified on the tapes were examples of nursing and nursing practice as it exists today. Ignoring these problems or wishing they were not there will not help the situation. Furthermore, when you graduate and become a paid employee, these conflicts will be even more pressing and troublesome to you than when you are a student and protected to some extent by the instructor. Through knowledge and understanding of the work system under which most

of nursing and health care is practiced, you can better choose your place of employment. You can begin to understand why some things happen as they do and, most important, you can better equip yourself to plan and implement changes within the system.

Some of these conflict situations were written up as problems for study and used by the students in informal rap sessions. They were also used on examinations to test knowledge and content in the area of leadership and organizations.[1]

## Phase 2: reidentification

The second phase was termed reidentification to indicate at least some return to bureaucratic system loyalty (students had higher bureaucratic loyalties upon entrance into school than at the end of their first year of nursing). Hopefully, it would also include the beginning of a bicultural redefinition of a work system that was an adaptive blend of choosing the bureaucratic mode when it was appropriate and the professional when it was more appropriate.

It is a fairly usual pattern for nursing students to either work for pay or as nurse's aides, particularly during the summer months. In the only study on this found, Paynich reports that in her sample of 68 junior and senior nursing students who worked during the summer, gaining self-confidence in giving nursing care was both the primary motivator and one of the chief benefits accruing from the experience. Earning money was the second-ranked factor; many of the students reported that they could have earned more money in other than nurse's aide jobs. The students participating in the research being reported here followed a similar pattern. Commonly, 80% to 90% of them sought summer employment, mostly as nurse's aides in general hospitals. Their motivations were mainly "to gain self-confidence," "to practice skills," "to test my skills out from under my instructor's eyes," and "to earn money." A previous study of State College nursing students (Kramer, 1968) showed that work experience as a nurse's aide had marked influence on the aspirant nurse as measured by her retention of aide-connected role models for at least as long as six months after graduation.

Based on these two factors (student nurses frequently work as aides during the summer, and this work experience has an influence on them), it was decided to use the summer nurse's aide work experience as an integral part of the Anticipatory Socialization program. Prior to planning this experience, four student nurses who were working as aides during the summer of 1966 were studied intensively. They were observed on the units, interviewed both formally and informally, and their opinions and attitudes sampled on a variety of measures. When they returned to school in the fall, their instructors were also questioned and interviewed regarding their attitudes toward these four nurses in particular. Faculty opinion was also sought regarding their perception of the advantages or disadvantages accruing to students who work as nurse's aides.

Based on this impressionistic data, as well as logical derivatives of the theory guiding this study, the following assessment was made of summer nurse's aide work experience and its potential impact upon the developing value system of student nurses. Summer aide work experience can be a danger to a budding professional value system. Many of the faculty perceived that such a work experience can lead to an entrenchment of work values at a time when professional values have not yet taken hold and that sometimes the entrenchment is so firm that it is difficult to dislodge. Another potential outcome of this work experience is that an unsatisfactory nurse's aide work experience can lead to a complete and premature rejection of all aspects of the bureaucratic work system. Either of these outcomes is undesirable. In the first, the student becomes an organization nurse focusing on the achievement of tasks and measuring her competence as a nurse by how quickly she can "dust and polish" the patients. Having been well rewarded for these activities during her summer experience, she has a great deal of difficulty in adjusting to the value and reward system of the instructors when she returns for the schoolyear. The other outcome, rejection of the bureaucratic system, is also very undesir-

able. In the earlier research (Kramer, 1966) it was demonstrated that some degree of loyalty and adherence to bureaucratic work principles was not only desirable but mandatory for survival. Most important, it was necessary to be an effective change agent within the system. One must believe that the system has some integrity and some value in order to effect change within it. In the exodus study described earlier, it was found that nurses who left nursing practice altogether had significantly lower bureaucratic scores than those who remained. It cannot be said that one causes the other, only that there is a relationship between the two.

The reidentification phase of the Reality Shock program consisted of monthly seminars available to all students in the experimental groups who were working for pay in the health care system during the summer between their first and second years in the school. Of the Classes of 1969 and 1970, 73% and 75% respectively, participated in this phase of the program. (Almost all of them were working as nurse's aides.) The purpose of this phase was to help the student maintain the delicate balance between two potentially antithetical value systems and to begin to ferret out a bicultural alternative for herself. The focus of seminar discussions was determined by the students, but there were specific readings, activities, and content presented. Amitai Etzioni's *Modern Organizations* (Englewood Cliffs, N. J., 1964, Prentice-Hall, Inc.) was used as a textbook. The learning experiences included recognition of values that the students were encountering that were different from values promulgated during the preceding school year. After students could identify these values and specify the behaviors that allowed or permitted the inference of these values, they would then attempt to see which of the systems (professional, bureaucratic, or some amalgamation of these) the values were consistent with. Students were continually encouraged to talk about their feelings toward their jobs and toward their emergent selves.

During the second month of the summer program, the concentration in the seminars was on identifying the bureaucratic system operation for what it was. The recognition that the bureaucratic system is quite efficient and effective when applied to things, but less so when applied to people, was sought. By this time students had been in their jobs long enough to know and to be able to analyze their work situations quite well. This provided opportunity to concentrate on the relative degree of bureaucratization as represented by the various hospitals in which the students were working. Students could also identify differences in the ways in which the bureaucratic system operated according to day, evening, and night shifts.

The seminars were usually held the third and fourth weeks of each of the summer months. By the end of approximately two months on the job most of these student nurse's aides were very comfortable in their jobs. Boredom had set in for a lot of them, mainly because of the prospect of doing incomplete, meaningless work. This led very naturally to a discussion of routine, monotony, and boredom as major undesirable consequences of work that is bureaucratically organized. Since they themselves were currently experiencing this, they could readily understand it. They could also recognize that it was not only the nurse's aide job that had succumbed to the bureaucratic principle of division of labor into effective time tasks (but often meaningless work tasks), but that the nurse role also often had many meaningless tasks, such as passing medications all day long.

From recognition of the problem, the instructor attempted to move the group to consider possible alternative resolutions. Although often the solution hit upon by the student was general and a sort of parroting of the team nurse concept—from each according to his ability to each according to his need—the students were encouraged to explore some of the newer possibilities such as participative management, adhocracy, and primary nursing.

A third major learning activity was the identification of a possible role model in the work environment. This was done at the end of the summer and was a useful tool in teaching and in evaluating the effectiveness of the summer program. Students were instructed to select someone in their work environment who came as close as possible to their present idea of the kind of nurse they would like to be. They then described her qualities, traits, and behaviors and conducted an interview with her to ascertain her opinions and attitudes. They analyzed her behavior and responses to conflict situations in terms of systems of work organization. The purpose of this activity was to help the students identify desirable bureaucratic and professional traits and behaviors and to see whether they were beginning to choose as role models nurses who were successfully bicultural.

It can be seen that the major goal of the summer work phase of the program was an attempt to bring about a reidentification of self from one who is a "budding professional nurse working in utopia" to one who sees herself as a "budding professional nurse working in the imperfect, sometimes illogical reality of today." Whether this goal was accomplished or not is difficult to assess. There were many periods of shared discouragement among the students and between the students and the instructor. Without a doubt, the students encountered shock. It registered on their faces and in their words: "I had no idea that this is the way it would be." "I don't see how I could be in clinical all last year and not see some of the stupid ways in which the jobs of nurses are divided." Sometimes the instructor wondered if she had gone too far with the shock situation and prayed that the students would return to school the following fall so that they could receive another injection of "professional icing."

## Phase 3: more conflict, but hope

The goal of phase 3 of the program was to continue to stimulate the students to constantly evaluate the professional goals and ideals they were continually ingesting and simultaneously to encourage them to think creatively and broadly about some of the possible changes in systems for the delivery of health care and the potential impact of the system on them as future practitioners. This phase of the program was conducted during the second of the three years in the nursing program and consisted of a total of 16 hours of lecture, seminars, and panel discussion, as well as a written paper.

Six hours were given as part of the regular curriculum, and consequently all students were exposed to it. The other 10 hours were specially planned seminars and panel discussions held in the evenings; they were open to all students but selectively attended.

During the second year in the professional program, the student had begun to enlarge her sphere of observation, cognizance, and potential influence. The Anticipatory Socialization program corresponded to this by enlarging her encounter with potential conflict situations engendered by the system as a whole. Cognitive input during this phase consisted of a theoretical consideration of patrimonial, bureaucratic, and professional systems of work organization particularly in respect to task organization (p. 13), types of role conflicts (inter- and intra-role conflict), and a study of some newer concepts of task organization such as proposed by Bennis. Other issues discussed in this phase consisted of physician-nurse conflicts, interdisciplinary conflicts, and nursing organization conflicts including possible conflicts between diploma and baccalaureate nurses. Not all conflicts to be encountered by the new nurse are professional-bureaucratic; it was considered important that the student realize this and begin to see things in the perspective that conflicts are multiple and interwoven and that techniques and skills used in the resolution of one conflict will transfer to others.

The evening seminar programs consisted of the following topics:

1. Potential physician-nurse conflict or support. Presentation by a panel consisting of one physician who was for baccalaureate education for nurses, one who was against baccalaureate education for nurses, and one who was willing to be convinced one way or the other.
2. The nurse and the law. Two presentations, one by a lawyer and the second by a nurse. Emphasis was on potential conflict between the law and "doing what's right for the patient." Presentations and discussion included such issues as the legal aspects of responsibility and accountability, health laws as they affect the professions, and case presentations on negligence and malpractice.
3. How others see you and what they expect. Presentation by a panel composed of head nurses, supervisors, and directors of nursing who represented viewpoints similar to those of the physician panel in no. 1.
4. What I could and could not accomplish. Presentation and discussion of stategies for action used by members of past graduating classes in their present nursing practice. Nurses were deliberately chosen to represent a variety of settings and and degrees of success.

### Optional summer program

This phase was not in the original plans or design but was added upon student demand. It was conducted during the summer between the second and third years, and was attended by 40% of the students in the Class of 1969 and 38% of the students in the Class of 1970. Again it consisted of three monthly seminars for those students who were working as either nurse's aides, licensed practical nurses, technicians, or in some health-connected job in either hospital or community agencies. The major purposes of this summer program were (1) to explore the professional-bureaucratic conflict as it is manifested in other professions and in other countries, and (2) to begin an investigation of theoretical models useful in formulating possible solutions to the conflict. Teaching-learning activities consisted of reading and analyzing reports of professional-bureaucratic conflict as it was encountered by professionals in at least one other country or one other profession. Students were also introduced to Glaser and Strauss's "awareness" model as a potential way of formulating solutions to conflict situations. Thibaut and Kelly's cost-reward model and Watson's change agent model were also introduced.

### Phase 4: affirmation

Phase 4 of the Anticipatory Socialization program consisted of 10 hours of lecture and seminars during the third and last year of the nursing program. The content focus was specifically on theoretical models useful in conflict resolution, role negotiation, and adaptations of the institutionally prescribed nurse role that might be useful in resolving conflict constructively and amalgamating the professional and bureaucratic systems of work organization. Students continued to study the values and behaviors of the medical center role models. Panel discussions of students who had graduated the preceding year also were held for the purpose of reinoculating the students to the conflict situations and reality shock that they would probably encounter. Emphasis was placed on individual nurse identification of her change agent style, and each student carried out a project designed to provide practice in this style and role. Since this phase of the program was made an integral part of the curriculum, all students in the experimental classes were exposed to it.[2]

Even though the program was planned in terms of distinct phases with a plan of what was to be included in each, the knowledge and attitudinal components were not always introduced at the same time to each seminar group. The attitudinal components in particular were undoubtedly differentially emphasized. In the next section, a summary of those knowledge and attitudinal components to which all students were exposed will be presented.

## KNOWLEDGE COMPONENTS

Just as the human body consists of an anatomy or structure and a physiology or function, so also did the Anticipatory Socialization program. The knowledge components were the structure or fabric upon and through which the attitudinal components functioned or were expressed. Knowledge alone is not enough; it is the ability to use knowledge that is power. Much of the use of knowledge is expressed through attitudes that are displayed in behaviors.

The knowledge and process components of the Anticipatory Socialization program were based on the observed discrepancies and differences between school and work values. They fell into six broad categories: (1) knowledge about the bureaucratic system as a method of work organization, (2) skills and strategies of role conflict resolution, (3) role negotiation, (4) knowledge of the postgraduation socialization process, (5) competency gap, and (6)

planned change strategies and practical leadership skills.

### Knowledge about the bureaucratic system as a method of work organization

To function effectively within a bureaucratic system, the neophyte nurse must first overcome the negative association with the word bureaucracy that she frequently has. Like other systems, although the bureaucratic system has limitations, it also has strengths. At best, work organized on a part-task basis provides coordinated, well-planned efficient care to large numbers of patients. At worst, it proves uncoordinated, fragmented care to large numbers of people. While the professional whole-task system of work organization at best provides more comprehensive care to fewer numbers of patients, at worst it provides less efficient care by providing some care that could better be provided by another system. Although the death of the bureaucratic system has been predicted, it is highly probable that we will keep many of its efficient features for some time to come.

The students in the Anticipatory Socialization program were taught the evolution of the bureaucratic system of work, the comparison and contrast of bureaucratic with patrimonial organizations and coming technocracies or adhocracies, and the comparisons between the professional and bureaucratic systems of work as outlined in Chapter 1. A number of exercises and activities were used to study the communication and power structures and the formal and informal systems operative in the many agencies within which students were having clinical experiences. By learning how to provide effective input into the bureaucratic system, the neophyte nurse gains not only increased power and sense of control but avenues of influence. It was also important for the student to understand where her professional values would probably conflict with bureaucratic values and the need for development of integrative strategies that would allow her to make effective compromises.

### Skills and strategies of role conflict resolution

In many ways, skills and strategies for managing role conflict vied with the above knowledge category to be the major focus of the whole program. It is not enough to present the professional-bureaucratic conflicts that are likely to occur, and it is certainly not enough to present the stock idealistic school solutions. Conflict management as discussed in social science literature was presented as well as the actual solutions developed and used by the model reference group of nurses. Discussion and analysis of solutions of the reference group nurses provided the opportunity to assess the degree to which they were effective in resolving conflicts in a constructive manner.

### Role negotiation

One very important skill for new graduate nurses is the ability to negotiate or carve out acceptable roles. To do this, at least two things are necessary: first, the nurse must have some knowledge available regarding potential roles and role behaviors; and second, she must have skill at establishing and maintaining desired identities both for herself and for others. This essentially means that the new graduate must develop empathy for her coworkers as well as for her patients. Stripping empathy of its affective overtones, this means that the neophyte must be able to correctly predict the impact that her various strategies or lines of action will have on other people's (staff or patients) definition of the situation. This is necessary in order to negotiate roles vis-a-vis others because they will act in terms of their definition of the situation. To put it more simply, the new graduate must know where she is coming from, where her coworkers are coming from, and how to correlate these two positions. In the practice and discussion of this aspect of the knowledge and skill component, role-taking maneuvers were particularly useful in exploring the roles of others (orderlies, nurse's aides, supervisors, older staff nurses, head nurses, and so on). In this way alternative actions and their potential outcomes could be explored with the purpose of increasing the new graduate's repertoire of responses and actions.

The second aspect of role negotiation was an in-depth exploration of role possibilities available now and in the future to the professional nurse. Perhaps the specific assignment given to the students will best illustrate the content and focus of this area:

Select any of the newly defined roles in nursing or paramedical careers described in the literature. Briefly describe the role. Take a stand on the issue of whether this new role will or will not improve the capability of the professional nurse to function effectively within a bureaucratic structure, and cite rationale for your position. Develop and describe conflict-reducing strategies that might work.

The bibliography on new nursing and paramedical roles included areas such as clinical nurse specialist, physician's assistants, liaison nurses, and extended nurse role.

### Knowledge of the postgraduation socialization process

To help students understand the need for role transformation and the socialization process that would probably occur following graduation, components of the postgraduation socialization process and potential reality shock were presented and discussed. Included was much of the cultural shock information presented in Chapter 1, Kelman's theory of influence in Chapter 2, and as much of the emergent theory of socialization as had evolved from the dairies and interviews at the time (Chapter 5). Foster particularly makes the point that "although there is no immunization that will prevent it [cultural shock], simply knowing that it exists . . . in itself reduces the severity of the attack." It was felt that by understanding some of the methods (the how of socialization), some of the sources (the agents), some of the reasons for socialization (the why or the intent), and the usual messages (content), the new graduate could be more active in influencing her own socialization and would suffer less from the incipient reality shock. If the new graduate is to put into practice some of her school-bred idealism, she will have to be selective in choosing which work values and norms she will adopt. She will also need to develop support for those of her values that are at variance with predominant work values.

An exercise that students found particularly

useful was an adaptation of the Asch experiments. Students in groups of five or six were presented with two different vignettes of professional-bureaucratic conflict situations similar to the opening paragraphs of Chapter 1. A list of five or six potential actions for each situation was also presented, along with the instructions that the group was to reach a unanimous decision regarding which of the alternatives best dealt with the problem. In the first situation, the groups were allowed to work on a problem as they normally would. In the second, however, one member of the group was preselected and instructed to support a deviant solution and to hold firm regardless of attempts by the group to sway her. The reactions of the group toward the deviant member and her feelings about being a deviant then constituted the focus of the larger group's discussion. (Sometimes the group discussions of the two situations were videotaped, which produced marked insight and understanding regarding the verbal and nonverbal reactions of group members.) The purpose of this exercise was to provide group members with both cognitive and experiential data regarding the consequences of deviancy such as they might encounter if they held out for team conferences or nursing care plans or individualized patient care in a work group that was opposed to these practices. The Asch experiments were useful in demonstrating the effectiveness of obtaining support from at least one other person before attempting strongly deviant behavior.

## Competency gap

One of the primary abilities new nurses must develop quickly is acquisition of knowledge in an informal setting. Part of the problem is that the new graduate has had little previous experience in gaining information in an unstructured setting. Expectations and sources are usually made quite clear to her in the school setting. The primary focus in closing the gap between knowledge acquisition in a structured and unstructured situation was on asking questions—who to ask, when, in what way? What kinds of questions yield the best information? What are some of the differences in quality of information depending on the

source you use? Exercises here included listening to taped dialogues of interactions between nurses to ascertain what messages were being sent and received and which messages and clues were being missed. Students were also encouraged to formulate for themselves lists of questions they would ask during an employment interview, both of a director of nursing and also of a staff or head nurse. Another activity included going into a ward or agency situation with which they were totally unfamiliar and ascertaining the kind of information they could acquire without talking to a single person but just by looking at assignment sheets and observing the flow of work, who talked to whom, and so on.

## Planned change strategies and practical leadership skills

All of the knowledge-skill components of the Anticipatory Socialization program could be taught under the general heading of leadership. However, there was considerable student resistance to the word leadership and to perceiving themselves as potential leaders in nursing. The focus of leadership was therefore shifted to the definition that leadership is any act of deliberative influence. Katz and Kahn's idea that leadership can and does take place on three levels (within existing structures, interpolation from the known, and creation of new structures or systems) was useful in helping the student understand that a nurse who effected a change within an existing ward structure was still enacting a leadership role; she did not have to completely revamp the entire hospital or agency to be a leader.

Within this frame of reference, the focus of this knowledge-skill component was on acquiring knowledge of the responsibilities and expectations of various nurse roles and practicing strategies to change aspects or behaviors of those roles. In the senior year of this nursing program each student had a planned leadership experience. For the students in the experimental groups, a special aspect of the program was effected. Staff nurses to serve as role models for the students were chosen jointly by the head nurse and the instructor on the basis that the staff nurses modeled professional nurse behavior and were judged to be effective change agents. Each student in her leadership experience was assigned to one of these role models. This was the nurse with whom the student worked, developed peer relationships, and hopefully would model. It was anticipated that in this way students would have the opportunity to observe both planned change strategies and practical leadership skills and to develop some of their own through practice. Consonant with the last objective, students were also required to develop, carry out, and write up at least one planned change activity they had engaged in, whether it was successful or not.

A particularly difficult area in day-to-day leadership activities is delegation of tasks. This is a particular problem to the neophyte professional who has been trained in a whole-task approach. First of all, she must recognize that she is likely to experience conflict in this area as a result of her school training and socialization. She must learn to discriminate which tasks are better approached through a whole-task perspective and which are more efficiently done on a part-task basis. (Unfortunately, many new nurses graduate with the idea that *all* tasks must be done on a whole-task basis.) The idea is not to choose or pledge allegiance to one or the other, but to be able to move back and forth between the two approaches as indicated by the resources, the tasks, and the needs involved—in a sense, to become bicultural.

Literature references on actual planned changes that nurses have made were particularly helpful. For an example see Lewis's report of four new nurses who really wanted to make a difference in the kind of care their patients received. Borman's discussion on marginal sources and routes of change would also be useful. It illustrates how less organized, more diffuse methods can accomplish effective change, and also points out that change is easier if one begins with marginal, less valued groups or with marginal values.

## ATTITUDINAL COMPONENTS

Describing the anatomy of the Anticipatory Socialization program is not sufficient for the reader to understand the total tenor; one must know the physiology also. How are things fitted together? Throughout the program, several dominant attitudes or themes prevailed and permeated all of the teaching-learning activities. In a sense, they formed the matrix or network that held the whole program together and gave it organismic unity.

*Theme I.* "If at first you don't succeed, keep trying." A technique or approach may not be effective at one point in time but may be highly effective later on. The receptivity of individuals may change, the climate may change, the people themselves may change. This point was also made recently by Huse and Beer in their discussion of an electic approach to organizational development.

*Theme II.* "People are unpredictable." What may not work in one situation may work in another. Don't give up readily. One must diagnose and treat each situation separately.

*Theme III.* "There are at least two alternatives. One can proceed indirectly by helping others do a better job or one can do the job himself." You may need to try either or both approaches, but the former is often more effective. For example, if you are having difficulty with your head nurse it is often more effective to help her do her job better than to do her job for her or to criticize her.

*Theme IV.* If there was one dominant theme, this was it. "Conflict is healthy and creative. Conflict is the order of the day." Rather than looking upon conflict as something bad, caused by troublemakers, view conflict as integral to change. Conflict is a potential source of growth; it is energy for equilibration or change. The way in which conflict is *managed* rather than suppressed, ignored, or avoided is the real issue. To manage conflict constructively and effectively, learn the major roles involved in conflict management—instigator, defendant, and mediator—and use them appropriately as strategies or lines of action.

*Theme V.* "Work that is meaningful is of paramount importance, both for yourself and for those with whom you work." Work and career choices are usually dictated by prospects of doing meaningful work rather than by economics or technology. There are a variety of approaches that can be used to make work meaningful for yourself and for others over whose work you may have some control (aides, orderlies, LPN's). When possible, construct work so that people can do a *whole* job, even though the job may be small. Encourage people to participate in decision-making; operationalize decision-making. Use conflict constructively to bring about change. This may mean playing the role of the instigator. You may also need to be an integrator.

*Theme VI.* "It is necessary to develop within oneself a tolerance for uncertainty, for ambiguity, for conflict." This is the mettle upon which growth and change is produced. Learn to accept and cherish that "unsettled" feeling. It is the spice of life.

*Theme VII.* "Development of interpersonal competence in several social contexts is necessary for maximum effectiveness." Interpersonal competence means ability to predict actions and reactions of others. When this can be done, the individual is in a position of managing situations, of being able to influence others in a positive direction (for example, persuading diabetic patients to follow their diet or other nurses to improve their standards of care). To predict the reactions of others, it is necessary to understand their value system. It may be necessary to reach for superordinate goals in order to influence others; ". . . knowledge by itself is nothing. It's the ability to sell knowledge to other people which is power" (Schein).

*Theme VIII.* "Learn to recognize when outside help and support is needed, and find someone who can provide that support." The new graduate has a responsibility for her own postgraduation socialization. She must initiate and obtain what she needs. Dare to be deviant, but try to get at least one other person to support you. Plan your deviancy.

## POSSIBLE REFERENCE GROUPS

A sample of nurses from the medical center sample provided the reference group whose values and behaviors the students in the experimental classes might hopefully model and to which they might anticipatorily socialize themselves. This group of nurses was selected from the total sample because they had a high bureaucratic–high professional role configuration, relatively low role deprivation, and were considered highly successful by their employers. It was judged that these were the most probable characteristics of the highly adaptive, bicultural, job-satisfied nurse. In addition to this model group, there were other potentially adaptive groups of nurses available: nurses who had high bureaucratic-low professional, low bureaucratic–high professional, and low bureaucratic–low professional role configurations. Within each of these groups there could be further subdivisions in respect to role deprivation and degree of success. Although it was the high bureaucratic–high professional group that constituted the desired models, true to the idea that freedom and wise choice consist in knowledge of the whole wide manifold of possibilities, the behaviors, characteristics and typical lines of action of the other groups were also presented to the students in the experimental classes. In this way they would have a basis for sifting, weighing, and choosing the path they wished to follow.

To properly orient the reader to the four major groups that will be presented here, the following diagram is presented. In the subsequent analysis and presentation, only role

## ROLE CONFIGURATIONS AND MAJOR CHARACTERISTICS OF NURSES ACCORDING TO SUBGROUPS

|  | LOW PROFESSIONAL ROLE CONCEPTION | HIGH PROFESSIONAL ROLE CONCEPTION |
|---|---|---|
| HIGH BUREAUCRATIC ROLE CONCEPTION | Organization Women | Bicultural Troublemakers |
| LOW BUREAUCRATIC ROLE CONCEPTION | Rutters | Lateral Arabesquers |

conceptions will be used to stratify the 220 nurses; levels of role deprivation and success will be discussed as differential characteristics of the nurses in the subgroups.

A description and composite picture of the nurses in each of the four main groups will be presented. This is the kind of material that was presented to the students, although not in the same kind of neat package as here. The characteristics and composite pictures were developing and being developed almost concurrently with the sessions in which they were being presented. Many times students were presented with vignettes of problems and solutions without any kind of appellations attached, that is, whether the nurse in question was high professional–low bureaucratic, high bureaucratic–low professional, and so forth.

There is always a danger in generalizing. However, it is often the only way in which the story of a fairly large group can be told. In this instance, the characteristics and behaviors of the 55 nurses in each of the four subgroups fell into fairly discrete and discernible patterns, so the danger was minimized. To minimize it even further, the data will be presented at two levels. First, an overall description of the demographic characteristics and parameters of the nurses in the particular subgroups will be presented: age, marital status, children, job position, success rating, dropout rate, and so on. Secondly, a composite or abstract of the behavioral choices, conflict resolution routes, and attitudinal characteristics of the group will be discussed. An attempt will be made to present the commonalities of the subgroup members as well as the range of deviation.

To further minimize the dangers inherent in generalization and the bias possibly operating to fit the data into the theoretical notions guiding the study, the composites for each of the four subgroups were abstracted and prepared by another nurse researcher[3] who had not been associated with the study previously. She had no part in the interviews or the data collection, so it was judged that she would be much freer from bias than would the investigator. The demographic characteristics are nominal and factual rather than interpretive

data, so it is less likely that bias would be operative there.

Since the high bureaucratic–high professional group, the *Bicultural Troublemakers*, has been mentioned previously in more detail than any of the other groups, it will be described last to demonstrate its relevancy as the desired model. The *Rutters*, or nurses characterized by a low bureaucratic–low professional orientation, will be presented first, followed by the *Organization Women* (high bureaucratic–low professional) and then the *Lateral Arabesquers* (low bureaucratic–high professional).

### Rutters

*Demographic characteristics and parameters.* The median age of the 55 nurses who started out in this group in 1968 was 28 years. They were the oldest of all the groups, although more than half (58%) were new graduates. (New graduates are defined as nurses graduating in the Classes of 1966 and 1967 who would have been out of school between one and two years at the time of the 1968 data collection.) Contrary to the other subgroups, almost half of these nurses were married, and many had small children. There was much evidence of outside interests and activities in this group of nurses; PTA, church, social, and local community activities leading the list. The group as a whole was either ambivalent or quite negative about returning to school for graduate education in nursing. In response to the question: "Are you glad you chose nursing as a career and would you choose it again?" almost three-fourths said: "It's OK," "It's a job," or "No." Mean role deprivation score was well below average (19.36), the second lowest of the four groups.

Almost all nurses in this group were staff nurses. Median number of job changes was fairly low (mean 2.5) when compared with that of the total group. Reasons for job change were either more money, better hours, or change in husband's job. Major reasons for working were "to provide family with a better standard of living," "to support myself," "to get some extra things we need around the house." The largest number of nurses in this group was classified by their employers as either average (44%) or less successful than average (36%).

The nurses in this group were the least likely of any of the groups to be members of professional organizations. About half of them reported that they read some nursing or medical journal, but only one quarter of them read it with any kind of regularity. Three fourths of these nurses had not purchased a nursing or medical book since graduation; over half of them had not taken any kind of professional course. The above results were obtained by questionnaire in late 1969 and early 1970. Most of the nurses would have been out of school at least three years by this time.

Two years after the initial look at this group of nurses, there was very little change in group membership (according to the 1968 median scores on the Corwin professional and bureaucratic role conception scales). The overall number remained almost the same (N = 52); 8 nurses shifted out and 5 shifted into the group. Most of them had remained in the staff nurse position. Mean role deprivation remained below the overall average, and the average or less successful than aver-

age nurse continued to predominate in the group. In fact, only 8 of the 52 nurses were labeled as highly successful. A particular characteristic of these 8 nurses, however, was a high performance on the Inner-directed Scale of the Shostrom Personal Orientation Inventory. Designed to measure the degree of self-actualization, this Inventory yields both a Support Scale (whether one's reactivity orientation is basically toward others or self) and a Time Competence Scale (the degree to which one is present-oriented and relates the past and future in a meaningful continuity). Contrary to the majority of the Rutters, the high-success nurses in the group were quite responsive to inner-direction.

In respect to dropout rate, the Rutters were second lowest (21%), with only the Organization Women having a lower dropout rate. Approximately 1 out of every 5 Rutters left nursing practice for some other occupation during the two years of the study between 1968 and 1970.

When these nurses were asked to identify the person who most influenced their nursing practice, there was no outstanding or primary position classification such as was found in

# THE RUTTERS

the other subgroups. The only categorical responses that exceeded that of the other three groups were "no one" or "a family member who is a nurse," but even here the percentage was low (12% to 15%). The same kind of lack of identifiable characteristics was apparent when the role behavior scores of this group were compared with those of the total group. They were not particularly professional, bureaucratic, or integrative in their behavior, having the lowest or second lowest score of the four groups on all three of these variables.

*Composite attitudinal and behavioral characteristics.* A direct antithesis to the high bureaucratic–high professional nurse, the Rutters evidenced minimal or no integration of professional-bureaucratic values and constructive conflict resolution behavior. For all intents and purposes, they seemed to have withdrawn from everything connected with the work situation. They had given up and consequently were in a virtual rut. This state was displayed by comments such as "I just don't let it bother me anymore," "I put in my eight hours and go home," or "I just get along with the staff, never tell them what to do, or what not to do."

The attitude displayed was so negative that indifference or complete rejection became the pattern of behavior. There seemed to be so little belief or commitment to the system or professional values as to warrant anything other than minimal behavior conformity. In some instances, performance seemed marginal or inadequate and moral support absent to the extent that opinions were withheld or even unformed. This could be attributed to actual lack of ability or feelings of alienation. For example, there was the nurse who talked about her work and the relationship with the technicians:

Our technicians are terribly good, all of them. None of them have any specific training. They are very bright kids who are willing and able to do anything and everything. It really does make you wonder why you need a nurse. (Med Ctr[9.3])

There were nurses who talked about idealism:

I have definitely lost all the ideal types of situations and everything that goes with it because I haven't found any of the ideal situations that the school would put you into. (Med Ctr[8.6])

• • •

When you graduate from school, you think you are going to be just a perfect nurse, but when you get into the swing of things you, well I don't know, you kinda incorporate what you learn in school but then it kinda loses its identity from what you learned in school. You don't think about it anymore. (Med Ctr[34.3])

There was another side to some few members of this group. They were the ones who rebelled. They had moved past the stages of being inactive or passive and had become advocates of fighting the system. In this mood, they attempted to expose and undermine the functioning power of the institution and profession by disagreeing, maligning, or leaving.

I had gotten this idea about nursing homes because we got them in the homes—you know, the patients who had to go home because of no Medicare. In the VNA I complained about it and told some of the families how they could help. They didn't like it. The administrator asked for my resignation . . . just like that. I didn't think it was fair. I convinced him to take my side. this began eating at me because I kept thinking: well, they are watching everything I do and one slip. . . . And there are so many touchy cases with this Medicare. It got to the point where I thought: well golly, somebody is going to report me. So I handed in my resignation. (Med Ctr[12.3])

A nurse who was asked if she planned to stay in nursing said:

I don't plan the future anymore. I used to have great plans. I just kinda take things as they come. I really don't know. I told my head nurse just yesterday, I think she realized that I never stay long in any place. She said: "Are you trying to tell me something?" I really don't know. (Med Ctr[9.3])

Nonacceptance of the values and expected behaviors within the system rendered the Rutters extremely unstable when changes were anticipated or introduced. When one had no stake, or minimal commitment to the ideals and values of the institution or of the profession, there was no sustaining power within the individual. They participated in but did not initiate activities to improve patient care or the delivery system.

There was a while when we were doing everything for a set of patients, regardless of what you are. If you were a nursing tech, you would care for a patient by yourself; if you were a nurse you would do the same. Somehow I couldn't buy the philosophy, but I went along with it. I didn't really care. (Med Ctr[28.2])

The low bureaucratic–low professional nurse is the parasite type who eats but brings no food of his own to the table, either for himself or others.

Nursing I thought was my life, and it was going to be no matter if I married or what have you. And now I value myself as a person, so I realize that maybe someday nursing may not have anything left for me and I might want to change to something else. (Med Ctr[12.3])

. . .

I came back to work. I know the reason you should have come back is because you love the patients and love the work. For me it was more getting out of the house and being with adults . . . my own personal stimulation and to earn money. (Med Ctr[9.4])

. . .

One of the reasons I chose this job was that it is only 15 minutes traveling time, other places are much more. It's OK . . . I am going to get my Master's in social work . . . I'm not really sure that is what I want. It's like I would like to get back to nursing, but I'm not sure where it is going and I really don't care anymore. (Med Ctr[21.4])

The outstanding characteristics of the nurses in this category was their lack of interest, understanding, and capabilities. They were merely existing in their positions and were of little benefit to the institution or to the profession. They attributed their frustrations and inabilities to others. They saw no faults in themselves and were content to have little or no involvement. This was evidenced by the following description in which the nurse talks about her nursing practice and giving care to a troublesome patient.

During the day we [nurses and technicians] do everything together. We [nurses] do most of the monitoring of the patients and they [technicians] do some research-type things. They help us start the patients and take them off and clean up afterwards. Then we order drugs for our patients. Some-

body goofs up so we give them enough to last a few days. Mostly it's vitamins or iron or something. But when it comes to the Seconal and sleeping pills, I worry a little bit. We do this occasionally; nobody says anything about things that count. I don't think anybody would pay attention.

On the evening shift when you have maybe one or two patients, we get them off by 10 o'clock in the evening but you have to sit there until 12 o'clock. In the daytime there are more people around and you have somebody to talk to. I guess there are other things I could do—help out on the wards—but why should I? The techs really gripe about having to stay over, but it really doesn't affect me at this point. I'm not personally involved, but it is terribly aggravating.

When we have a troublesome patient, it would be one who is very ill—bleeding or shocking or both. Of course we have some personality problems too. They get very troublesome. And we rotate on them. We stand them as long as we can and then we send someone else in. (Med Ctr[9.3])

The style of conflict resolution behavior for the Rutters was fairly diverse. A good number of them appear to be in a burned-out condition of sustained apathy.

I just don't care anymore; it's too much of an uphill fight. I tried for awhile, but now, well you know, what's the use. It's better if you just don't think about it. (Med Ctr[4.2])

Others appeared to have made a conscious choice decision when faced with conflict.

Look, I soon learned that if I fought for what I believe is good patient care it would be one constant hassle and head-banging session. So I said "forget it." There's more to life than just work. I decided I'd come, do my job, and forget it. I live for after work hours. (Med Ctr[19.6])

A third kind of seeming resolution was characterized by what might be called the iceberg spirit—ideas and frustrations pretty well covered up, but at least lip service to the hope that maybe, eventually someday, things will change. However, the change was not to be initiated by the nurse who manifested this kind of spirit.

I think I'm seen as constant sour grapes, and perhaps I am. I'm not happy, not even content; but I have to work, and it might as well be here as anywhere else. I keep thinking that maybe someday something will happen that I can nurse like I was taught in school. Trouble is, it's been so long since I really talked to or did some of the nice things for patients, I'm not sure I'd remember how. (Med Ctr[26.4])

No matter what the style of conflict resolution behavior adopted, the end result seemed to be that the nurse was seen by herself and by others to be in a rut—reasonably content with the status quo and unwilling to become involved in making any changes or improvements. These nurses were not particularly mobile: "I'll only work as long as I have to." "Since I have to work, it might as well be here as anywhere else."

### Organization Women

*Demographic characteristics and parameters.* This subgroup of 55 nurses had a median age of 23 years, the second oldest of the four groups. They were either single or married (one third), but without small children. They were career oriented in the sense that they had the longest tenure in their jobs (median of a little over 6 years), and there were more of these nurses in head nurse and supervisory positions than in any of the other subgroups. They also intended to remain in their jobs longer. Often their career patterns included several promotions within the organization, from staff nurse to assistant head nurse to head nurse and so on. Only a few nurses in this group had returned to school for education beyond the baccalaureate degree. The Organization Women had the fewest number of job changes of any of the four groups (mean of 1.9 jobs since graduation), although they had more job transfers within the same organization than any other group. Reasons for job changes were usually advancement, increased salary, or better hours. These nurses were about evenly divided in respect to their reasons for working: "I'm working because I want to, it's fulfilling and self-satisfying," and "I have to work to support myself or my family, but I really like it." There was considerably more involvement, investment, and commitment apparent in this group than in the Rutter group. In response to questions about liking nursing and choosing it again, there was a resounding "Yes, I love it." Mean role deprivation score (17.91) was lower for the Organization Women than for any other group, indicating that these nurses found the actual job situation more compatible with their role conceptions than any of the other nurses. Over half of the nurses (N = 32) in this group were classified by their employers as average; another fourth were classified as highly successful. In spite of the relatively high median age, this subgroup had the largest percentage of new graduates (65%). This perhaps reflects a finding in an earlier study that new graduates quickly raise their bureaucratic loyalties and drop their professional ideals upon graduation.

The Organization Women were second lowest among the four groups in loyalty to the profession of nursing, as evidenced by membership and activity in professional organizations such as the American Nurses' Association (ANA) and National League for Nurses (NLN). Fewer than one third reported they were members; less than 10% said they were active. Over two thirds of the high bureaucratic–low professional nurses, however, reported that they read some medical or nursing journal, although only 46% said that this was done on a regular basis. The Organization Women are also not keen book-buyers or course-takers. They were second only to the Rutters in the number who reported not having purchased any professional book since graduation (68%) and not having taken any kind of course, either for professional or personal improvement since graduation (36%). As might be expected, one characteristic of this group was the relatively large number who purchased books on personnel management and counseling (12.5%).

By 1970 the ranks of this group of nurses had increased by almost 50% (55 in 1968 to 75 in 1970). This means that, among the total sample of 220 nurses, more nurses had changed their value orientations in this direction than in any other direction. From 1968 to 1970, 46 of the nurses in the total sample of 220 had received administrative promotions (staff nurse to head nurse to supervisor). Of these,

35 (76%) were in the Organization Women subgroup. Concomitant with the high promotion rate, another outstanding characteristic of this subgroup was that over half of them (54%) identified an organization person (head nurse, supervisor, or director of nursing) as being the person who most influenced their nursing practice. The mean role deprivation scores of the old and new Organization Women was 17.49, still markedly below that of any of the high professional subgroups. This indicates again that a high bureaucratic–low professional role conception is one that is quite compatible with the reality work score. Even with the swell in ranks, over half (51%) of the nurses in this group were considered highly successful, another 43% were average. Because of the large number of high-success nurses in this group, the degree of self-actualization as measured by the Personal Orientation Inventory (POI) test was higher than the mean for the total group; the complete analysis of the POI data showed that high success, regardless of role conception, was associated with high self-actualization scores.

The Organization Women had the lowest dropout rate of any of the four groups of nurses. Approximately one out of every six Organization Women (15%) left nursing practice during the two years of the study between 1968 and 1970. Only three of these nurses went into teaching; the others left to go into other occupations such as business, accounting, personnel management, and the like.

As might be expected, the Organization Women were dominant among the four subgroups in their choice of bureaucratic behavior when faced with conflict situations. They scored significantly higher than their counterparts (low bureaucratic–high professional) on the bureaucratic role behavior scales, usually choosing behavior such as checking the routine or procedure book or asking the supervisor to work out a conflict.

*Composite attitudinal and behavioral characteristics.* The high bureaucratic–low professional groups of nurses have accepted and integrated bureaucratic values, but have minimal or no integration of professional ideals—at least professional ideals the way they are gen-

erally taught in school and as measured by the Corwin role conception scale. (It is quite possible that many of these nurses are professional bureaucrats as described by Reissman.) These nurses have not withdrawn from the system, either literally or figuratively; they were competent and skilled in the behavioral expectations of the institution, and this constituted their way of resolving a part of their role conflict. It consequently afforded them a relatively low degree of role deprivation.

I just love nursing. It's different than what I was taught in school, but oh so much better. So much better organized. If you really just learn what's expected of you and do that, everything goes so much better and the job gets done. I think more patients get better care that way. [What way?] When things are organized and everyone does his job according to the rules and procedures. (Med Ctr[98.6])

In the process of developing this identification with the organization there was evidence that the Organization Women were influenced by work-centered role models to a greater extent than were any of the other groups.

I guess the person who influenced me the most was a HN I had. She was an old Army nurse and ran a tight ship. She had to be in control of all 30 patients and the personnel. One new HN is good also. She's getting routines all established on paper. (Med Ctr[19.1])

This influence extended to the point where they sought out active guidance and support from authority figures within the organization.

When I first started out I had a lot of problems: getting across to the people that I wanted certain things done, that I wanted a patient by the end of the evening to be well kept. The environment for the next shift would be good. At first, I think, they resented this. I had a lot of help from the supervisor and finally we got together and now they know what I want. (Med Ctr[10.5])

Because the Organization Women valued the rewards inherent in the display of properly acceptable bureaucratic behavior, there was a resultant adaptive conformity. There was job satisfaction, which came from a positive attitude toward the job and its rewards. This allowed the individual some fulfillment of the need for self-actualization in her work.

I kind of like to have the authority of the supervisor, get the people to see about their nursing care, to check on things, posting orders, check on charting, find out how things are charted, and try to keep a little peace up there. With so many law-suits and stuff, they are just kind of starting here in the Midwest. (Med Ctr[20.4])

. . .

I think the floor was run pretty sloppy; it irked me. Some nights would pass slow, nothing happening. The nurses just sat around too much. They were all parttime housewives; they liked to come to work just so they could sit. They admitted this to me. It really bothered me. (Med Ctr[17.3])

Oddly enough, there was satisfaction in spite of the awareness of constraining influences on their personal affairs.

I feel more responsible to the hospital than I do to home. I get calls during my days off, but I don't mind; the unit must be run properly. Staffing and supervising personnel are important if I'm to do the job well. I get tough with the personnel at times to keep them functioning properly. (Med Ctr[20.4])

The positive attitude toward the job did not extend to nursing as a profession; in fact, it was just the opposite. The rewards from endorsing the values of the profession did not appear to be important to the high bureaucratic–low professional members.

Only reason I took the VNA job was because it was a day job and it was fulltime. It wasn't because I liked the work. I hated the work. I just hated it. It was changing catheters and visiting old people. I don't like taking care of really sick people. I don't like doing nursing things. (Med Ctr[17.1])

In spite of the adoption of bureaucratic values, the members of this group were not necessarily the most stable staff members. The commitment may be to extrinsic factors rather than to intrinsic organizational values, which then places self-interest in a priority position over principle. This kind of dedication becomes somewhat shaky when better opportunities are promised such as more

money, better hours, less demanding working conditions, prestige, or less conflict.

Salary is important. I like to work, but I can't stand shift work. I like to have things run well; here they do. I have good salary, time off, vacations, sick leave, promotions, and a lot of praise for my work. I'm not really committed to anything at this time; I'd go somewhere else if they offered more money. I wouldn't go to school if you paid me. (Med Ctr[4.2])

Another example of this instability became apparent when pressures were increased. Since the nurses in the subgroup had only limited investment in professional values, there was the inclination to defect when the risk of performance escalated. Resultant behavior was manifested by leaving, inactivity, waiting for the crisis to subside, or switching to another unit within the institution.

You would be worried about staffing problems, people being ill, heavy patient overload, doctors yelling—things like this that I think that as a staff nurse I really didn't appreciate it. I decided to go back to school to teach. [How do you think teaching is going to help those kinds of things?] I think a lot of these things can be helped by proper organization and looking at patient care. Now staffing—you really are not going to do that much about it. I think if the RN's are properly taught, I think there can be better organization of the staff. I'm going back to school to learn how to teach students and nurses better organization. (Med Ctr[5.5])

. . .

I got along. At times I became a bit unhappy in ICU and I would almost dread going to work . . . it's just a hectic pace. I just got tired and wished for awhile that I was not in nursing. We had some disagreement among the group, which is not good. After I got into recovery I completely enjoyed nursing again. It was just the change of pace that I needed. (Med Ctr[36.4])

The previous types of responses render the system somewhat vulnerable in the advent of change. The worker may recognize possible advantages in staying with the system and may become active in supporting the revision process or she might also work against it.

Apparently here they are going to make the head

nurses have a Master's. Now that is what I hear, you know this is what they tell me. See, this doesn't make sense to me. I think it is very true . . . you work in a hospital five years . . . what I am trying to say, you get more education so you get paid more for doing an adequate job. And so people who have been here maybe two or three years before me, well I think that is important and I think they should be paid for this experience, if you have worked ten to fifteen years. . . . It is kind of different if you were a trainee. If you have a degree you get paid more. That is what I said the other day. There's no point in harping on this education bit because I don't think you get that much out of it. (Med Ctr[2.6])

A composite picture of the nurse in this category showed a hard-working skilled performer who valued the system and its rewards, would work extra hours to display expected behavior, maintained order and the status quo. Yet this worker would leave one agency or change units within the agency or "even go back to school" in order to have fewer demands for professional performance.

A fairly typical response concerning nursing practice and a troublesome patient was expressed as follows:

When I changed my position, I began to see the hospital more as a total unit rather than the unit being the revolving thing. I see the need for standardizing some of the procedures that go throughout the hospital. I float people. They are expected to do a job, and they get to a unit and they have to spend the first two hours learning how that unit is different. It is not fair to them and it is not fair to the patient and it is not fair to the other staff members because when they need help they have to take one of their own away so that they can tell the one who is supposed to help. Suddenly it hits me—I don't know if I read it or someone told me about it or what—it's the patient who suffers if he has to learn the procedure new or over each time it is done for him because people aren't following a general pattern. (Med Ctr[24.6])

. . .

I divided them into two categories, but I think of each as a troublesome patient. A patient who is perhaps very fearful and expresses this in ways of refusing care, negating treatment, and being in general a pain in the neck. I would also classify as a troublesome patient someone who required a lot of physical care. You needed more than one person, but not two, to take care of them. (Med Ctr[21.3])

There is little to say about the Organization Women and conflict resolution. For the most part they reported or expressed little conflict. They had found their niche, and generally were quite happy and contented with nursing. What conflict they did express was with "people who don't do their jobs right, who didn't follow the rules and procedures that are set forth," "things and people that aren't organized . . . or standardized." Lack of organization distressed them, but for the most part they seemed to have been able to subjugate or obliterate conflict springing from a discrepancy between school and work values.

### Lateral Arabesquers

*Demographic characteristics and parameters.* The youngest of the four subgroups (median age 22), almost all of these 55 nurses were single at the time of initial interviewing and testing (1968). Employed predominantly as staff nurses, their relatively brief career patterns showed a marked tendency toward job hopping. As a group, they had the highest number of job changes of any subgroup: mean of 3.58 jobs with a range of two to nine jobs within a two-year period. About 40% of the nurses in this group were new graduates as previously defined. The dominant success rating of these nurses by their employers was that they were less successful than average (67%). Only about one fifth (22%) were rated as being highly successful.

Many of the nurses in this subgroup expressed positive intentions of returning to graduate school to go into teaching or "to do something else in nursing or out where I can get more satisfaction." Since teaching, with or without graduate preparation, can be viewed as a pseudopromotion in which employees, incompetent in one system, sidestep into another position with a new title and a new workplace, this group was named the Lateral Arabesquers (Peter, 1969). "I can't stand this; I'm going back to school. There must be a better way." These sentiments as well as a vehement

"No" in response to the question: "Are you glad you chose nursing as a career?" depict the hurt, confusion, and moral outrage characteristics of Lateral Arabesquers. About one third of the nurses who did not respond negatively to the above question were either ambivalent or said: "Yes on the whole, but not nursing as it's practiced here. I've got to find some other place where it's done like I was taught in school." As might be expected, the mean role deprivation score of this subgroup was very high (35.84)—the highest of any of the subgroups.

The Lateral Arabesquers had the second highest percentage of membership in professional nursing organizations (42.58%), with 12.5% reporting a moderate to high degree of activity. Almost two thirds of them said that they read professional nursing or medical journals, and 40% reported that they read with some degree of regularity. This group of nurses was the highest book-buyers among the four groups. This behavior is seemingly consistent with the value they place on formal education. They also were quite active course-takers, with fewer than one fourth of them not having taken either a professional or personal course since graduation.

At the 1970 testing and interview period, two years after the initial data collection, only 41 nurses remained in this group. This might well be because retention of this kind of role configuration in the work scene is exceedingly painful; also, many of them had left nursing practice. Over half (51%) of the 41 nurses who professed a low bureaucratic–high professional orientation had left nursing within the two years from 1968 to 1970, more than in any of the other subgroups. Of the nurses who remained, most were staff nurses. There were few promotions, either administrative or clinical, in this group, although about 40% of the nurses said they would like to have had a promotion or felt they deserved one. "Yes, I'd like to be promoted to head nurse; maybe then I could be in a position where I could do something, make some changes."

Although in 1968 most of Lateral Arabesquers were rated as being less successful than average, there was no really dominant rating in 1970. Thirty-nine percent were rated as less successful than average, 30% as average, and 31% as highly successful. Their mean role deprivation scores continued to be very high (31.58), and there was little evidence of self-actualization as manifested by Inner-directed and Time Competence scores. They had quite low Inner-directed scores when compared with those of the rest of the total group.

Did the nurses in this group make the lateral arabesques they indicated they intended to do in 1968? Very definitely so. Almost one third of the group (29.72%) had gone into teaching or graduate school to prepare for teaching because: "I can't nurse the way I've been taught; I might as well teach others how to do things right." Accompanying this lateral arabesque was a high retention of former nursing faculty or instructors as role models. When asked to identify the person who had the most influence on their nursing practice, 35% of these nurses (higher than any other group) specified a former nursing school instructor.

As their counterparts (high bureaucratic–low professional) chose almost exclusively bureaucratic behavior in conflict situations, the Lateral Arabesquers reported that they would enact almost exclusively professional behaviors such as discussing the problem with a colleague or another professional or making an independent decision or judgment when faced with a conflict. They had the most extreme scores of any of the four subgroups: very high professional, very low bureaucratic, and very low integrative role behaviors. On all three variables they were either the highest or lowest of the four subgroups. Whereas the Rutters (low bureaucratic–low professional) presented a picture of low-keyed blandness, the Lateral Arabesquers (low bureaucratic–high professional) seemed to be volatile extremists.

*Composite attitudinal and behavior characteristics.* In the low bureaucratic–high professional group, there was minimal or no integration of bureaucratic values, but a high commitment to values of the profession. Withdrawal seemed to be almost predetermined for some members of this subgroup because they did not have the acceptable bureaucratic behaviors and were apt to be rejected by and rejecting of those who held such behavior in high regard.

The staff is a long-standing group and they have lots of power. I think I might be able to compromise somewhat, but not much. (Med Ctr[29.5])

.  .  .

My last evaluation was like somebody taking a knife to you and completely ripping you apart. This head nurse I was telling you about was real spiteful, who was always telling me I should do this, but not willing to do anything herself. Big talker, no action. She said I was not dependable and all that—just my whole attitude. (Med Ctr [25.3])

It would be unfair to say that the low bureaucratic–high professional nurses were not competent just because they were frequently viewed as such by co-workers. They were incompetent, at least interpersonally, in the work subculture. They might have been quite skilled but their behavior demonstrated only marginal involvement because of their role conflict and dedication to intrinsic values that to them were most important. There is evidence, though, that during crisis situations the energy expended was sufficiently high to compensate for any lack of technical performance. They seemed to have internalized the values of the profession and worked to maintain them. The rewards were internal.

I had one situation with a patient that was very satisfying; it was challenging I think because, you know, I was really involved with her. (Med Ctr[6.2])

Their attitude toward nursing in general may be positive, but the bureaucratic structure was subject to reproach. There was job satisfaction mainly when the nurses in this group were able to work within a structure where responsibility was given, risks could be taken, and their value appreciated.

I became interested and applied for this job . . . I guess because of a friend of mine. When they changed the ward I was working in, it was very chaotic and I didn't want to get involved in that kind of situation. Then this friend was so enthused about this center—it was so interesting. She said you could really do things there and use your own judgment . . . and she was right. It's much better here. (Med Ctr[14.4])

.  .  .

I know that my head nurse doesn't think I'm too good a nurse . . . I had a code blue the other day and I was scared to death, but I did all right—worked my tail off. The head nurse said I handled

# LATERAL ARABESQUERS

it very efficiently but that's not what's important, you know. I mean I took the time to let the family know what was happening. I felt good about doing that. (Med Ctr[22.2])

When dissatisfaction was expressed, it was felt that the administrative hierarchy placed restrictions upon them through policies, working conditions, and relationships that were interpreted as rigid, unnecessary, or strained.

I have difficulty being a HN in the present structure; I am thinking more and more about going back to school . . . get more preparation. But I'm not sure I can use it; you know, I feel some of the preparation isn't being used now and I don't want to get more preparation and have that go to waste too. (Med Ctr[16.6])

. . .

It's almost as though they have whipped it [dedication] out of me with all their rules and regulations and policies. (Med Ctr[17.6])

Their dissatisfaction is also attributed to their educational preparation.

We're taught it all through school; and then to come to work in the same hospital where you were taught all this stuff and then to find that it is almost completely opposite . . . and you feel as if you are in a constant battle. (Med Ctr[25.3])

There were very volatile and profuse expressions of role deprivation in this group of nurses. When role deprivation is high there is a correspondingly high possibility that job change or even a complete change of profession will be sought. The Lateral Arabesquers did become the jobhoppers, constantly looking for the ideal situation or environment. They most frequently pirouetted into inservice, teaching, or situations where they were able to work alone or with a very small staff.

I job hopped, so it looks . . . and it has bothered me. But my opinion is real: nursing, for me, is very dissatisfying . . . They knew it when I was tired of clerical duties. I wanted to get back to real nursing. This was in my letter of resignation and my reasons for resigning . . . I got into private duty and I'd say I've found my niche in nursing. I enjoy it. I do complete patient care and I learn an awful lot. (Med Ctr[25.3])

. . .

I think I remember saying in my thesis committee or my orals the same reason that I was dissatisfied with the situation over at the hospital. I felt frustrated and couldn't do anything, and I thought I could work a different kind of change by going into teaching. (Med Ctr[1.2])

Several nurses commented when asked about decisions to return to school.

It came out of the fact that I became quite discouraged with nursing over at [X Medical Center]. Just before I quit I was in the process of looking into something different in nursing, such as office nurse, school nurse, or PHN, and maybe I wasn't looking too hard. I went to one office and I'm not sure what it was—racial. Suddenly the job wasn't so open. I got very discouraged and frustrated with nursing, and my husband said: "If you want to switch out of nursing since you are becoming discouraged, you can go back to school." So I thought it would be a good idea—and I have always said if I hadn't been a nurse that I might like to be a kindergarten teacher—so that's what I'm doing. (Med Ctr[16.4])

. . .

I've thought about going to school and I've thought now and then about taking courses, but not in nursing. I'm not using half of what I've already learned now. I get so frustrated. I know what good patient care is and how to do it myself, but I don't know how to sell others on it. (Med Ctr [17.6])

Not infrequently the Lateral Arabesque nurse verbalized that one "must know the system in order to be able to make changes within it." She related some attempts at change that she had tried. For the most part, though, the low bureaucratic–high professional nurses were in a critical stage and seemed to have little tolerance for the stress that accompanies change initiation.

The head nurse here . . . she's good and everyone praises her and she's good, but I see a lot of things that I don't think she does correctly, especially in her approach to patients. She's very . . . like this is *my* intensive care unit, and visitors get two minutes out of an hour to visit, and rules are rules. But the one thing I object to, how come she's the head nurse when she doesn't initiate anything? She never asks us for an opinion or a suggestion of how we might do something better or anything. If you do something wrong she'll tell you;

I've never been told that I've done anything right. Nothing has been changed in the 10 months I've been in here. (Med Ctr[17.6])

Among reasons given for leaving was:

Well, I talked to them already about it, in fact the director and supervisors, that I am thinking about leaving and, you know, what I told them is pretty much what I told you. I just decided, you know, cause of these administrative hassles and wanting to get more involved with families and the fact that, well, the director always said: "Why can't you do that here?" Well, you know, I can do that here to some extent every once in awhile but, you know, it is like if I have to beg and plead, well forget it. (Med Ctr[23.3])

The nurses in this subgroup were usually unhappy people trying to find a place for themselves. They were committed and enjoyed nursing in its abstract sense. However, they wanted to work where the structure allowed them freedom. As a result they were highly mobile, leaving one job after another, carrying with them a great deal of frustration about unpleasant working conditions, unsatisfactory performance ratings, poor attitudes, and a need to continue their pursuit of an idealized conception of good nursing care. The following comments pertain to the practice of nursing and working with a troublesome patient.

If I could, I would almost rather go backwards than forwards. I would almost rather be an LVN; they get to take care of patients. Even in the position of staff nurse, you don't usually do as much patient care as I would like to do. I really like to work with the patients. I really do. We have two teams and we have all of our own patients. The ward is divided. You have one team. We have a charge nurse. We do get to do some patient care, but there is a lot of paperwork. We have a ward clerk, but the nurse does a great deal of paperwork. The ward clerk does the charts, puts temps in, she does check charts for surgery, answers the phone, and runs errands. If we need things from the lab or the blood bank, the ward clerk goes and gets it. Everyone seems to be busy. I don't care for paperwork. I don't feel that is why I went to school. (Med Ctr[5.1])

· · ·

I guess really the most challenging ones are not the patients with difficult medical problems, you know, if they can be improved. I think really the patients with the emotional, personal problems are really challenging because you don't have a lot of time that you can spend to talk with them like you would like to. You feel like you have to cut them short or you haven't done as much as you could, and it is a challenge to help them if you can. (Med Ctr[20.5])

As the name implies, conflict resolution for low bureaucratic–high professional nurses was a lateral arabesque into a safe, more idealistically structured environment where the values closer to those learned in school still prevailed. Another mode of conflict resolution for this group of nurses was flight out of nursing into jobs perceived as being more challenging and satisfying. Perhaps the nurses who sidestepped into teaching or fled the nursing scene were the lucky ones. For those who remained, the pain of moral outrage, rejection, hostility, and frustration persisted; there appeared to be little hope in sight.

I don't know what I'm going to do. I can't afford to go back to school to prepare for something entirely different from nursing. I don't see any point in getting more nursing education; I'm not using half of what I've got already. The last three jobs I've had, you know, the care and conditions are so bad I'm miserable all the time. The only way I can handle it is just to block it out. I know it's not fair to you, but that's why I agreed to participate in this study. [Why was that?] I'm so mad at the nursing profession, at my school of nursing for teaching me things I can't use and do. I think it's the way I was taught that is making me so miserable now. It's already been four years and five jobs, and nothing's getting better. I haven't told this to my old nursing instructors . . . I don't think they'd listen anyway. I thought I'd feel better if I told you. (Med Ctr[3.6])

### Bicultural Troublemakers

*Demographic characteristics and parameters.* In 1968 the median age of the 55 nurses in this group was 23 years, the same as the median age for the entire sample. About one fourth of the nurses were married, but only a few of them had small children. Most of the nurses in this subgroup were in staff nurse positions, although there were a few head nurses and definitely more nurses in autonomous clinical nurse positions than in any of the other subgroups. They had a mean number of three job changes but quite a few job transfers; in fact, they were second only to the high bureaucratic–low professional subgroup in this characteristic.

One outstanding characteristic was that 71% of them were rated as being highly successful. (This was the largest single rating for any of the four subgroups.) This high-success appellation was earned in spite of the fact that this group of nurses had relatively high role deprivation scores (32.53). Second only to the low bureaucratic–high professional group in role deprivation, it would seem that for the most part these nurses were aware of the conflict between school and work values, had managed to make the best of both systems and thereby became bicultural, and were effective in doing this as manifested by their high success ratings. Informally, they also expressed satisfaction with nursing as a career, the most common expression captured by phrases such as "I'm pleased, but . . . " "things could be better," "nursing has a long way to go," "there's lots of changes I'd like to make." The six nurses in the high professional–high bureaucratic subgroup who were rated less successful than average, however, expressed strong feelings of conflict and dissatisfaction. There apparently is a relationship between ability to handle the conflicting value systems and perception by others of being successful.

The appellation "troublemakers" was attached to this group because of the many remarks made by directors of nursing, supervisors, or co-workers about these nurses. Said with a mixture of fondness, admiration, and exasperation, the frequent comment was: "She's a troublemaker; she's constantly into things, wanting to change this, that, or the other thing. But she's got a lot of good ideas and seems to know how to get things through." Possibly because this kind of behavior takes time to develop, there were proportionately fewer new graduates (34%) in this subgroup than in any of the others. The high bureaucratic–low professional cell, for example, with which the bicultural nurses shared high

bureaucratic beliefs, had 50% more new graduates than the high bureaucratic–high professional cell. Apparently, adoption of bureaucratic values and relinquishment of professional values can be done easier and quicker than adopting bureaucratic values while simultaneously holding onto one's professional beliefs.

About one fourth of the nurses in the high bureaucratic–high professional subgroup expressed intentions of returning for graduate work in nursing, but only "when I'm ready," "after I've tried things out a bit more." This was the group of nurses who were the most likely to say: "I don't want to teach until I've had several years of experience first; I was taught by faculty who didn't have experience, and I don't want to be that kind of teacher."

The Bicultural Troublemakers headed the list of the four groups with regard to membership and activity in professional organizations (56% and 27%, respectively). They were also the group that reported the most community organization activity (39%). Over four fifths of them (83%) reported reading professional or medical journals, 66% on a regular basis. Three fifths of them purchased professional books, and all but 17% had taken some kind of course since graduation. (A complete summary and comparison of the four groups on the above characteristics can be found in Table 3-1.)

By 1970 the size of this subgroup had been reduced from 55 to 41 nurses. They still tended to be in staff nurse or clinically promoted positions, although about 20% were in head nurse positions. The proportion with high success ratings had gone up even higher, to 80%, and the nurses in this subgroup scored higher on all factors of self-actualization than any of the other subgroups. The analysis showed, however, that this was probably due to their high success classification, not to their role configuration. Mean role deprivation scores were still high (31.36). The shrinkage in the number of nurses with this kind of role configuration was due to a rather high dropout rate from nursing (41%), of which over half went into teaching or graduate school. The proclivity of the high bureaucratic–high professional nurses for returning to graduate school was high: six times

**Table 3-1.** Comparison of Rutters, Organization Women, Lateral Arabesquers, and Bicultural Troublemakers on degree of activity in professional organizations, amount and frequency of reading, books purchased, and courses taken°

| | LBHP (N = 40) | | HBLP (N = 72) | | HBHP (N = 41) | | LBLP (N = 48) | |
|---|---|---|---|---|---|---|---|---|
| | NO. | PERCENT | NO. | PERCENT | NO. | PERCENT | NO. | PERCENT |
| Member of ANA-NLN | 17 | 42.5 | 23 | 31.9 | 23 | 56.0 | 9 | 18.7 |
| Active in professional organization | 5 | 12.5 | 7 | 9.7 | 11 | 26.8 | 4 | 8.3 |
| Member of community organization | 5 | 12.5 | 12 | 16.6 | 16 | 39.0 | 6 | 12.5 |
| Professional journals | | | | | | | | |
| None | 13 | 32.5 | 22 | 30.5 | 6 | 14.6 | 22 | 45.8 |
| AJN or medical | 26 | 65.0 | 50 | 69.4 | 34 | 82.9 | 24 | 50.0 |
| Light professional | 1 | 2.5 | 0 | 00.0 | 1 | 2.4 | 2 | 4.1 |
| Frequency of reading | | | | | | | | |
| Not at all | 12 | 30.0 | 21 | 29.1 | 5 | 12.1 | 21 | 43.7 |
| Occasionally, 1 or 2 articles | 12 | 30.0 | 18 | 25.0 | 9 | 21.9 | 14 | 29.1 |
| Most, all, regularly | 16 | 40.0 | 33 | 45.8 | 27 | 65.8 | 13 | 27.0 |
| Books purchased | | | | | | | | |
| None | 12 | 30.0 | 49 | 68.0 | 15 | 36.5 | 36 | 75.0 |
| Nursing, medical | 26 | 65.0 | 14 | 19.4 | 25 | 60.9 | 12 | 25.0 |
| Reference, dictionary, or interest only | 2 | 5.0 | 9 | 12.5 | 1 | 2.4 | 0 | 00.0 |
| Courses taken | | | | | | | | |
| None | 9 | 22.5 | 26 | 36.1 | 7 | 17.0 | 25 | 52.0 |
| Professional only | 11 | 27.5 | 18 | 25.0 | 12 | 29.2 | 12 | 25.0 |
| Professional plus other | 15 | 37.5 | 15 | 20.8 | 16 | 39.0 | 3 | 6.2 |
| Other only | 5 | 12.5 | 13 | 18.0 | 6 | 14.6 | 8 | 16.6 |

°Data collected in late 1969 and early 1970. Abbreviations: LBHP, low bureaucratic–high professional; HBLP, high bureaucratic–low professional; HBHP, high bureaucratic–high professional; LBLP, low bureaucratic–low professional.

that of the high bureaucratic–high professional but not as high as the low bureaucratic–high professional. Major differences between the high bureaucratic–high professional graduate school returnees and those with low bureaucratic–high professional orientation, however, were the number of years between baccalaureate graduation and graduate preparation, and the focus of graduate study. The Bicultural Troublemakers tended to work at least two years before returning to school and were judged to be highly successful nurses at the time they quit work. The Lateral Arabesquers worked much shorter periods of time, had histories of job hopping, were seen as being less successful than average, and gave evidence during interviews that returning to school was an escape from intolerable practice conditions. More high bureaucratic–high professional nurses declared intentions to become clinical nurse specialists than did low bureaucratic–high professional nurses, who preferred baccalaureate faculty teaching positions.

Like their direct counterparts (low bureaucratic–low professional), the high bureaucratic–high professional nurses were quite variable in their responses to the request to name the person who had the most influence on their nursing practice: 29% specified head nurse or supervisor, 14% said a former nursing instructor, and 12% each said colleagues or no one.

The biculturalism of this group was particularly evident in their reported choices of action when presented with conflict situations such as found on the role behavior scales. They were the highest of the four subgroups—significantly higher than the low bureaucratic–high professional subgroup—in their reported use of integrative behavior choices. This kind of behavior represented compromise or judicious breaking of rules and routines. The troublemaker also maintained relatively high professional and bureaucratic role behavior choices, second to the low bureaucratic–high professional on professional, to the high bureaucratic–low professional subgroup on bureaucratic.

*Composite attitudinal and behavioral characteristics.* The role models desired for the Anticipatory Socialization program were in the high bureaucratic–high professional subgroup. These nurses had internalized the values of both the bureaucratic and professional systems and exhibited the behavior consistent with the expectations of each. Support and commitment were inherent in their actions because decisions pertaining to behavior were based on judicious weighing of several alternatives, not automatic responses. It is not intended to portray these nurses as being superhuman and nondemanding. There was definite awareness of the inequities and inconsistencies of both the bureaucratic and professional systems of work; yet there was the ability to assess a situation, make a decision, and assume the responsibility for actions. The principle took precedence over self-interest or blind allegiance to a particular work system. It was not always apparent which came first.

I think two years ago I wouldn't have wanted the responsibility of it. Before I became HN I was very much ready to let anybody else do anything and I just wanted to work on my job. Taking a HN position, I really became more interested in all the other things that were going on besides my little job. I think that did change my whole viewpoint. It changed my attitude about the situation too. I don't think I would have wanted the responsibility before—it would have been just that. Now I kind of enjoy it; I have influence as well as power. (Med Ctr[19.2])

Role deprivation was quite high for this group of nurses but, due to their intrinsic school-bred value commitment, they also managed to internalize the nursing work values to the extent that they were highly functional. This ability was somehow enhanced or intensified by the system, which in turn rewarded the nurse, who then had her attitude toward nursing and the system positively re-

inforced. For instance, in the handling of role expectations:

I just usually got upset. I have just got to stop myself and say: "You can only do the best you can." So I got about five different things that I have to do . . . I tell the people what I'm going to do and the reason why I'm going to do it, and that's all I can do. (Med Ctr[19.6])

· · ·

I definitely think I have changed. I think I have become more involved with the patients . . . I am far more conscious of the procedures and policies now than I ever was. I used to be the complete rebel and I still am a bit, but I can see where they have a definite purpose to protect both patients and nursing staff and I am becoming pretty strict about this myself. There are some things that I agree that can be done right in a thousand different ways. If the hospital has one way . . . I might find there are grounds for it . . . I at least look now. Like they have a poor isolation technique at [X] Hospital and I squawked about it and it has changed some . . . but it has definitely changed, and I am far more conscious of this kind of thing. (Med Ctr[29.6])

Job satisfaction seemed to be high, yet members of this group did not lessen their efforts to make the position better and more rewarding. Integration of both sets of values did not come easily, but there was evidence that growth-producing role conflict resolution behavior had been put into action.

I love my job. There are frustrations about it, of course, but neoadministration and I have bucked each other every now and then but it's the only way to get changes, and I've gotten a few. Keeps them in good balance, really have a good relationship, but you are still fighting them for what you want, and you know you can win sometimes. With every hassle I feel I learn and grow. (Med Ctr[25.5])

· · ·

I think getting into a rut could happen in this job very easily. I think if you are not challenged, moderately at least, then you can get in a rut. And sometimes I think of some of the directors . . . I see them in a rut. You have to be sincere and you have to keep going over why you are really here. You have to think of the patients and why you are here. I would get bored if I did just sit in a chair all day. (Med Ctr[26.2])

Interesting behaviors were displayed by these group members. They could take risks, use their experiences to relate to patients, stand up to the administration, and accept responsibility. They enjoyed their work and didn't consider extrinsic work factors as prime influences in their decisions if they interfered with their own value system. They could relate to co-workers, support their abilities, and constructively criticize their inabilities. They were creative and welcomed challenge. In many cases they sought out their own challenges. What better role models can be found to support and sustain the nursing profession and the values of the neophyte graduate nurse?

Well, I thought about going back to school. At that time I was frustrated and thought I was interested in teaching. I don't know why I changed my mind except I really enjoy hospital nursing and think I can do more here to really make a difference in the kind of care patients get. The hours and salary would be nice, but being happy in your work is more important. I don't have to run away now. (Med Ctr[2.2])

. . .

I think when I was in school I really used to wonder how important a nurse was and what they did; and I think I really had an idea they were physician assistants, *not* as they are evolving now. Nursing is something very separate and very vital. You know, it is something that I guess you learn when you learn confidence . . . you finally realize it is really important. (Med Ctr[29.4])

The nurses who comprise this group were not content with nursing and health care as it presently is. They believed in the institution and the profession and exerted tremendous effort toward making it work. Realistic aspects of the situation were given consideration as decisions were made, responsibilities assumed, and concern for others evidenced. They "made waves" and hung on tenaciously to get results. This was exemplified by the nurse who talked about her nursing practice and view of a troublesome patient.

Two years ago . . . what I had been taught and what I learned in working wasn't very well jelled. I knew theory, but I didn't know . . . maybe it is right and maybe it is wrong; so then I learned a couple of ways and decided which was better. Before, I wasn't able to say . . . now I know I am right. I am willing to take risks . . . I believe in what I think. If I don't know, I would say: "I would be inclined to do it this way. Do you have any other ideas or preferred ways of doing it?" At least you are telling that person that you are not wiping out all their routines.

A troublesome patient is one that doesn't lie there quietly and not say a word and let you do whatever you want to. Maybe an aggressive patient, someone who has been sick for a long time and is reacting the same way any person would react. If they lie there and be quiet and shut up, a judgment is made, but not by me. They are considered good patients, but if they fight they are bad. Really, his self image is shot. He can't even relate as we expect to anything. They are troublesome but they are the challenge. (Med Ctr[27.4])

### Looking at them all together

It is often helpful to look at the whole as well as individual parts. The following is a summary and comparison of characteristics of the nurses in all four subgroups.

1. Nurses with high success ratings were found most often in the groups reporting high bureaucratic orientations, either high bureaucratic–low professional or high bureaucratic–high professional.
2. Married nurses with small children tended to be highly represented in the low bureaucratic–low professional category; single nurses were most numerous in the low bureaucratic–high professional subgroup.
3. Nurses with a high professional orientation had the highest dropout rate and the most job changes; a high bureaucratic orientation was associated with job transfers within the same organization.
4. Nurses with high bureaucratic–low professional orientation tended to be in administratively promoted positions more frequently than any of the other groups; the high bureaucratic–high professional nurses tended to be in unusual and clinically promoted positions more often than the others.
5. The high bureaucratic–low professional nurses expressed the most job and nursing satisfaction in response to open-

ended questions; they also had the lowest role deprivation scores. Both the high bureaucratic–high professional and the low bureaucratic-high professional groups had high role deprivation scores; the latter also expressed much job dissatisfaction in response to open-ended questions.

6. Nurses rated as highly successful were consistently higher on all three components of self-actualization than were the other groups regardless of their role configurations.

7. The low bureaucratic–high professional nurses were most likely to return to graduate school to prepare to be teachers or go into teaching without graduate preparation. The high bureaucratic–high professional subgroup also had a fairly high school-return rate, but they worked longer first and reasons given were to become clinical nurse specialists or nurse practitioners rather than teachers.

8. There was a lower percentage of new graduates in the high bureaucratic–high professional and low bureaucratic–high professional cells than in the other two. This may be because it takes awhile to work out the conflict and compatible marriage between high bureaucratic–high professional role concepts and because many of the nurses with low bureaucratic–high professional role concepts leave nursing practice or go into teaching very rapidly after graduation.

## DID THE ANTICIPATORY SOCIALIZATION PROGRAM WORK?

Before looking to see whether the events anticipated actually occurred, we must ask and answer the question: Were the people who took the Anticipatory Socialization program affected by its anatomy and physiology? Did they feel it? Glaser and Nitko stress the point that it is not enough to measure the degree to which the objectives of a study are attained, that is, to measure the values of the dependent variable; attention must also be given to the adequacy of implementing the practice or program or treatment, that is,

the effectiveness of the independent variable. They further suggest that specific criteria should be provided that indicate just how the program should function and how specific features of the program should look when the program is in actual operation.

To follow through on this suggestion, two factors were studied. Recall that the treatment variable—the Anticipatory Socialization program—was designed as an inoculating agent. The first phase in particular, the shock phase, was intended to cause some self-doubt and anxiety. If this treatment were successful, one predictable effect might be change in the withdrawal patterns of students from this school of nursing.[4] There would not necessarily be a total increase in withdrawals, but if the students were introduced head on into some of the perhaps unpleasant realities of the work world, it is quite likely that some students with borderline involvement or commitment might withdraw earlier in the program rather than later on.

### Rate of attrition

An attrition study was done on the basic students in the control Class of 1968, the two experimental Classes of 1969 and 1970, and also one class on either side of those involved in this study, the Classes of 1967 and 1971. Table 3-2 shows the differences in time of withdrawal for students in these various classes. Inspection of this data indicated both similarities and differences in the attrition patterns for the five classes. The overall attrition rate for the five classes was quite similar, ranging from 20.5% for the Class of 1970 to 32.2% for the Class of 1971. The chi square $(\chi^2)$ value of 4.05 was not significant. Therefore, it can be concluded that there were no differences in the overall attrition rates among the five classes of students. This had been expected.

A difference that had been expected, but that was not confirmed by the data, was that the students in the Classes of 1969 and 1970 would withdraw from the program at an earlier date than would the students in the other classes. The total number of students withdrawing during the first year of the program ranged from six in the Class of 1968 to eleven

**Table 3-2.** Differences in time of withdrawal for students

| Class and treatment | First year | | | | Second year | | | | Third year | | Attrition rate | | Reentered and completed a program° | |
| | Mid | | End | | Mid | | End | | | | | | | |
| | NO. | PERCENT | NO. | PERCENT | NO. | PERCENT | NO. | PERCENT | NO. | PERCENT | NO. | PERCENT | NO. | PERCENT |
| 1967—Not in study (Entering N =66) | 2 | 3.0 | 5 | 7.6 | 3 (1) | 4.5 | 5 | 7.6 | — | — | 16 | 24.2 | 1 | 1.5 |
| 1968—Control class (Entering N =61) | 3 | 4.9 | 3 | 4.9 | 5 | 8.2 | 6 | 9.8 | — | — | 17 | 27.8 | — | — |
| 1969—Received Anticipatory Socialization program (Entering N = 72) | 4 (2) | 5.6 | 3 (1) | 4.1 | 2 (1) | 2.8 | 1 | 1.4 | 0 (1) | — | 15 | 20.8 | 5 | 6.9 |
| 1970—Received Anticipatory Socialization program (Entering N = 78) | 5 (3) | 6.4 | 3 | 3.8 | 2 (2) | 2.6 | — (1) | — | — | — | 16 | 20.5 | 6 | 7.7 |
| 1971—Not in study (Entering N = 84) | 5 | 6.0 | 5 | 6.0 | 7 (1) | 8.3 | 7 | 8.3 | 2 | 2.4 | 27 | 32.1 | 1 | 1.1 |

°Number of students from that class who reentered and completed a nursing program within two years of the time they would ordinarily have graduated; four of the thirteen completed their education in programs other than at the University of California.
(  ) Signifies the number and time at which reentered students withdrew.
$\chi^2$ between withdrew and completed = 4.05 (NS at .05 level).
$\chi^2$ between withdrew in first year and other years = 7.37 (p = .05, df 4, $\chi^2$ = 9.49).

in the Class of 1970. Chi square analysis was not significant. Therefore it must be concluded that the five classes were similar both in total attrition rate and in attrition rate during the first year.

Although the students in the two experimental classes (1969 and 1970) did not withdraw earlier, they did appear to differ from the other classes in that they either withdrew during their first year or not at all. The second-year withdrawals ranged from four in the Class of 1969 to fifteen in the Class of 1971. Most important, the second-year withdrawals appeared to clump into two groups: those from the Classes of 1969 and 1970, with a low of five and six withdrawals, and those from the other three classes with nine, eleven, and fifteen withdrawals during this year. It seems that being a member of a class exposed to the Anticipatory Socialization program made one more likely to either withdraw during the first year of the nursing program or not at all.

Another area in which there was a difference among the five classes was in the number of students who withdrew and later reentered and completed a nursing program. A total of eleven students from the Classes of 1969 and 1970 followed this pattern, while only two students from the other three classes combined did so. This was an unexpected and unpredicted finding and one in which there is some evidence that the Anticipatory Socialization program was directly involved. The reasons for withdrawal for all students were recorded in regular exit interviews done by the faculty responsible for the student at the time of withdrawal. Tabulations of these reasons showed no noticeable difference among classes, using the usual categories found in the literature: academic failure, personal reasons, health, and so on. Intuitively, little faith can be placed on this kind of analysis because it is generally recognized that a person's reasons or motivations for major life decisions are highly complex and difficult to categorize. More insightful data on the reasons for withdrawal and possible effect of the Reality Shock program were obtained from followup questionnaires and reentrance interviews with nine of the students who withdrew and subsequently reentered the program.

The questionnaires were sent about six months after they left school and asked the former students a number of open-ended questions about their feelings, attitudes, and cognitions about nursing, and about their specific program. It also asked them what their current activities were and their plans for the future. Those who reentered were also interviewed shortly thereafter (but not as a prerequisite for readmission to the program).

The number is too small to analyze the data quantitatively, but dominant themes emerged from the data. Of the eleven reentering students from the Classes of 1969 and 1970 who had had at least part of the Anticipatory Socialization program, a dominant theme abstracted from questionnaires and interviews emerged.

I didn't think I would like it. When I heard those tapes of the new graduates, I was really shocked. I didn't think nursing would be like that at all. I decided that I didn't want it that way, so I quit; but I've always wanted to be a nurse, so I got a job as an aide. I'd worked as an aide before, but this time I really opened my eyes and looked. I talked a lot to new graduates at the hospital too. And it isn't all rosy. I found out that there are a lot of things we're taught here that are good and should be done, but they're not. And sometimes there's really good reasons for not giving good care, and other times it's because people don't care or don't know how. They just don't think it's important. I'm ready now to accept nursing as it is and try and become the best nurse I can and do something to make patients get better care, at least in the little corner of the world where I live. (NG:BS[6]1/70)

This does not mean that all reentrants left because of shock or dislike for nursing. Some left for obvious health reasons or to get married or to have babies. But even among the latter, traces of the above theme were discernible.

I left because I wanted to get married and be with my husband. But, to be honest, I really wasn't liking nursing very much anyway; I was quite confused and shook up at the time. I came in

here with one idea of nursing. The faculty feeds you an altogether different brand, and then in bits and pieces I got another angle on it. [What do you mean by the bits and pieces?] Oh, in some of the seminars we heard tapes of nurses telling how it was, and then on the units sometimes you'd see things that made you realize nursing wasn't like your instructor said it was. (NG:BS [10]4/71)

Although tentative, these questionnaire and interview data do lend credence to the idea that the Reality Shock program was effective in getting at least some of the students to take a closer look at nursing and the differential ways in which it was practiced. It appears that one possible effect of exposure to the program was a greater tendency to delay completion of the formal nursing education program until one had a chance "to go out and look things over for myself." (All but two of the thirteen students worked as nurse's aides during the period before reentrance.)

In summary then, the five classes of students were similar in respect to overall withdrawal rates and withdrawal rate during the first year. They differed in that the two experimental classes had significantly lower withdrawal rates following the first year and they also had higher reentry rates than any of the other classes. Although suggestive, this withdrawal data does not permit the conclusion that the Anticipatory Socialization program *caused* the changes in attrition pattern. The patterns for the two experimental classes look different and are not incompatible with changes that might be expected from a program like the Anticipatory Socialization program, but a cause and effect relationship cannot be established. It is possible that other factors may have been operative. It is impossible to identify all possible relevant factors; attempts were made to maintain constancy only in the programs for the Classes of 1968, 1969, and 1970. All that can be said is that one of the major factors that was different between the experimental classes and the others was the Anticipatory Socialization program, and the changes in the withdrawal pattern were consistent with implementation of this program.

## Changes in values

Another way of assessing whether the Anticipatory Socialization program took hold was to see whether the students who took it picked up the same conceptions as those who did not have the program. Looking at the professed loyalty to work organizational values at periodic intervals during the educational program permitted an assessment of this. Utilizing the Corwin Likert scales described earlier, all students in the Classes of 1968, 1969, and 1970 were tested within the first week of entrance into the school (T1), at the beginning of the second year (T3), and at the end of the third year within one month of graduation (T4).° The students in the Classes of 1967 and 1971 were tested at graduation only. If the Anticipatory Socialization program had an effect on the students in the Classes of 1969 and 1970, it would be expected that their bureaucratic scores would show an increase in comparison to the Class of 1968. It was anticipated that professional scores for all classes would rise due to the general professional socializing experience of the nursing program. Because of the incompatibility of these two systems and the reality confrontation, it was expected that if the above predictions held the role deprivation scores would be higher for the students in the two experimental classes. The mean scores of the classes at stipulated time periods are presented in Appendix C, Table C-2.

Analyses were done in two ways: over time between T1, T3, and T4 for each class, and between classes. Contrary to expectations, the results indicated a significant decrease in the mean scores for the classes of 1968, 1969, and 1970 on the bureaucratic role conception scale from entrance to graduation, although the drop for the Class of 1968 was significantly greater than that for the Classes of 1969 and 1970 (Appendix C, Tables C-2 and C-5). It must therefore be concluded that if the Antic-

ipatory Socialization program had an effect on students' valuation of bureaucratic work principles, it was in the direction of helping them to maintain some of the loyalty to these principles that they had when they entered the program rather than increasing this loyalty after they were in the program.

The data indicated that the prediction in respect to the increase in commitment to professional work principles was upheld. There was a significant increase for all three classes on this dimension from T1 to T3. It can be concluded, therefore, that at least as measured by the role conception scales used in this study the faculty were successful in professionally socializing these students. Furthermore, most of this change in professional loyalties occurred early in the program. These findings are consistent with those of Davis and Olesen.

There are some data to support the inference that a nurse training program may be effective in socializing the student into a service role conception. (This conception corresponds on a number of dimensions to what is usually described as the lay image of nursing.) The findings were definitely inconsistent. There was no change in service role conception scores for either the Class of 1968 or 1969; the Class of 1970 showed a significant increase in mean score from T1 to T4. Davis and Olesen also reported a minor and inconsistent trend away from lay images in nursing. Perhaps it is that some normative commitment to this role dimension is required (which would explain the rapid service socialization of the Class of 1970), after which individual differences in "person" and "self" dimensions are permitted.

In the interclass analyses (Appendix C, Table C-2) a significant difference at T1 was noted between the mean score of the Class of 1970 and the combined means of the Classes of 1968 and 1969 on service role conception scale (p. 59). Beginning with the midway testing period, the expected increase in role deprivation for the Classes of 1969 and 1970 began to show. It was not possible to analyze this variable over time, because most beginning nursing students do not have sufficient information to perceive a reality to nursing

---

°The T2 designation was used for a random sample of students from the Classes of 1969 and 1970 who were given the Role Conception scales at the end of the first year in the program. This was done to assess the effect of a summer work experience on students' role conceptions.

and consequently cannot answer the role deprivation scales. The interclass analyses on this variable, however, showed that the experimental classes had a significantly higher mean role deprivation score than did the control class. This lends credence to the inference that the Anticipatory Socialization program was operative and effective in familiarizing students with the discrepant values they were likely to meet in the work world. Although a mean role deprivation score of 26 is not within the shock range, it does represent at least some greater awareness of incipient value conflict than does a score of 23.[5]

At the graduation testing (T4), complete over-class analysis was possible (Appendix C, Table C-2). Here are seen some interesting findings. There was even greater confirmation of the inference that the Anticipatory Socialization program was doing something to help students retain some loyalty to bureaucratic work principles. All three of the classes that did not have the Anticipatory Socialization program had significantly lower mean bureaucratic role conception scores than did the two experimental classes. All five classes had high professional orientations at graduation; there was essentially no difference among them on this variable. As expected, there was a significant difference between the classes that had the Anticipatory Socialization program and those that did not in respect to the total role deprivation variable. Whether this was due to the interaction effect of high professional and high bureaucratic values, as the theory would dictate, or whether it was due directly to the Anticipatory Socialization program is not known. In all likelihood, because of the way in which the measurement of this variable is derived, it is probably the former.

There were some differences noted between the two experimental classes. The role deprivation scores of the Class of 1970 were significantly higher; professional and service role conception scores were also higher than those of the Class of 1969. One possible reason for the higher role deprivation scores was that professional role conception is known to be the instrumental factor in raising role deprivation scores. Another factor might be that

perhaps the Anticipatory Socialization program was taught more effectively the second time. There was definitely more detailed experiential data available from the medical center reference group, and certainly the teacher was better prepared to handle the students' questions and reactions. Whether these factors made the difference can be speculated but not answered by the data.

In summary then, there is supporting evidence that permits the inference that the implementation of the Anticipatory Socialization program was adequate. The data indicate that the students in the experimental classes did not relinquish bureaucratic loyalties to the same extent as did the control class. They seemed to acquire a commitment to professional and service values equal to that of the control group, and they reported more discrepancy between preconceived role and actual role than did the control class. Experiencing this discrepancy while in school was one of the aims of the Anticipatory Socialization program. It was hypothesized that this would lessen students' reality shock after graduation.

### Differences according to extent of participation

There were five phases to the Anticipatory Socialization program. It was possible for students to participate in one, several, or all of the phases. Was there a difference in the attitudinal behavior of those who chose to participate in different amounts of the program?

In the evaluation of the adequacy and implementation of the Anticipatory Socialization program, there are many facets that need to be examined. The sequencing and content of the program, the methods of delivery, the format and packaging, the abilities, motivation, and readiness of the student are but a few. For the most part these were outside the purview of the present research; the Anticipatory Socialization program was conceptualized as a total package with a stipulated delivery strategy.[6] In the original design of the study, there were plans for evaluating the differential effectiveness of the program along two dimensions: the teacher variable and the effect of differential exposure.

It had been conjectured that if the Anticipatory Socialization program were effective it might be so because of the positional authority and status of the investigator (Assistant Dean in charge of the undergraduate program). To determine this, it had been planned to simultaneously replicate this study at a state college nursing program in the same city, with the research assistant rather than the investigator teaching the Anticipatory Socialization program to these students. This would not only have provided a control for the teacher variable, but would also have increased the external validity of the study since the students in the state college program come from a different population than do the students at the University of California.

Steps were taken to implement this aspect of the research design. The program was favorably received by the faculty of the state college. They were willing to allocate program time for inclusion of the leadership seminar content. Mechanics of classes, time, and so forth, were all worked out. Arrangements were made to present the research assistant as a regular member of the state faculty to minimize possible Hawthorne effects. The Anticipatory Socialization program was taught for approximately one semester to the 54 students who entered their sophomore year in the state college program in September 1968. Unfortunately for the study, there was considerable social turmoil on this campus during that time. This, coupled with the extended illness of the research assistant, required the termination of this export phase of the project. This is regrettable since it now leaves many questions unanswered, but even its brief existence helped to substantiate the fact that the program could be exported and was well received by nurse faculty.

Another variable in which a planned assessment was built into the design was the possible effects of differential exposure to varying amounts of the Reality Shock program. Recall that the subjects in this study had the choice of participating or not participating in various activities of the program. The major

part of the program included bimonthly seminars during the first year, six hours of class in the second year, and ten hours in the third year. This was a part of the academic program. In the crossbreak analysis that follows, it was assumed that all students in the experimental classes were exposed to the above, although in this particular nursing program students had the option of attending classes or not.

A crossbreak analysis on role conception and role deprivation scores of the students in the experimental classes according to the extent to which they elected to participate in the Anticipatory Socialization program was done. For this analysis, the students in the two experimental classes were grouped together. One group consisted of those students who had only the part of the Anticipatory Socialization program that was included as a regular part of the curriculum. For convenience in designation, this group will be called "curriculum only." It consisted of 35 of the 116 students in the combined Classes of 1969 and 1970. Another group, called "curriculum plus summer," was composed of 36 students who had the curriculum part and elected to participate in at least one of the summer programs. The last group, called "entire program," consisted of 45 students who had the curriculum part, two summers, and at least two evening participations.

Analysis of the role conception and role deprivation scores of the students according to whether they had the curriculum only, curriculum plus summer, or entire program (Appendix C, Table C-6) indicated that the students who had minimum participation in the Reality Shock program had significantly lower professional role conception scores than did the students in the other two groups. This may well mean that this group of students was less involved in the total school scene than were the students in the other groups. The other variable on which the three groups differed markedly was in total role deprivation. On this variable, the curriculum-only group had significantly lower role deprivation scores at graduation than did the curriculum-plus-summer group. The latter had significantly lower scores than did the maximum participation group. Therefore, the greater the exposure to the Anticipatory Socialization program, the greater the role deprivation. This is highly important and seems to indicate that the extent of participation in the program is positively correlated with achievement of desired results of the program.

## SUMMARY

The nature and substantive content and strategies of the Anticipatory Socialization program have been presented. Although this program served as the independent variable of this research study, the emphasis was on presenting the overall idea and plan rather than the detailed procedures that would be needed for replication.

Data on attrition rates and patterns and differential scoring between classes on the role conception and deprivation scales were presented to substantiate the contention that the Anticipatory Socialization program was adequately implemented. The final section presented a crossbreak analysis of scale scores for students who elected differential amounts of the Anticipatory Socialization program. The next chapter will move into the evaluative phase of the effects of the Anticipatory Socialization program on the students' chosen work locale, retention, and operationalization of professional values.

## NOTES

1. I wish to acknowledge the help of a baccalaureate student from the Class of 1967 in this regard. Miss Sharon Mindlin, a second-year student at the time, assisted in the preparation of these conflict situations. She listened to over 150 tape recordings and selected situations that she judged would have particular interest and appeal for students. These were then modified to eliminate identifying names and characteristics and were used in the leadership seminars or on examinations.
2. Three sections of this Anticipatory Socialization program were made an integral part of the nursing curriculum for the Classes of 1969 and 1970: the first-year leadership seminars, 6 hours of class in the second year, and 10 hours in the third year. The control Class of 1968 had first-year leadership seminars that were lectures focused on characteristics of groups and leadership styles; in the second year they had lectures on ecology and seminars on the effects of different kinds of leadership; in the third year they had lectures on the change agent process.

3. I wish to acknowledge the splendid contribution to this study made by Mrs. Mary Lawrence, R.M.M.S., who did the very tedious and time-consuming work of listening to the tape-recorded interviews, reading and rereading the typescripts, and then preparing the composite pictures of the nurses in each of the four subgroups.
4. I am grateful to the Dean of the School of Nursing, Helen Nahm, for pointing out this logical prediction on the occasion of the initial discussion of this project with her.
5. Over a series of studies utilizing this same tool, it has been found that the mean role deprivation score of graduate nurses after working for at least one year is about 23; the shock stage of reality shock is associated with scores above 30. See Appendix B for a summary of mean scores for various populations.
6. The delivery strategy used in this study was an inoculation strategy following the experimental results of McGuire and associates. Another possibility would be the situation-simulation approach described by Froelich and Bishop (A method for guiding professional socialization in medical education, Br. J. Med. Educ. 3:192-196, 1969). Orme and Wender (Anticipatory socialization for psychotherapy: method and rationale, Am. J. Psychiatry 124(9):1202-1212, March 1968) favor a direct, explicit approach to accomplish this kind of socialization. Danielian (Live simulation of affect-laden cultural cognition. Conflict Resolution 9(3):312-324) follows the cultural assimilation approach and suggests a method of live simulations.

## REFERENCES

Asch, S. E.: Effects of group pressure upon the modification and distortion of judgements. In Cartwright, D., and Zander, A.: Group dynamics research and theory, ed. 2, New York, 1962, Harper & Row, Publishers.

Bates, B.: Nurse-physician teamwork, Medical Care 4:69-80, 1966.

Bates, B., and Chamberlin, R.: Physician leadership as perceived by nurses, Nurs. Res. 19(6):534-539, 1970.

Bennis, W.: The coming death of bureaucracy. In Think magazine, published by IBM Corp. A Notes and Quotes reprint, Hartford, 1966, Connecticut General Life Insurance Co., Inc.

Bennis, W.: Post-bureaucratic leadership, Trans-Action 6:44, July 1969.

Borman, L. D.: The marginal route of a mental hospital innovation, Human Organization 29(1):63-69, 1970.

Davis, F., and Olesen, V.: Baccalaureate students' images of nursing. Nurs. Res. 13(1):8-15, 1964.

Ewing, D. W.: Tension can be an asset, Harvard Business Review, September-October, 1964, p. 71.

Ford, R.: The obstinate employee, Psychology Today 3:32-34, November 1969.

Foster, G.: Traditional cultures and the impact of technological change, New York, 1962, Harper & Row, Publishers, pp. 64-217.

Glaser, B., and Strauss, A.: Awareness of dying, Chicago, 1965, Aldine-Atherton, Inc.

Glaser, R., and Nitko, A. J.: Measurement in learning and instruction, American Council on Education, Washington, D. C., 1971, pp. 663-665.

Huse, E., and Beer, M.: Eclectic approach to organizational development, Harvard Business Review, October, 1971, pp. 103-112.

Janis, I.: Psychodynamic aspects of stress tolerance. In Klausner, S., editor: The quest for self-control, New York, 1965, The Free Press.

Janis, I.: Effects of fear arousal on attitude change; recent developments in theory and experimental research. In Berkowitz, L., editor: Advances in experimental social psychology, vol. 3, New York, 1967, Academic Press.

Katz, D., and Kahn, R.: The social psychology of organizations, New York, 1966, John Wiley & Sons, Inc.

Kramer, M.: Some effects of exposure to employing bureaucracies on the role conceptions and role deprivation of neophyte collegiate nurses, unpublished doctoral dissertation, 1966, Stanford University.

Kramer, M.: Role models, role conceptions, and role deprivation, Nurs. Res. 17(2):115-20, 1968.

Kramer, M.: Collegiate graduate nurses in medical center hospitals; mutual challenge or duel, Nurs. Res. 18(3): 196-210, 1969.

Kramer, M., McDonnell, C., and Reed, J. L.: Self-actualization and role adaptation of baccalaureate degree nurses, Nurs. Res. 21(2), March-April 1972.

Lewis, E.: Four nurses who wanted to make a difference, Am. J. Nurs. 69:777-782, April 1969.

McGregor, D.: The human side of enterprise, New York, 1960, McGraw-Hill Book Co.

Manthey, M.: Primary nursing is alive and well in the hospital, Am. J. Nurs. 73(1):83-87, 1973.

Manthey, M., and associates: Primary nursing, Nursing Forum 9(1):64-83, 1970.

Manthey, M., and Kramer, M.: A dialogue on primary nursing, Nursing Forum 9(4):356-379, 1970.

Paynich, M. L.: Why do basic nursing students work in nursing? Nursing Outlook 19(4):242-245, 1971.

Peplau, H. E.: Nurse-doctor relationships, Nursing Forum 5(1):60-75, 1966.

Peter, L. J., and Hull, R.: The Peter principle, New York, 1969, Bantam Books, Inc.

Reissman, L.: A study of role conceptions in bureaucracy, Social Forces 27:305-310, 1949.

Schein, E. H.: Organizational socialization and the profession of management, Industrial Management Review 9(2):1-16, 1968.

Shostrom, E. L.: Inventory for the measurement of self-actualization, Educational Psychological Measurement 24:207-218, Summer 1964.

Stein, L.: The doctor-nurse game, Am. J. Nurs. 68(1): 101-105, 1968.

Thibaut, J., and Kelly, H.: Social psychology of groups, New York, 1959, John Wiley & Sons, Inc.

Watson, G., editor: Concepts for social change, 1967, National Training Laboratories, NEA.

Weinstein, E.: The development of interpersonal competence. In Goslin, D. A., editor: Handbook of socialization theory and research, Chicago, 1969, Rand McNally & Co.

## CHAPTER FOUR

# EFFECTS OF THE ANTICIPATORY SOCIALIZATION PROGRAM

From several studies, it is known that student nurses graduate with high professional value orientations but that they lose or abdicate these professional values rather quickly when they begin to practice nursing. Davis and Olesen found that the school socialization process was instrumental to some degree in promoting the development of this professional orientation. In the present study it was found that there was a significant increase in professional value orientation for the students in both the control and experimental groups from the intake to the graduation testing. It can be concluded, therefore, that the probability is very high that an aspirant nurse will develop a high professional role orientation during the process of socialization into becoming a nurse. Upon employment she must increase her loyalty to the bureaucratic system of work. If she attempts to do this while retaining her professional loyalties, it it likely that she will experience considerable role deprivation. This reported perception of the nurse work world as being different from the role of the nurse taught in school is what brings about conflict, frustration, and intense dissatisfaction. Unless the nurse has developed within her behavioral repertoire adaptive ways of responding to the resultant conflict, that is, integrative role behaviors, the probability is high that she will either flee the work scene or abdicate her professional values. The purpose of the Anticipatory Socialization program was to confront student nurses with some of the shocks of the reality world and to equip them with integrative strategies that hopefully

would help them to articulate the school and work value orientations in such a way that the professional values would be put into operation.

Was the Anticipatory Socialization program successful in doing this? What effect did this vehicle have on the places we planned to visit on this journey? At each junction some anticipated events had been forecast—much the same way in which a vacation trip is planned so that you can arrive in a particular city for some special event (like Mardi Gras in New Orleans). Let us review what was expected and then see what actually happened.

1. *Role deprivation school junction:* If collegiate student nurses are provided the exposure to and opportunity to work out professional-bureaucratic work conflicts with guidance and support during the school socialization period, reality shock and role deprivation will be experienced as part of the school period.

2. *Role deprivation work junction:* Collegiate student nurses who had the Anticipatory Socialization program will experience less role deprivation upon employment than will a comparable group of nurses who did not have this program.

3. *Job turnover and exodus junction:* A higher percentage of the collegiate student nurses who had the Anticipatory Socialization program will remain in hospital work two years after graduation than will a comparable group who did not have the program.

4. *Integrative role behavior junction:* A higher percentage of collegiate nurses who had the Anticipatory Socialization program will report use of integrative role strategies than will a comparable group who did not have the program.

5. *Professional loyalty and behavior junction:* A higher percentage of collegiate student nurses who had the Anticipatory Socialization program will retain professional nurse role conceptions and behaviors upon employment than will a comparable group who did not have the program.

A brief word of explanation about the general procedure used in the data analysis of this study is in order. For all tests of the hypothesis in which both the independent and dependent variable data were of interval nature, the usual procedure was first to do an analysis of variance over all three classes. If the F ratio was significant, a Scheffé procedure was done between the various combinations of means of the three classes.

## ANTICIPATED EVENTS
### Role deprivation school junction

This hypothesis was tested by comparing the role deprivation scores of the control group with those of the experimental group of student nurses at the graduation testing. If student nurses had been protected and not exposed to reality conflicts in such a way that they could perceive that conflict was inevitable and that they had best learn strategies to manage it, then one would expect their role deprivation scores to be relatively low at graduation. This was the usual situation found in tests of several classes of collegiate nurses. (See Appendix C, Table C-2, for graduation role deprivation scores of students in the Classes of 1967 and 1971 at the University of California School of Nursing.) If student nurses, such as those in the Classes of 1969 and 1970, had a program in which they were deliberately exposed to conflict situations and presented with alternative strategies for managing conflicts, then it was expected that their role deprivation scores would be higher upon graduation than those of their counterparts who had not had the program. As can be seen in Table 4-1, this was the case. The mean role deprivation score of 23.65 for the Class of 1968 was significantly lower than that for either the Class of 1969 or 1970. Hypothesis I was therefore accepted.

There is also some less methodically collected data that supports the conclusion to this hypothesis. Faculty perceive and talk about classes of students as though there were a group personality, a syntality. From expressions in faculty meetings and other informal meetings, it was fairly commonly agreed among the faculty of this school of nursing that the students in the Class of 1968 were calm, poised, docile, intelligent nurses. The Class of 1969? "They're good nurses, but a lot of them are troublemakers." "They're a much more resistive and feisty class than last year. In many ways they seem much more unhappy and discontent with nursing than any class I've ever taught." "That Class of 1970—they're going to have problems. They're good nurses, but they constantly question whether what the faculty is doing for them is the best way for them to learn how to be nurses. They seem much more concerned about how they're going to do on their first jobs, whether they'll make the grade, and how much will be different from school." "They're sort of an anxious group, I'd say, and I get the feeling that they don't completely trust the faculty. They're like last year's class in that respect." The above were a few quotes from groups of faculty who had taught students in all three classes. This data was useful in rounding out the picture that the faculty observed that there were some differences in the syntality of the control and experimental classes. It is not contended that all of the observations made by the faculty were necessarily attributable to the Anticipatory Socialization program. The important point is that, without knowing the hypothesis or even the general design of the study, faculty did observe and comment upon their perceptions of differences in the three classes of students, and these differences did fit the expectations of the research.

Table 4-1. Significance of mean differences in role conception and role deprivation scores for nurses in Classes of 1968, 1969, 1970 at graduation and one-year after employment: ANOVA

| | Class of 1968 | | Class of 1969 | | Class of 1970 | | F | Scheffé° |
|---|---|---|---|---|---|---|---|---|
| | X | SD | X | SD | X | SD | | |
| Graduation (T4) (N = 161) | | | | | | | | |
| Bureaucratic role conception | 15.93 | 2.60 | 17.79 | 4.71 | 17.39 | 2.95 | 3.60† | 3.0317 ± .19 |
| Professional role conception | 30.29 | 3.57 | 30.11 | 3.17 | 31.13 | 3.72 | 1.42 | |
| Service role conception | 28.53 | 2.55 | 28.48 | 2.49 | 29.12 | 2.88 | 1.02 | |
| Bureaucratic role deprivation | 5.84 | 2.94 | 6.53 | 3.48 | 7.30 | 3.59 | 2.42 | |
| Professional role deprivation | 9.18 | 2.90 | 10.11 | 4.71 | 11.85 | 4.69 | 5.33† | 1.7986 ± .22 |
| Service role deprivation | 8.58 | 4.10 | 9.65 | 4.81 | 10.03 | 4.42 | 1.40 | |
| Total role deprivation | 23.65 | 7.00 | 26.28 | 10.86 | 29.03 | 10.13 | 4.02† | .0050 ± .2148 |
| One-year after employment (N = 152) | | | | | | | | |
| Bureaucratic role conception | 19.35 | 2.57 | 18.13 | 2.77 | 18.27 | 3.55 | 2.23 | |
| Professional role conception | 29.63 | 2.63 | 30.58 | 3.55 | 30.13 | 3.88 | 0.91 | |
| Service role conception | 28.19 | 2.52 | 27.91 | 2.98 | 29.05 | 2.62 | 2.62 | |
| Bureaucratic role deprivation | 7.00 | 3.67 | 6.09 | 3.14 | 5.64 | 2.79 | 2.27 | |
| Professional role deprivation | 12.81 | 5.31 | 10.30 | 3.74 | 10.20 | 4.20 | 5.26† | 2.5649 ± .11 |
| Service role deprivation | 9.05 | 4.13 | 7.16 | 4.26 | 8.07 | 4.39 | 2.39 | |
| Total role deprivation | 28.86 | 10.54 | 23.55 | 9.48 | 23.91 | 9.59 | 4.21‡ | 5.1316 ± .65 |

°All Scheffé procedures were done on the difference between Class of 1968 mean and the combined means of Classes of 1969 and 1970.

†Sig. at >.05 level for df 3, 150; F value is 3.06.

‡Sig. at >.01 level for df 2, 150; F value is 4.75.

## Role deprivation work junction

A more important test of whether or not the Anticipatory Socialization program was effective in reducing role deprivation and corresponding reality shock was to look at the differences in the postemployment role deprivation scores of those who had had the program as compared with those who had not. It had been noted in the past that role deprivation scores increase markedly upon employment and that this increase is associated with reality shock symptoms and with "flight from nursing practice" behavior. Presumably, if the Anticipatory Socialization program were effective, the nurses would experience at least some of the shock and deprivation during the preservice socialization experience and not suddenly upon graduation. Therefore, the postemployment scores of those who had the Anticipatory Socialization program would show a drop from graduation when compared with those who had not had the program. The differences in mean role deprivation scores from graduation to one year after graduation are presented in Table 4-2.

There was a significant difference in the direction predicted for the nurses in the Classes of 1968 and 1970; for the nurses in the Class of 1969, the difference was in the direction predicted but was not significant. For the Class of 1968, professional role deprivation was the component that accounted for the increase in total role deprivation. For the Classes of 1969 and 1970, service role deprivation contributed most to the decrease in total role deprivation. This means that while their concept of the nurse role with regard to devotion and loyalty to the patient remained relatively unchanged from graduation to one year after employment, these nurses found conditions in actual practice *more* consonant with their service role conception than they had at graduation. This was an unexpected finding and one that had not been encountered in prior research. If this finding had also held for the Class of 1968, one possible explanation might have been the dominant emphasis on research and education with less on patient care that is prevalent in large medical center hospitals such as the one

**Table 4-2.** Significance of mean differences in BPS scores for nurses in Classes of 1968, 1969, and 1970 at graduation and after one year: paired t's°

| Scale | Class of 1968 (N = 43) | | | Class of 1969 (N = 53) | | | Class of 1970 (N = 56) | | |
|---|---|---|---|---|---|---|---|---|---|
| | $M_D$ | $O_{MD}$ | t | $M_D$ | $O_{MD}$ | t | $M_D$ | $O_{MD}$ | t |
| Bureaucratic role conception | 3.4418 | .4174 | 8.245† | 0.3208 | .7769 | .412 | 0.5730 | .3996 | 1.433 |
| Professional role conception | −0.6744 | .5394 | 1.250 | 0.3208 | .4232 | .758 | −0.4281 | .4008 | 1.068 |
| Service role conception | −0.6512 | .3659 | 1.779 | −0.5283 | .3946 | 1.338 | 0.0893 | .3867 | .230 |
| Bureaucratic role deprivation | 1.000 | .5687 | 1.758 | 0.0943 | .5450 | .173 | −0.6607 | .4982 | 1.326 |
| Professional role deprivation | 3.6744 | .8109 | 4.531† | 0.2830 | .6737 | .420 | −0.6071 | .6323 | .960 |
| Service role deprivation | 0.3953 | .8640 | .457 | −2.3962 | .7697 | 3.113† | −1.8750 | .7208 | 2.601‡ |
| Total role deprivation | 4.9767 | 1.7430 | 2.855‡ | −2.1132 | 1.4747 | 1.432 | −4.2678 | 1.4932 | 2.858† |

°Formula for paired t test: $\dfrac{M_D}{O_{MD}}$ where est. $O_{MD} = \sqrt{\dfrac{SD}{N-1}}$ . Hays, W. L.: Statistics for psychologists. New York, 1963, Holt, Rinehart & Winston, p. 335.

†Sig at >.01 level for 40 df on two-tailed test.

‡Sig at >.02 level for 40 df on two-tailed test.

in which these students had the bulk of their clinical practice. Perhaps the significant decrease in service role deprivation is somehow related to the assumption of a position in which the nurse feels as though she personally can implement practices advantageous to the patients, whereas in the student role she was hampered from doing so. It certainly was an interesting finding and one that awaits further study.

It can be said that the students who did not have the Anticipatory Socialization program experienced considerably more role deprivation, and presumably reality shock, upon employment than did the students in the Class of 1970 who did have the program. Hypothesis II is partially accepted.

The test of the second hypothesis was not completely satisfactory. One of the most immediate criticisms that comes to mind was that because the role deprivation scales have too low a ceiling the observed nurses reached the ceiling at graduation and could not show greater increase upon employment. This is true for some individuals. The role deprivation scales have a ceiling score of 88. Several of the students in the experimental group had almost reached that ceiling at the graduation testing; their postemployment test scores tended to remain at the same level. It is possible that if the test had had a higher ceiling the scores would have been higher and, consequently, the mean score of the experimental group would have been higher. It should be possible to get some clues as to whether or not this was the case by looking at these nurses as individuals. This was done, but unfortunately there was no discernible pattern. Of the six nurses in which the ceiling problem seemed to be occurring, two remained in the same place of employment for the entire two years of the followup study. They reported that they were "not necessarily content, but alive and happy and really doing something." This is verified by their employers who reported that they were "happy troublemakers who really care about patients and are always trying something new." It seems that these two are quite successful products of the Anticipatory Socialization program and psychologi-

cally are simply capable of tolerating a great deal more conflict and deprivation than the usual new graduate.

Three of the six nurses fit the expected picture and pattern. They had high role deprivation scores at graduation and the same high scores one year later. They held on to their graduation high professional scores, but lowered their graduation high bureaucratic scores, so that one year after employment they were low bureaucratic–high professional and high role deprivation. They were all still working, but two had become job hoppers, two were working in public health, and none reported themselves as being particularly happy with their jobs or with nursing. It must be concluded that the Anticipatory Socialization program was not effective in reducing their role deprivation.

Another cause for dissatisfaction is a possible boomerang effect—role deprivation scores went down because things were not as bad as the students had been led to believe.[1] This is a reality distortion in the opposite direction and is not necessarily desirable because some anxiety and challenge is necessary to develop integrative role behavior and to stimulate and motivate change.

### Job turnover and exodus junction

The rationale for this hypothesis was fairly straightforward. If an individual is happy in his work and feels he is making a contribution, he will stay in his job longer than someone who is not. It is a well-known fact that most nurses start out in hospital work and that many graduates, particularly collegiate graduate nurses, do not stay long. The average length of stay has been variously quoted. In a study done by Stanford of the nurses at Moffitt Hospital, which is the medical center hospital associated with the University of California School of Nursing in San Francisco, it was found that the average length of stay of staff nurses was six months.[2] Did the nurses in the experimental group remain in hospital work longer than the nurses in the control group?

This hypothesis was submitted to several tests. In the Class of 1968, all but eleven of the nurses chose hospital staff nursing as their initial work locale. Of the eleven, six started out in public health nursing, four were in doctors' offices or private duty, and one was in teaching. In the Class of 1969, all but five nurses chose hospital staff nursing as their initial position; the five began in public health. In the Class of 1970, seven chose public health or school nursing as their first job; all others went into hospital staff nursing. No matter what the setting of initial job choice, the tenure in the initial job should provide some indication of the nurses' relative degree of satisfaction with the job and with nursing. Tables 4-3, 4-4, and 4-5 show the dispersion

**Table 4-3.** Number and percent of graduates of 1968 according to tenure of initial job and stated reason for leaving: N = 43°

| Number of months in initial job | Still in initial job | | Returned to graduate school | | Left for voluntary reasons | | Left for involuntary reasons | | Total | |
|---|---|---|---|---|---|---|---|---|---|---|
| | NO. | PERCENT | NO. | PERCENT | NO. | PERCENT | NO. | PERCENT | NO. | PERCENT |
| 1-3 | 0 | 0.0 | 3 | 6.97 | 16 | 37.21 | 1 | 2.33 | 20 | 46.51 |
| 4-6 | 0 | 0.0 | 0 | 0.0 | 7 | 16.28 | 1 | 2.33 | 8 | 18.61 |
| 7-11 | 0 | 0.0 | 1 | 2.33 | 4 | 9.30 | 2 | 4.65 | 7 | 16.28 |
| 12-18 | 0 | 0.0 | 0 | 0.0 | 2 | 4.65 | 1 | 2.32 | 3 | 6.97 |
| 19-23 | 5 | 11.63 | 0 | 0.0 | 0 | 0.0 | 0 | 0.0 | 5 | 11.63 |
| Total | 5 | 11.63 | 4 | 9.30 | 29 | 67.44 | 5 | 11.63 | 43 | 100.00 |

°Two members of the Class of 1968 have not worked since graduation.

**Table 4-4.** Number and percent of graduates of 1969 according to tenure of initial job and stated reason for leaving: N = 55°

| Number of months in initial job | Still in initial job | | Returned to graduate school | | Left for voluntary reasons | | Left for involuntary reasons | | Total | |
|---|---|---|---|---|---|---|---|---|---|---|
| | NO. | PERCENT | NO. | PERCENT | NO. | PERCENT | NO. | PERCENT | NO. | PERCENT |
| 1-3 | 0 | 0.0 | 5 | 9.09 | 0 | 0.0 | 1 | 1.82 | 6 | 10.91 |
| 4-6 | 0 | 0.0 | 0 | 0.0 | 2 | 3.64 | 0 | 0.0 | 2 | 3.64 |
| 7-11 | 2† | 3.64 | 0 | 0.0 | 2 | 3.64 | 2 | 3.63 | 6 | 10.91 |
| 12-18 | 2† | 3.64 | 4 | 7.27 | 8 | 14.54 | 7 | 12.73 | 21 | 38.18 |
| 19-23 | 18‡ | 32.72 | 0 | 0.0 | 1 | 1.82 | 1 | 1.82 | 20 | 36.36 |
| Total | 22 | 40.00 | 9 | 16.36 | 13 | 23.64 | 11 | 20.00 | 55 | 100.00 |

°Two members of the Class of 1969 have not worked since graduation.
†Three members of this class went directly into graduate school, so their initial employment began after M.S. Graduation; one graduate did not work for 13 months after graduation.
‡Analysis was done at two-year postgraduation anniversary. Within three months after that date three members of this class left their initial place of employment and returned to graduate school.

**Table 4-5.** Number and percent of graduates of 1970 according to tenure of initial job and stated reason for leaving: N = 59°

| Number of months in initial job | Still in initial job | | Returned to graduate school | | Left for voluntary reasons | | Left for involuntary reasons | | Total | |
|---|---|---|---|---|---|---|---|---|---|---|
| | NO. | PERCENT | NO. | PERCENT | NO. | PERCENT | NO. | PERCENT | NO. | PERCENT |
| 1-3 | 0 | 0.0 | 0 | 0.0 | 3 | 5.08 | 0 | 0.0 | 3 | 5.08 |
| 4-6 | 0 | 0.0 | 0 | 0.0 | 3 | 5.08 | 4 | 6.78 | 7 | 11.86 |
| 7-11 | 2° | 3.39 | 2 | 3.39 | 3 | 5.08 | 1 | 1.69 | 8 | 13.56 |
| 12-18 | 0 | 0.0 | 1 | 1.69 | 8 | 13.56 | 7 | 11.86 | 16 | 27.12 |
| 19-23 | 23° | 38.98 | 0 | 0.0 | 1 | 1.69 | 1 | 1.69 | 25 | 42.37 |
| Total | 25 | 42.37 | 3 | 5.08 | 18 | 30.51 | 13 | 22.03 | 59 | 100.00 |

°One nurse was working part time in each group.

of the graduates from the Classes of 1968, 1969, and 1970 at the two-year postemployment followup. A chi square $(\chi^2)$ determination of the number of nurses in each class according to the number of months working in initial job (the total columns of each table) was significant at greater than the .05 level. Significantly more nurses in the classes of 1969 and 1970 remained longer in their initial jobs than did the nurses in the Class of 1968. The most marked difference was the fact that almost 50% of the nurses in the Class of 1968 changed jobs between one and three months after starting them, while over 60% of the nurses in the other two classes remained in their initial jobs for periods of one to two years. This finding is highly important based on the one notion that a person must remain in a position for at least some extended period of time in order to develop social power and exert influence.

It is also important to look at reasons for job changes. Coupling a nurse's given reasons for leaving her initial job with place of residence, it was possible to evolve two distinct categories. *Voluntary job change* was any change in which the nurse subsequently took another job in the same city without changing her place of residence, one in which an unmarried nurse stated that she was free to travel anywhere she wished, or one in which a nurse left a job for which a nurse's license was required for one where it was not required. *Involuntary job changes* mainly were for marriage or because a husband was transferred although, particularly for the Class of 1970, this also included job layoffs or terminations due to lack of financial support for projects. If the data in Tables 4-3, 4-4, and 4-5 are analyzed according to voluntary and involuntary reasons for change from initial job, another significant difference between classes emerges. More members of the Class of 1968 left their initial job voluntarily than did nurses in the other two classes. Two-thirds of the members of the Class of 1968, as compared with about one fourth of the members of the other two classes, left their jobs for voluntary reasons. Coupling high voluntary job turnover with low tenure on initial job

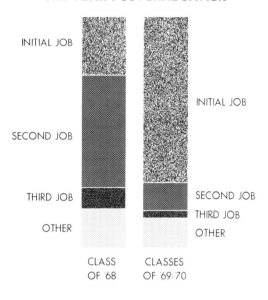

## NUMBER OF JOB CHANGES AT ONE YEAR POSTGRADUATION

CLASS OF '68

CLASSES OF '69-70

would lend support to the inference that the nurses in the Classes of 1969 and 1970 were less dissatisfied with nursing and with their jobs in nursing than the nurses in the Class of 1968.

To fully test this hypothesis, it is not enough to look at tenure in initial job or reasons for leaving. The extent of movement over time is also of importance. The figures above and on the following page illustrate the number of job changes of the nurses in the three classes from the time of graduation to one and two years postemployment. Analyses indicated that there were marked differences between the classes. Significantly more of the nurses in the Classes of 1969 and 1970 remained in their initial jobs longer than did those in the Class of 1968, and they did significantly less job hopping at the two-year period than did the control class. Only one nurse in each of the experimental classes held four jobs, as compared with five in the Class of 1968.

Another factor of difference is that by the time of the second year postemployment followup six nurses from the Class of 1968 were working in or preparing for occupations outside of nursing. No members of the other two classes were doing so. As of this writing, eight

## NUMBER OF JOB CHANGES AT TWO YEAR POSTGRADUATION

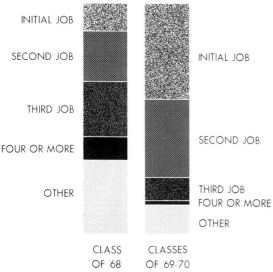

INITIAL JOB

SECOND JOB

THIRD JOB

FOUR OR MORE

OTHER

INITIAL JOB

SECOND JOB

THIRD JOB
FOUR OR MORE

OTHER

CLASS OF '68    CLASSES OF '69-70

members of the Class of 1968, none in the Class of 1969, and one in the Class of 1970 are now employed or studying outside of nursing.

Coupling these two factors—the frequent job hopping and the beginning exodus from nursing practice—we begin to see a pattern for the Class of 1968 similar to that uncovered in the nationwide medical center sample of nurses studied. In that sample, those nurses who withdrew from nursing practice for reasons of dissatisfaction (labeled dropouts) had a mean number of job changes during a two-year period of 4 as compared with 2.7 for nondropouts. It would seem, then, that the Class of 1968 was well on its way to verifying this observed pattern, while the nurses in the Classes of 1969 and 1970 appeared to be heading for a more stable work pattern.

Hypothesis III stated that more of the nurses who had had the Anticipatory Socialization program would remain in hospital work two years after graduation than those who did not. The rationale for this was that if the Anticipatory Socialization program were effective the nurses would have learned how to get along, how to make changes, how to influence and make a contribution, and how to constructively manage conflict. If they did this they would not have to initiate flight behavior, or at least not as often as those who did not have the program. This hypothesis was upheld. The nurses in the classes that had the Anticipatory Socialization program remained in their initial jobs longer, remained in hospital nursing longer, did less job hopping, and had fewer job changes for voluntary reasons than did the nurses in the control Class of 1968.

Although not as complete data is available because of limitations in time and money, it appears that the nurses who graduated from the Class of 1971 will follow in the same kind of pattern as the Class of 1968. This was expected since they did not have the Anticipatory Socialization program. As of one-year postgraduation followup, three of the gradu-

## GRADUATES WORKING OUT OF NURSING

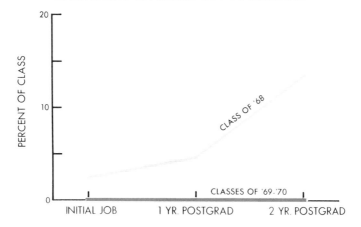

## GRADUATES WORKING IN HOSPITALS

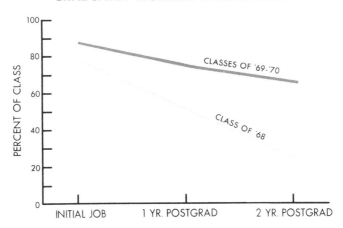

ates of this class have left nursing; over half are already in their second or third job.

Although not hypothesized, there was another aspect of job choice and movement that became evident in studying the career patterns of these three classes of nurses. More nurses in both of the experimental classes had job transfers, that is, same organization but assignment to a different ward or unit, than did the nurses in the Class of 1968 (Appendix C, Table C-7). Job transfers within an institution may be one possible way of managing conflict. This was borne out by the comments from some of the nurses when questioned as to why they had requested job transfers.

There was no point in running away. Things weren't going too well, so I thought if I'd work on another ward for a little while until I could regroup myself that I could then return to 4 East and do a better job. I think I kind of made a fool of myself ranting and raving. I wanted to get away from it for awhile. (NG:BS/6[703]10/70)

•  •  •

My reason for asking for a transfer? I was beginning to get a bit bored. But I know a lot of the ropes here. I know how to get things done. It seemed I could make more of an influence by staying here but getting some new kind of stimulation, which is what I wanted, by getting a transfer. It's worked out fine. I can use what I've learned to get the job done, but I have the stimulation of a whole new field opening up. It also kind of gives you a second chance with some of the people re-

lationships that you might have bungled the first time. (NG:BS/12[918]6/70)

There is a great deal more that needs to be explored in this area; both nurse practitioners and nursing service administration might keep this possibility in mind.

Before the results of Hypotheses IV and V are presented, there is a problem with the statement of Hypothesis III that needs to be pointed out and discussed: it lacks clarity and definitiveness. Simply predicting that the effectiveness of the Anticipatory Socialization program would be measurable by the number of nurses who remained in hospital work two years after graduation does not take into account the work pattern of the nurses (or the potential trajectory) during those two years. For example, according to the way the hypothesis was originally stated, the Anticipatory Socialization program would have been considered to be equally as effective for a nurse who remained in the same hospital job for the entire two years as for a nurse who changed jobs four times during those two years but was in hospital work at the time of the two-year checkup. Through study, knowledge, and experience gained from the research process during the period from inception of the hypothesis in 1964 and testing in 1972, I realized that it was not retention in hospital work as such that was the variable of interest. Rather it was the length of time in any kind of nursing position, and particularly whether the career pattern indicated flight from hospital nursing as the usual conflict resolution pattern. Although this lack of early and definitive hypothesis statement was troublesome, the following conclusion related to the idea of this hypothesis is well supported. Nurses who had the Anticipatory Socialization program had more stable career patterns two years after graduation as manifested by less job hopping, fewer voluntary job changes, longer retention in their initial jobs, and less flight from hospital nursing behavior than did the nurses who did not have the Anticipatory Socialization Program. Hypothesis III is accepted.

### Integrative role behavior junction

This hypothesis stated that those nurses who had had the Anticipatory Socialization program would report higher integrative role behavior scores after employment than would those who had not had the program. This relationship was predicted on the basis that if people are vicariously exposed to conflicts and constructive conflict resolution they will develop similar means of resolve when they subsequently find themselves in conflict situations. Having developed these kinds of strategies, they would select them when confronted with a written test designed to elicit choice behavior.

Integrative role behavior was defined as an effective compromise between behavioral choices that clearly support professional values and those that clearly reflect allegiance to bureaucratic values. They are the kinds of behaviors that a nurse who is attempting to operationalize professional values in a bureaucratic setting would choose. Inferentially, the use of integrative role behaviors permits the assumption that some degree of growth-producing conflict resolution behavior and biculturalism was taking place.

The role behavior scales consisted of a series of seven conflict situations in which the respondent was asked to state the extent to which she would elect to enact certain behaviors (p. 54).

A potential problem of exposure and memory in the validity of the role behavior scales was recognized from the onset, and measures were taken to eliminate or at least control this as a possible source of error. The nurses in the Anticipatory Socialization program simply had more exposure to and practice in managing conflict situations, at least on a vicarious level. Furthermore, it was desired that the conflict situations on the role behavior test be real ones drawn from actual conflicts as reported by practicing nurses. Care had to be taken not to expose the students in the Anticipatory Socialization program to the same conflict situations they would encounter on the test, or the test would have become a memory test rather than a test of behavior choice. To avoid this, all summer, evening, and leadership seminars were tape recorded, and an index was made of the kind and substance of conflict situations discussed. When the role behavior scales were to be developed, only the broad outlines of the conflict situations to be developed were sketched. These then were illustrated with actual conflict situations taken directly from the verbatim typescripts of some of the medical center interviews, making sure that none of the examples chosen were the ones that had been presented to or discussed in any of the seminars. The research assistant on this project, who did not teach any of the Anticipatory Socialization program, was then urged to select other examples of conflict situations, or modify some of those already selected, for use in the role behavior scales. It was then judged that the role behavior scales were free of investigator bias toward inclusion of conflict situations presented and discussed in the Anticipatory Socialization program.

As an additional step to mitigate the memory factor and increase the probability that differences noted between the control and experimental classes were due to real differences in conflict management, rather than sheer exposure and recall of conflict situations from the Anticipatory Socialization program, it was decided at the time the study was designed that the role behavior scales would not be administered until the very end of the study (two years after employment). It was judged that the memory factor would be quite diluted by then, if indeed it were still operative at all.

Was there a difference in reported integrative role behavior choices to conflict situations between the two groups of nurses? The control Class of 1968 had a mean role behavior score of 44.10, while the combined mean of the two experimental classes was 46.93 (high mean indicates high choice of integrative role behaviors). Analysis indicated that this was a significant difference (Appendix C, Table C-8). It was therefore concluded that the nurses who had had the Anticipatory Socialization program selected more integrative behavior choices to conflict situations two years after graduation than did those who had not had the program. Hypothesis IV was accepted.

### Professional loyalty and behavior junction

This hypothesis stated that those nurses who had had the Anticipatory Socialization program would retain and profess more loyalty to the professional system of work organization after employment than would those nurses who had not had the program. In prior research it had been established that upon employment new graduate nurses attempt to hold onto their professional ideals while at the same time raising their loyalty to the bureaucratic work system. When this occurs, marked conflict results and role deprivation is reported. One way, and in fact the usual way of resolving the conflict and mitigating the discomfort accompanying the conflict, is to abdicate professional values. There is evidence to support the contention that the longer one practices nursing the less one's loyalty to professional work principles remains.

The purpose of this study was two-pronged.

Allaying conflict and reality shock was one goal that could be achieved quite readily. By training the nurses of tomorrow in the part-task bureaucratic work system, little conflict between the training environment and work would be encountered. The second goal is what makes achievement of the first one difficult. The desire was for the nurses to confront and manage the expected conflict situations in a growth-producing manner, in a way such that they would not abdicate their professional values. The goal was not the fusion or absorption of professional values but their retention and operationalization in a whole new way—a way in which the new graduate was not bound to either rigid bureaucratic or professional responses but was free to respond in a creative way to meet the unique situational demands.

The hypothesis that the anticipatorily socialized nurses would retain greater professional loyalty than those not anticipatorily socialized was tested in several ways. Scores of the nurses on the Corwin professional role conception scales one year after employment were analyzed. Comparisons of the two groups on the professional component of the role behavior scales taken two years after employment were also made. These data are presented in Table 4-6. Analyses indicate that there were no significant differences between the Class of 1968 and the combined Classes of 1969 and 1970 on either of these measures. Although the experimental classes had a higher mean professional role conception score (30.35 as compared with 29.63), the difference was not statistically significant. The same was true of the performance of the two groups on the

**Table 4-6.** Significance of differences in mean professional role conception and professional role behavior scores of nurses one and two years after graduation: ANOVA

| Scale | SS | df | MS | F |
|---|---|---|---|---|
| Professional role conception one year after graduation | | | | |
|   Variance between classes | 21.78 | 2 | 10.89 | |
|   Variance within classes | 1775.04 | 149 | 11.91 | 0.91 |
|   Total | 1796.82 | 151 | | |
| Professional role behavior two years after graduation | | | | |
|   Variance between classes | 21.11 | 2 | 10.55 | |
|   Variance within classes | 3119.65 | 145 | 21.51 | 0.4906 |
|   Total | 3140.76 | 147 | | |

professional role behavior scales a year later. The mean score of 34.07 for the Class of 1968 was not significantly different from the mean score of 33.89 for the combined Classes of 1969 and 1970.

Since the hypothesis stated that there would be a retention in professional values over time, it was considered desirable to look at what happened from graduation to one year after employment. Was there a loss or gain in loyalty to the professional system? Here again, the picture is pretty much the same. Table 4-1 on p. 106 shows that although the Class of 1968 had some decrease in professional role conception scores from graduation to a year later, neither the difference for this class nor the small amounts of difference in the two experimental classes were significant. This was not as expected, nor was it in line with my findings in the earlier study of baccalaureate nurses from the California State College nursing programs or Hogan's 1972 cross-sectional sample of collegiate nurses. Apparently some factor was operating to help these nurses retain their professional loyalties. It was expected that the Anticipatory Socialization program would help the nurses in the group that had it, but an explanation is wanting for the nurses in the Class of 1968. The only possibility that can be proffered is that their high withdrawal rate from nursing practice and their very frequent job hopping helped them to hold onto their professional values longer than anticipated.

Loyalty to the professional system of work can be retained and expressed in ways other than scores on written tests. Although leaving nursing practice in pursuit of graduate education may be evidence of maladjustment and unresolved conflict, it can also be regarded as a manifestation of greater involvement and commitment to one's profession. Analysis of the number and percentage of graduates from all classes, according to the time of their return for graduate education in nursing during the two years of postgraduation followup, indicated few differences (Appendix C, Table C-9).

A major problem encountered was that this research, concerned as it was with a compre-hensive picture of the possible relationship between a specifically planned education program and a variety of attitudes and career behaviors, opened onto a vista of concern so wide that a thorough examination and measurement of each variable was staggering in scope. Most previous studies had focused on professionalism as a criterion variable from only a unitary, usually indirect perspective, that is, a self-reported scale of some type. This study did that in looking at the role conception and role behavior scale scores, but it also attempted to take into account a wide range of other relevant factors. The questions of concern were: Did the nurses who had the Anticipatory Socialization program behave and act more professionally? How could this be determined? Were they able to influence others more effectively than the nurses who had not had the program? It was decided to limit the vista of concern to four specific areas: (1) a variable called professionalism, composed of commonly agreed upon behavioral indices of professional people, (2) change agent activity, (3) the degree of self-actualization of the nurses as measured by performance on a psychological test, and (4) a variable called empathic ability, a proxy for interpersonal competence. These four plus the role conception and role behavior scale scores already reported comprise the test of the fifth hypothesis.

*Were they professional?* A necessary attribute of any profession is a lifelong commitment of its members to continued learning. The latter can be defined as any event or process in which an individual undertakes voluntarily, alone or in groups, to increase his knowledge, skill, or sensitivity. This attribute is of particular importance in an occupational group, such as nursing, in which members are deeply involved in a struggle to upgrade not only their practice but also the contribution their practice can make to the betterment of mankind through improved health care and maintenance. Technological advancement, the rapid increase in scientific knowledge, and the shortened time lapse between scientific discovery and clinical application have made it imperative for nurses to engage in continued learning. Nursing leaders have long recognized and repeatedly stressed the importance of commitment to continued learning for nurses. In the construction of an index of professionalism, the following kinds of activities, judged to represent commitment to continued learning, were included: enrollment in professional courses, subscription to professional journals, purchase of professional books, and numbers of hours per week devoted to professional reading.

In most industrial societies, the voluntary associations of professional groups play an influential role in helping to shape policy and opinion, both of society and of their own members. Furthermore, these voluntary professional associations are the source of professional stimulation and sharing as well as collegial support and validation. Wilensky notes that the rise of professional organizations is one of the first and most influential factors in the emergence of a profession. For these reasons, membership in the American Nurses' Association and other professional organizations such as the National League for Nurses or Sigma Theta Tau, offices held, and extent of attendance at meetings and activities were also included in the Index of Professionalism.

Other criteria used in the Professional Index were selected on the basis that they have been included in other indexes and are generally considered to reflect professional activity. These criteria included publications in professional journals, speeches on health-related issues to professional and lay groups, and participation on committees within the employing organization that have as their goal the advancement of professional behavior and activity.

The final Index of Professionalism and weighting of the factors on the Index was described on pp. 56-57 of Chapter 2. The data needed to classify the nurses in both the experimental and control groups on the factors of this Index were obtained from a mail questionnaire completed by the nurses at the one-year postemployment followup. Confirmation of intraorganizational committee activity was forthcoming from interviews held with the nurses' supervisors and co-workers. An Index score was obtained for each nurse individually by scoring her on each factor and then summing all factors. Total possible Index of Professionalism score was 29, with a high score indicating more professional behavior than a low score.

Was there a difference in the Index of Professionalism scores between the nurses who

**Table 4-7.** Number and percentage of nurses in classes according to Professional Index

| Professional Index score | Class of 1968 (N = 43) | | Class of 1969 (N = 53) | | Class of 1970 (N = 55) | |
|---|---|---|---|---|---|---|
| | NO. | PERCENT | NO. | PERCENT | NO. | PERCENT |
| 0-1 | 7 | 16.28 | 5 | 9.43 | 2 | 3.64 |
| 2-3 | 7 | 16.28 | 9 | 16.98 | 8 | 14.54 |
| 4-5 | 12 | 27.91 | 12 | 22.64 | 13 | 23.64 |
| 6-7 | 9 | 20.93 | 7 | 13.21 | 10 | 18.18 |
| 8-9 | 5 | 11.63 | 7 | 13.21 | 7 | 12.73 |
| 10-11 | 0 | 0.0 | 2 | 3.78 | 8 | 14.54 |
| 12-13 | 3 | 6.97 | 4 | 7.55 | 4 | 7.27 |
| 14-15 | 0 | 0.0 | 2 | 3.77 | 2 | 3.64 |
| 16-17 | 0 | 0.0 | 3 | 5.66 | 0 | 0.0 |
| 18-19 | 0 | 0.0 | 2 | 3.77 | 1 | 1.82 |

| Between classes | Mann-Whitney U | Rank sums | Probability (1-tailed test) |
|---|---|---|---|
| 1968-1969 | 935.50 | 1884.50 | .06 |
| 1968-1970 | 860.00 | 1806.00 | .01 |
| 1969-1970 | 1355.00 | 2786.00 | .26 |

had had the Anticipatory Socialization program and those who had not? The results are presented in Table 4-7.[3]

Analysis showed that the nurses in the Class of 1970 had significantly higher (U = 860.0) Professional Index scores than the nurses in the Class of 1968. The difference score for the nurses in the Class of 1969 approached the criterion level of .05; there was no significant difference between the Classes of 1969 and 1970 on this variable.

Before proceeding to the results of the next test of this hypothesis, perhaps a word is in order about the professionalism of nurses in general as measured by performance on the criteria of this Professional Index. If we view these 151 nurses as a microcosm of all new graduate nurses, how healthy is the state of the profession? Nursing looks fairly good when it comes to taking courses. A large number of the courses taken by the nurses were ICU and CCU courses given by the employing organizations, usually during on-duty time, but over half of the nurses taking courses took them on their own time away from work.

There apparently has been some improvement in the amount of time nurses spend in professional reading per week. Compared with the 1963 Habenstein and Christ and 1967 Simms reports, there are more nurses reading professionally now than a decade ago (for example, 87% nonreaders in 1963 as compared with 37% in this sample). Interpretation of the results of involvement and frequency of participation in professional organizations of this group of nurses must be viewed in respect to involvement of nurses in general and as compared with other professionals. In 1969 less than one third of the nation's employed nurses were members of their national professional organization (American Nurses' Association). This figure has remained pretty much the same since then and can be compared with the fact than 43% of the nurses in this sample reported that they belonged to their professional organization. However, when compared with other professional groups (even professional groups like teachers, who are also considered to be semiprofessional), this is a very poor showing. Professional organization membership in other professional groups generally ranges from 75% to 98%.

*Did they effect any changes?* The primary objective of this research was to help new graduate nurses retain their professional idealism and be functional and interpersonally competent within bureaucratic work settings. To do this, they had to become operative and successful change agents. One of the major premises in the selection of change activity as a measure of operationalization of professional values was that successful influence via change activity is indicative of one's effective functioning within a social system. It is an indication that a person has come to grips with the human side of the organization, has an active commitment and involvement in that aspect of the health care system associated with his job, cares enough to work within the system to change it.

A change activity was defined as an attempt to influence one or more people in a desired and preplanned direction. One measure of the effectiveness of change agent activity was the knowledge other people have of the change attempted. If no one else is cognizant of having been influenced by you or cognizant that you have tried to influence others, then either you have not been attempting to influence or else the influence has not been effective.

Considerable attention is directed toward preparation of change agents in the professional education of many new graduates. It is probably safe to assume that this is an almost universal goal of nursing education. This goal usually is implemented through lecture and discussion of the principles of change, the ways, steps, and procedures in effecting change, and so on. Sometimes students are encouraged or assigned to enact change agent activity in the clinical setting. Seldom, however, is clinical change agent activity modeled for them by their instructors. To be an effective change agent model, one must be involved in and be an integral part of the work setting and have social power and influence. Since most nursing instructors are not an integral part of the work setting and seldom have this kind of power, they are unable to model change activity for the students.

The Anticipatory Socialization program described in Chapter 3 contained some principles of change agent theory, but rather than teaching change agent principles in their theoretical purity, the main focus was on extension of the principles into lines of action, into pragmatic strategies for doing. One of the premises was that to be an effective change agent one needed both knowledge and skills; one needed to be able to predict the actions and reactions of others in situations; one needed to know the principles of work organization of the bureaucratic system to be able to exert influence within that system. Formalized theoretical input was important but useless without actual or vicarious exposure and modeling of practical and realistic ways in which the theory could be made operational. To accomplish this, the experiences of the medical center reference group nurses were used. The following field notes exemplify how this type of change agent activity was taught. They are taken from one of the tape-recorded seminars of the Anticipatory Socialization program.

The group had been discussing how one went about getting things done or making changes when the immediate supervisor was a block. They had described from their own experiences numerous ways in which supervisors could and did block—either directly by saying "No," indirectly by withholding necessary information that you would need to proceed, or by playing the waiting game: "We'll see" or "I'll ask so and so about it," and then never doing it. The seminar leader had also introduced the problem of premature commitment and how difficult it was to back down, retreat, or reverse direction without losing face once a commitment has been made. This latter concept was difficult for these young students to understand and accept since it was quite foreign to their ideal of open and complete honesty in interpersonal relations. After discussing it for awhile they decided that, at least for some people, this was a personal value they would have to accept and work with in order to effect change. The Asch research in this area helped considerably in getting the group to understand this point

since much of this research had used college-age students as subjects.

After more discussion of how one goes about getting some change through an obdurate or blocking supervisor, the group asked for a concrete example. As one girl said, "Our instructors are always talking about this and we know the theory, but I've never seen anyone really do it."

The following incident was presented to the students as an example, as related by a reference group nurse who was head nurse in a 30-bed pediatric unit at the time of this interview.

What did I do? You mean about getting the nursing office to go along with the home visit? [Yes.] Well, it was kind of a long process. We'd all [the staff on the pediatric unit] decided that this is what we wanted to do, that those kids coming in for open-hearts and their folks really weren't getting enough information and they couldn't *hear* us when we tried to explain things to them after they got here. The best thing was for us to go out and visit them before they came into the hospital for the surgery. The surgeons and pediatricians thought this was a great idea and said: "Go to it." They even offered to go see [Mrs. X, the DNS] for us, but I knew that that was a power play that would leave a bad taste in her mouth. I also felt pretty sure that [DNS] wouldn't be the stumbling block. She seemed pretty much on the ball every time I've talked with her. She doesn't know much about patient care, but she knows that she doesn't and doesn't try and pretend. She's reasonable and I really thought if I could explain it to her logically and rationally that she'd go along with letting us make home visits on duty time. We figured from past experience, you know, that the real problem was [Mrs. Y, the supervisor]. She's very negative, against everything. I know I'm probably exaggerating, but that's the way she seems to me. Everything I ask her—Can I do this? Can we have medicuts? Can the diet kitchen serve smaller portions of food to the kids?—everything is a real big deal. [What happens when you ask her?] Oh, she doesn't usually say "No" right off. She puts me off for a couple of weeks, and every time I bug her about it she comes up with a reason why we can't do it or a "We'll see" thing. Ideas die aborning with her. You can never quite say that she's opposed to things, but that's the way it comes out.

[So what did you do about this home visit idea?]

Well, I decided that it would be a real delaying action to go through [Mrs. Y.] but yet she's my supervisor and that's the way you're supposed to do it. Besides, if I went directly to [DNS] it would sort of put both her and [supervisor] on the spot. So one day I casually mentioned to my supervisor that I had read about this, and what did she think about it—sort of in the abstract, not telling her how far we already were in the planning of it: you know, what I told you earlier about how we'd worked out with [the doctor's] office nurse to call us about one month before an open-heart was scheduled and so on. [Yes, I remember. What was the supervisor's reaction?] In the abstract, I'd found that she's more open to ideas. She asked some questions and said that that sounded like a good idea, but that of course it must require a lot of coordination, and you'd have this problem to work out and that one and so on. I just listened and sort of tried to end the conversation by getting her to repeat again that she thought it was a good idea—sort of on a positive note, you know. And then I particularly tried to remember some of her exact words—the positive ones, the ones in favor of the idea. [Yes, then what?] Well, here's where we got sneaky—but it worked! Jill [ward secretary on pediatrics] is a good friend of [Mrs. Z., the secretary in the nursing office]. You know, they have lunch together and that sort of thing. Well, we set it up so that [secretary] would call Jill when [DNS] was going to go to the dining room for coffee. This took a little doing because she didn't go every day, and lots of times she'd have some visitors with her. We had to get her alone or with just one other person with her. Well, after several attempts we finally made it. The idea was that as soon as we knew she was going to coffee a couple of us would dash down the back steps and get either in front or in back of her in the coffee line. We sandwiched her in between Carol and I and started very casually, you know, started telling her about the patients, and about Joey—you know, the little boy with the open-heart I was telling you about—and we kept up a steady conversation so that she really had no choice but to sit down and have coffee with us. So, we started in and told her about the idea, and I told her that I had talked with [the supervisor]. I didn't tell her exactly what I said or what Jan had said, just that I had talked with her about it. I could see she was really "go." Well about that time, we spied [supervisor] coming into the dining room and we knew we had to take care of that problem or we'd get all kinds of blocks thrown up

before we got started. So Carol dashed over and invited [supervisor] to have coffee with us. I even bought [DNS] another cup of coffee so she wouldn't leave. When [supervisor] sits down, I open things up by saying: "We've been talking about that idea I talked with you about the other day—you remember, the floor nurses making preoperative visits on the children scheduled for open-heart surgery." Then I went right on and said that [DNS] thought it was a good idea, and then I looked right at [supervisor] and quoted some of the positive things she had said when I talked to her. Well, she was sort of trapped. She could hardly disagree when her boss was so enthusiastic about the idea and when I made it sound like she also had approved of the idea when I had talked with her earlier. Carol and I made sure that before we finished coffee we not only had permission but that it was understood we were going to make the first visit on Friday. I think they were kind of impressed with all the arrangements and plans we had already worked out.

It can readily be seen that this example provided opportunity for extensive discussion, not only of change agent theory but, most important, of pragmatic modes of operationalizing it.

Another seldom discussed aspect considered in the seminar is the unique and individualistic abilities and limitations of each person in developing an effective change agent style of operation. Some can do the kind of thing the nurse in the above sample did; others do not have that kind of personality and must work out different modes of operation.

Since it was judged possible to test the fifth hypothesis by looking at change agent activity, the question now is: Were there any differences in the scope and effectiveness of change agent activity for the nurses who had the Anticipatory Socialization program when compared with those who did not?

One year after employment, all nurses in the three classes were contacted for an interview. They were also asked to arrange for their head nurse and a co-worker of their choice to also be interviewed briefly. During these tape-recorded interviews a question was asked as to whether there have been "any new things or projects or approaches which (nurse subject) has tried to get going." (Because of some negative connotation or a possible "halo" effect occasioned just by mention of the word, it was judged desirable not to use the words change agent or change.) Subsequent probes were designed to elicit details such as the degree of success of the project, how many followers it had, or things that were attempted but were not successful.

The change agent data thus elicited, plus any other change agent data that came out spontaneously or in response to other questions in the interview schedule, were analyzed along three major categorical dimensions. The first category was the *nature* of the change itself, as distinguished from the process of bringing about the change. Nature of change was defined in terms of the goal or objective of the change:

1. Attitudinal change: to bring about a change in someone's attitude (patient groups, physician, nurse, administration).
2. Technical change: to introduce a change in some technical aspect of work such as introducing a new intravaneous clamp or a new dressing tray.
3. Informational change: to bring about a knowledge increase or correction of erroneous knowledge to a patient, physician, other staff.
4. Procedural change: to bring about a change in routine or policy such as the hours for giving medications or new Kardex procedures.
5. Environmental change: to bring about some alteration or improvement in the environment of the patients or staff, such as deroaching the coffee area or getting the volunteers to paint murals in the pediatric ward.

The second category, *effectiveness of change agent activity*, was concerned with the degree of goal accomplishment, that is, whether others followed the change suggestion, the length of time it was in effect, and whether the nurse persisted in the face of resistance. Dimensions identified were:

1. Change seemed to be stabilizing. Others followed her. Nurse judged it highly effective and head nurse or co-worker did also.

2. Others followed her suggestions and change agent activity. It has been in effect for over one month. The nurse judged the change to be effective.
3. The change was effective for less than one month, then was reversed or substantially altered.
4. There were some alliances or followers of the change activity, but resistance was at a high level and change never really got through.
5. Resistance was encountered at all levels, but some concerted action was made by the nurse. She didn't give up without trying.

The last category of analysis, *recipient of change agent activity* was concerned with identification of the benefactor of the change. This was not necessarily who the nurse worked with to bring about the change, but who was going to directly benefit from the change. The possible parameters identified here were:

1. Employee or staff centered: The direct benefactors of the change are fellow staff members, physicians, and so forth. This could be on a unit or total agency level. Example: teaching the nurse's aides how to take blood pressures.
2. Environment centered: Expected result of the change is improved working conditions for the staff. Can be on a unit or total agency level. Example: replacement of hooks to hang isolation gowns.
3. System centered—unit: Expected result is a policy or a program change for the ward, unit, or immediate working area. Benefactors are patients or groups of patients, but the effect is indirect, that is, through a policy, routine, or procedure change. Example: taking temperatures later in the morning so patients get more rest. This is more general; it is based on a principle (sick people need rest) rather than a response to specific identified patient problems.
4. System centered—hospital or agency: Same as No. 3 except that expected change affects a department, several wards, or the whole hospital or agency. Example: initiating a change in the hours

and procedure for discharging patients.

5. Patient centered: The direct benefactor of the change is an individual patient. Examples: hanging bright-colored curtains around children's beds to cheer them up; procuring pediatric urine collection bags to replace the colostomy bags now used for urine collection.

The analysis of the typescripts for all dimensions of change agent activity was done by two nurse coders not previously associated with the project and who were not aware of the purpose of the study or the hypotheses. Typescripts were coded with numbers known only by me. The typescripts for the nurses in the various classes were deliberately mixed up before being submitted to the coders. Each of them was trained in the classification protocol; training sessions were held until the coder felt comfortable in doing the task. They worked independently, classifying and coding all change agent activities identified in each typescript. Points of discrepancy in the coding format were clarified. Most of the discrepancy was due to instances in which the information on the typescript was incomplete or vague. Using a stratified random sample of 33% of the typescripts from each class, the two coders, working independently, agreed on the following percentages of the change incidents:

| | |
|---|---|
| Nature of the change | 96% agreement |
| Effectiveness of change agent activity | 87% agreement |
| Recipient of change agent activity | 90% agreement |

The coders reported little difficulty in identifying change incidents or activities from the typescripts or in classifying them into unit changes (a change centered or located on a single or specific unit) and agency changes (attempts at influence that were directed beyond the local station or area of assignment). For the 32 nurses interviewed in the Class of 1968 a total of 33 change activities were identified; for the Class of 1969 there were 113 change activities; and for the Class of 1970 there were 127 change activities. There were no differences among the classes in respect to proportion of unit and agency changes. For all classes, it was about a 70:30 split in favor of unit changes.

Table 4-8 summarizes the sources of reported change agent activities. There was more than one change activity identified in the typescripts of some of the nurses. Classification into source category was done on the basis of at least half of the changes identified in the typescript of the interview with the nurse being verified by comments in the typescripts with the head nurse and co-workers.

Analysis of these data indicate that there was a significant relationship between class membership and source of reported change agent activity. The relationship exceeds chance expectations in two areas. There were more nurses from the Class of 1968 and fewer nurses from the Class of 1970 in the "No change activity reported" category than would be expected by chance. The second area in which findings exceeded chance was the number of nurses in the Class of 1968 whose change activities were not reported or verified by head nurses or co-workers. This was a particularly meaningful finding since it was in this area that the difference was expected between the nurses who had had the Anticipatory Socialization program and those who

**Table 4-8.** Number and percent of nurses' change agent activities according to the source of the report of the activity

| | Class of 1968 (N = 32) | | Class of 1969 (N = 42) | | Class of 1970 (N = 54) | |
|---|---|---|---|---|---|---|
| Change activity reported by graduate only | 11 | 34.37 | 11 | 26.19 | 22 | 40.74 |
| Change activity verified or reported by head nurse or co-worker | 7 | 21.88 | 13 | 30.95 | 22 | 40.74 |
| Change activity reported by graduate and others were different | 1 | 3.13 | 5 | 11.91 | 7 | 12.96 |
| No change activity reported by graduate or others | 13 | 40.62 | 13 | 30.95 | 3 | 5.56 |

$\chi^2 = 18.6$ (p = .05, df 6, $\chi^2 = 12.59$)

**Table 4-9.** Number and percent of change activities according to effectiveness of change

| Effectiveness of change | Class of 1968 | | Class of 1969 | | Class of 1970 | |
|---|---|---|---|---|---|---|
| | NO. | PERCENT | NO. | PERCENT | NO. | PERCENT |
| Very effective | 7 | 21.21 | 48 | 42.48 | 62 | 48.82 |
| Some adherents | 6 | 18.18 | 30 | 26.55 | 31 | 24.41 |
| Effective but reversed | 6 | 18.18 | 6 | 5.31 | 3 | 2.36 |
| Ineffective | 7 | 21.21 | 19 | 16.82 | 16 | 12.60 |
| Much resistance | 5 | 15.15 | 5 | 5.31 | 10 | 7.87 |
| Insufficient information | 2 | 6.06 | 4 | 3.08 | 5 | 3.94 |

$\chi^2 = 22.38$ (p = .05, df 10, $\chi^2 = 18.31$)

had not. It was anticipated that more nurses from the Classes of 1969 and 1970 would have change activities verified by others because it was conjectured that the Anticipatory Socialization program would help them to be more effective change agents. The data support this expectation.

There is a problem with the validity of these data, however. More nurses in the Classes of 1969 and 1970 arranged for the interviews with their head nurses and co-workers than did the nurses in the Class of 1968. (Of the Class of 1968, 21 [47%] of the 32 nurses who were interviewed one year after employment arranged for interviews with a head nurse or co-worker; of the Class of 1969, 30 [52%] of the 42 nurses did so; 41 [69%] of the nurses in the Class of 1970 did.) This was in large measure a function of the frequent job hopping of the nurses in the Class of 1968. "I'd be glad for you to talk with my head nurse and with a co-worker, but I've been there such a short time I don't think people know me that well yet." This comment of one of the nurses in the control class illustrates the problem. It stands to reason that if fewer head nurses and co-workers were interviewed for the nurses in this class, there would be less opportunity for verification of change activity. It is also obvious that there was less opportunity for the nurses in the Class of 1968 to effect change since most of them had shorter tenure in their jobs when compared with the nurses in the other classes. There is undoubtedly a positive relationship between length of time in a job, change agent activity, and judgments of the effectiveness of that activity. The data must be interpreted with this relationship in mind.

Another way to get at the effectiveness of change agent activity was simply to use the criteria of effectiveness (p. 120) and rate all change activities according to these criteria. This was what the coders did. Table 4-9 indicates that there was a significant relationship between class membership and effectiveness of change activities. Fewer of the changes reported by the nurses in the Class of 1968 were rated as being "very effective" than would have occurred by chance. More changes from the nurses in this group were classified as "effective but reversed" or "much resistance" than would have been expected if only chance were operating.

The data presented in Tables 4-8 and 4-9 strongly support the contention that the nurses who had had the Anticipatory Socialization program were more effective change agents, and consequently were more influential in operationalizing their professional values, than the nurses who had not had the Anticipatory Socialization program.

An additional attempt was made to get at some rating of the nurse's overall change agent style and activity by having the coder-judge rate the typescript of the nurse, supplemented by that of the head nurse and co-worker if they were done, in terms of this variable. What was the estimate of change agent activity? Was this nurse a constant troublemaker, always into things? Was she quiet and passive, careful not to make waves? The results are presented in Table 4-10. Analysis indicates that the overall estimate of change agent activity was not independent of class membership. There were more nurses rated "enthusiastic" in the Class of 1970 than would be

**Table 4-10.** Overall estimate of change agent activity by classes

| Estimate | Class of 1968 (N = 32) | | Class of 1969 (N = 42) | | Class of 1970 (N = 54) | |
|---|---|---|---|---|---|---|
| | NO. | PERCENT | NO. | PERCENT | NO. | PERCENT |
| Constant troublemaker | 1 | 3.13 | 5 | 11.91 | 7 | 12.96 |
| Enthusiastic | 5 | 15.63 | 10 | 23.81 | 22 | 40.74 |
| Makes suggestions° | 9 | 28.12 | 13 | 30.95 | 18 | 33.33 |
| Causes no trouble° | 4 | 12.50 | 1 | 2.38 | 4 | 7.41 |
| No reported change activity | 13 | 40.62 | 13 | 30.95 | 3 | 5.56 |

°Collapsed for analysis. $\chi^2 = 20.10$ (p = .05, df 6, $\chi^2 = 12.59$)

expected by chance. There were also more nurses in the Class of 1970 and fewer in the Class of 1968 who reported no change agent activity than would be expected by chance.

Look briefly at some of the other dimensions of change agent activity and see if there were any differences among classes. Change activities were analyzed according to nature of change and recipient of change (p. 120); also, the nurse herself was rated in terms of the extent to which she appeared to be either involved or alienated from her job and her perceived power and control in the job. Analysis according to these perspectives showed no relationship with class membership. For all classes, technical and environmental changes were lowest, ranging from 3% to 14%. Other employees were the dominant recipients of change activity for all classes, with 65% of the 273 change activities reported for all classes. Patients did not fare so well; only 20.5% of all change activities were directed toward their immediate benefit. There were also no significant differences between classes in terms of degree of involvement; about 20% of the nurses in each class were rated as being frustrated or alienated. In terms of the degree of perceived power and control over job, about one fourth of the members of the Classes of 1969 and 1970 were rated as already having reached a stage of anomie or they were "fighting a losing game"; 38% of the Class of 1968 were rated as such. The lack of difference shown between the classes on the above variables may well be due as much or more to the crudity of the measuring instruments as to the actual lack of differences. These are very important and potentially fruitful ways

of looking at and measuring one's professional effectiveness in a job; they remain to be better defined and developed.

*Were they in touch with others?* There are two other dimensions that have a potential bearing on or are a reflection of biculturalism and operationalization of professional values. One of these was suggested by the literature on interpersonal competence and role-taking that was reviewed earlier. Based on the notion that to be effective in a situation one must be empathic, (1) a person must be able to define a situation as others see it, and (2) he must be able to predict accurately the actions and reactions of others in order to exert influence in a desired direction. Dymond reported studies on the validity and reliability of a tool developed to measure the degree of empathy between two or more individuals. Her basic methodology was used in this research. In the one-year postgraduation interview each nurse in the study was requested to rate herself on three factors from several perspectives: (1) as she sees herself, (2) as she thinks her head nurse sees her, (3) as she thinks her co-workers see her, and (4) as she thinks her head nurse (or co-worker)° sees herself. The three factors used were: loyal employee, autonomous practitioner, and skilled worker. Head nurses and co-workers were requested to do the same

°For all empathy ratings, only one or the other was used; that is, if a particular nurse subject had arranged for interviews with both her head nurse and a co-worker, only one was randomly entered into the empathy score tabulations. This was done so that there would be equivalency among nurses since about one third of the nurses did not have interviews from both head nurses and co-workers.

**Table 4-11.** Degree of empathy of nurses by classes

| | Class of 1968 (N = 21) | | Class of 1969 (N = 30) | | Class of 1970 (N = 41) | |
|---|---|---|---|---|---|---|
| | NO. | PERCENT | NO. | PERCENT | NO. | PERCENT |
| None (Score 0) | 12 | 57.14 | 3 | 10.00 | 13 | 31.71 |
| Low (Score 1 or 2) | 4 | 19.05 | 10 | 33.33 | 12 | 29.27 |
| Medium (Score 3 or 4) | 3 | 14.29 | 8 | 26.67 | 6 | 14.63 |
| High (Score 5 or 6) | 2 | 9.52 | 9 | 30.00 | 10 | 24.39 |

$\chi^2 = 13.94$ (p = .05, df = 6, $\chi^2 = 10.64$)

task. This method yielded a potential empathy score of 0 to 6. A score was given if there was exact correspondence between the way in which the nurse thinks her supervisor (or co-worker) sees herself and the way that the supervisor actually does see herself. Another score was given if there was exact correspondence between the way in which the nurse thinks her supervisor sees her and the way in which the supervisor states that she sees the nurse.

Results of the empathy testing are presented in Table 4-11. Analysis indicates that empathy, as measured by the above questions, was not independent of class membership. There was a significant difference between the classes on this variable. There were more nurses in the Classes of 1969 and 1970 who were able to correctly predict their head nurse's or co-worker's perception of them, and who were accurate in their perception of the head nurse or co-worker, than in the Class of 1968. The nurses in the Class of 1969 were particularly empathic, as evidenced by the low percentage of them who had a zero empathy score. It is a little unusual that they surpassed the Class of 1970 on this variable since on almost all other variables the nurses in the Class of 1970 displayed a slight edge over the nurses in the Class of 1969. To the extent that being able to define self and the situation as the other person sees it is necessary to be effective in introducing change and influencing others, it can be said that the nurses in the Classes of 1969 and 1970 were better able to opera-

tionalize their professional value system than were the nurses in the Class of 1968.

*Were they in touch with themselves?* The last aspect of the variable of operationalization of professional values that was investigated was the extent of self-actualization. This aspect of personality was first discussed by Goldstein. Maslow describes self-actualization as becoming more and more what one is capable of becoming. The process of "becoming" requires that the individual make full use of unique talents and potentials by going beyond his immediate needs and realizing more fully the higher needs of esteem, cognition, and self-actualization. A person who is functioning on his highest level is self-actualizing or self-realizing such qualities and is free from the emotional and inhibitive restraints held by persons who function on a lower level. Based on this rationale, it seemed logical to conjecture that nurses who had learned how to manage conflict in a growth-producing manner, who had attained some degree of biculturalism, who had some built-in protection against reality shock (all desired outcomes of the Anticipatory Socialization program) would be more self-actualized than nurses who had not had such a program. Heckmat and Theiss demonstrated that highly self-actualized people are more resistant to enculturation than low self-actualizing people. They think this occurs because the source of effective reinforcement for one's values and behaviors moves from an external to an internal source. If adjustment to the first work experience is viewed as an enculturation process, it should be possible to predict that the nurses in the Classes of 1969 and 1970 would be more resistant to enculturation and hence more self-actualized.

Shostrom, enlarging upon the work of Maslow and Perls, developed a tool to measure the values and behaviors thought to be of importance in the development of an actualizer. This tool, the Personal Orientation Inventory (POI), was administered to all nurses in the three classes two years after employment. The POI is composed of 150 two-choice comparative value and behavior judgments, scored into two subscales: I, that is, whether an individual is oriented to inner direction or outer direction, and time competence (Tc), the degree to which an individual is present-oriented and relates the past and future in a meaningful continuity. The scores on the scales are interpreted on the basis of norms established for self-actualizers and for certain personality categories. The test is self-administered; high scores are in the direction of a self-actualized personality.

Analysis of the Tc and I scores (considered to be the best indicators of the total test) of the nurses according to class membership indicated that there was no significant difference (Appendix C, Table C-10). The Class of 1969 and the Class of 1970 had higher mean scores on both the Tc and I scales than did the Class of 1968, but the difference in variance was not great enough to rule out chance. It therefore had to be concluded that differences in scores were not related to class membership. The nurses who had had the Anticipatory Socialization program were no more or less self-actualized than the nurses who did not have the program. (For a report on a multivariate analysis of all of the variables used to assess the construct operationalization of professional values, see Appendix D.)

## Summary of anticipated events at various junctions

A summary is in order before proceeding further. This is especially so for the fifth hypothesis, which had two official tests and several contributory inspections. Hypothesis V stated that nurses who had the Anticipatory Socialization program would retain professional nurse role conceptions upon employment while nurses who did not have the program would relinquish them. The latter aspect of this hypothesis was based upon previous research. The hypothesis was tested by looking at the comparative scores of the two groups of nurses on the professional role conception and professional role behavior scales one and two years after employment. The scores over time, from graduation to one year followup on both groups of nurses, were also studied. Results indicated that there was not a significant drop for either the control or the experimental classes. Both groups retained essentially the same degree of professional loyalty as they had had at graduation. The hypothesis was rejected.

To enlarge the hypothesis to include not only retention but also operationalization of professional values, several subsidiary tests and analyses were done. An Index of Professionalism, consisting of nine generally accepted criteria of professionalism, was constructed. An index score was generated. Analysis showed that nurses in the classes of 1969 and 1970 reported more professional behaviors such as attending courses, subscribing to and reading professional books and journals, professional organizational activity, and so on, than did the nurses in the Class of 1968. Dimensions of change agent activity were investigated in some depth. The students in the experimental classes described more change activities. More of these were verified by head nurse–supervisor or co-worker, the activity itself was more successful, and the nurses were rated as being more enthusiastic than the nurses in the control class. There were no differences on the other dimensions of change agent activity studied. A study of possible difference in empathic ability as a precursor to interpersonal competence indicated that more nurses in the Classes of 1969 and 1970 were able to correctly predict how their supervisor or co-worker would rate them and would rate themselves on three items (loyal employee, skilled worker, autonomous practitioner) than the nurses in the Class of 1968.

It was thought that the nurses who had had the Anticipatory Socialization program would be more self-actualized than those nurses who had not had the program. Analysis of scores on the Shostrom Personal Orientation Inventory, a tool designed to measure self-actualization, indicated no difference between classes.

Hypothesis IV predicted that a higher percentage of the nurses who had had the Anticipatory program would report use of integrative role strategies than would those who had not had the program. This hypothesis was tested through analysis of scores on a test of behavior choices in conflict situations. There was a significant difference between classes, with the nurses in the experimental group scoring significantly higher. The hypothesis was accepted.

In Hypothesis III the question was raised as to the effects of the Anticipatory Socialization program on the chosen work locale and career pattern of the two groups of nurses. When submitted to analysis, it was found that the nurses in the Classes of 1969 and 1970 remained in their initial jobs longer, did less job hopping, did not flee the hospital work locale, remained in nursing practice, and were less likely to leave their jobs for voluntary reasons than did the nurses in the Class of 1968. The hypothesis was accepted.

Do collegiate nurses who have had the Anticipatory Socialization program experience less role deprivation upon employment than nurses who have not had the program? The second hypothesis predicted that they would. The first hypothesis predicted that the role deprivation scores of those who had had the Anticipatory Socialization program would rise during the school period (and not later as is usually the case). Both of these hypotheses were upheld. The nurses in the Classes of 1969 and 1970 had significantly higher role deprivation scores during school than did the Class of 1968. For the Class of 1969, scores remained the same a year after graduation; the Class of 1970 showed a significant decrease.

## EMPLOYER EVALUATION

Quantitative scores and pencil marks on paper are important: they tell you a good deal about what is happening and if something was successful or not. When it comes to the problem under study here, there is another group of people to be heard from— very important people who are not often asked the question "What do you think of the product being prepared in schools of nursing today?" In an attempt to ask and answer that question, the employers of the nurses in the class sample were contacted.

Employer evaluation of work performance is subject to all of the usual biases and pitfalls. However, such evaluation is a real and necessary fact. Although we judge ourselves and our work performance, we are still influenced and affected by what others think of us. For this reason it was deemed important to obtain an employer's view of each nurse subject within the following considerations. First, it should be a representation or description of how the nurse subject was viewed by her employer after she had had as much experience as the research design allowed (two years). The second consideration was that the nurse should have been in a position long enough to have become adjusted to it before an employer evaluation was sought. This is a difficult time period to assess, but there seems to be general agreement among directors of nursing that it takes about six months for a new graduate to become thoroughly oriented; on subsequent jobs it seems realistic that it would take less time. The third criteria governing the employer evaluations was that they should be completed by the individual who has the most knowledge and opportunity to observe the work of the nurse being evaluated. This would usually be the person who is in a head nurse or supervisor capacity, but it could vary with the particular position. The fourth criteria for obtaining employer evaluations of the nurses was that they should be obtained either while the nurse was still actively employed in the position or within a very short period of time after termination. For purposes of this study, the latter was defined as within one month so as to increase the potential accuracy of the evaluation rather than rely on memory. In addition to the above criteria, the usual criteria of anonymity, as well as assurances to the employer that the evaluation would not in any way be placed in the former student's file or be used in any way that would harm the individual in subsequent job employment or getting into graduate school, also prevailed.[4]

To obtain employer evaluations on all subjects within the considerations outlined above, the following procedure was used.

1. Employer evaluations were obtained for each nurse subject within one month of termination for each job that was held for at least six months. The evaluation that covered the six-month period closest to the two-year followup was the one used in the analysis.
2. At the two-year followup, an evaluation was obtained from the current employer of each nurse subject if the nurse had been employed in that position for longer than six months.

The above procedure resulted in a total of 197 employer evaluations for the 161 nurses in all three classes. Those subjects who changed jobs frequently would have more evaluations than those who did not; the maximum number of evaluations possible for the two-year period was four, but only one evaluation was used for each nurse. Employer evaluations were obtained for 87% (N = 39) of the members of the Class of 1968, 91% (N = 52) of the Class of 1969, and 90% (N = 53) of the Class of 1970. The smaller percentage of evaluations for the Class of 1968 was because of the larger number of nurses in this class who were working out of nursing or who changed jobs so frequently that they did not have at least a six-month tenure on any job.

Of the 144 evaluations for the nurses in all classes, over 90% (N = 132) were completed by head nurses and supervisors; the remainder were completed by a variety of people: coordinators, clinical nurse specialists, consultants, directors of in-service, and so on. There was no difference between classes in respect to the position of the person completing the questionnaire. Over three fourths (N = 111) of the nurses' evaluations were based on employment in an inpatient setting, either general hospitals, specialty hospitals, or nursing homes; the remainder were based upon employment

in health departments, schools, and clinics.

All employer evaluations were obtained by writing to the director or administrative head of the agency or hospital employing the graduate, requesting that the evaluation form be transmitted to the immediate supervisor of the nurse for completion. A stamped, self-addressed envelope labeled Confidential so that it would not be opened by anyone other than the research staff was included for the evaluation form return. If the form was not returned within three weeks, a reminder was sent to the director of nurses. The employers and people designated to complete these evaluation forms were most gracious and cooperative. During the course of the four years in which this data was collected, only six employers failed to return the form.

## Description of employer evaluation form

Constructed from forms described in the literature by other investigators and from an intensive study of nurse evaluation forms used by hospitals and public health agencies, the employer evaluation form used in this study consisted of three parts. One part contained factual data that could be verified from records: length of employment, unit assignment, presence and length of in-service orientation program, number of days of illness and absence from work, promotion, and salary increases based on merit. A second part consisted of general perceptual data, subjective in nature. Items on this part included the respondent's perception of the performance of a nurse in comparison with others, the nurse's differential loyalties, the importance the nurse placed on others' perceptions of her work, and perception of general behavioral characteristics of the nurse subject. The third and last part of the employer evaluation form, the function section, was composed of data midway between factual, verifiable information and general perceptual data. It consisted of a rating scale in which the respondent was asked to rate the nurse subject as to whether her performance was above, the same, or below that of other nurses on a list of 30 common nurse functions. These 30 functions had been abstracted from the literature. Two nurses,[5] highly knowledgeable about the literature on differentiation between professional and technical nurse functions, independently classified all of the functions into three subcategories:

**professional** those activities most consistent with the idea of the professional nurse as described in the literature.
**technical** those activities most consistent with the idea of the technical nurse as described in the literature.
**baseline** those activities that cannot be differentiated into either professional or technical. They are common, baseline activities that are inherent in the concept "nurse," regardless of what adjective precedes "nurse," and are expected of all nurses.

In an attempt to ascertain some estimate of the reliability of this employer evaluation form, eight head nurses were asked at two different time periods to complete the forms on nurses working on their units. This was not a random sample or random selection. I attended a head nurses' meeting at one institution and requested that they complete the forms on their staff at that time, utilizing code names known only to them. Three weeks later at another meeting the same head nurses were given blank forms and the list of code names they had used on their previous evaluations and were requested to complete the forms once more. Since the head nurses could not accurately complete the factual section because they did not have employee records available to them at the meetings, test-retest reliability coefficients were computed for the function and perceptual sections of the form only. The head nurses completed the paired evaluation forms for 23 staff nurses on their units. Reliability coefficient for the function section of the form ranged from .76 to .92, with a median of .77. On the perceptual section the range was from .64 to .90, with a median of .72. It was concluded that the form was sufficiently consistent for the purposes of this study.

Use of the employer evaluation form was in the nature of a fishing expedition. Nothing so formal as hypotheses had been proposed, although there were some ideas or conjectures that guided both the formulation of the form and the analysis. These ideas and the results will be presented according to the three main sections of the form.

*Factual data.* A major emphasis in this section was on orientation programs: Does your agency have one? Did the nurse participate in it? Did she need more than the ordinary amount of orientation? The purpose in obtaining this information was twofold. It was important to know whether the graduates from the three classes had an equal chance at adjustment as measured by the presence of an orientation program, and it was thought that needing more than the ordinary amount of orientation would be indicative of poor adjustment. Analysis of data by class indicated no real differences between classes. Of the agencies represented by the nurse subjects in all three classes, 92% offered orientation programs; 87% of the nurses participated in them; 22% were reported as needing additional orientation. Most of the latter was concerned with special units, such as the operating room, intensive care unit, nursery for premature babies, and so on. Chi square analysis indicated no difference according to class membership. There was no difference in numerical count between classes when the evaluator was asked if there were "things you expect graduate nurses to be able to do for which this nurse was not prepared?" Forty-one percent of the evaluators said "Yes." Expecting the nurse to be able to perform skills such as giving intravenous medication, catheterizations, and the like, headed the list of specifics (44%), followed by accepting responsibility (19%) and organizational skills (14%).

Another aspect of the factual section was questions about extent of illness and absence, promotions offered, and salary increases based on merit. It was conjectured that unhappy, disillusioned nurses would be more likely to absent themselves from work more frequently than happy, successful nurses. There was some evidence of class differences in response to the question: How many days has this nurse been ill or absent from work during the past year, or since her employment if less than one year? Although the range for each class was about the same (zero to 39 or 41 days), the mean number of days of absence from work was 6.1 for the Class of 1968, 5.5 for the Class of 1969, and 4.4 for the Class of 1970 (Appendix

C, Table C-11). This data take on even more significance when one realizes that for the Classes of 1969 and 1970 the figure represents a yearly average of absence from work, while for the Class of 1968 the figure undoubtedly represents less than a year since fewer members of this class of nurses remained in any job for as long as a year.

It was thought that salary increases on the basis of merit would be indicative of perceived success on the job. There was no difference between classes on this data; only a total of five nurses received such merit increases, but there were a large number of notations to the effect that this was because they had not been employed long enough yet. This point leads to the question of whether the merit increases were really for merit or for length of tenure.

Turned-down promotions, particularly to traditionally administrative positions such as assistant head nurse or head nurse, were thought to be indicative of high value placement on direct patient care. The study of the medical center nurses had indicated that in the two-year period from first to second interview (1968 to 1970) many of them had abdicated promoted positions in favor of bedside staff nursing, often on the same unit. Results of the analysis of the data obtained on the employer evaluation form indicated no significant difference between classes. Approximately one fourth of the nurses in each class had been offered promotions that they had rejected.

*Perceptual data.* This section contained a myriad of variables, the only commonality being that they depended upon the evaluator's perception and comparative evaluation of a nurse by whatever criteria the evaluator assumed were constant and general. One of the first questions in this section dealt with the evaluator's perception of the performance of the nurse when compared with other baccalaureate, diploma, or Associate Arts graduates who had about the same amount of experience as the nurse being evaluated. Table 4-12 shows the percentage of each class of nurses who were evaluated as being above, the same, or below other nurses with the specified educational preparation. Analysis indicates only one

**Table 4-12.** Percent of nurses according to employers' perceptions of their performance in comparison with others

| Performance compared with other graduates | Class of 1968 (N = 39) | | | | Class of 1969 (N = 52) | | | | Class of 1970 (N = 53) | | | | Total (N = 144) | | | |
|---|---|---|---|---|---|---|---|---|---|---|---|---|---|---|---|---|
| | SA | S | SB | NA | SA | S | SB | NA | SA | S | SB | NA | SA | S | SB | NA |
| Baccalaureate | 35.9 | 59.0 | 5.1 | 0.0 | 42.3 | 46.2 | 11.5 | 0.0 | 56.6 | 34.0 | 9.4 | 0.0 | 45.8 | 45.1 | 9.0 | 0.0 |
| Diploma | 43.6 | 43.6 | 5.1 | 7.7 | 48.1 | 34.6 | 15.4 | 1.9 | 58.5 | 35.8 | 5.7 | 0.0 | 50.7 | 37.5 | 9.0 | 2.1 |
| Associate Arts | 48.7 | 25.6 | 2.6 | 23.1 | 59.6 | 25.0 | 5.8 | 9.6 | 64.2 | 28.3 | 0.0 | 7.6 | 58.3 | 26.4 | 2.8 | 12.6 |

SA, somewhat above other nurses with the same amount of experience; S, about the same as other nurses with the same amount of experience; SB, somewhat below other nurses with the same amount of experience; NA, no basis for comparison.
Chi square on comparison with Associate Arts graduates: $\chi^2 = 13.23$ ($\chi^2$ at .05 for 6 df = 10.64).
Chi square on comparison with diploma graduates: $\chi^2 = 5.42$ ($\chi^2$ at .05 for 4 df° = 7.78). °NA cell eliminated in $\chi^2$ analysis because of small cell size.
Chi square on comparison with baccalaureate graduates: $\chi^2 = 5.81$ ($\chi^2$ at .05 for 4 df = 7.78).

area of difference. The nurses in the Class of 1969 (to some extent) and Class of 1970 (to a greater extent) were perceived as being somewhat better performers than Associate Arts graduates. However, this finding could well be a function of historical development. The high percentage of evaluators who indicated that they had no basis for comparing the graduates of 1968 to Associate Arts graduates might well indicate that in 1969 and 1970 (when the forms were being completed on the nurses in the Class of 1968) the ranks of nurses still contained too few Associate Arts graduates to make comparison meaningful or possible.

Further inspection of Table 4-12 indicates a more subtle message, however. Whether it can be identified or defined, or whether or not it is openly voiced, it is apparent that the evaluators (most of whom were head nurses) do in fact expect different kinds of performance from graduates prepared in different educational programs. Looking at only the "somewhat above" column, for example, there appears to be a hierarchy of expectation, with the expectations for the baccalaureate graduate being the highest, then the diploma graduate, and then the Associate Arts graduate. For each class, the percentage distribution decreases in the same direction and by about the same magnitude. To clarify, 36% of the nurses in the Class of 1968 were rated as being somewhat above the performance expected of the baccalaureate-prepared nurse; but 44% were above that expected of the diploma nurse, and 49% were above that expected of the Associate Arts graduate. Therefore, the expectations for the baccalaureate-prepared nurse must be higher than those for the diploma and for the Associate Arts graduate. It would be helpful if these expectations could be expressed in more definitive and practical terms.

A second major area of the perceptual section was concerned with the evaluator's perception of the nurse's loyalties and of the importance that the nurse placed on the opinion of specified others' perception of her as a nurse. Analysis of the percentage and rank order of loyalties and importance placed on work by class and for the classes combined

indicated no significant difference (Appendix C, Table C-12 and C-13). Nurses in all three classes were perceived as maintaining primary loyalty to themselves, to patients, to co-workers, head nurses, employing agencies, physicians, and former teachers, in descending order. There were also no differences between classes in respect to the perception of importance placed on them as nurses. Patients ranked first, followed in order by head nurses, co-workers, physicians, relatives, and former teachers. This does not appear to be a particularly fruitful line of inquiry except to note that there is apparently a marked difference in the employer's valuation of the importance of former teachers and in the new graduate's valuation of them.

If the Anticipatory Socialization program were effective in helping the nurses in the Classes of 1969 and 1970 become professionally operative within their work situation, then there should be some differences noted between these nurses and those in the Class of 1968 with respect to some general behavioral characteristics. Questions along this line constituted the third area in the perceptual section of the employer evaluation form. The evaluators were asked to rate the nurses as to whether they perceived them primarily as leaders, followers, or loners; whether they seemed to be in a rut, constantly stimulated, or in between; whether they were disillusioned with nursing, happy, or in between; and whether they tended to follow, resist, or wiggle through rules. Two other questions—whether the nurse liked to work mainly with patients or with personnel and whether her standards were perceived as being higher, the same, or lower than other nurses—were asked to get some idea as to whether conflict management might have been achieved at the expense of value capitulation. If so, it would be expected that those nurses who were leaders, happy with nursing, and constantly stimulated would be perceived as having lower standards and liking to work more with personnel than with patients. The summary of the data with respect to the above questions is presented in Table 4-13.

The responses to each question were first

**Table 4-13.** Number and percent of nurses according to employers' perception of behavior and preferences

| Behavior and preferences | Class of 1968 | | Class of 1969 | | Class of 1970 | | Total | |
|---|---|---|---|---|---|---|---|---|
| | NO. | PERCENT | NO. | PERCENT | NO. | PERCENT | NO. | PERCENT |
| Is she a | | | | | | | | |
| leader | 15 | 38.4 | 34 | 65.3 | 39 | 73.5 | 88 | 61.1 |
| follower | 17 | 43.5 | 9 | 17.3 | 7 | 13.2 | 33 | 22.9 |
| loner | 6 | 15.3 | 8 | 15.3 | 7 | 13.2 | 21 | 14.5 |
| not applicable | 1 | 2.5 | 1 | 1.9 | — | — | 2 | 1.3 |
| She likes to | | | | | | | | |
| work with patients | 27 | 69.2 | 37 | 71.1 | 42 | 79.2 | 106 | 73.6 |
| work with personnel | 11 | 28.2 | 11 | 21.1 | 11 | 20.7 | 33 | 22.9 |
| not applicable | 1 | 2.5 | 4 | 7.6 | — | — | 5 | 3.4 |
| She is | | | | | | | | |
| in a rut | 2 | 5.1 | 4 | 7.6 | 2 | 3.7 | 8 | 5.5 |
| constantly stimulated | 11 | 28.2 | 29 | 55.7 | 35 | 66.0 | 75 | 52.0 |
| in between | 26 | 66.6 | 17 | 32.6 | 16 | 30.1 | 59 | 40.9 |
| not applicable | — | — | 2 | 3.8 | — | — | 2 | 1.3 |
| She is | | | | | | | | |
| disillusioned with nursing | 11 | 28.2 | 6 | 11.5 | 2 | 3.7 | 19 | 13.1 |
| happy with nursing | 14 | 35.8 | 20 | 38.4 | 33 | 62.2 | 67 | 46.5 |
| in between | 13 | 33.3 | 24 | 46.1 | 18 | 33.9 | 55 | 38.1 |
| not applicable | 1 | 2.5 | 2 | 3.8 | — | — | 3 | 2.0 |
| Nursing standards are | | | | | | | | |
| higher | 17 | 43.5 | 25 | 48.0 | 31 | 58.4 | 73 | 50.6 |
| the same | 20 | 51.2 | 24 | 46.1 | 21 | 39.6 | 65 | 45.1 |
| lower | 1 | 2.5 | 1 | 1.9 | 1 | 1.8 | 3 | 2.0 |
| not applicable | 1 | 2.5 | 2 | 3.8 | — | — | 3 | 2.0 |
| Rules and regulations | | | | | | | | |
| follows | 35 | 89.7 | 39 | 75.0 | 32 | 60.3 | 106 | 73.6 |
| resists | 1 | 2.5 | 1 | 1.9 | 1 | 1.8 | 3 | 2.0 |
| wiggles through | 1 | 2.5 | 5 | 9.6 | 10 | 18.8 | 16 | 11.1 |
| other | 2 | 5.1 | 7 | 13.4 | 10 | 18.8 | 19 | 13.1 |

submitted to chi square analysis. If it was found that there was a significant association between response and class membership, a McNemar significance of difference test between proportions was done to ascertain the major area of difference. Results indicated that:

1. There were significantly more nurses perceived as leaders in the Classes of 1969 and 1970 than in the Class of 1968.
2. A higher percentage of the nurses in the Class of 1968 were perceived as being in between a rut and constantly stimulated than in the Classes of 1969 and 1970.
3. There were proportionately more nurses in the Class of 1968 perceived as being disillusioned with nursing than in the Class of 1970.
4. Although not statistically significant, the Class of 1970 gives more evidence of bicultural compromising-type behavior as evidenced by a higher proportion of "wigglers" and written-in lines of action than the nurses in the other two classes.
5. There were no differences between the nurses in the three classes as to employers' perceptions of their standards or in their preference for working with patients over personnel.

*Functions.* The last major section of the employer evaluation form was concerned with the immediate supervisor's perception of a nurse's ability to carry out what the literature terms as professional and technical functions of the nurse. This data was to be obtained by the evaluator's rating of the nurse on 30 func-

**Table 4-14.** Percent of nurses evaluated according to specified technical, professional, and baseline

| Functions | Class of 1968 (N = 39) | | | |
|---|---|---|---|---|
| | SA | S | SB | NA |
| **Technical** | | | | |
| Carrying out nursing techniques | 12.8 | 66.7 | 7.7 | 12.8 |
| Positioning and making patients comfortable | 12.8 | 51.3 | 5.1 | 30.8 |
| Operating special equipment, such as oxygen, suction, and irrigating equipment | 20.5 | 46.2 | 7.7 | 25.6 |
| Making decisions regarding patient care° | 51.3 | 38.5 | 7.7 | 2.6 |
| Observing signs, symptoms, and changes in patient's condition° | 25.6 | 59.0 | 2.6 | 12.8 |
| Reporting signs, symptoms, and changes in patient's condition° | 33.3 | 53.8 | 2.6 | 10.3 |
| Recognizing need for assistance from other health workers | 33.3 | 53.8 | 5.1 | 7.7 |
| Working within rules and policies of organization° | 25.6 | 69.2 | 5.1 | 0.0 |
| **Professional** | | | | |
| Planning and providing comprehensive nursing care° | 38.5 | 51.3 | 0.0 | 10.3 |
| Assisting patients to make maximum contribution toward health and recovery° | 35.9 | 41.0 | 2.6 | 20.5 |
| Working with other health team members to meet health needs of individuals | 46.2 | 38.5 | 2.6 | 12.8 |
| Working with other health team members to meet health needs of families and larger social groups | 28.2 | 51.3 | 0.0 | 20.5 |
| Giving advice or assistance to other nursing personnel† | 15.4 | 66.7 | 7.7 | 10.3 |
| Directing work of other nursing personnel | 20.5 | 41.0 | 10.3 | 28.2 |
| Evaluating work of other nursing personnel | 15.4 | 46.2 | 7.7 | 30.8 |
| Developing individualized nursing care plans | 28.2 | 51.3 | 5.1 | 15.4 |
| Leading team conferences | 17.9 | 46.2 | 5.1 | 30.8 |
| Showing awareness of needs and activities of total health care system of which she is a part° | 17.9 | 66.7 | 10.3 | 5.1 |
| Initiating appropriate activity to change rules and regulations when necessary | 12.8 | 64.1 | 5.1 | 17.9 |
| Suggesting and following through ways to improve patient care or operation‡ | 12.8 | 53.8 | 12.8 | 20.5 |
| Reading professional journals | 25.6 | 41.0 | 7.7 | 25.6 |
| Functioning in a charge or head nurse capacity | 10.3 | 33.3 | 12.8 | 43.6 |
| **Baseline** | | | | |
| Explaining procedures and treatments to patients° | 48.7 | 38.5 | 0.0 | 12.8 |
| Identifying patient problems and nursing needs° | 46.2 | 48.7 | 2.6 | 2.6 |
| Meeting psychological needs of patients° | 35.9 | 53.8 | 2.6 | 7.7 |
| Making positive contribution to overall goals of work group of which she is a member | 43.6 | 46.2 | 7.7 | 2.6 |
| Understanding of professional ethics° | 28.2 | 61.5 | 5.1 | 5.1 |
| Enacting a sense of responsibility° | 53.8 | 41.0 | 5.1 | 0.0 |
| Listening to patients, their families and relatives° | 38.5 | 53.8 | 0.0 | 7.7 |
| Participating in committee work of organization | 20.5 | 43.6 | 10.3 | 25.6 |

SA, somewhat above other graduate nurses who have had a comparable amount of work experience; S, about the same as other graduate nurses who have had a comparable amount of work experience; SB, somewhat below other graduate nurses who have had a comparable amount of work experience; NA, no opportunity to observe or not applicable in this situation.
°SB, and NA were eliminated from chi square analysis of these functions so that expected frequency would meet minimum requirements.
†$\chi^2 = 16.84$ (p = .05, df 6, $\chi^2 = 12.59$).
‡$\chi^2 = 17.63$ (p = .05, df 6, $\chi^2 = 12.59$).

functions

| | Class of 1969 (N = 52) | | | | Class of 1970 (N = 53) | | | | Total (N = 144) | | |
|---|---|---|---|---|---|---|---|---|---|---|---|---|
| SA | S | SB | NA | SA | S | SB | NA | SA | S | SB | NA |
| 19.2 | 48.1 | 9.6 | 23.1 | 32.1 | 49.1 | 3.8 | 15.1 | 22.2 | 53.5 | 6.9 | 17.4 |
| 17.3 | 51.9 | 5.8 | 25.0 | 35.8 | 47.2 | 1.9 | 15.1 | 22.9 | 50.0 | 4.2 | 22.9 |
| 13.5 | 44.2 | 13.5 | 28.8 | 28.3 | 45.3 | 9.4 | 17.0 | 20.8 | 45.1 | 10.4 | 23.6 |
| 40.4 | 44.2 | 7.7 | 7.7 | 45.3 | 45.3 | 5.7 | 3.8 | 45.1 | 43.1 | 6.9 | 4.9 |
| 36.5 | 51.9 | 3.8 | 7.7 | 49.1 | 43.4 | 0.0 | 7.5 | 38.2 | 50.7 | 2.1 | 9.0 |
| 26.9 | 59.6 | 5.8 | 7.7 | 45.3 | 49.1 | 0.0 | 5.7 | 35.4 | 54.2 | 2.8 | 7.6 |
| 32.7 | 55.8 | 5.8 | 5.8 | 41.5 | 50.9 | 5.7 | 1.9 | 36.1 | 53.5 | 5.6 | 4.9 |
| 23.1 | 69.2 | 5.8 | 1.9 | 24.5 | 69.8 | 3.8 | 1.9 | 24.3 | 69.4 | 4.9 | 1.4 |
| 44.2 | 38.5 | 9.6 | 7.7 | 35.8 | 49.1 | 5.7 | 9.4 | 39.6 | 45.8 | 5.6 | 9.0 |
| 38.5 | 53.8 | 7.7 | 0.0 | 39.6 | 45.3 | 5.7 | 9.4 | 38.2 | 47.2 | 5.6 | 9.0 |
| 36.5 | 48.1 | 3.8 | 11.5 | 47.2 | 47.2 | 3.8 | 1.9 | 43.1 | 45.1 | 3.5 | 8.3 |
| 32.7 | 42.3 | 5.8 | 19.2 | 37.7 | 47.2 | 3.8 | 11.3 | 33.3 | 46.5 | 3.5 | 16.7 |
| 28.8 | 42.3 | 21.2 | 7.7 | 39.6 | 52.8 | 7.5 | 0.0 | 29.2 | 52.8 | 12.5 | 5.6 |
| 25.0 | 38.5 | 17.3 | 19.2 | 34.0 | 45.3 | 13.2 | 7.5 | 27.1 | 41.7 | 13.9 | 17.4 |
| 23.1 | 34.6 | 13.5 | 28.8 | 22.6 | 52.8 | 11.3 | 13.2 | 20.8 | 44.4 | 11.1 | 23.6 |
| 36.5 | 46.2 | 9.6 | 7.7 | 41.5 | 41.5 | 3.8 | 13.2 | 36.1 | 45.8 | 6.3 | 11.8 |
| 25.0 | 36.5 | 11.5 | 26.9 | 24.5 | 37.7 | 9.4 | 28.3 | 22.9 | 39.6 | 9.0 | 28.5 |
| 32.7 | 55.8 | 7.7 | 3.8 | 41.5 | 56.6 | 1.9 | 0.0 | 31.9 | 59.0 | 6.3 | 2.8 |
| 26.9 | 40.4 | 15.4 | 17.3 | 28.3 | 54.7 | 7.5 | 9.4 | 23.6 | 52.1 | 9.7 | 14.6 |
| 34.6 | 44.2 | 9.6 | 11.5 | 47.2 | 45.3 | 1.9 | 5.7 | 33.3 | 47.2 | 7.6 | 11.8 |
| 26.9 | 34.6 | 5.8 | 32.7 | 32.1 | 37.7 | 1.9 | 28.3 | 28.5 | 37.5 | 4.9 | 29.2 |
| 19.2 | 26.9 | 17.3 | 36.5 | 28.3 | 37.7 | 7.5 | 26.4 | 20.1 | 32.6 | 12.5 | 34.7 |
| 34.6 | 55.8 | 1.9 | 7.7 | 47.2 | 45.3 | 3.8 | 3.8 | 43.1 | 47.2 | 2.1 | 7.6 |
| 50.0 | 40.4 | 7.7 | 1.9 | 62.3 | 32.1 | 0.0 | 5.7 | 53.5 | 39.6 | 3.5 | 3.5 |
| 50.0 | 46.2 | 3.8 | 0.0 | 54.7 | 35.8 | 3.8 | 5.7 | 47.9 | 44.4 | 3.5 | 4.2 |
| 42.3 | 42.3 | 11.5 | 3.8 | 52.8 | 39.6 | 7.5 | 0.0 | 46.5 | 42.4 | 9.0 | 2.1 |
| 36.5 | 59.6 | 3.8 | 0.0 | 39.6 | 54.7 | 3.8 | 1.9 | 35.4 | 58.3 | 4.2 | 2.1 |
| 36.5 | 50.0 | 11.5 | 1.9 | 60.4 | 37.7 | 1.9 | 0.0 | 50.0 | 43.1 | 6.3 | 0.7 |
| 40.4 | 53.8 | 1.9 | 3.8 | 50.9 | 43.4 | 1.9 | 3.8 | 43.8 | 50.0 | 1.4 | 4.9 |
| 26.9 | 32.7 | 11.5 | 28.8 | 28.3 | 39.6 | 3.8 | 28.3 | 25.7 | 38.2 | 8.3 | 27.8 |

tions according to her perception of whether the nurse performed them somewhat above, the same as, or somewhat below that of other graduates who had had a comparable amount of experience. No specific differences as a result of the Anticipatory Socialization program were forecast; it was hoped that they would be rated as performing professional functions at least as well as those nurses in the Class of 1968. The data was sought mainly to find out if the Anticipatory Socialization program and the emphasis on understanding and valuation of bureaucratic work principles had diminished the professional aspects of job performance to any marked degree.

A summary of the percentage of nurses evaluated according to each of the functions by class is presented in Table 4-14. The functions listed in the table are abbreviated from those actually listed on the employer evaluation form. The data were analyzed by summing each nurse's score (with 1 point for below, 2 for same, and 3 for above) for each of the three functional categories—technical, professional, and baseline. Total scores were then ranked by class, and Kruskal-Wallis Analysis of Variance by ranks by classes was done (Appendix C, Table C-14). Results indicated that only within the professional category was there any significant difference by class (at $>.05$ level). A followup Mann Whitney U (Appendix C, Table C-15) indicated that the Class of 1970 had significantly higher professional rank scores than did the Class of 1968. There were no other differences between classes or any differences on any of the other functions.

## SUMMARY

In this chapter I have reported on the results of a program designed to help new graduate nurses manage the anticipated conflict between work and school values that generally confronts them on their first job. Five hypotheses were submitted to testing. It was concluded that the Anticipatory Socialization program to which the nurses in the Classes of 1969 and 1970 were exposed was effective in raising perceived role deprivation while in school, decreasing role deprivation

upon employment, increasing the length of time that nurses remained in their initial jobs and in nursing practice, and helping nurses to develop integrative role strategies useful in managing conflict. There is evidence to support the conclusion that the nurses who had the Anticipatory Socialization program were better able to operationalize their professional values and to experience some measure of job success. Although the nurses who did not have the program did not abdicate their professional values as expected, the nurses in the experimental group reported more behavior consistent with that usually understood to be professional (for example, professional reading, activity in professional organizations), were more active and more successful change agents, and had higher empathic ratings than did the nurses who did not have the Anticipatory Socialization program.

Results of assessments of work performance and behavior by employers done two years after graduation indicated that the nurses who had the Anticipatory Socialization program had fewer days of absence from work and were perceived as being happier, more stimulated, and exerting more leadership than the nurses who did not have the program. The nurses in the experimental Class of 1970 were also rated as better performers on professional job functions than the nurses in the control Class of 1968. This difference is generally consistent with other findings that indicate that the program was slightly more effective for the nurses in the Class of 1970 than for those in the Class of 1969, probably because it was better developed and taught to that class.

## NOTES

1. Reality shock is not completely analogous to role deprivation. It is quite possible for a nurse to feel and report role deprivation and not be shocked by it. In other words, she is role deprived but she expected to be and learned that she would be all the way through school. She is role deprived but has been saved the "shock" experience. It is contended that this is better than someone who is both role deprived and "shocked." The former individual is much further along in effecting some kind of resolution. At least she knows what the score is and is prepared to accept it for what it is.

2. This information was obtained from "The University

of California Hospitals Nursing Service Personnel Turnover Study, January 1, 1967 to December 31, 1967" (an unpublished report prepared jointly by the Nursing Research Field Center, Division of Nursing, Bureau of Health Manpower and Education, National Institute of Health, and University of California at San Francisco Nursing Service).

3. The reader might be interested in the performance of this group of baccalaureate nurses on some of the specific criteria comprising the index. Almost two thirds (62%) of the 151 nurses in the combined three classes took some kind of professional course during their first year of employment. ICU and CCU courses were very popular, but about half of them took some additional college or continuing education course. About one third (31%) of the nurses did not subscribe to any kind of professional journals; the others subscribed to between one and four journals. *American Journal of Nursing* was the most popular, followed in order by *Nursing Outlook, RN, Nursing Research,* and *Nursing Clinics of North America.* A little over half (53%) purchased some kind of book for their professional library during their first year of employment. Books on nursing techniques and procedures vied with books on clinical nursing to head the list. They were closely followed by books in sociology and psychology. Over one third of the nurses (37%) reported that they did no professional reading or only about one hour per week. Another fourth (27%), however, were quite serious professional readers, spending eight or more hours a week. This does, however, include 15 nurses who were in graduate school at the time the questionnaire was completed. Almost half (45%) of the nurses reported that they did not belong to any professional organization; another fourth (27%) stated that they were members but not active. The state nurses' organization was the dominant organization to which they belonged (43%). Of the 151 nurses, only 16 (11%) were what might be called very active members, engaging in some kind of activity of the professional organization at least once a month. Eight nurses were officers in some kind of professional organization. Nineteen (13%) were engaged in some kind of professional activity within the employing organization, usually a professional performance or nursing audit committee. There were 25 (17%) active speechgivers, many of them giving more than one talk or presentation. Topics varied markedly from "Care of the Teeth" to "Coronary Care after Discharge" to "The New Graduate in the Working Situation."

4. The students in this study signed release forms for this and all other aspects of the study. Agreement to continue with much of the followup study was dependent upon the nurse's returning questionnaires, arranging for interviews, and the like. Written authorization was not obtained for this; it was assumed that if a nurse arranged for an interview she was in fact giving permission for the interview.

5. I wish to acknowledge the help and cooperation of Dr. Shirley Chater and Dr. Holly Wilson who performed this most valuable service.

## REFERENCES

American Nurses' Association: Facts about nursing; a statistical summary, New York, 1969, The Association.

Corwin, R.: Role conception and mobility aspirations; a study in the formation and transformation of nursing identities, unpublished doctoral dissertation, 1960, University of Minnesota.

Corwin, R.: Militant professionalism, New York, 1970, Appleton-Century-Crofts.

Davis, F., and Olesen, V.: Baccalaureate students' images of nursing, Nurs. Res. 13(1):8-15, 1964.

Dymond, R. F.: A scale for the measurement of empathic ability, J. Consult. Clin. Psychol. 13:127-133, 1949.

Etzioni, A.: The semi-professions and their organizations, New York, 1969, The Free Press.

Glass, H.: Teaching behavior in the nursing laboratory in selected baccalaureate nursing programs in Canada, doctoral dissertation, New York, 1971, Columbia University, Teachers College.

Goldstein, K.: Organism, New York, 1939, American Book Co.

Habenstein, R., and Christ, E.: Professionalizer, traditionalizer, and utilizer, ed. 2, Columbia, Mo., 1963, University of Missouri, p. 153.

Hayter, J.: A follow-up study of graduates of the baccalaureate degree program in nursing, Nurs. Res. 12(1): 45-47, 1963.

Hekmat, H., and Theiss, M.: Self-actualization and modification of affective self-disclosures during a social conditioning interview, Journal of Counseling Psychology 18:101-105, 1971.

Hogan, C.: Registered nurses' completion of a bachelor of science degree in nursing—its effect on their attitude toward the nursing profession, doctoral dissertation, St. Louis, 1972, St. Louis University.

Huse, E. F., and Beer, M.: Eclectic approach to organizational development, Harvard Business Review, October, 1971, pp. 103-112.
ber, 1971, pp. 103-112.

Kramer, M.: Some effects of exposure to employing bureaucracies on the role conceptions and role deprivation of neophyte collegiate nurses, unpublished doctoral dissertation, June 1966, Stanford University.

Kramer, M.: Role models, role conceptions, and role deprivation, Nurs. Res. 17(2):115-120, 1968.

Kramer, M.: The new graduate speaks—again, Am. J. Nurs. 69(9):1903-1907, 1969.

Kramer, M., and Baker, C.: The exodus; can we prevent it? J. Nurs. Administration, May-June 1971, pp. 15-29.

Malone, M.: The dilemma of a professional in a bureaucracy, Nursing Forum 3(4):36-60, 1964.

Maslow, A. H.: Motivation and personality, New York, 1954, Harper & Row, Publishers.

Perls, F.: Ego, hunger, and aggression, London, 1947, George Allen and Unwin.

Shostrom, E. L.: Man the manipulator, Nashville, Tenn., 1967, Abingdon Press.

Simms, L.: The hospital staff nurse position as viewed by baccalaureate graduates in nursing. In Fox, D. J., and Kelley, R. L., editors: The research process in nursing, New York, 1967, Appleton-Century-Crofts, pp. 459-477.

Wilensky, H. L.: Professionalization of everyone, Am. J. Sociol. **70:**142-144, 1964.

## CHAPTER FIVE

# POSTGRADUATION NURSE SOCIALIZATION
## An emergent theory

It was noted in the Preface of this book that, whenever appropriate, research decisions and methodological approaches would be shared with the reader. This chapter begins with a discussion of the similarities and differences between case histories and case studies as used in behavioral science research and then proceeds with a theory of postgraduation nurse socialization utilizing both of these approaches.

A case history is not the same as a case study.[1] A case history is a full story about one social unit, such as a person, status, organization, process, group, or relationship. It covers some specific span or interlude in the life of that social unit. Letters from Lynn, the case history to be presented in this chapter, is the story of the postgraduation socialization experiences of one graduate nurse during her first year of employment. The research goal in a case history is to obtain the full story for its own sake; the story is frequently accompanied by a theoretical commentary that interprets, elucidates, and explicates elements of the story line.

Typically, case histories are quite long because of the full explication of the event or process under focus. They are usually about a single case, although it is possible to do multiple case histories when the analyst has a theory that integrates them. Multiple cases, however, are the rule in the case-study approach. This is a requisite base for the broader generalities that are derived from comparisons.

In contrast to case histories, case studies focus on analytic abstractions and constructions obtained from multiple sources. The purpose of the case-study approach is to describe, verify, and generate theory. It is neither necessary nor desirable to present the full story line; only the data needed to illustrate or substantiate the constructions designed by the abstract purposes of the researcher are presented. The process of analytic abstracting eliminates any confusion over the various stories represented by the different cases. In a case study the story is subordinated to abstract purpose.

In summary, theory is generally applied to case histories (usually in separate commentaries), whereas the purposes of case studies are to generate and verify theory, with the story selectively interwoven with the theory as evidence and illustration. In the first part of this chapter a theory of postgraduation socialization, abstracted from the literature as well as from systematically collected case studies, will be presented. Subsequently, a case history of one graduate will be presented, along with theoretical commentary interpreting various aspects of the new graduate's story.

## ROLE TRANSFORMATION FROM STUDENT TO GRADUATE NURSE

Socialization, the process by which one learns to perform his various roles adequately, is continuous throughout life. Although individuals enter the adult world with some anticipatory socialization, the socialization experienced in childhood is not enough to meet the demands of later years; adult socialization is needed. Chief among the roles for which adult socialization is needed is the occupational role; an adult must learn what others will demand of him in his role and what he will come to demand of himself.

Newly graduated nurses face a period of crisis. They may have received some anticipatory socialization into the occupation of nursing, but the likelihood is that socialization during the school period focused on the norms, values, and general nurse role behaviors that the *faculty* believed to be necessary components of the nurse role. Rarely does the student nurse see the instructor function as a nurse. The neophytes have yet to face the behavioral expectations of the nurse work force, the expectations of their supervisors. Role transformation, the process wherein one changes the behavioral expression of a role, is the next order of business. How does this come about? Who are the instrumental figures in it?

Although much has been written about the difficulties encountered by new graduate nurses, about the high and differing expectations held of the new graduate by nursing service administrators and educators, and about working conditions conducive to greater job satisfaction, the process of postgraduation professional nurse socialization has hardly been explored. Answers are needed to questions such as: Are neophyte nurses aware of the imminent occurrence of the postgraduation socialization process and its dimensions? Is there a relationship between successful role transformation and future contribution in the profession? Is it patterned and predictive? Can it be made more planned and deliberative and, therefore, not more restrictive but more constructive? Is there discontinuity between pre- and postgraduate socialization which calls for great role transformation? The purpose of this section of the chapter will be to describe and analyze the process of postgraduation professional socialization for a group of newly graduated baccalaureate nurses during their first year of work as nurses. We will take a look at their role transformation and hopefully begin to get some answers to the above questions.

The data were obtained from several sources. At my request, six new baccalaureate nurses wrote diaries of their experiences, feel-ings, and impressions and their analysis of their work situation and adjustment to it. These were sent to me at regular intervals, usually about every two or three weeks. This was a convenience and volunteer sample. The only requisites were that the nurses be new graduates, able to express themselves in writing and willing to do so. Given these qualifications, the six nurses were selected to obtain geographical and work-setting variability: Far West, Mountain states, Midwest, South, and East. Four of the nurses worked in hospitals; two worked in public health departments. Most of the data and propositions offered here will be based upon and abstracted from these diaries, as well as from retrospective data about the first year of nurse employment obtained through 1½-hour tape-recorded interviews with 127 new graduate nurses from the Classes of 1968, 1969, and 1970. The one-year postgraduation work settings of these 127 nurses were mainly in hospitals (82%) and mainly in California, although 17% were working out of state.

The concept of adult socialization can be approached from at least four different perspectives. First, *who is being socialized?* A good portion of the writing and research in this area has been concerned with the deviant adult—the criminal returning to a noncriminal way of life, the cure of the drug addict, the effect of therapy on the emotionally ill. There has also been considerable work focused on socializees with changing physical or social status; for example, the disabled veteran, the consequences of physical stigma, the analyses of the impact of illness on a person, the effect of abrupt downward social mobility, and the consequences of radical changes in married states, such as widowhood. Of concern here will be the nondeviant adult who is being socialized into a work setting and role.

An area of active study and research interest has been the *agents of socialization*, both formal and informal. Who are they? Which of them are effective and which are not? What is the relationship between diffuse status characteristics of the socializer and effectiveness as a socialization agent? Also of interest is the visibility of the agents and the preparation of the socialization agent for his task.

A third major area of study in adult socialization is the relative effectiveness of different *methods of socialization*—various lengths of speeches, effects of drugs, devices to influence war prisoners, different types of models, exhortations, and so on. In addition to these methods of socialization, there is also the concern as to whether the socialization agent is internal or external: Is the socialization self-initiated or does it arise from external pressures?

The *content of the demands* made upon the adult in the socialization process constitutes the fourth major area of study. What is the nature of the socialization demands? Are they mainly knowledge, skills, attitudes, or processes? Do the demands arise in response to technological changes, new levels of worker aspirations, or shift in expectations of role alters?

The following descriptive analysis of the postgraduation socialization experiences of new baccalaureate nurses will focus on the nondeviant adult from the perspectives of who is socializing her, by what methods, and the content of the socialization experience. This report is not intended to be exhaustive or inclusive. It is only a beginning; the limited data preclude the formation of anything but tentative conclusions.

## SOCIALIZATION AGENTS

Who are the socialization agents of the neophyte nurse during her postgraduation socialization experience? The daily socialization of the new graduate is truly labyrinthine. Many of the inputs compete for time and attention; many are conflicting in their messages. Although we usually think of community as an economic, political, or physical aggregate, it is just as valid and more to our purposes to think of the community into which the new graduate is immersed as a socialization community. Within this community it is readily possible to identify clusters of people who have a vested interest in influencing the behavior and values of the neophyte nurse as she begins her process of role transformation.

*Nurse's aides.* It was evident that nurse's aides are major socialization agents for the new graduate. This was borne out by comments in the diaries and from the nurses who were interviewed. They reported much surprise about various aspects of their relationships with aides—"they have so much power," "they're so competent; they can show you how to do most anything," "they're incompetent," "you just better do things their way or you're in real trouble," "the supervisor backs the nurse's aides, not the nurses," and so on.

Boy, was that ever a surprise! It's the nurse's aide who gives you the skinny about what you are to do, not do. And, it's not only the *things* they expect you to do, it's other stuff too—like how hard you should work, how involved you can get with the patients, how much time is too much or too little for lunch or to spend with a certain patient. (NG:BS/2[D3]

Although the messages are mixed, it is clear that the nurse's aide group as socializers conveys both norms and behaviors to the new graduate. An analysis of the data reported by Gale in her study of the coordination between the nurse's aide and staff nurse role would seem to indicate that the effectiveness of the nurse's aide as a socializer is limited to this initial postgraduation socialization period rather than running extensively throughout the ensuing work period. Initially, the nurse's aide seems to function as almost the dominant socializer; but Gale found that after role specific behaviors have been learned the two groups (nurses and nurse's aides) tended to develop separate subcultural norms and role expectations and that, in fact, these two roles were not particularly well coordinated.

Look more closely at this initial view and socializing function of the nurse's aide group. The illustration° on the following page captures the essence of the new graduate's per-

---

°From: University of California hospitals nursing service personnel turnover study; January 1, 1967, to December 31, 1967, unpublished report prepared jointly by the Nursing Research Field Center, Division of Nursing Bureau of Health Manpower and Education, National Institute of Health, and University of California at San Francisco Nursing Service. Permission granted by the Nursing Research Field Center.

MEDIAN YEARS OF:
AGE ——24—34—37
EXPERIENCE—2⅔—4—9
TENURE— ½—2½—5⅓

NURSING RESEARCH FIELD CENTER
Division of Nursing 1965

RN LVN NA

ceptions of the "power and might" of the nurse's aide and LVN. Both the interview data and the diaries contained much about this perceived power relationship.

The aides are older and have had so much experience; yet I'm the person who is responsible, in charge, and supposed to tell them what to do —it's crazy! (NG:BS/2[D2])

In addition to the power-and-might perspective, there was also evidence that the nurse's aide might well be the person who begins the "back region" socialization of the new graduate. Goffman has presented a description and analysis of social interaction in terms of the means used by people to control the impressions others receive of them. This he calls impression management and describes it as follows:

We find a team of performers who cooperate to present to an audience a given definition of the situation. This will include the conception of own team and of audience and assumptions concerning the ethos that is to be maintained by rules of politeness and decorum. We often find a division into back region, where the performance is presented. Access to these regions is controlled in order to prevent the audience from seeing backstage and to prevent outsiders from coming into a performance that is not addressed to them. Among members of the team we find that familiarity prevails, solidarity is likely to develop, and

that secrets that could give the show away are shared and kept.°

Translated into the context of nursing, the result is somewhat as follows. The new nurse comes to the unit, often accompanied by someone from in-service education (the official formal socializers of the new graduate, frequently perceived as "sticklers for procedures and principles, but they are definitely not 'Ivory Tower' and unrealistic like our instructors were."). While she is being oriented, there is often a hands-off policy practiced by both aides and other staff nurses. Within the line of vision of the newcomer, policies and procedures are performed according to the book. The neophyte is presented with the "front region" of the ward or agency activity. The impression given to outsiders—at this point, both the newcomer and in-service education—is carefully managed.

Little by little, though, the nurse's aide (or the community worker in the case of one of the nurse diarists who was working in a public health agency) provides the neophyte with glimpses of the back region.

I don't know . . . it was very subtle. When I said that I was going to withhold the pain medication until I got a renew order, the aide just looked sort of funny, kind of surprised like . . . I don't know. It was really little things, little messages I got, that made me suspect . . . so one day I said to Margie [the aide]: "Isn't this the way others do it?" And she shrugged her shoulders and walked away. I think she said something like: "Well, you'll find out." So I decided I'd better really find out what was going on. But that's not easy to do . . . it took me almost a month and a half before I got through. (NG:BS/4[D4])

The nurse's aide seems to provide sufficient clues to motivate the neophyte to suspect that some type of image management might be going on. It is quite possible that this is all that the nurse's aide group knows—that there is a back region. They might lack detailed information as to the precepts of the back region; the specific precepts of the back region

°Goffman, E.: The presentation of self in everyday life, New York, 1959, © Doubleday & Co., Inc., p. 238.

seemed to come more from LVN's and other staff nurses.

Perhaps the key to the breakthrough to the back region reality comes for the new graduate when she enacts some kind of behavior or verbalizes some attitude that is not quite to the letter of the law, not quite in keeping with idealistic norms learned in school. Examples of such behavior cited by the nurses included giving a medication without an order, taking medications ordered for one patient to start doses for another, or not doing treatments or monitorings that were ordered.

Today I got the word from Jane [nurse's aide] and Mrs. C. [LVN] about which doctors you call out on nights and which you go ahead and give the med and they'll cover you on. I don't know what to think. Miss J. [head nurse] hasn't ever said anything. Should I listen to what the aides say, do it my way, or ask the head nurse?

[Two weeks later] You know, it's really funny. I mentioned about calling out the doctors on nights in the dressing room today, and was saying how upset the aides were that I just didn't go ahead and give the med repeat. They're upset because when the patients don't sleep they have to work harder and it interferes with their almost constant nap. All the nurses agreed with me and said that, yes, you really should call the doctors to get a repeat on sleeping pills and everything before you give an unprescribed med. Later, Marie, who overheard the conversation, told me that when Martha and Sue were on nights, they never did. It seems all kind of hush, hush, you know; and I don't know what to think or expect.

[Three weeks later] I went to coffee with Lil today and confided to her that I had repeated Mr. Jones' Demerol last night without an order. I told her I was worried and felt guilty about it; did she think it would be OK? She said not to worry. Then she opened up and really gave me the dope —not only about this med situation but lots of other stuff too. I felt like I'd made it. The older nurses can really make things easier for you if they want to.

[One week later] I feel good. Mary [an RN] stopped me in the hall, smiled, and said I was really getting with it. Then she asked if the med problem had worked itself out. I said "Yes." Then she winked at me and said "Good." She also told me some of the other things you can do with different doctors' patients. I don't know what I did, or why they're finally *really* telling me; I guess

I'll just count my blessings and let it go at that. (NG:BS/4 and 5[D3])

It is also quite possible that if the neophyte does not give the appropriate cues, if she continues to "mouth the school lines," as one staff nurse put it, she will never get to the back-region reality. It is as though the socializers were unsuccessful, so a more or less constant image management ensues. Image management is an unstable social situation that is extremely taxing. It is likely that before long the neophyte will recieve unintended glimpses of back-region reality. If she chooses to ignore and not pursue these further, a mutual pretense awareness context will probably develop in which both parties mutually agree to ignore discrepant information. Consider, for example, the comments of this graduate after working one year on the same unit.

I gradually found out what they wanted me to do —and I tried for awhile—but that just wasn't my idea of nursing. [Would you give me an example of this?] They felt they deserved an hour or an hour and a half for lunch. We were supposed to rush through the baths, and then often there wouldn't be enough time for formula demonstration before we had to rush the babies out. I was never really one of them because I wouldn't do things their way. (NG:BS/12[D5])

*Physicians.* Another highly instrumental socializing agent for the new nurse is the physician. Without a doubt, he is effective in shaping the new nurse's behavior, particularly around technical performances. Gale found that nurse's aides reported that experienced staff nurses placed optimum priority on diagnostic tests and technical procedures as ordered by physicians. The physician was also effective in shaping the corresponding attitudes and norms of the new nurse toward technical care as most important. In this respect, his socialization reinforces that of many head nurses and supervisors, who also place priority on technical tasks: "Are your temps and treatments done? Are they recorded? That's the only thing my head nurse ever says to me."

If the nurse's professional beliefs were strong enough, or if there was some outside support, it seemed that eventually some of the earlier school socialization might reassert itself.

Golly gee, I really was an idiot when I first started here. You know, I was wrapped up, so concerned that I *had* to learn all these disease things—diseases I'd never heard about in school—and lab tests and skills . . . because the doctors expected you to know. [What did they expect you to know?] How to set up for an LP and IV setups and helping them with exams and tests. They didn't particularly pressure you on the disease things, come to think of it . . . it was interesting to me and I wanted to learn it . . . but anyway, after a few months I had had enough of that. I'd learned a lot and, what's more, I knew I *could* learn what I didn't know. So I guess in a way you'd say I came back to nursing and began concentrating on the patient as a person, you know, rather than the "choley in 316." (NG:BS/12[723]6/71)

*Patients.* The data did not indicate that the patient was as strong a socializing agent for nurses as for physicians. Olmsted and Paget believe that the young physician is most likely to be socialized by his own patients; if he ever learns an adequate set of performance behaviors, he learns them on his own in interaction with his patients. Intuitively one would also expect this to be true for nurses, but evidence for this kind of socialization was not found in the diary data. Perhaps this is because nurses have earlier and more direct contact with patients during their school socialization than do physicians. The patient is central in pregraduate socialization. Individualized, comprehensive, patient-centered care is the dominant theme in nursing schools. Upon graduation comes the realization that there are other strong influences upon nursing. Patients do not appear to have the power or relevance to continue the nurse's socialization.

I still get pretty maudlin about service and all that. I realize there certainly is a lot more trivia involved in keeping the unit operating, but certainly not all that running around taking care of people's every little need all the time. There are other relationships you have to keep up with—people you work with, the ward secretary, all the doctors that come in. It's just not the nurse-patient relationship that is central and that keeps the ward running. (NG:BS/2[3]8/71)

. . .

Well, in school we were always taught patient-centered and family-centered care. But here sometimes it's not very much patient-centered. In school we were taught that you put patient priority above anything else, but in a hospital, in natural practice, it is just not true. Maybe it's because this is a teaching school and we have so many people, doctors, and so many different kinds of people coming in and out. Sometimes we ignore patients. (NG:AD/2[4]8/71)

Perhaps patients and nurse-patient relationships were not described as central socialization agents because the socialization of the nurse is not as segmented (into student professional, intern, resident, worker) as is that of her medical colleagues. Since the last part of the nurse role socialization is done as a paid employee (rather than as an intern or resident), the nurse may well be more attuned to other nurses' and employer's demands during this critical role transformation period than is the physician.

*Formal socializers.* In the postgraduation socialization, there are probably only two groups of personnel within the socialization community who could be termed formal socializers in the sense that they have the positional authority and responsibility for the task. These two groups are in-service education instructors and head nurses. Included in the last category would also be assistant head nurses and charge nurses, dependent upon the shift on which the nurse works.

The data on the role of the in-service education instructor as a socializing agent was confusing; no pattern was discernible. Most of the new graduates were exposed to such socializers, but their power and effectiveness was highly variable.

[Mrs. G.] was great. She really looked out after me and sort of protected me. Later on, I found that she was one of the few people in the place that I could really talk to. She was the only one who had even the foggiest notion of what I was talking about. She couldn't do anything, but it helped to talk to her. (NG:BS/6[D5])

. . .

You mean the staff development people? They're OK. There's this one little old lady who's really a riot, though. She comes up with all her pamphlets and booklets and tells us we should be doing this and that. She's so nice; so we listen to her and give her a cup of coffee and she goes away happy . . . I kind of feel like patting her on the head, you know what I mean? I hope I don't have to work when I'm that old. (Med Ctr:BS[812]7/68)

Generally speaking, in-service educators were perceived as being "nonthreatening," "good people to ask questions of," and ones who "don't make you feel so dumb," and they helped immensely in making implicit expectations explicit.

I think probably the staff development people were the most helpful. We had asked for some things from the staff on the floor, like the routines and how the floor runs from dawn to dusk. And it never happened; we didn't get it until we had a meeting with the staff development people. They got the staff together for us, and then we got some things put out in the open . . . found out exactly what we were supposed to be doing. (NG:BS/2[16]8/71)

One new graduate analyzed the seeming lack of power and effectiveness of staff development or in-service education (the two appellations are used interchangeably) personnel in this way.

There's something I was mulling over in my head. At the first meeting, Helen [in-service instructor] went over the administrative setup and who reports to who and who really has political clout in nursing administration. Staff development doesn't, and they like it that way because they are then perceived as nonthreatening. The other side of that coin is that they are perceived as noneffective. The thing I remember about the change theory from school was that, to get people to change, it's not that you appeal to their rationality and that they see the correctness of all that. What is going to effect them personally is something that they pay the most attention to first off. So, without any kind of political clout, without feeling, even if it's the slightest kind of threat, most nurses see that it's possible in an organization to just go on and on and never change. Like, M. can come to our conferences and talk until the cow comes home about nursing care plans and stuff like that, but until people see that this kind of thing is expected of a nurse now—it's in the job description, that this is the job she's hired for, that this is the job she's expected to do and that it's included on her evaluation—until they really understand that, I

don't think it's reasonable to expect people to change. (NG:BS/2[3]8/71)

As might be expected, the charge and head nurses were dominant socializers, particularly in the area of role specific behaviors. A few generalizations from the data were quite conclusive. The neophyte expected the head nurse to be a teacher; she expected her to tell her what to do and how to do it. Perhaps because of these role expectations, the new graduates reported considerable vicarious socialization from the head nurses—more so than from any other socialization agent.

I heard [the head nurse] chewing out Martha. Boy, did I learn something from that. (NG:AD/3[18]3/69)

Almost all of the specific socialization incidents reported by the diarists concerned role behaviors rather than attitudes or norms. In fact, it was only after the diarists were specifically asked "What influence, if any, does your head nurse have on you?" that there was much data forthcoming at all. This should not be wrongly interpreted as meaning there was no influence; rather it would seem that the influence was so pervasive and expected as to be not worthy of mentioning in a diary.

*Other socializers.* Many of the key socialization agents of the community never came in contact with the new nurses. Two groups of personnel in particular fit into this category. One might be called top-level administration, and consisted of the hospital or agency administrator, the board of directors, and the director of nursing. The other group was the top man in a particular service, such as the chief of staff of pediatrics. The socialization influence of both of these groups was largely through memo, notice, letter, or directive or by word-of-mouth, and had subsequently been committed to the card file in large, bold print, usually in red.

DO NOT MOVE BEDS FROM
ONE FLOOR TO ANOTHER!

NO EATING IN THE LINEN ROOM:
THAT MEANS YOU!

DR. T. SAYS NOT TO USE ALCOHOL
BATHS ON ANY CHILDREN.

Although given in absentia, there was little doubt that the fiats had some impact or they would not have been reported. Consequently, it seems that these nonvisible groups were effective as socializing agents.

A further explanatory word about the director of nurses is in order. This individual tended to be an enigma to most of the nurses. The administrative fiats quoted above were usually ascribed to someone in a middle-management position or to the hospital administrator rather than to the director of nursing. The director of nursing as a socializing agent tended to be perceived with fear or absentee power.

I don't know who she is; I've never met her, but Janie has and she tells me that it's best to avoid her altogether. Just follow the edicts or you're bound to lose. (Med Ctr:BS/13[1123]1/70)

This attitude was by no means universal. In fact, there was evidence that some graduate nurses deliberately sought out the director of nursing, acquainted her with their needs and desires, and sometimes used her to help them accomplish their goals. The important point is that perception of her as a socializing agent seems to be all or none, either total avoidance or deliberate seeking.

**Perception of socialization agents**

It is one matter for the new graduate to perceive the influential people in her postgraduation socialization process. Also of interest was the new graduate's perception of the extent to which the people with whom she worked perceived that their socialization functions were consonant with her expectations. There were frequent notations in the diaries and interviews to the effect that often fellow staff nurses saw their socialization role incongruently from what apparently were the neophytes' expectations.

You're just going to have to pick it up on your own. I don't have time to teach you every little thing . . . You should have learned that in school . . . It's faster for me to do it than to show you how to do it . . . That's such a "mickey-mouse" thing— go ask Mrs. A. [nurse's aide] to show you how to do it. (NG:BS/4[D#4])

This does not mean that fellow staff nurses were not socialization agents; indeed, the above were strong socialization messages about what the nurse saw as important in her role. The difference is between deliberative, planned socialization that is congruent with belief systems and with the neophyte's expectations and unplanned, nondeliberative, incongruent socialization as exemplified by the above excerpt. A significant question is whether unplanned socialization is what we want—always keeping in mind, of course, that the new graduates of today are the postgraduation socialization agents of tomorrow.

It would be inaccurate to leave the reader with the notion that none of the socialization agents willingly accepted or included this function in their role concepts. This was certainly not true.

I've found that the doctors, particularly some of the house staff, are so anxious to teach you; they'll discourse on almost anything at great length. Some of the staff nurses and the head nurse will also, if it's quiet and they have the time. They don't really see it as their job, though, to teach and help me. The aides and LPN's are very helpful and will gladly show you what they know. There's one other RN who will really go out of her way to help the new person get started, but only one. (NG:BS/3[D#3])

It does come through, however, that the extent of incorporation of socialization as a function of one's role was variable: warmly embraced by some, ignored by others of the socialization agents.

**METHODS OF SOCIALIZATION**

The question of when to intervene and when to allow the socializee to generate his own initiative toward growth and development is the most important value judgment that socialization agents must make. Another important decision is the election of appropriate methods to meet goals. Once socialization goals have been clarified, it is potentially possible to derive multiple appropriate action designs. For example, if what is desired is a change in attitude, then the research and corresponding action designs of communication theorists such as Hovland and associates, Hovland and Weiss, Kelman and Hovland, and Luchins are most appropriate. Goals must be defined and appropriate socialization strategies selected to create the conditions necessary for the attitudinal, cognitive, or behavior changes desired. During the postgraduate socialization period, neophyte nurses seemed to encounter three major problems related to methods of socialization. The first of these difficulties concerned the shift from formal to informal modes of socialization and from formal to informal learner roles. In the school socialization period the dominant method was direct and expository. Expectations were clearly and concisely presented; the performance standard was usually made quite explicit through rules and regulations, course objectives, and so on. This picture changes radically when the neophyte becomes involved in the socializing context of the work environment. Here, methods of socialization are informal; expectations and performance standards are much more vague and implicit. In her first job the new graduate expects to test herself and to learn something. Yet formally the role and expectations of the new graduate are that of worker, not learner. So immediately she is confronted with the problem of meeting her learner expectations (which are set in the context of the formal learner role to which she is accustomed) within the formal role of worker.

In a similar vein, another problem confronting the new nurse during this postgraduation socialization period is what appears to be inadequate feedback on her performance. Accustomed previously to an almost constant feedback environment (grades, faculty evaluations, and so forth), the new socialization setting is often characterized by a paucity of feedback or, at best, very general implicit feedback.

My supervisor? I don't feel she is interested. She hasn't once asked me about my work; never once has she asked me what I am doing or about my work. I haven't gotten one bit of feedback, and it really upsets me. (NG:BS/12[754]12/70)

A third problem area encountered by the new graduate nurse stemmed from the ongoing process that is the main subject of this book. For many of the nurses, the involvement in the reality shock experience was so great that they could not perceive, hear, or assimilate many of the socialization messages sent their way. When this happened, confusion and distrust emanated from both the socializee and the socializing agent. The latter was of the opinion that she had given appropriate messages to the newcomer, so she was consequently quite surprised to hear the newcomer say: 'I had no idea you were displeased with my work.'' The neophyte, on the other hand, reported that she was not even aware that she had received any feedback on her work whatsoever.

Well, really everything was fine. It came as a bolt out of the blue. It was about two days before my evaluation conference that I found out that my supervisor wasn't going to recommend me for a permanent position. [This was in a public health department wherein after one year of probation nurses were either kept on temporary status or placed on permanent status, depending upon their evaluation.] I really thought everything was fine. I had worked hard and really gave what I thought was good care to my patients. Oh, I made mistakes, but they weren't world-shattering and I didn't make the same one twice. I just couldn't understand it. I wasn't happy in the job—it came as quite a shock to find out what real nursing was —but I liked some parts of the job and I wanted to keep it. I just couldn't believe it when she told me my work was poor and that she was not going to recommend me.

With this nurse's permission, I talked with the supervisor about this incident, who said:

I don't know why it was such a surprise to M. She must have known she was in trouble all along. She certainly had been told often enough, and not just by me. I've heard the other nurses tell her too. [Can you give me some examples of the kinds of things she did that got her into trouble?] Well certainly. One thing, she was lazy. She thought she had too big a caseload, so she closed out many of the long-term cases that didn't seem to be making any progress. She didn't check this with anyone; she just did it. I told her about it, and I also heard her team leader tell her, but she just persisted in doing it anyway. We lose money when nurses do that, you know. And if we don't have money, we can't operate. I know she says she wasn't told about this all along, but that's not true.

During a subsequent interview with the new graduate in her home (she had been let go from the public health department position and was awaiting a new job), she said:

There were so many things that really bugged me about that job, and there was nothing I could do about them. Sometimes I could just scream. Ridiculous things like carrying thousands of patients in your caseload who didn't need or want you, and you weren't doing anything for them, and everybody knew it; but you had to pad your caseload just to bring in certain kinds of funds. I was in turmoil the whole time I worked there, but I sure didn't know there was anything wrong with my work or that I wasn't giving good nursing care. (NG:BS/12[59]6/67)

Analysis of the preceding excerpts illustrates the point that the new nurse was being evaluated on the basis of backstage reality—the most implicit of all expectations. Staff nurses (and supervisors), unaware that they are socialization agents, do not understand the neophytes confusion between back- and frontstage reality. They are probably not even aware that this difference exists or that evaluation guidelines that are so clear to them are not at all clear to the new graduate. They are also probably unaware that they are evaluating on backstage reality. From the perspective of the neophyte who is operating on the basis of frontstage reality and expects an evaluation based on that, a staff public health nurse does have the autonomy and responsibility to make decisions regarding her patient caseload and the needs of the patients in it. From the viewpoint of the personnel operating in the backstage reality, it is understandable that it is necessary for all nurses to maintain a patient caseload of a size that will support the organization. It is incongruous to them that failure to do this would not occasion a negative evaluation. But for the new graduate in the throes of reality shock, who has not yet achieved entrance to the backstage reality, whose perceptions are clouded by the emotions generated by moral outrage, this basis for evaluation is incomprehensible.

This problem of widely variant or discrepant perceptions is so crucial to an understanding of the postgraduation socialization process that perhaps another example would help in bringing to the surface the marked differences in the perceptions of the socializee and the socializer. In the following excerpts, the same incident is described by a new graduate and by her head nurse. From the perspective of the neophyte nurse:

The head nurse gives lip service that she wants to be open and receptive, but every time Sue or I suggest something we get: "We don't do it that way here." There are some things that I find irrelevant and rather unimportant that I am informed by my head nurse are duties and must be performed at all times . . . daily bathing of every single patient on the unit. There are some days when I think that there is something else you can do for that kid that is much more important than making sure he gets bathed from head to foot. I have a real gripe with Mary [the head nurse] about this—not the bathing itself, but her approach to it. She won't approach me directly but she says to me: "The aides complain you don't give a bath every day." The only time I skip baths is like some of the teenagers. I feel they should have a choice in it. Like if they skip a bath for one day, I really can't see any harm in it, but Mary is there with "everyone has to take a bath every day for the duration of their stay here" kind of thing. Another reason I sometimes skip a bath is for a kid who has been awake all night long with some kind of problem or is in pain or something. If he's asleep, I can't see waking him up to give him a bath, and in the afternoon there are visitors and I am not going to kick the visitors out to give that kid a bath. But as far as Mary is concerned he should be awakened and given a bath because baths must be done every day and this is hospital policy. (NG:BS/12[705]6/71)

The same issue from the perspective of the head nurse:

When she first came, she wasn't a very good bedside nurse. She was unsure of herself and disorganized. Her knowledge was very good. She has a good background, I could tell. But as far as her practical bedside nursing, it is still not up to par. She asks questions and seems to have the medical knowledge. She knows the diseases and drugs. And when the other nurses ask her questions she has the answers. She does have good suggestions, but her nursing is just not up to par. [Can you give me an example?] Well, for awhile there she wasn't bathing the patients every day.

I finally asked her about it and she said it isn't that important, that other things are more important. I said that in this institution it is, that everybody does get cleaned up. I have to constantly remind her of it. She didn't do it deliberately; it just didn't hit her. I thought I would try and look and see what she was doing instead. She would spend time talking with patients, which is good. But I feel that you can talk with a patient and still carry on your nursing care. So I tried to tell her: "Now look, organize your work. Why don't you do this one first and this one second, and so forth." But she seemed to have a need to continue to learn and work things out for herself. It's the little things, but the little things are important too. And it was hard on the others. The nurse's aides—they've been here a long time and they know the routines and policies—would do her work for her because they didn't want to see Johnny not bathed. They would go and do it for her. I had a couple of conferences with her about this and she has improved. She is not one to make excuses. She never complained.

Here we can see that for the head nurse the backstage reality upon which she was operating and judging the neophyte was that all patients must be cleaned up every day. She knows that she will look good and will be judged by her superiors on the basis of whether all patients are "dusted and polished" every day, the ward looks neat and tidy, and she is able to accomplish this with the staff allowed her by the front office (with difficulty, of course, which is why everyone must look busy at all times in case the supervisor comes onto the ward.)

It is quite possible that the head nurse knows and mouths the rhetoric of the front-stage reality: "It's most important to give individualized patient care," "Plan and give care to each patient according to his needs," and so on. In fact, during other parts of this interview the head nurse did state this rhetoric. The problem is that the new graduate actually believes, acts, and lives by this rhetoric of the frontstage reality that she has been taught. Furthermore, she expects to be evaluated on this basis. It is no wonder that there is surprise when not only is the praise not forthcoming but instead there is blame!

Another of the ways in which reality shock and the resultant attempts at conflict resolu-

tion interferred with the perception of the socialization messages being sent is illustrated by the following excerpt.

At first, and for what seemed like a long time—maybe it wasn't, but it seemed like it was ages—I was so overwhelmed by all I had to learn. I was amazed. I had no idea of how much I didn't know. It's really quite a shock, you know, to be out on your own after being coddled in school for so long. Well, I was so bogged down in learning all this stuff: Routines, and what this doctor likes, and skills and procedures—IVP's, EKG's, setup things like that. Well, I guess I was just so wrapped up in myself and in learning all this stuff that I guess I just didn't listen or hear what people were saying to me. I found that out from an aide. She had told me something about a patient, and instead of answering her I told her about these new orders. She thought what she was telling me was important and she told me that I just didn't listen. After that I stopped to think about it and suddenly realized that I was going at such full tilt all the time that I didn't hear. (NG:BS/9[D2])

The diaries of the other nurses also contained references to feedback information that they had apparently not heard or heard inaccurately, particularly while they were in the moral outrage phase of reality shock. Sometimes this information was positive feedback: "I told you a couple of months ago that you were doing fine, just fine. Why are you so surprised to hear it now?" In no instance, however, in the more than 550 interviews that I have conducted with nurses all over the country or in many conversations and more than 100 formal interviews with head nurses, supervisors, and directors of nursing, has any word ever been mentioned that the new nurse was perceived as being in culture or reality shock, that she might not be hearing a message because of shock interference. Yet there is much evidence that reality shock is prevalent and that it is a marked deterrent to effective postgraduation socialization.

### Formal method

*Exposition.* The dominant socialization method was simple straightforward exposition or demonstration: "She showed me how to do it" or "She told me to do it this way." The kind of content communicated in this way was mainly skills and knowledge rather than norms, attitudes, or values. The head nurse or immediate supervisor was generally perceived as having the most power in this kind of socialization encounter. In-service education instructors, the other group of formal work socializers, were perceived as having some power but as being too far removed from the reality situation to have operational authority.

I know we learned it that way in orientation; but the head nurse showed this better way, and on the floor it works better that way. (NG:BS/1[913]7/69)

### Informal methods

The informal methods of socialization used were quite varied and were generally used to transmit value and attitudinal messages. Although it is not possible to indicate the extent to which either the socializer or the socializee was cognizant of these methods or of their use to achieve a preestablished goal, there can be little doubt that they were effective, or they would not have been remembered and reported. Among the more or less informal methods reported by the neophyte nurses were the following.

*Do nothing.* Schein noted in his interviews with college graduates after they had been on the job for six months to one year that almost all of them in one way or another stated that he was shocked by the degree to which his good ideas were rejected. Often there was no argument or analysis of the idea; just nothing happened. This same phenomenon was described repeatedly by the nurses in their diaries and interviews.

It's a great control method. When I suggest something and the other RN's think it's too school-bookish or they just don't want to do it, they smile and say what a good idea it is and then just don't do it. I phoned the pharmacy and asked the pharmacist if he would send up the leaflets on all the new drugs we were giving—none of us ever knew what we were giving; we kept asking one another and no one knew. So he said "sure," he'd send them up, and he did. I faithfully put them together in a looseleaf binder and indexed it and everything. I showed others my system. When I came back from a week's vacation not a thing had been done and the book was shoved way back in the corner of the drawer. (NG:BS/8[D4])

The do-nothing method is extremely effective in socializing the new graduate to the dominant and desired behaviors of the unit or agency. It tells her which problems and information to report and which to ignore. It can rapidly socialize her into the proverbial rut; she quickly learns which behavior is rewarded and expected.

*Nonverbal.* Another effective method of socialization, but one in which the content of the message is subject to more ambiguity than in the do-nothing method, is nonverbal communication.

Oh, the nonverbal messages—frowns, raised eyebrows, and so on—they really get to you. They shape you up fast. My head nurse rarely talks to me or others either. She communicates almost completely with eyebrows, shoulders, and hand gestures. (NG:BS/12[738]12/70)

*Assignments.* Perhaps it would be more accurate to call assignment of work tasks a socialization tool. One young nurse related how she really enjoyed being assigned to admit new patients.

It gave me a chance to really relate with the patients, conduct an admission interview, and really do some good nursing. Well, that assignment didn't last long! It took me more time to admit people than the other nurses, so after that I was never assigned to admit patients again. I got the message as to what was wanted. (NG:BS/12[908]6/70)

*Breakdown.* The next method of socialization is difficult to describe because in many respects it is so abhorrent. For want of a better term, it will be called breakdown because that is what the nurses termed it. Actually it seems quite close to what Dornbusch describes as the stripping process. It usually consists of face-to-face confrontations in which the individual is psychologically stripped in such a way as to lose face, self-esteem, and confidence. He is stripped of his old values and beliefs. Presumably the idea is that when this occurs the neophyte will then be ready to listen and to take on the new values and behavior patterns that he "should." Needless to say, this procedure is devastating to the ego, and if the ego is weak it can do substantial harm. It certainly does not appear to be effective in doing anything other than driving nurses out of nursing practice. An illustration from one the case studies will exemplify this method.

One night a girl didn't want to float because it was a floor where she had a lot of problems before, and besides we were really busy that night. The team leader that night was a new graduate like I was, and she relayed the message to the girl [a nurse's aide] that the supervisor wanted her to float to 3 West. The nurse's aide explained why she didn't want to go, and we agreed but we didn't see anything we could do about it. So the girl called the supervisor herself and explained. We were all called in the next day, and in front of the day shift the supervisor blasted us royally—about not going through the chain of command, and that if there was a question about floating that it should be the team leader's responsibility to talk to the supervisor, and that you don't get to the supervisor unless you talk to the head nurse first. She didn't ask us what happened or any of the facts; she just blasted us over and over again. I finally broke down and cried, and she said: "Oh, that is just what I wanted. *Now* there is some response here. Now you will begin to listen." Then she began all over again. She said that because the nurse's aide called the supervisor that that meant that the team leaders didn't have enough power. I challenged that because we are all new graduates on evenings and we haven't learned all that is acceptable and not acceptable yet. And the nurse's aide had been there for ten years and knew what things were. That got her very upset and she began blasting away again. I was so upset I broke down again, and that again made her very happy. She said that meant I was willing to learn. (NG:BS/12[736]5/71)

*Questions.* The last and prevalent method of socialization that was used appeared to be quite effective; through repetitive questioning the neophyte nurse learned what was valued and rewarded in the organization. Consider this comment by a new graduate in a public health department.

My supervisor hasn't once asked me about my work. [What does she ask you?] She asks me why I am wearing a blue ribbon in my hair or why I have gold buttons on my coat; she asks me why I am late or why I want to go home—all of these rules type of things that as far as I am concerned they're a lot less important than the patient care.

And I feel I am doing good patient care. (NG: BS/12[754]12/70)

By the kinds of questions asked of the neophyte by physicians, the head nurse, aides, other nurses, and so on, the new nurse learns what others expect of her in her new role. In time, with rewards and identification, this is what she comes to expect of herself.

The diary cases studied actually contained only one incidence in which it seemed that the neophyte was aware of this process.

I didn't realize how much I had changed. I realized that my instructor's questions, "How do I feel about something," "What do I think about this patient's plan of care," had been replaced by "What's his BP, I & O?" or "Who's got the narcotic key?" These are the only things we say to one another now. No one asks me about plans of patient care anymore—that's not important. (NG: BS/9[D2])

A side study done in connection with this research study further illustrates the impact of questioning as a means of socialization. Both the medical center and the class samples of nurses were asked the following questions during their respective interviews; "What are the three questions your head nurse or supervisor most frequently asks you?" and "What are the three questions you most frequently ask of the people responsible to you?" Responses to these questions were categorized under the areas of patient care, system maintenance, and personnel development. Results showed that within the responses to each set of interview questions the highest percentages were within the system maintenance category. Since the nature of the questions asked by one's supervisor in a work setting gives an indication of the values that are primary and rewarded within that setting, it can be seen that questioning can and is an effective method of socialization. It was inferred from the results of this study that nurses are socialized to place primary emphasis on the completion of tasks and on keeping the organization running.

## CONTENT OF SOCIALIZATION EXPERIENCES

It is almost impossible to talk about who does the socialization (the agent) and how it is done (the method) without at the same time indicating the message—what is transmitted. Some of the content of the socialization experience has already been noted in excerpts presented earlier: how much time to take for certain activities, attitudes toward work, skills and procedures, speed, getting tasks done, and so on.

### Normative: the "shoulds"

Brim provides a famework in which to analyze the content of the new nurse's socialization experience. He notes that the function of childhood socialization is to develop the personality, to provide the child with a sense of identity. Childhood socialization produces a core of attitudes, values, and norms that have to do with the child as a person, with his relationships to others, and with the world about him. Adult socialization, on the other hand, is concerned with the learning of role appropriate *behaviors*. These behaviors are learned in the context of acting out specific roles (wife, mother, nurse). It is with what the role occupant in fact does and thinks rather than what he *should* do and think that adult socialization is all about. Olmsted and Paget enlarge upon this distinction by noting that much *professional* socialization is concerned with providing the student with a core of attitudes, values, and norms that have as their content what professional educators believe the aspirants should and should not do and think in a variety of situations. Nursing schools are concerned with the attitudes and values generalized to the abstract role of professional nurse, not to the specific role of public health nurse or pediatric nurse. Behaviors appropriate to such specific roles are at best given only peripheral attention. Further socialization must be forthcoming in the postgraduation socialization period to equip the neophyte professional with role specific behaviors.

Upon entering the work scene, the neophyte nurse sees herself equipped with a truckload of "shoulds" and a paper bag of role appropriate behaviors. There is also every indication that her employers and co-workers see her in much the same light. It is to be expected that there will always be some degree of conflict between previously learned values and behaviors and emergent requirements and expectations. Mediating such conflict can be viewed as a major purpose of adult socialization.

It is logical to analyze the content of socialization messages in terms of values or norms ("shoulds") and role appropriate behaviors. Some of the "shoulds" learned in the postgraduation socialization are an extension of the preservice socialization period, others are not.

I think the majority of nurses really care about the patients, and in that way work is like school. But you know, one thing I found out—and this was a big surprise—there are some nurses who just don't care. Nursing is a job and they could care less whether they helped the patient or not. (NG:BS/12[719]6/71)

Another theme that was started in the preservice setting and consistently recognized and continued in the work setting was responsibility. "I'm responsible! I knew it before, but now I'm *really* responsible."

One of the major normative values learned, and one that constituted a real surprise for many of the new graduates, was that there are doctors and nurses who are incompetent and that the system tolerates this incompetence. "Doctors don't give a damn!" "I was flabbergasted at the incompetent nurses and that everyone knows about it and nothing can be done!" "I had no idea there could be such incompetent head nurses and that they would receive the support of administration." It seems as though the new graduate learns very quickly to differentiate levels of competence; often it comes as a surprise to her to find that she has the knowledge and insight to be able to do this. "I didn't know I'd be able to tell you who was a good doctor or nurse and who wasn't, but I can!"

In line with this value are many of the comments that new collegiate graduate nurses make about diploma graduate nurses with whom they work.

Some diploma nurses are very good. It's not the education but what she does with it that makes the difference. I've seen good and bad from both kinds of programs. I think the B.S. girl has more background to work with, but it all depends on how competent they are. You can have a diploma girl that doesn't have the educational background, but if she reads and asks questions she can run circles around the other ones. It all depends on their competence. (NG:BS/11[D # 1])

This differentiation of competence was also instrumental in valuation of feedback mechanisms. In the process of adult socialization, the new graduate learns that positive feedback from a particular physician or nurse is to be valued, yet from another "it is as worthless as a chest suction system with a hole in it!" One of the criteria of valuation is the perceived competence of the individual providing the feedback; positive affect toward that person is not a necessary ingredient in the feedback.

[Dr. S.] is really obnoxious! He scores F on personality, but he really knows his stuff. He's a terrific surgeon—everybody says so. If he tells me I've done well with his patient, or something like that, I'm on Cloud 9 for weeks. That's much more important to me than a compliment from [Dr. T.]. He compliments all the girls all the time. He's so stupid, it doesn't mean anything. I don't know how he made it through med school. (NG:BS/8[D # 3])

The following is another normative learning abstracted from the diaries and interviews.

It came as a big surprise to me when it finally dawned on me that we're not really here for the patients! We [Who's we?]—the patients, the nurses, the hospital, this whole place—are here mainly to service the doctors! That was a real explosion when that got through to me. That's the criteria for decision-making here: does it help the doctor, not does it make things any easier or better for the patient or his family. We're here to help the doctors learn, to provide them with good experience, or to wait on them hand and foot. This whole system is really crazy! (Med Ctr:BS [1841]9/68)

While many of the nurses who focused on this learning followed it up with qualitative remarks such as: "This is changing somewhat; [Judy] and [Jill] told me it used to be much worse" or "I know that eventually the patient will receive some benefit," it was particularly meaningful to note that not all the nurses who encountered this surprise were opposed to

this attitude. Several of them stated that although it was a surprise, "I've come to realize that this is the way it should be" and "things run better and smoother when you keep the doctors happy; that's what's really important."

Based on the previous discussion, is a pattern developing? Although some normative learnings, such as accepting responsibility, were similar in both the school and the work setting, others were dissimilar. Some of these dissimilar values were that nurses can and should judge the value of the work of other professionals and that the value of work is directly related to the perceived competence of the individual doing the evaluation. There was also evidence of a beginning value shift from seeing the patient as the sine qua non to the legitimacy of fostering the work of the physician as the primary goal of the organization.

Three of the above similar and dissimilar values emphasize traditional professional values. The increased valuation of service to the physicians' goals may not necessarily be a negative instance, although certainly increased valuation of research and teaching would be more in line with usually accepted professional tenets. Perhaps nurses perceive that the interests of the patients are more quickly and favorably advanced through serving the physician than could be accomplished directly. If so, norms acquired during the postgraduation socialization period appear to be consistent with the professional system of work.

But, there is another side to the picture: "You've got to get your work done on time." "If you'd get yourself organized, you'd be done by lunchtime." Speed and organization were dominant value themes reported frequently. Many times the competence referred to in the above section was on the basis of getting things done quickly rather than with effective judgment based on desired outcome of the operation. "Speed and getting tasks done is all-holy! That's the basis for judging yourself and the basis on which everyone else judges you."

Another normative area in which there was some dissimilarity between school and work was the emerging criterion upon which one was supposed to base decisions for task accomplishment. This criterion could be conceived on a continuum. At the high end was whether or not a particular task would be instrumental in preserving biological life. "First thing to do is that which will keep the patient alive." The second place on the continuum was the performance of those tasks that had been ordered by the physician. Here the water of decision-making was a little muddier because it depended to some extent on which physician had written the order. The status of the physician (visiting man, resident, intern) was also important, as was the affect of the nurses toward the particular physician and how important the nurses thought the order was.

How do I make my decisions as to what to do when I'm busy? Well first, the life-or-death thing; then next is to do the doctor's orders—but you do the residents' orders before the interns", and then too it depends upon how much respect you have for the doctor who does the ordering and also if you think the patient needs it . . . like a q 4-hour blood pressure, ordered by a new intern on a patient that I don't think needs it, gets very low priority. (Med Ctr:BS/[1011]1/70)

Closely vying·with and at times nudging the second-place position of doctor's orders is a phenomenon called routine or policy. "It's our routine here." "That's established policy in this agency." Sometimes this criterion received a higher priority than doctor's orders.

When an intern—or even sometimes a visiting man, but you have to be more careful there—orders something that's against the routine, you know, like a blood test at a peculiar time, well, you just make the adjustment in it and then later on when I see him I'll tell him what I've done. (NG:BS/11[D#3])

The rationale for conforming closely to established routines and procedures is not necessarily robotism; it may be done out of consideration of personnel comfort and security.

It's a big headache if you don't [carry out the routine]. And it's not that I think it's so important, but my supervisor has told me several times that she won't support me unless I do. You're supposed to know agency policies and carry them out in spite of what your personal judgment tells you. No, there's not much recourse that I can see. (NG:BS/10[D#6])

Perhaps the young graduate finds the safety of carrying out routine preferable to the excitement and challenge of thinking.

Low on the priority list for task accomplishments were items termed emotional support, teaching patients, and talking and listening to patients. This tended to vary slightly with the setting, but was reported to occur in psychiatric as well as general hospital settings. When support and listening behavior was perceived as being role inappropriate, it was particularly disturbing to the neophyte. A number of new graduate nurses indicated that their head nurse, supervisor, or co-workers "really believe in psychological support of the patients; and they do try and do it, but only when everything else that has to be done is done."

Another underlying normative theme prevalent in both the diaries and the interviews was despairingly stated by one of the new graduate nurses as follows: "The message I get is: 'When you stop making suggestions and coming up with things you want to change, we know then that you have finally adjusted to the work situation.' "[2] Schein noted in his study of college graduates that they reported a marked resistance on the part of their colleagues to new ideas.

Not all of the respondents identified this theme of adjustment as clearly as the above excerpt. Many said things such as: "You have to be careful about making suggestions. My supervisor heads them off by saying: 'After you've learned your district thoroughly, then I'll listen to your suggestions but not before,' " or "Making suggestions is viewed as your inability to adjust to the present state of affairs," or "new ideas really threaten the people here; they think you're trying to show off your education."

Perhaps the area of normative learning in which there was the most divergence between school and work socialization was that concerned with the extent of involvement with patients and their families deemed appropriate for a nurse.

Little things, like I asked if I could do home visiting on my own time with some of these patients or visit some of the nursing homes and stuff. It would benefit the patient and would really stimulate me. So I asked my head nurse and she said that wasn't nursing, that that was inappropriate and I was getting too involved. She said that if I was unhappy in this job why don't I find something else—"Why don't you become a social worker?" (NG:BS/12[736]6/71)

In another instance a co-worker stated the following in response to the question: What are some of the areas in which you think [X] needs to improve?

Her ambition. Getting involved in too many things and taking patients' problems home with her. Maybe that's all right in school, but not here. She becomes upset and concerned about her patients. Like, we have a patient who is dying now with Hodgkins'. She was working on another ward today and she came over to visit him. Now, this is not good. I feel that we do have to become emotionally detached, and I feel that this is still a problem with her.

These kinds of normative themes—primacy of speed and organization, task accomplishment and its underlying priority criterion, negativism toward suggestions, superiority of the present way of doing things, noninvolvement with patients beyond some ill-defined normative parameter—are all antithetical to the professional system of work into which the new graduate received her early socialization. They represent marked discontinuities in the socialization experience. To the extent that they conflict with values that have been internalized from her prior socialization, intrarole conflict will result.

### Behavioral: the "do's"

The other major category of content in adult socialization, and the one to which adult socialization is primarily geared, is role specific behavior. In this respect the postgraduation socialization experience was tremendously successful. Quantitatively, the learning of role specific behaviors (as nursing is currently practiced) constitutes the bulk of the learning that occurs in the first nursing job after graduation. How to carry out diagnostic tests and execute skills and procedures headed the list of role appropriate behaviors learned. Closely following this category was another large group of behaviors termed routines and

administrative detail. Included here were not only those behaviors esoteric to a given institution—which slips to fill out for a CBS, what kind of census form is needed, operation permits, and so on—but also the usual routines of individual physicians, institutions, and kinds of patients. The special likes and dislikes of particular physicians, the routine on nights, and the usual procedures to be followed in the care of cardiac, postoperative, or radium-implant patients illustrate these three kinds of routines. In respect to routines for particular kinds of patients, the young graduates voiced much concern and hostility because they had not been exposed to these role appropriate behaviors while in school. In the case of the other two kinds of routines they appeared to be tolerant and unconcerned about their ignorance, and perhaps rightly so.

I think it's OK that we don't know details about hospital and doctors' routines, just so we know that there are such things and that they are going to make a difference on the kind of care you can give. Also, these change with every place you work and you can learn them there. But we definitely should have learned the care of patients who all have similar conditions, things wrong with them. (NG:BS/12[940]6/70)

Perhaps what this young graduate was suggesting is that in the school socialization the aspirant nurse needs to learn how to develop group nursing care plans for patients with common "sets of limitations." As described by Graham, this process is effected as follows: problems common to specific groups of patients (for example, comatose patients) are identified; group care plans consist of specific actions helpful in the solution of these problems, principles or rationale for the specific actions, priorities under certain conditions, and alternative courses of action. The learning of this kind of role specific behavior would indeed help the new nurse to become functional more quickly. There was no question that hospital-agency and physician routines were role specific behaviors that need to be learned, but it is probably true that they are excess cognitive baggage during the school socialization period.

An area of content in the postgraduation

socialization experience that was both normative and role specific was "keeping busy," "seeing work to be done." This content was decidedly discontinuous with the content and norms of the school socialization.

When I was in school, and you weren't busy or your patient was off somewhere, you were expected to read charts or go to the library or set up a conference or something . . . you certainly weren't expected to look for busywork to do! (NG:BS/6[D6])

Except possibly for the area of helping one another, the content and normative expectation of keeping busy and seeing work to be done was a real surprise to the new graduate and one that many had difficulty in learning. The normative aspect of this socialization content appears to be the traditional value that a busy nurse is a good nurse, but it also included the perhaps not so subtle message that nursing is "doing" and "activity," that talking or listening to patients or reading or studying is not part of the staff nurse role.

[What are some things that you have found that are different?] Specific assignments with very specific things to do. As a student you're sort of oblivious as to what the rest of the staff are doing and what needs to be done totally to make the unit run. You're not concerned with that. You're concerned with your particular assignment and you do that and then read or go to the library. But you don't realize that that's only a very tiny part of what's going on, you know—totally. My big problem was not knowing what had to be done. I'd finish my patient assignment or passing meds and then I'd stop and talk or play with the kids. My head nurse was constantly at me with: "Can't you see that there's these other things to be done?" And I'd say: "No, I really couldn't." (NG:BS/12[705]6/71)

Closely related to the socialization content of seeing work to be done was the discovery that nursing is a continuous repetition of tasks. This knowledge was markedly discrepant from the earlier school socialization experience.

In school everything was so new to me, and I thought that was the way nursing would be. It was at first, but after a few months I found that nursing is repetition with only one tenth innovation. That's almost opposite of what I somehow

got from my instructors in school. Sometimes I get so bored doing the same thing over and over again I could scream. (NG:BS/3[D1])

We see, then, that contrary to the "normatives" and the "shoulds," the "do" socialization content focused on role-specific behavior and on two values or perspectives that are contrary to school socialization values.

## CYCLICAL NATURE OF POSTGRADUATION SOCIALIZATION

The preceding sections of this chapter have been concerned with an analysis of the agents, methods, and content of socialization of the new graduate nurse in her first work experience. Another factor that emerged from the diary and interview data was the cyclical nature of the postgraduation socialization experience. This cyclical process seemed to have several phases: an initial position, a reversal, and then an alignment somewhat similar to the initial position on ideas about standards, school-bred idealism, and the place of the nurse in the health care system.

Well, it sort of went in a circle. In school I had been taught to have standards and to live up to these and judge yourself and your work by these standards. Then when I started working I found out everybody has different standards, and I was driving myself crazy trying to live up to them all. Now I've decided that it's myself I have to live with and that I have good standards and those are the ones I'll try to live up to. (NG:BS/12[737] 12/70)

• • •

I think I've almost gone the circle. That job at [X] I found dreary and boring—the whole thing. It was so impossible [the kind of care that you had to give]. And now I'm not that convinced at all that I can give the kind of care that I think people should have. I think I can, but I'm not sure. I think I really went through a period where I disliked nursing. I just didn't think that all the ideas from school were that realistic, but now I think maybe they are. (NG:BS/12[757]12/70)

• • •

They've gone in a cycle. When I graduated I thought nursing could rule the world. That patient-healing was more dependent on nursing and what was done day to day—a doctor just diagnoses and treats; it is the nurse who coordinates things, regardless of whether it is with the hierarchy or with the doctors at the top. That there could be some grassroots power—if all the nurses were united together they could change things. At [X] there aren't enough people who want to fight the system, so after two months I wanted to quit and go back to school just to get another degree and have more power in the situation. I could obviously see the ones who sit at the top with the Master's are the supervisors or in-service trainers and the people on the wards don't communicate with them. I am sure glad now that I didn't go back, because it is bad enough to have the education and not have the work experience; they respect experience quite a bit. Now if I go back, I've thought about not nursing, but psychology. (NG:BS/12[951]6/69)

## PROCESS OF SOCIALIZATION

From additional insights into the overall scope and possible patterns of the postgraduation socialization process discernible from the diary entries, a process of socialization was developed. This process is circular in nature, with many opportunities for exit and reentry. The various phases overlap; they certainly are not as distinct and deliberative as they will appear when described. All subjects did not record events that would permit the conclusion that they were going through each step of the process. There was, however, sufficient evidence to suggest that the following description of the postgraduation socialization process will serve as a beginning guide to this exceedingly complex process.

One other point that is important to clarify concerns the temporal feature of the proposed process. Brim notes that behaviors and values are transformed gradually through a process of personality drift. Minor changes in expectations that an individual holds for himself occur subtly and over a period of time. The resultant day-to-day alterations in behavior lead to a cumulative change that makes him much different from what he was at the start. The pace of this temporal and change process is affected both by the individual and institutional factors; only the description of the phases and their sequencing will be attempted here.

## Phase 1: skill and routine mastery

In the beginning phase, the neophyte appears on the job scene flushed with excitement. She has secured a goal (license, diploma, degree) for which she spent several years preparing. There is a fascination and an exhilaration at "having arrived." The entrant may feel a sense of power with the newly acquired status. There is a kind of all-pervasive, diffuse euphoria—like a honeymoon. Everything is beautiful and wonderful. There is little discrimination and judgment in assessing either people, working conditions, or nursing practices. The newcomer is elated by the symbols of her new economic independence (a paycheck) and also by the realities of the newfound worker role ("When I have a day off, it's really a day off; I don't have to study or write a paper or anything.").

This period of diffuse, generalized euphoria is usually brief (although in some individuals it is amazing how long it can last!). Then some of the realities of the worker role begin to assert themselves, both on and off the job. "I had no idea how tired you get after eight hours of work!" "When can I make a dentist appointment?" On the job, the neophyte is usually overwhelmed with the tremendous amount of material she must learn and has terrible feelings of inadequacy and lack of confidence. In some people, this may manifest itself by an outward show of bravado and overconfidence. The immediate solution to this perceived gap in knowledge and skills is to throw oneself completely into the mastery of skills, routines, and procedures. This is often the path chosen by the neophyte. Since many new graduates see their first job as a test or proving ground (Chapter 6 will elaborate on this), skill mastery becomes one of the items on the neophyte's self-constructed test. However, it is also the area in which her goals are most consonant with those of the organization. Many nurses judge other nurses by their competency in performing diverse and complex technical skills. For this reason, it is difficult to determine whether in fact the neophyte comes to the employing organization with skill mastery as one of the items on her self-constructed test or whether it is placed there soon after arrival because of the expectations of others in her environment.

Often the new graduate's total immersion in and concentration on skills is done to the total abdication of many of the human elements that were once so central. This can be a temporary abdication, but sometimes it is permanent. The skill mastery is often accompanied by a change in attitudes toward the patients, toward what they see is happening: "It's for his own good. It's better to get it done and over with quickly; he wouldn't understand even if I explained it to him." This rationalization process might well be necessary to relieve the dissonance the new graduate undoubtedly feels between her old values and the newly acquired ones of efficiency, mastery, and technical competence. All too often new graduates succumb to the powerful influence of behavior upon beliefs. When behavior changes (emphasis on skill performance and mastery), cognitive dissonance is relieved if values and beliefs change also (task performance is more important than continuity of care).

With the attempt to master skills and routines comes reality-testing and feedback and a disappearance of the one-sided positive glow of the honeymoon period. Reality-testing comes from serious goal-seeking: "My immediate goal is to learn all the routines, get myself organized, and become a skilled, competent nurse." The neophyte will probably not meet much resistance to accomplishment of this goal; in fact she will usually get considerable help and feedback, both internally and externally, as to how she is doing. Most new graduates can assess for themselves whether or not they are meeting their own expectations of setting up medications quickly, getting treatments done on time, and so forth. There is a measureable and easily observable quality to the success of skills such as catheterization (either you got the catheter into the urethra or you didn't), so there generally is no problem in reality-testing of skill mastery.

The problem lies in other areas. There may be some shock and letdown feeling when the new nurse discovers the extent of her skill incompetency. With the mastery of some skills comes the recognition of all the many more that need to be attained. (It is probably here that the real meaning of the technological explosion in medical care is realized by the new nurse.) To compensate for this, the neophyte may well have to revamp her goals. What she saw initially as a short-term interim goal ("Learn the skills and routines so that I can do them readily and easily and then be able to concentrate on the more important aspects of nursing such as individualized patient care.") shifts in importance and perspective ("It will take me at least a year to master all the skills I need to know.").

A second problem encountered in reality-testing during this skill mastery phase is concerned with the external feedback that the neophyte is likely to receive. She will probably receive both help and positive feedback from co-workers for placing skill mastery high on her list of goals (although she will frequently encounter negative criticism such as: "Didn't you learn how to do that in school?") and will not meet too much resistance in achieving this goal. Resistance and reality shock, however, will set in when she finds that skill and task accomplishment are often perceived by others as ends rather than as means to an end. Where the neophyte expected to master skills and then move on to putting into practice the individualized and comprehensive patient care she was taught in school, she finds that these goals are often not shared by others in her work environment. She received positive feedback for skill mastery, yet there is either negative or no feedback when she elects to listen and talk with Mr. Jones and his family rather than help the treatment nurse with the two o'clock treatments.

The last area in which reality-testing may engender the beginnings of shock is seen in increased ability to judge, to evaluate, to discriminate the quality of the work of others: "Some nurses and doctors are better than others" or, even more profound, "Some nurses do things correctly; others do not" and "Some doctors make mistakes!" The rose-colored glasses are removed and the real world with all its imperfections is open for critical inspection and appraisal. The new graduate expects to be judged and evaluated by others, but for many the harsh reality that they have the knowledge to discriminate between good and poor medical and nursing care is a shocking and sobering experience.

For a few new graduates there may be some immediate awareness of the dynamics of this skill mastery phase. They may be aware of their shift in behavior and perhaps temporary abdication of values. For most, though, the evidence seems to indicate that, at least initially, the neophyte is unaware of the abdication of values or even of the conflict in values. This insight comes later.

When I first came I had so much to learn: routines, procedures, how to do rectals—just everything. The first thing I did was I really knuckled under and learned these. I was still aware of what was going on, but now that I am into the system, I don't know, you find yourself picking up the same attitudes. It is really awful. The people that I notice that make me nervous the most are the new people because they register a shock at some of the awful kinds of things that go on. All of a sudden I realize that I'm not shocked at this anymore, but I remember I had the same shocks when I first came. The assembly-line approach here is really gross, but the emotional response wears off. You get so wrapped up in doing the physical skills that you get calloused to the situation. (NG: BS/12[745]5/71)

It is possible for a nurse to become arrested in her growth at this skill and routine mastery phase. She develops tremendous technical proficiency and receives rewards, admiration, and respect from others for it. Usually, however, because we are all social beings working in a social environment, even the most technically skilled nurses move on to or are already involved in the next phase in the socialization cycle.

## Phase 2: social integration

The second phase frequently overlaps the skill and routine mastery phase; and in some settings where there is not a high demand for accomplishment of physical tasks and procedures (for example, a psychiatric setting) this phase may completely replace the first

one. Concern in this phase is with getting along with co-workers and getting in with the group. Mastering interpersonal relationships and achieving knowledge and participation in back-region reality is paramount. Feedback on degree of success is measured by invitations to "coffee," lunch, parties or showers and by being asked one's opinion or advice on a variety of matters. While perhaps not at the conscious level, undoubtedly the skill mastery of Phase 1 is the ticket of entry to achieving Phase 2.

During this phase it is likely that the new graduate is quite concerned with the image she presents to others. Throughout the period of encountering and learning to work with others a newcomer becomes very conscious of the continual assessments and evaluations she is making. This serves to make her aware of the fact that others are continually evaluating her; consequently, she feels the need and desire to manage the impression she is giving them. As she becomes aware of the back-region reality and the techniques used by others to maintain desired images to outsiders, such as relatives of patients, new nurses, supervisors, and representatives from the main office, she realizes that she is quickly coming to a point of choice. Being a new graduate enables her to hold on to the neophyte role for awhile, but that role will not be tolerated by others for very long. She is at a point of choice between managing an impression of approachability or attractiveness or some combination of these. In the role of learner she was highly approachable (it makes others feel good to help or teach someone who says they don't know how to do something). This aided her social integration. If she moves out of that role and begins to demonstrate competence (and particularly if that competence exceeds in theoretical score the competence of those around her), she becomes highly attractive but more unapproachable. High attractiveness and resulting low approachability block social integration (Blau, 1960).

I didn't know which way to turn. Once I got the hang of the monitors, I knew not only how to do it but I knew the theory behind it—what a P wave meant. And I'd ask the doctors questions, but I could see the other nurses just rolling their eyes every time I did because they couldn't understand his explanations. Sometimes I could hear them talking about something—you know, like what a lab test meant—but they wouldn't ask me. I'd know what it meant, but I found out that they didn't like it when I'd offer to explain it. They'd say something like: "I guess you learned that in college, huh?" It wasn't so much what they said but how they said it. I never did really get in with them. Somewhere along the line I made a wrong turn. I was always an outsider. (NG: BS/12[819]6/69)

Another new graduate shares her solution to the problem of social integration within the working group:

I was having a terrible time trying to get "in" with the group. Maybe it was because I was so wrapped up in learning all about the diseases and routines and the procedures I had never learned in school. I didn't have time or energy to socialize with the others. But then I think it was that once I mastered these other things I could offer to help others, and then I made friends. The idea is to zip through your work so you can offer to help others, and then you are seen as someone who is really efficient and helpful. (NG:BS/8[D#5])

It is quite possible for arrested exploration to occur at the end of this phase of the cycle, particularly if the neophyte nurse never accepted the school-bred professional ideals. Such an individual would find the characteristic Phase 1 emphasis on task and routine accomplishment very satisfying. Successful mastery of this phase, coupled with satisfactory social integration into the working group, would set the climate for fixation at this phase of the cycle. Such an individual may advance into the administrative hierarchy because she has been successful at two of the primary requisites for such promotion: mastery of skills, routines, and tasks and the ability to get along with others.[3] Or she may simply settle down into a comfortable niche, do her job, and enact externally directed nurse behavior. It is highly unlikely for a neophyte nurse with any degree of professional socialization to become fixated in this phase. Although happy here for awhile, she would soon become bored and begin to question: "There's got to be more to nursing than just this. What about all that stuff I was

taught in school?" The climate is now set for the onslaught of shock, outrage, and rejection.

### Phase 3: moral outrage

The third phase in the cycle of socialization is characterized by anger, frustration, and intense discomfort. There is the sudden realization that "I can't really practice nursing the way I've been taught; just passing meds and doing treatments is not my idea of nursing."

In this phase the neophyte sees everything in terms of ideals—"shoulds"—with a very fuzzy idea of the appropriate corresponding behavior. She seemed to have few if any role models during her school socialization experience to demonstrate the reality operationalization of the "shoulds." It is quite a natural feeling that she expresses when she says she feels that she has been left holding the bag (of "shoulds").

Accompanying this moral outrage is a marked lack in perception and possibly distorted assessment. The new graduate frequently is so busy sending out her program of "shoulds"—being evangelistic—that she has no energy left to receive the input of others. This phase is characterized by feelings of tremendous upheaval and turmoil. Moral outrage can go on for quite some time or it may end quickly, depending upon the reaction of others in the immediate work situation as well as the conflict resolution resources and strategies of the individual. It is probably the period of greatest vulnerability and the most decisive in respect to the eventual outcome of the satisfaction and effectiveness of the neophyte nurse.

Because the cultural suffering and energy drain in this phase are too great for the individual and the emotion generated by the outrage too disruptive for the system, it is difficult to remain actively outraged for very long. She may "burn out," sinking into apathy and "quiet despair" as the only way that the unresolved conflict can be tolerated. There is a tendency to blame the system globally for all one's problems, yet frequently the concept of "system" cannot be defined. Nurses who choose to remain fixated in this phase feel a deep and painful loss. Interpersonally incompetent, they are not able to either resolve their own conflict or influence others in the organization to make changes efficacious to improved patient care. Personal mental health is often maintained by those who drift into this stage of quiet despair through interests and activities outside the job. The job increasingly is viewed as "something to be gotten through," a "temporary moment in my life." Each day on the unit or in the agency reopens the stab of pain and scratches the nettle of despair: "This isn't the way things should be! Why don't they do it the right way?"

If the sufferer lacks the courage, insight, and ability to even attempt conflict resolution, she can remain in this chronic state of morale outrage. Her only other choice is to move into the phase of conflict resolution.

## Phase 4: conflict resolution

The conflict resolution phase is characterized by evaluation and choice. An analysis of the diary and interview data, as well as potential resolutions suggested in the literature on culture shock, generated the development of the following typology of reality shock resolution.

One type of conflict resolution is termed *behavioral capitulation.* This means that the nurse solves the problem of conflicting value systems by holding onto her school-bred values but compromising her behavior. This capitulation can be a more or less complete sellout, but characteristically the nurse continues to voice her old values: "I know I'm a washout, but it's too big to fight. I know how to give better nursing care—and the patients should have it—but I just can't do it. It takes too much out of me. Maybe someday." Rosow describes individuals who have maintained loyalty to the desired value system but not to the behavior as chameleons. He particularly notes that such individuals are the most fertile group of potential power for social change. They have held onto their value systems and await only the necessary time and climate to spring into action. This is all well and good in theory, but study of the medical center nurses over four- and five-year periods shows that this is not what happens. School-bred

professional values seem to gradually erode. Nurses who had once professed strong patient loyalty and professional commitment gradually, over subsequent contacts, spoke increasingly as technical bureaucrats—no longer striving to learn and improve themselves, but content with getting the job done and earning enough money to buy things they needed for their homes.

Another aspect of the behavioral capitulation type of conflict resolution is seen in those nurses who *withdraw* from nursing practice. This includes nurses who leave for such non–health-related jobs as secretary, librarian, horse trainers, elementary educator, and so on. They have resolved their conflict by running away from it, although they almost always retain their original school-bred professional values. This type of conflict resolution also includes those nurses who retreat to the Ivory Tower of school, wherein they can enact behaviors more consistent with the values they hold. Although they may not actually engage in nurse behavior themselves, they are in a position where they can pass the cherished values (if not the corresponding role appropriate behavior) to the next generation. Behavioral capitulators usually begin their retreat by enrolling in graduate school, then becoming faculty members of schools of nursing.[4]

Why not go to graduate school? It's this or I leave nursing altogether. In fact, I do think that teaching in a college program is leaving nursing. I've been so disgusted with how I've had to practice nursing for the last four years that I've got to do something. I'm hoping teaching will be better than nursing. At least it pays more and the hours are better . . . and if you can't be happy in your work you might at least get paid well to be miserable. (Med Ctr:BS[3733]2/68)

"Competence, like truth, beauty and contact lenses, is in the eye of the beholder." From the perspective of the nurse employing organization (hospital or public health agency), this kind of conflict resolution can be seen as a *lateral arabesque,* that is, a pseudopromotion consisting of a new title and a new workplace, because the individual was incompetent in his old position. Many nurse faculty openly admit:

I couldn't cut it. I know they thought I was disorganized and couldn't carry my share of the load. And looking at it from their eyes, I probably was. I couldn't see any sense to it—running around doing only bits and pieces for seven or eight patients when almost each one of them needed my fulltime attention. I decided I would be happier in teaching where I could have more influence and teach students what good nursing care really is.

Peter speaks of the lateral arabesque as an apparent exception to his principle that "in a hierarchy, every employee tends to rise to his level of incompetence." He then proceeds to demonstrate that, in fact, the individual in a lateral arabesque position has risen to his level of incompetence. From the view of the employing organization, nurses who pirouette into teaching (for example, in-service education or a formal education program) because they were unhappy or unsuccessful in the work setting have in fact reached their level of incompetence. Unable to operationalize their professional value system in the real work scene, they are shunted or have shunted themselves off into the lateral arabesque position wherein they minimally interfere with the real workers who are getting the job done.

A second major type of conflict resolution—*value capitulation*—is the reverse of behavioral capitulation. After experiencing the throes of moral outrage for awhile, the nurse becomes convinced that the work setting values are more operational and result in the best possible care for the largest number of people. Consequently, they are to be preferred to the nonoperational school-bred idealistic values, which are thrown overboard. This kind of conflict resolution choice not infrequently results in immediate tension reduction, which is very rewarding and reinforcing.

I know I'm not the same kind of nurse as when I graduated—I'm less idealistic, more practical. But I've decided that that's the way it has to be. That one-to-one individualized stuff may work in school, but you just have to be more practical and realistic here. (Med Ctr:BS[3322]8/70)

If this is the route chosen, the process of identification and internalization (p. 34) commences. This then helps to actively per-

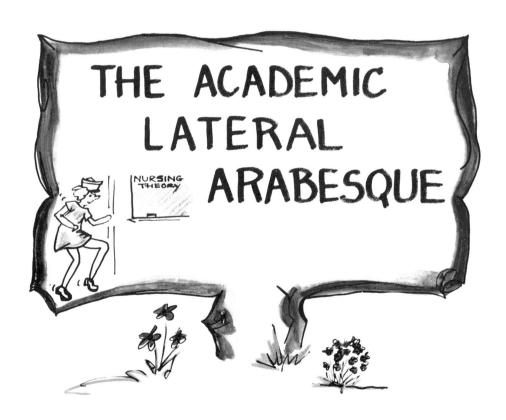

petuate the route for future socializees because it provides role models for other neophytes to identify with when they are in the conflict resolution stage of the cycle of socialization. It was also noted that often the nurses who chose this route of conflict resolution had contact with traditional nurse role models, particularly in their own families.

Abdication of school values and overconformity to the work-promulgaged value system can be seen as a version of *going native.* Cleveland and associates describe shocked individuals who go native as "snugglers"—people who want to belong. They are prepared to pay what they think is the price of belonging: the rejection of their school-bred values. The neophyte nurse, socialized into a professional work system, finds herself in conflict with the subcultural values of the work setting. Because she wants to belong and to reduce the conflict, she elects to abdicate the professional work system values. This choice may be personally functional and effective but, as with individuals in culture shock, "if they really go native they find their effectiveness is blunted; they have been sent, after all, not to embrace the whole of the local culture but to effect fundamental changes in that culture." In a way, so also has the nurse graduate. There are many people who believe that the impetus for improvement in the quality of health care lies with her.

Some nurses elect to resolve the conflict between school and work values by rejecting both sets of values. This might be called the *plague on both your houses* solution. The reaction to moral outrage is: "If you can't agree, then I won't believe either of you." This choice manifests itself in behavior that is just conforming enough to hold onto the job. The individual frequently declares himself in a rut and is perceived by others as doing the minimum to get by and having no investment or involvement in the job. Complacency is the order of the day.

I'm in a rut. I know it and so does everyone else. But I really don't care. It takes too much time and energy to get out. I'll continue like this for a couple of years and quit nursing just as soon as we can financially manage without my working. (Med Ctr:BS[2732]4/70)

This route choice is not particularly effective or profitable and certainly not growth-producing for either the individual or the organization.

Another type of conflict resolution followed by a fairly large number of nurses might be called *going it alone.* One of the conflicting value systems—in this instance the school-bred professionalism—is made psychologically dominant. In this way one can think of others as irrelevant and stop listening to them, thus diminishing or avoiding the pain of completing the conflict resolution process. Behaviorally, this route is similar to the protective isolationism seen in people suffering from culture shock, when they wall themselves off from the distress of input not in line with their home values. Going it alone is manifested by the seeking out of geographically isolated units or shifts in which one can enact his professional values or by isolating oneself psychologically from conflicting value messages. The selective perception and dominant choice of the school-bred values are usually fostered and assisted by the presence of some outside source of support to these values; for example, a continuing relationship with a former nursing school instructor, a close friend in graduate school, or some other professional usually one more autonomous than nurses. Coupled with this retention of values is corresponding behavior perceived by the individual as being role appropriate but frequently perceived by co-workers as being detrimental to the system. This is a situation in which the nurse decides that she's going to "do her own thing," "nurse as she's been taught," no matter what the consequencies. "I'm going to give the best possible nursing care to my patients that I can, and never mind the rest. If I have too many patients, I'll pick one or two of those and really nurse them and do just the minimal for the others."

*Biculturalism* is the name given to the last type of conflict resolution used by neophytes to resolve the value discrepancy that produced moral outrage and rejection. Perhaps the best descriptive phrase for the orientation of this group is from the Johann prose (p. 27). The nurse in this group pursues a "mutuality of distinct initiatives as an on-going project."

She has neither fused her values with those of the organization, allowed herself or her values to be absorbed by the system, nor abdicated her professional values or behaviors. She is a nurse whose stance is: "I can see why she made the decision she did; following a standard or routine is probably the best way of ensuring the safety of all the patients. However, there are some patients for which this procedure is detrimental or at best ineffective. Let's see how we can work together to accomplish both the safety of all patients and the individual care of patients."

In this approach the nurse has learned that she possesses a value orientation that is perhaps different from the dominant one in the work organization, but that she has the responsibility to listen to and seek out the ideas of others as resource material in effecting a viable integration of both value systems. She has learned that she is not just a target of influence and pressure from others, but that she is in a reciprocal relationship with others and has the right and responsibility to attempt to influence them and to direct their influence

attempts on her. She has learned a basic posture of interdependence with respect to the conflicting value systems.

Within the bicultural type, several strategies were apparent. Some nurses attempted to find a mutual rapprochement of divergent values through a quiet, subtle process of influence. Characteristic of this *inside fighter* approach was a breakdown or invasion of the opposition informally prior to suggesting or advocating a change. Another strategy was to simply role model the desired change and attempt to demonstrate through behavior the potential integration seen as possible.

I really thought it was important to do nursing histories on the patients. For about a month or so I did them religiously, hoping that the others would see that they were helpful and beneficial to the patient and follow suit. But they didn't, so I decided I'd have to use a different approach. One by one Elaine [another RN], who thought the same way as I about them, and I set out to line up the opposition—like they do in politics. I drank more cups of coffee that week. I'd invite someone to "coffee" and then start explaining nursing his-

BICULTURALISM

tories and showing them how to do them. That was a lot of the problem; they didn't know how to do them and didn't want to admit it. Anyway, when the head nurse brought it up for a staff vote it went through fine; but most important, they're really doing them and using them. That's what I think is great. (NG:BS/12[708]7/71)

. . .

I decided I just had to mount a campaign against all these ridiculous rules, like in this hospital nurses cannot do specific gravities. So they charge the patient a dollar to send it down to the lab when it can be done in two seconds on the ward and save the patient the expense. So I started this questioning campaign: "Why?" (It's a rule.") "Can't the rule be changed?" ("No.") "Why?", and so on. Finally, I don't know if it was just to shut me up or what but she [the head nurse] got it changed. I praised her to the hilt for this and told one of the relatives how she had done this in front of her so she could hear it. Then I started on something else—getting the isolation procedures changed, I think. After the first one, the others came much easier. I just work behind the scenes and let her take all the credit. With my ideas and her power, we're getting somewhere. (NG: BS/12[705]6/71)

Another pattern of behavior that could be abstracted from the reports and observations of nurses who chose to resolve conflict by becoming bicultural was that of *overt risk-taking*.

At first my head nurse didn't see any need for all of the emotional and psychological support. And there was a lot of this business: "We've got to get all this work done; we've got to get these patients bathed by 9:30." And I say "phooey." One of the other nurses who trained in a hospital program ten years ago comes to the floor. She is oriented in July and was told: "You have to have all the patients bathed by 9:30." I come to work in September, and in October we are sitting down to coffee and she says: "I just don't know if I can keep working; I can't keep up with all the work." I said: "What's the problem?" And she says: "I can't bathe four patients by 9:30 and get the meds out." I said: "So what? Bathe them at 11:00 or 1:00. What difference does it make?" I said: "Look, it doesn't make any difference. You have to set priorities and deal with them that way. If we get an amnio in, or if someone is upset and crying, it's more important to take care of that than to get baths done by 11:00." It blew her mind. She

could not understand that you could do this; that administration said: "This is the way it is going to be"; that you could say: "OK, I accept that, but there are these other things." At first the head nurse was a bit taken back, but I just joked it off and said: "I'm not very efficient; it takes me longer than 9:30 to do up my patients." But then she saw the kind of care I was giving, even if it was in the afternoon, so she didn't say anything more about it. Now she even tells others about it. (NG:BS/12[942]6/70)

Some of the bicultural strivers preferred to use positional authority and power to achieve their mutuality of initiatives goal. This was a relatively little-used choice option, probably because of some undesirable consequences or because the nurses were not yet in positions of power. The idea behind the *power users* was to acquire a position of authority and then, operating from this power base, institutionalize some of the school-bred values that had been held in abeyance until the power position was achieved. In a sense, this is what Lippitt calls "compartmentalizing loyalty." To avoid the stress of conflicting loyalty pressures, confrontation is postponed until a power position has been achieved.

This route choice appears to be effective only or mainly if the power base can be achieved rather quickly after first starting the job, before compartmentalization can become permanent and one's set of values are lost through nonuse (similar to the chameleon type of conflict resolution). This route also requires considerable ego strength and internalization of the school-bred values to resist encroachment, fusion, or absorption during the "waiting period." The major problem in the use of this method of achieving biculturalism is that once the nurse is in the position of power (for example, head nurse) there is tremendous pressure to abdicate school values and internalize work values. This pressure is both external, from one's peer group, and internal, through the process of identification and internalization (p. 27).

Another variation of power-user methods is illustrated in the extensive interview excerpt related on p. 118. Here we saw the nurse using the system—the established hierarchy of power—as a means to achieve her goals. She very carefully kept within the organizational tenets of going up the ladder, following the chain of command, but at the same time she maneuvered the situation in such a way that she made *her* influence felt as well as that of the director of nursing.

## SUMMARY

Based primarily upon the case study data presented in six nurse diaries, the primary socializing agents for the new graduate seemed to be the nurse's aides, orderlies, and LVN's (particularly initially and for attitudes and norms) and physicians and head nurses (for role specific behaviors, particularly in the technical realm). The nurse's aide appeared to be particularly influential in assisting the neophyte to break through the image management phase of the new community. The staff nurse may have assisted in this, but the diaries contained few mentions of perceptions of other staff nurses as socialization agents. Although this data was of help in the beginning formation of a theory of postgraduation socialization, it is not enough. If ideas for planned, constructive socialization are to be developed, it is necessary to continue to identify who the socialization agents are and the key problems facing them. Dominant among the problems is formulating articulate socialization goals. What are the objectives that will best help the organization achieve its goals? How can the organization help the socializee attain her goals? Another goal must be the adequate preparation of the socialization agent for her task. If nurses are not presently recognizing themselves in this role, how can a change be effected?

The problem of formulating and pursuing appropriate socialization goals was made even more complex by the fact that the one being socialized was continuously in the process of formulating new sets of personal goals and values. These came about from the neophyte's efforts to cope with and use the input from the great variety of experiences she was having with numerous socialization agents and also from her attempts to cope with her own internal experiences of maturation and prob-

lem-solving experimentation. The new nurse developed and reconstructed her own expectations, hopes, and demands as she interacted with socialization agents. She initiated input as well as received it. The sensitive socialization agent had to accept and support this development of personalized initiative and identify as well as take responsibility for representing the values and expectations of the larger society.

A variety of methods was used to socialize the new graduate in her first work experience. All of them appeared to be effective to some degree, although the neophyte was not always aware of their use or effectiveness. There were little data in the diaries to give any indication whether particular methods were consciously chosen by the socializers to achieve specific goals.

The effectiveness of methods of socialization was tempered by three major problems that the neophyte nurse was aware of and vocalized fluently. First, feedback on the quality or quantity of work is informal and implicit; thus it is much more difficult for the new graduate to discern and interpret correctly. Second, the cue sensitivity of the neophyte is markedly diminished, particularly during the moral outrage and rejection phases of reality shock, and frequently messages are missed or misinterpreted. A third major problem is the frontstage-backstage discrepancy. If the evaluation feedback received by the new graduate has its source in backstage values, and if she has not yet learned or come to appreciate those values, then she will not have a framework for receiving or interpreting these evaluative messages.

In analyzing the content of the socialization messages, as illustrated by the case study diaries and the interviews, one dominant theme appeared to emerge. In spite of the emphasis on the value of competence, which is consistent with the professional mode of organizing work, the majority of both the normative and behavioral content messages sent to the neophyte in the work setting were different or discontinuous from those emphasized in the school setting. The dominant focus of the postgraduation socialization ex-

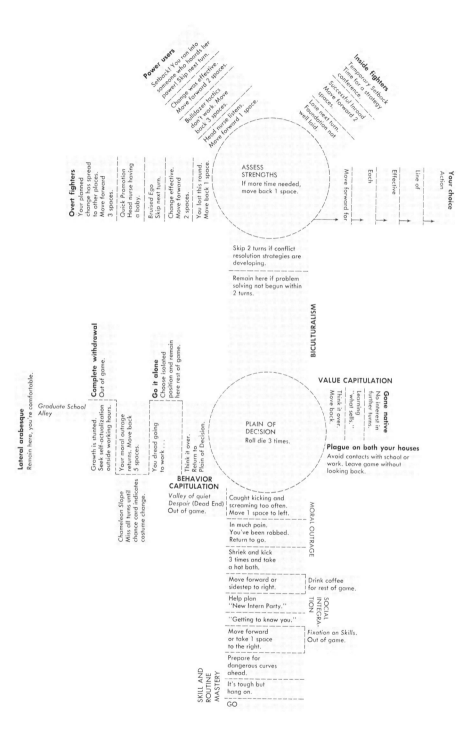

perience was on speed, organization, and role specific behaviors such as organizing and giving physical care to six or eight patients, completing forms and records, passing medications, and so on. Two other socialization content areas reflecting both norms and behaviors[5] were the positive valuation of keeping busy and the discovery and tolerance of nursing as a series of repetitive tasks.

Based on case study diaries, interviews, and field observations, an attempt was made to explicate and describe the postgraduation socialization cycle. It begins with a phase in which the primary emphasis is on mastery of skills and routines; this is closely followed by vigorous attempts to become socially integrated within the working group. The moral outrage phase is the explosive peak of reality shock and rejection. This highly vulnerable period will hopefully lead into the phase of conflict resolution. Unfortunately, some neophytes do not get beyond it, choosing to quickly exit from nursing or electing to remain in "burned out" moral outrage.

A typology of conflict resolution based upon the actual experiences of neophyte nurses was described and illustrated through excerpts of tape-recorded interviews. Although obviously overlapping, and certainly not mutually exclusive within one individual, this typology consisted of withdrawal, lateral arabesque, going native, plague on both your houses, going it alone, and biculturalism. The bicultural strategies of inside fighters, overt risk takers, and power users were described. The diagram on p. 165, in game form, presents the various options of the postgraduation socialization process.

## CASE HISTORY OF A NEW GRADUATE

In the last section of this chapter will be presented the story of the trials, successes, feelings, hopes, and aspirations of one new graduate nurse as she stepped out into the work world. A theoretical commentary will be presented periodically throughout the case history in the form of a dialogue between Kramer and Benner. The interruption to the flow of the case history will be kept at a minimum; the story as Lynn tells it is so rich and articulate that it can well stand alone.

Initially at my request this new graduate began the account of her experiences almost immediately after beginning her first job. However, as she states in one of her later letters: "I started writing these because you asked me to; now I'm doing it for myself. It helps a lot in trying to get myself straightened out to put my thoughts down on paper and to know that someone is reading them and cares."

### LETTERS FROM LYNN
*by*
LYNN MALONEY PITTIER

*Late September, 1970*

After I started my job, it became obvious that I could never get any of the nurses in the orthopedic surgical ward excited about nursing or even cooperative with some of the things I wanted to initiate, like nursing histories. I started them, but they remained on the Kardex unused except for extra space to write other things. . . . Also, this orthopedic ward would not have provided me with the technical skills that my classmates and I craved so far. The patients were mostly postamputees awaiting a prosthesis fitting. The two weeks that I served on the floor involved the care of fifteen to twenty patients. I was floored! The care was minimal, granted, but with so many I felt like a guard pacing up and down the halls. So many of these young Viet Nam amputees needed someone to sit down with them and just talk. Some had histories of battle neurosis and poor adjustment to their disablements. But you just couldn't spend any time on these problems even to scratch any surface. It sort of made me think back when I was in school and all the time I spent on some of the wards, and also in visiting families, trying to think up patient problems to satisfy the instructor. And here were all these problems staring me in the face, and I had neither time nor energy to do anything about them. . . . All in all, I requested a transfer to the coronary care unit. I was refused for two weeks because of my inexperience, but they finally put me in; I really had to talk them into it.

This area really fascinates me. I've been coming home every night and studying the EKG's and reading almost more than when I was in school. The nurses are really super and the physicians in the unit constantly seem to be explaining what they are doing and why. All one has to do to get an EKG explanation is to look ponderingly at a strip. Also, the chief cardiologist expects the nurses to follow him on rounds of the four-patient ward and listen in and possibly participate in patient discussions. I can't help but really enjoy each day here; it is an area that we sort of trained for all along with the one-to-one patient-nurse relationships, observational responsibilities that are valued, and heavy psychosocial aspects of the disease encountered. As far as technical skills go, the patients have constant IV's running which the nurses initiate and restart. We give IV meds, draw all our own blood, and defibrillate those in ventricular fibrillation if there are no doctors handy. Yesterday I was drawing my first blood from a jugular intercath and managed to squirt blood all over my entire uniform and the patient. He was really concerned that he would have to pay for the additional embellishments on the polka dot sheets and laughed and laughed about it.

The most valued skill in the CCU is observational in nature. This is rather in contrast to the orthopedic station where I reported some swollen lymph nodes and an earache and sore throat to the resident physician (surgeon), who sharply informed me that he was a surgeon not a medical man. Think of the problems I may have encountered if I would have taken it to the medical man myself! . . .

My impressions with my first job really convince me that all that psych emphasis wasn't so in vain. On the other ward I really felt like a middleman who had to understand and then deal appropriately with every staff member. The surgical residents were really uptight and defensive as a whole on that ward, and the nurses were really aggravating the situation in trying to meet with some satisfaction for themselves. Then the LPN's, who were two men, had to maintain their position both as men and nurses. By the time the IPR with the staff members are waded through, it's no wonder lots of people have no energy left for that poor patient labelled difficult. And with a 40-bed-ward–five staff ratio, it may be understandable that one tends to become involved with the struggling interpersonal relationships between the staff members, including the doctors. Anyway, it seemed to be often the case that the difficult doctor received more time than the difficult patient. The CCU is as different as night and day. There is nothing but praise and respect for the physicians, with no competition raging. And patient care is really *the* issue. It really excites me! And when the nurses go home it isn't with the sigh of relief that the day is over.

Actually the switch to this ward is a blessing for me. I was never very satisfied in nursing school and seemed to look for each clinical as perhaps a little more satisfying, which it wasn't really. By the end of basic training I felt like I couldn't leave the academic setting until something caught my interest about nursing on a long-term basis. Going to [X] with physiology-type electives made me even more uneasy about the profession as a lifelong career. (Does this sound like Chapter 3 of Search for Tomorrow?) The upshot of this is the crucial importance of this first job. As it stands now, I'm neck deep in nursing and was fearful of hating my compulsory one year of clinical experience. (One year seems to be the magic number which was quoted to me ad nauseum as I applied for various jobs for which I was refused.) See, I was already avoiding the hospital setting before ever really encountering it. My supposed clinical expertise in medical-surgical nursing also necessitates a bit of experience if it is to mean anything to me or the nursing world. The dramatic end to this episode is that I really *do* like what I am doing in the hospital, and it looks as though this may last on a day-to-day basis.

## COMMENTARY

KRAMER: It looks as though Lynn didn't go through any kind of a honeymoon phase on that orthopedic unit, doesn't it?

BENNER: No, I don't think she did. I think there might be several reasons for that since she did experience a rather striking honeymoon period in the CCU. First, Lynn did not choose to be in the orthopedic unit as a place where she would like to try out her new status, whereas she did have a decision commitment to the CCU. She had to fight to get into the CCU and I think this initial commitment, which stems from her own choice, gave her a positive view of the CCU even before she entered the unit. And second, I think that the CCU met the testing criteria that Lynn had set up for herself.

KRAMER: Let's look at some of the examples Lynn gives us of her honeymoon phase in the CCU.

BENNER: Lynn begins her work in the CCU with all the characteristic enthusiasm and fascination that can occur with a new environment.

> The nurses are really super and the physicians in the unit constantly seem to be explaining what they are doing and why. All one has to do to get an EKG explanation is to look ponderingly at a strip. Also the chief cardiologist expects the nurses to follow him on rounds of the four-patient ward and listen in and possibly participate in patient discussions. I can't help but really enjoy each day here.

Lynn exhibits the wholesale praise and acceptance that is characteristic of the honeymoon phase.

> The CCU is as different as night and day. There is nothing but praise and respect for the physicians, with no competition raging. And patient care is really *the* issue. It really excites me! And when the nurses go home it isn't with the sigh of relief that the day is over. Actually the switch to this ward is a blessing for me.

This wholesale acceptance and praise is almost like a "Cook's tour mentality." There is not yet enough reality testing in the new environment to provide a critical, more balanced view. Expectations of what the environment will provide soar. And these high expectations are fertile ground for the impending crash of reality shock. It is at the point of serious navigation and goal-seeking that the honeymoon phase wanes. Because the initial euphoria of the honeymoon phase does not allow for cue sensitivity and accurate perception of social reality of the new social system, the entrant gathers very little objective information. The excitement and "high" with the new environment's potential contributions and assets effectively block energy for receiving and accurately processing information about the prevalent cultural values and norms in the new social system. The resulting absence of information makes goal accomplishment in the new social system next to impossible. The entrant bumps up against reality in the form of blocked goal achievement.

Did you notice that the doctors seemed to treat the nurses differently on the orthopedic and CCU?

KRAMER; Yes, that's right. In both instances the physicians were socilization agents; however, the message they imparted to Lynn was markedly different. In the CCU, Lynn perceives the MD's saying: "I am competent; I'm here to teach you; come follow and listen. The care of the patient is most important." In contrast, on the orthopedic unit Lynn picks up the messages: "Don't bother me unless it's my specialty; I'm a little unsure of myself; the most important thing is to keep *me* happy, not necessarily the patients."

In terms of socialization content, Lynn also seems to be getting two distinct messages: one, that technical and observational skills are very important in CCU and, second, that IPR with staff is of primary importance on the orthopedic unit. Lynn's initial preoccupation with skills is predictable. Almost all new graduates go

through this—mainly because, at least at this point in time, skills and techniques are exactly the job specific behaviors that most new graduates have not developed to any degree of proficiency in school. On the orthopedic ward, Lynn mentions staff's IPR as one of her first new learnings; this usually comes after skill mastery in the socialization cycle. I think we might watch to see when and if IPR moves into paramount concern for Lynn in the CCU.

BENNER: Yes, at this point both Lynn and her perception of the CCU staff seems to be almost completely focused on the patient.

*Early November, 1970*

My request for the CCU was based on: (1) being initially refused when suggesting it, because of lack of experience. I usually aim for that which is just out of my reach; (2) it was really painfully evident that any concentrated nurse-patient relationships would be an impossibility when one is so overloaded with technical tasks and patients like I was on the orthopedic unit; (3) our CCU has a maximum patient load of four—there is ample time to really learn the technical and emergency skills and also to enjoy the one-to-one relationships I became so accustomed to in nursing school; (4) the night duty was by choice; the family situation demanded it; the choice was not only situational but voluntary. I really enjoyed an isolated independence. On days, there are a million secretarial and task-oriented types of duties which consume much time. At night it is more patient-observation oriented. And very imporant for me now are the free hours in which I read and study the progress notes. I am really frustrated if my workday is not constructive for me in some way. At night one is able to sit at the bedside and listen for the gallop of rales reported in the physician's notes. My goal is to become clinically competent enough to observe subtle changes as they occur in the patient. For example, if on Saturday night I begin to hear that gallop for the first time, or an existing one becomes louder, I may be picking up the first signs of congestive heart failure. It will eventually be a function of the nurse to report the CHF anyway when the clinical signs are more overt, so why let the patient progress that far if one can avoid it. Then, aside from the patient, I try to read at least one article a night or go over EKG's. On days, one just doesn't sit down to read; there is always someone coming through—and we *must* look productive. Even before I ever worked, hospital nursing represented a form of stagnation, a job with a ceiling on it. I still feel this can easily happen as a person settles into the rut of the workaday world. You may hear this from lots of students who approach their first job; I fear lapsing into mediocrity. So progressing means more to me than performing well on the job, and this area is ideally suited with respect to the number of patients and shift to seek the satisfaction needed to keep me out of that rut. I can't help feeling that this is one more transitional stage in my education, but I'm not sure exactly just what I'm eventually going to go after. So much for rationale in job selection.

Since I've begun working in the unit with a relatively limited and close-knit group of girls, the Blau article you sent me has become increasingly relevant. It's funny that I can currently and in retrospect analyze the social interactions. However, I seem to go through every pitfall mentioned which is inhibitive to attractiveness. One requirement for security in the nursing role as I see it has been focused on acquiring clinical competence. In my zeal to learn EKG's, for example, I approached the understanding of them by the 12-lead interpretation. Fine. People on all sides of me were pushing the literature but it wasn't anticipated that I would immediately be so thorough. I didn't realize at the time that I was a threat. The head nurse would occasionally ask me a question which I would really answer as completely as I could. Blau states that the social processes generated by excessive concern with making a good impression actually set up an impasse to integration within a group. That's me! Further, I complicated the scene with what Blau terms self-deprecation. (That's a great article, incidently, and one which has increasing relevance as my socialization in the unit progresses.) I feel as though I've really blown it with the head nurse, who is obviously uneasy around me. The socialization or social integration into this group really deserves ten pages. And, interestingly, a large part of one's on-the-job energies are focused on the maintenance of interrelationships with colleagues.

### Late November, 1970

I feel quite guilty about this delay, but I had just reached the point of exhaustion. One could see it coming when I averaged about two to three hours sleep a day. I am a person who, when given an hour, will plan two hours' worth of projects. There were so many things that I planned to do after graduation which I have been compulsively fitting in during sleeping hours. Now I have to face the reality of limiting myself. I am finding this to be true in nursing too. Throughout my edu-

cation I migrated toward the sciences, but I found it hard to become attached to any specific area. So here I find myself in one of the most specialized aspects of hospital nursing. . . . I think about this a lot. At some point in time, and preferably in the near future, I should direct my energies toward that which I want to pursue in depth over a long period.

This brings me into the unit where I now work. When I first entered the CCU my attentions were focused mainly on the oscilloscope. I read like mad to catch up with the other nurses and was, I'll have to admit, awed and curious about the expertise which supposedly sets this group apart from the rest of the staff at this hospital. (I imagine this may hold true at many establishments.) During my orientation the emphasis was on the arrhythmias. The nurses still seem to concentrate on this as opposed to the clinical aspects of cardiac pathology. They seem to rise to the challenge of the electrocardiographic diagnosis but not to a paralleling clinical type of diagnostic skill. Perhaps one reason for this is delegated responsibility. The physician will inquire about the current rhythm a patient has been in, and the nurse is expected to have interpreted both the type and relative significance of the rhythm. The physician would never inquire about the patient's progressive rales or heart gallop. *So the physician is the major determiner of the type of interest and responsibility the nurses in this circumstance assume.* After the first two to three weeks on nights, I got tired of looking at the oscilloscope and began to spend more time with the patients. My clinical expertise was low, as I had really seen very little. So Mike, my husband, proceeded to teach me about how to approach a patient. His method is logical, concise, and of course oriented toward the diagnosis of the patient's physical problem. So in trots our new CCU nurse, working from head to foot, and then comparing my results with the progress notes. This didn't seem to be what I was looking for at the time, so I migrated more toward the patient as a *person-patient*.

At this point in time I was beginning to get tremendously tired and lapsed, if you will, into that which came naturally (considering my U. of C. nurturing). There *is* a process . . . I am becoming more cognizant of it all the time. As above, I can see my interests and needs changing on about a weekly basis. It's not something one can really change, and the observation of one's self can be somewhat embarrassing at times. A lot of the interpersonal transitions I have found are very much dependent upon the interplay of defenses. Before I get into this, though, I have also found that the process of becoming that type of professional one will be is very much related to a person's needs to compensate for inadequacies, real or perceived. I have found that I am quite aggressive but unsure of myself. My confidence is usually proportional to whatever level of competence I have in a given area. So in areas where I feel quite insecure I become intense. This holds true for skiing or any activity I happen to engage in. Once the threat is over and I have, I guess, conquered my fear for a subject, I typically migrate to another area of threat. One would be amazed at the number of varied challenges I have attacked. The staff in the CCU did not see me as being particularly defensive; in fact they saw me as being quite sure of myself. Both the RN that I oriented with and the head nurse made this clear to me a couple of times when I expressed my feelings of inadequacies. Apparently part of my particular way of handling an uptight situation is to appear somewhat confident. This was a shock to me as I always perceived myself as one who was entirely too passive and apologetic for my actions. . . .

At any rate, my functional rapport with the staff is, in retrospect, rather poor. I apparently set myself up as a threat while attempting to integrate myself at their level of competence within too short a period of time. The head nurse is a shy girl who finds leadership a hardship, I think. I was an instant threat to her and increased the initial gap by trying to impress her with my progress in learning my assigned task of interpreting EKG's. In addition, when we both attempted to establish some sort of social rapport, I again distanced myself by exposing too many of my interests. Perhaps this was also an attempt to prove myelf. It was almost immediately evident that she was intensely uneasy around me. This has a tendency to snowball when one begins to respond with a similar uneasiness and confusion. Comments made by her which were, I felt, inconsistent with her good nature included: "I hope you won't get bored with this unit." "The books you bring are *very* impressive." "I don't know why I'm explaining these to *you*; you probably know more about them than I do" (EKG's). After the tone of her voice, which smacked with as much sarcasm as I'm sure she could muster, I was shattered and sat down at home to have a good cry. She is just not given to sarcasm and is friendly with the whole crew. So I guessed that the major problem was my own and cooled it completely. The other new RN, Sue, and the head nurse immediately hit if off. And it was interesting to me that I went to a cardiology convention where I just happened to sit in the only

seat left, which was next to Sue and the head nurse. In retrospect, that was quite a coincidence —and a bit embarrassing for them, I think. They told me that they had tried to contact me; they hadn't. Everyone is typically told about education opportunities. Since that time I have eliminated any real attempt at social rapport. Instead, I have focused on strictly giving reports and consciously avoiding a defensive attitude. It's like we are friendly business partners but avoid personal involvement. Her uneasiness seems to be subsiding a lot and I know mine is. I hide my book in my purse before she arrives in the morning . . . and make an attempt to use her as a resource, which I think she needs. I'm also so conscious of the situation that care is taken to be subtle. I am still a threat to her; if I avoided any activity that posed a threat I wouldn't be satisfying my needs in this role. My report, for instance, is well prepared and inclusive of the psychosocial status of the patient. I really enjoy giving a comprehensive account of the night's events, pertinent progress notes, etc., in hopes of increasing continuity of care with special emphasis on how the patient feels about his progress or prognosis. Sound textbooky? This is the area where most of our current contact is made. According to Blau, I've passed through the state of caring so much about acceptance that I defensively acted in ways to interfere with it:

1. I avoid self-deprecating modesty. I don't apologize for what I don't know anymore. And I don't give defensive rationalizations for each action. I am increasingly quiet about the little decisions I make and simply present what has been done at report time.

2. I've gradually reduced the social aspects of staff interaction for a more businesslike congeniality. I'm less uptight and *less solicitous of their good will toward me.*

3. I was expending great amounts of energy in the social interactions with the staff which I now direct toward my patients.

4. I can still see myself as trying to impress, perhaps now by silently not allowing them to see my persistent weaknesses. For instance, if something is bothering me about a procedure or medication, I keep it to myself until I get home where I look it up or ask Mike. The point where I am now has allowed the tenseness between head nurse and me to lie down a bit.

Now to my LPN. I wrote you a couple of pages about her one day that I couldn't have possibly sent at the time. They're handwritten at the end of this and represent complete abandonment of objectivity. I simply hated her for about two weeks. And about that time the above tensions with the head nurse were brewing. I began by attempting to make myself acceptable to her by using her as a resource. She took right over by carefully explaining "how *we* do things here." Well, considering my defenses and desire to move in in my own way, I instantly resented her authoritarian attitude. So I cut the questions with such comments as: "I think Mr. X needs a repeat of his Seconal, don't you?" Any opening I gave her was used so that I began to wonder who was making the decisions. And every morning at five she insists upon waking up the patients for TPR and weights. It's not so bad that she wakes them up ... she makes them get out of bed on those darn scales, which wakes them up for sure. A couple of times I've requested that she not get started until six, which would give her plenty of time to finish. My emotional agitation about it made me so tense that I was fearful of my tone of voice and decided to cool it until I could get my bearings. Obviously there was more to it than the five o'clock arousal. Although I haven't been getting these diaries jotted down, they have been a tremendous help in seeing what is happening. I think about situations by saying: "Dear Miss Kramer. . . ." And you know, I analyze the situation as a person looking in at what is really taking place. By doing this I finally could figure out that this LPN has no idea in the world what I am upset about, if she is even aware of that. Her Filipino background makes her very old-country in the way she approaches things. I began to understand her nursing actions when she related her life style to me. Her marriage was arranged, her children are ruled with an iron hand, and she wouldn't let her daughter be Prom Queen at a Catholic girls' school because she didn't want this senior to meet any boys until after college. There are set ways to do things.

Then I really did give her too much credit for thinking, and would get secretly angry when she didn't. That statement isn't sarcastic, but I expected her to problem-solve each little problem. Some people, I guess, find their security in performing on a schedule which they are assigned to do, and without question or deviation in style. When I could see this, my anger cooled down a lot.

Also, I really tried to set up an initial rapport with my LPN which incorporated the social. And it was again very energy-consuming to try and make conversation with an older lady with whom I had nothing in common. When I began to feel comfortable with the silent periods, my tension

subsided a lot. Now we can go for four-hour stretches where I may be reading and getting the hourly B/P and she goes about her tasks. She is also a quiet woman who enjoys the silences, I think. Our relationship is much improved now. And I think it is curious that she was perhaps unaware of the majority of the turmoil that I have been experiencing. . . .

I haven't even reached the poor man in the bed yet, but in writing this I can see that he is only about 25% of my concerns now. I sound pretty bad to myself as I write along, but I try so hard on a constant basis. The patients themselves have been approached in a number of different ways, progressively since I started. I was at first fearful of "breaking" the man with the vulnerable heart and hidden vessels. Now it seems like all the veins are pipelines ready to be tapped. And the patients aren't breakable but were, for a while, becoming interesting specimens for learning on. I even began to try for veins I couldn't see. But when I wasn't as successful I decided to stop. Then I was hot for hearing rales, cardiac auscultations, etc. And finally I settled back with the patient himself. I've run the gamut of nursing approaches all in two months' time.

*One week later*

One thing I am beginning to miss on the job is any kind of good old nursing conversations. I mean, you can't really discuss with anyone what you see as happening: the inadequacies, advances, or even, really, patient progression. There is a loneliness about being unable to discuss one's interests. It is also a cause for frustration. As a novice I am keenly interested in becoming proficient within my role. Coming fresh from school, I am still close to participant learning ... hashing things out with my colleagues. Gaining the type of proficiency I need or value requires a close association with those I work with. For example, this hospital organization is complex in terms of administration. The nursing services seem really top-heavy with administrators and deficient in concern for quality patient care. Ever since I began working I have been interested in the function each of these administrators play. I have asked many different RN's what the DNS actually does on a day-to-day basis and her overall function. There is a consensus of discontent about her, and the answer is typically a complaint. I was directed to the formal write-up of job descriptions ... the formal job description is just ambiguous enough to tell me very little.

Lesson number 34 on the job has also been to

*avoid* mentioning any reading you've done either in the past or recently. It is superthreat number 1. This is again an area where one feels alone. The real excitement I feel about this job is supported by, and sort of proportional to, what I learn. I read an article the other day about the dangers of strokes caused by arrhythmias. These strokes are especially common in the elderly and occur when the perfusion to the brain is temporarily decreased. We can sit there watching the oscilloscope and because of the patterns tell when perfusion is decreased somewhat. This is really exciting to me that in a susceptible person we can be alerted to this danger and act appropriately when the situation arises.

The nurses don't want to hear these things though . . . it's a threat to them. I may still be approaching things awkwardly enough to be stifling those interesting conversations that could go on. I'll have to keep this in mind.

I wonder if part of the new graduate's disenchantment is due in part to the assignment of night duty. The autonomy of nights seems at first a reward in itself. After all the schooling one really gets a chance to try herself out without displaying to the world a knack for making all those initial mistakes. And aside from getting the routine down in an efficient way, I wanted to try *myself* out—establishing and becoming comfortable with nurse-patient communications, being able to throw away one's nursing notes and rewrite them when needed, taking time to organize and establish a regimen for giving report, spending extra time listening to hearts and seeing what edema really looks like all over the body. The nurse-patient communication style really does take time. What I mean is that I have a particular way of expressing *myself*. This was never used for what it could be before. In school one could always think about and psychologically prepare for most of the patient contacts, but now I have to do it more quickly.

COMMENTARY

BENNER: Lynn's November diary entries have a different flavor than her October entries. It's as if she's begun her journey for real and she is very involved in finding out the kind of nurse she has become and is becoming. I really get the feeling in this section that Lynn is caught up in developing her proving ground.

KRAMER: Yes, Lynn seems unusual in that she had quite clear conceptions of what is important in *her* self-constructed test or proving ground. She says that she viewed this job as an opportunity:

1. To develop one-to-one relationships which she felt that she was trained for in school.
2. To make observations that are valued.
3. To develop clinical diagnostic skills.
4. To attend to psychosocial aspects of illness.
5. To practice and become expert in "important" high-level technical skills such as IV's, drawing blood, defibrillating patients.
6. To be able to learn . . . and perceive progress in her accomplishments.

BENNER: Those are very clear, explicit objectives In terms of technical skills, Lynn did differentiate between technical skills in the CCU which she valued and technical skills on the orthopedic unit which she did not value.

KRAMER: Apparently the orthopedic unit was a totally unacceptable proving ground. Lynn is able to point out that the orthopedic unit did not meet the conditions which were important to her test on several counts. The number of "important" technical skills is one of the missing pieces, I think. Do you think that if Lynn had had school socialization which valued and taught the strategies of influencing others to effect better patient care, rather than one-to-one relationships with patients, that she might have perceived the orthopedic unit as an ideal place to test herself?

BENNER: I think she might have. That's a thought-provoking question. One of her objectives was to attend to psychosocial aspects of illness; certainly she perceived more than enough psychosocial needs on the orthopedic unit.

KRAMER: But her perception only served to frustrate and overwhelm her. She could not meet patients' psychosocial needs in the *way* that she was prepared to meet them—on a one-to-one basis. After her sensitive perceptions of psychosocial needs on the orthopedic unit she is left with the proverbial empty bag. She lacked a repertoire of approaches to plan and execute interventions through others.

BENNER: So her sensitivity only served to frustrate her?

KRAMER: Exactly. Let's get back to the testing idea.

BENNER: I am primarily aware of the test that Lynn is constructing for herself. This is in contrast with some of the new graduates I have worked with in the Reality Shock program. They seemed more aware of the tests constructed by their work group. Are you seeing any evidence of the staff constructing tests for Lynn?

KRAMER: A little, but they seem quite subtle at this point. Rather than tests, they seem to be almost daring Lynn to be competent without making them feel threatened.

Lynn, however, is becoming much more aware of other socialization agents in her environment. There's still the physician and he continues to send "skills are important" messages, but also there's this message:

> The physician will inquire about the current rhythm a patient has been in, and the nurse is expected to have interpreted both the type and relative significance of the rhythm. The physician would never inquire about the patient's progressive rales or heart gallop. *So the physician is the major determiner of the type of interest and responsibility the nurses in this circumstance assume.* [Italics in original].

From this statement, we can see that Lynn is quite cognizant of the physician as a socialization agent and of questioning as a method of socialization. We can also see that Lynn is less willing to buy the physician's socialization messages wholesale now than she was during the honeymoon phase. She is now thinking for herself and appears to be rejecting them somewhat.

As was evident in much of the diary material described earlier, aides and LVN's are highly instrumental socialization agents. And we see this with Lynn also. It's evident that the LVN Lynn is working with is sending some strong socilization messages.

BENNER: Yes, she really tried to cut Lynn into the backstage reality, didn't she? She took right over by carefully explaining "how *we* do things here."

KRAMER: We don't know whether Lynn was aware of this possible entree into the backregion, but it is evident that Lynn knew what she wanted:

> Considering my defenses and desire to move in in my own way, I instantly resented her authoritarian attitude. So I cut the questions with such comments as. . . .

And then there's Lynn's attempt to influence the aide, to effect change; but unfortunately she was not yet powerful enough in the social system to be able to do so.

BENNER: I think that Lynn is beginning to be anxious to make contributions, to be able to effect change, to make a difference in the situation she finds herself in.

KRAMER: Yes, I think that Lynn's quest for competency in her new situation comes across in her desire to be clinically competent enough "to observe subtle changes."

BENNER: Lynn identifies that she has created distance between herself and other staff members. I think that Lynn's quest for competency plus her reality shock distanced her from other staff members and interfered with her reception of their socialization.

KRAMER: That could be. She saw herself as an almost instant threat to the head nurse; this produced uneasiness and distrust in both her and the head nurse. The more Lynn tried, the greater the distance grew, until finally the snowballing produced comments from the head nurse such as:

> I hope you won't get bored with this unit. The books you bring are *very* impressive. I don't know why I'm explaining these to *you*; you probably know more about them than I do.

These are very strong socialization messages that the head nurse is sending, but because Lynn is not yet ready to accept the notion that she must learn to deal with the human side of the organization, she has difficulty interpreting them correctly.

BENNER: How true. I think part of the reason for Lynn's difficulty in interpreting the messages correctly stems from her reality shock which began to set in in late November:

> I had just reached the point of exhaustion . . . Now I have to face the reality of limiting myself. I am finding this to be true in nursing too. Throughout my education I migrated toward the sciences, but I found it hard to become attached to any specific area. So here I find myself in one of the most specialized aspects of hospital nursing. I think about this a lot. . . . At some point in time, and preferably in the near future, I should direct my energies toward that which I want to pursue in depth over a long period. . . .
>
> At any rate, my functional rapport with the staff is, in retrospect, rather poor. I apparently set myself up as a threat while attempting to integrate myself at their level of competence within too short a time.

Although this beginning rejection is not as strong as it will be within a week or two, it is a strong contrast to the initial euphoria and wholesale acceptance and praise Lynn felt upon entering the CCU. It is clear from the above excerpts that she no longer sees the CCU through rose-colored glasses.

KRAMER: What do you think triggered the reality shock phase for Lynn?

BENNER: It is not clear from Lynn's diary what all the triggering events for the wholesale rejection and reality shock were. One can postulate that she had a series of value clashes and that her different values served to alienate her from her co-workers. As you noted, she did not accept the physician's socialization in regards to the importance of oscilloscope observations and interpretation. This may well have been one of the differences that served to alienate her from her co-workers. I think that Lynn's description of her value clash with her LPN is also instructive:

> And every morning at five she insists upon waking up the patients for TPR and weights . . . A couple of times I've requested that she not get started until six which would give her plenty of time to finish. *My emotional agitation about it made me so tense that I was fearful of my tone of voice and decided to cool it until I could get my bearings. Obviously there was more to it than the five o'clock arousal.* [Italics added.]

The LPN's task orientation clashed with Lynn's patient-centered orientation. Lynn was correct in concluding that there was more to it than the five o'clock arousal. The task orientation clashed with a whole set of school-bred values having to do with putting patients' needs before task accomplishment. Lynn was not prepared for the set of responses that this one activity of the LPN evoked. Lynn's wholesale rejection and criticism is characteristic of the lack of objective appraisal of this phase of reality shock. Lynn found this to be so and is candid in her realization.

> Now to my LPN. I wrote you a couple of pages about her one day that I couldn't have possibly sent at the time. They're handwritten at the end of this and represent complete abandonment of objectivity. I simply hated her for about two weeks.

KRAMER: At least Lynn is aware of her predicament, her abandonment of objectivity. I think Lynn also has some longing or idealizing of the past.

> One thing I am beginning to miss on the job is *any kind of good old nursing conversations.* [Italics added.] I mean, you can't really discuss with anyone what you see as happening: the inadequacies, advances, or even, really, patient progression.

BENNER: That's a good point since one of the hallmarks of the rejection phase of reality shock is the longing for familiar symbols and idealization of the past. Here Lynn is longing for the collegial relationships experienced in nursing school. The diary itself is one means of maintaining the school ties. In fact, Lynn's view of school is now more positive, and she has a hard time reconstructing why she and her colleagues were chronically unhappy about this thing or that.

KRAMER: But side by side with this rejection stage of reality shock I also see signs of increasing empathy and recovery, for example in her analysis of her interaction with the LPN. She is aware that the LPN has "no idea in the world what I am upset about." Notice Lynn's increased empathy and role-taking of the LPN:

> Some people I guess find their security in performing on a schedule that which they are assigned to do and without question or deviation in style. When I could see this, my anger cooled down a lot.

BENNER: There is evidence that writing the diary helped Lynn increase her objectivity and empathy. I remember in the last commentary that you raised the question of whether Lynn would begin to get involved in interpersonal relationships with the staff—you know, to move from seeing everything as patient focus to accepting the fact that some time and energy must also be devoted to dealing with the human side of the organization.

KRAMER: Lynn does seem to be struggling with the necessity of dealing with the human side of the organization. Schein points out that school teaches the student to rationalize away the human side of the organization. Rational goal achievement without all the familiar work group personality constraints is learned by the student. And some students never learn to accept the human side of the organization. In his survey of business school graduates Schein found that the new graduates expressed a strong wish to exist in a world that by their own definition was totally rational. Oftentimes someone who would view a complex technical problem as a great challenge would find the human problem unworthy of his efforts.

Lynn was taught to value the worth of solving difficult interpersonal problems with patients in nursing school; however, she did not learn to equally value solving difficult interpersonal problems with staff members.

> By the time the IPR with the staff members are waded through, it's no wonder lots of people have no energy left for that poor patient labelled difficult. And with a 40-bed-ward–five staff ratio, it may be understandable that one tends to become involved with the struggling interpersonal relationships between the staff members, including the doctors. Anyway, it seemed to be often the case that the difficult doctor received more time than the difficult patient.

BENNER: Lynn's initial reaction—or perhaps it was a planned action in view of how well she is in touch with herself and her strengths and weaknesses—to this perceived pull and tug between the task and maintenance goals of an organization was to pull out: "I really enjoy the isolated independence on night duty in CCU." And initially she believed that the patient would be the central issue in the CCU.

KRAMER: This view was not to last long. Within about two weeks after entering the CCU she realized that she could devote about "ten pages to socialization and social integration into the work group." She states with some surprise: "And interestingly, a large part of one's on-the-job energies are focused on the maintenance of interrelationships with colleagues." The point here is that Lynn was not prepared for and found it difficult to accept that she would have to devote energies to the human side of the organization—the interpersonal relationships and acceptance gaining with staff members.

BENNER: One senses some of the isolation Lynn has chosen and feels when she talks about "the staff," "they saw me," "I set myself up . . . while attempting . . . their." Later on she notes:

I've gradually reduced the social aspects of staff interaction for a more businesslike congeniality. I'm less uptight and less solicitous of their good will toward me.

KRAMER: Yes, she still believes that she can gain acceptance on a purely rational, professional basis and attempts to seek respect rather than acceptance. But this does not work for Lynn in this small unit. Still in November she notes:

There is a loneliness about being unable to discuss one's interests. It is also a cause for frustration. As a novice I am keenly interested in becoming proficient within my role. Coming fresh from school, I am still close to participation learning . . . hashing things out with my colleagues. Gaining the type of proficiency I need or value requires a close association with those I work with. Lesson number 34 on the job has also been to *avoid* mentioning any reading you've done either in the past or recently. It is superthreat number 1. This is again an area where one feels alone.

*Early December, 1970*

I have just completed a seven-day run of nights. As I mentioned before, I live a full life during the day. I wonder how many of the girls who enjoy a fast pace on the job also continue the pace at home. I have this thing about energy spent being spent constructively. If I spend an hour doing something and it is either not some-

thing learned or constructive, it is time wasted. Because of this, routine is frustrating; housework is boring, and I consequently undertake more projects to keep me somewhat satisfied. You were right about the effect of home life on the quality of work done while on the job. On day seven a compulsion for good patient care is obscured by exhaustion. . . .

Hospital nursing is something I probably won't stay with for very long. There is a ceiling to it.

*Two days later*

I feel closed in on the job. I don't even think I am practicing anywhere near my peak. I have been horribly depressed for the past week; most of it is due to my dissatisfaction with work. I often wonder why I ended up in nursing when I find interpersonal relations so unmanageable. Perhaps this is what you may find in the nurse who seeks satisfaction in the emergency care situation.

In addition to the limited setting I'm in, I am also on permanent nights. And I'm beginning to wonder just how pathological that decision was. Even still, I find the interpersonal staff relations more energy-consuming than the patient-care activities on a busy night.

Perhaps it's just my generation, but I absolutely abhor the clenches that the establishment has on one's activities. . . . Right now, specifics matter very little. It's a feeling of wanting to break out and throw one's arms all over the place just to prove that there is room and the energy can be spent any way it wants to!

I mentioned the ceiling that is inherent in hospital nursing. The ceiling is low and the four walls around it seem to be thick to me right now. There isn't anywhere in the system where one can advance to free expression. Higher positions seem to mean more money and more precisely defined roles.

*Three days later*

It is becoming interesting to me that every time I write about my job, my attitude toward it is completely different from the time before. The exhaustion finally did catch up with me and it seems to be affecting my performance at work to a greater degree than I would have expected. The first part of patient care to be neglected or given lower priority has been the patient's emotional status. Somehow, giving physical care requires less of one's energies than does standing for long intervals at the bedside allowing the patient to talk it out. Even more difficult is the attempt to help the patient express what he is shouting covertly. The problem with attending less to the patient's emotional needs for the past week is that job satisfaction has decreased even more. I go home feeling very little in the way of accomplishment. . . .

Although our unit is strictly set up for coronary patients, the doctors like to send their patients who require close observation in to us. There is no ICU yet, and out on the ward close observation is difficult due to lack of help. The doctors complain about the nursing care out on the wards. I spent several days out there and came back to my comfortable four-bed, carpeted unit feeling that they are really super women who have been beaten down by the overwhelming number of patients and tasks to be done. I was really slow out there in comparison to the aide I was helping. I inwardly criticized her for whizzing through those patients without saying anything to them or asking how they were. Then *I* got behind on all my duties. The concern for poor Mr. Jones quickly passed in the effort to get that next patient weighed or something.

The medical ward where I relieved is chronic in the sense that most of the men seem to be there for at least two to three weeks. And yet there is much less interpersonal interaction than we have in our emergency unit. So for this hospital, with consideration of the work load, there is much more opportunity for one-to-one nurse-patient contact in CCU. . . .

Actually, nights are much less ideal than I originally thought for patient observation. I hesitate to completely wake up my patients with bright lights to look at their coloring, veins, etc., unless they are critical or already unable to sleep. This means that I can't really follow a progression throughout the night like I should. But once these apprehensive fellows finally do get to sleep on their second sleeper, it's a mortal sin to wake them up. Consequently, I find myself waiting until morning to really check them out. Sometimes this worries me; I'm caught between good nursing care and a little compassion for the patient. Also, one real lure of the unit originally was the constant presence of doctors and medical students. They stand around six to ten at a time hashing out what is happening to the patient. It is also an area where the attendings pull out the chalk and give quasi-lectures which we could bend an ear to. Every day I see new diagrams on the little blackboard in the unit and sort of feel bad about missing that session that went with it. I do have more time to read the progress notes, which isn't quite the same.

There are many more small everyday realizations which are beginning to sum up dissatisfaction. I don't feel that I am doing a very good job.

I'm carrying out all the activities that the job description requires . . . I really try to be conscientious. But I feel as though I am helping the unit to hold its own without advancing.

*Late December, 1970*

This portion should really have a different sound from the last few days of entry. I've had some sleep. . . .

My purpose in this first position in the CCU is to gain experience so that I may comfortably move into some other area of nursing. As I said previously, I am still a bit unsure just where I am heading. The important point about this as it relates to this job is that it is less a "job" than another learning experience for me. It is like an extension of my student clinicals, except that it is my first effort to show myself what I am made of and what I can expect with my future career as a result of it. . . . I am consciously critical of my failings as a leader, innovator, and with interpersonal staff relations. . . . Within the clinical situation, I have felt closed in for many reasons. One of these is the authoritarian structure I must function in. I mentioned the cooling process I quickly went through when I felt that I was threatening the head nurse. She was not, at the time, a person to be alienated from, especially while she was orienting me and probably somewhat influential in my socialization with the staff. Lately my fears of alienation have been overshadowed by the frustrations felt about not progressing. Also the head nurse is talking of some good innovations in the charting format.

In the new charting format there will be a space allocated to nurse-patient teaching. Hopefully it will be specific enough to be really effective. Our charting is really extensive; it covers one page on both sides (I'll include one). The change will be a real positive step in one-to-one involvement. Also I bet it will open up a lot more awareness about the patient's emotional status than is now recognized. I had two strong personal feelings about her change: (1) I felt a sting . . . that she had thought of it first, and (2) I felt a relief or relieved to perhaps be able to add something without social penalty. What's this bit with my preoccupation about being accepted?????

I feel I have so much to offer, so many things I'd like to suggest—things that I really think would help the patient, but . . . But what? I don't want to threaten them. I want so much to be accepted. For instance, there is a constant awareness of the EKG and significant changes in the rhythm. This is as it should be. However, another very important aspect of nursing care is patient's hydration. We usually seem to blindly follow the physician's orders about fluid restrictions, flow rate of the intravenous fluids, etc. Or if we don't, we sort of sneak our opinion in without charting what we've done. At least I've found myself doing it. Twice now since I've begun in the unit we have overloaded a patient with IV fluids unnecessarily by following the doctor's orders. Even worse, I recall saying at report: "This man will be overloaded if we keep up the fluids at this rate." The day nurse agreed with me, but both of us continued the fluids. We slowed them down so that we were behind, but we should have included in our notes or comments to the doctors that we were doing it intentionally and given our rationale. The last fellow I've had was totally miserable 24 hours out of the day because he was allowed 75 cc per shift. His tongue was dry and furrowed despite almost constant applications of swabs to his mouth. He groaned continually. I gradually just cheated. The doctor increased the IV's to a good rate but not the oral intake. I poured out some of the fast running D5/W and gave him an equivalent amount of $H_2O$ with some Jell-O for osmotic purposes. Bad, bad, bad. There is a neat article in the December *AJN* about the clinical application of fluids and electrolytes for nurses. In it Voda suggests that nurses be responsible somewhat for the consequences of the intravenous fluids that they monitor, just as they are responsible for the medications given with respect to dosage, allergic responses, etc. The upshot of this is that I would like to introduce the article to the girls at work and perhaps we could together prevent these unnecessary fluid disasters. Every person in our unit is constantly on IV's so that medications can be administered through the veins. Hydration is our business . . . but I'm afraid to introduce it—the social penalty.

Since the last letter my relations with the staff have again completely changed. I'm just more relaxed. Things seem to fall into place better and when I request the aide to do something or get something it is not quite so stiff. Also my permanent LVN is on vacation and I have a breather from the continual problem about the patients being awakened every four hours, never to get to sleep after five.

### COMMENTARY

KRAMER: Lynn begins her December diary entries by commenting on the pull of her home role demands versus the pull of work role demands. In both settings she, like most professionals, finds routine trying.

BENNER: Lynn's feeling of rejection for the hospital seem to have increased too:

> Hospital nursing is something I probably won't stay with for very long. There is a ceiling to it. . . .
> [Two days later] I feel closed in on the job. I don't even think I am practicing anywhere near my peak. I have been horribly depressed for the past week; most of it is due to my dissatisfaction with work. . . .

KRAMER: Sounds like a combination of moral outrage and despair, doesn't it? This is also the first hint from Lynn that she sees flight as an acceptable alternative in coping with the high level of frustration she is experiencing.

BENNER: It's not hard to empathize with her frustration, especially when you take into consideration the high degree of investment Lynn has made in her job.

KRAMER: Yes. Lynn is also tuned into the fact that she brought with her some bias against the organization, which may be above and beyond the discomfort she is experiencing with this other method of organizing work. Lynn says it better than I can:

> Perhaps it's just my generation, but I absolutely abhor the clenches that the establishment has on one's activities. Right now, specifics matter very little. It's a feeling of wanting to break out and throw one's arms all over the place just to prove that there is room and the energy can be spent any way it wants to!
> I mentioned the ceiling that is inherent in hospital nursing. The ceiling is low and the four walls around it seem to be thick to me right now. There isn't anywhere in the system where one can advance to free expression. Higher positions seem to mean more money and more precisely defined roles.

BENNER: Given Lynn's level of activity plus this amount of frustration, it is little wonder that fatigue is a persistent problem.

KRAMER: I think that Lynn's lack of interpersonal power in her social system is beginning to take its toll, too. Perhaps she is experiencing frustration from a lack of interpersonal competence in this social system. By interpersonal competence, I mean the ability to bring about desired effects through being able to predict how one's actions will affect and be interpreted by others. At this point Lynn feels powerless to bring about desired effects in her new social system, and understandably so.

BENNER: Feeling powerless is probably one of the most trying parts of being new in a social system. And for Lynn, without the feeling of being able to make a difference or effect change, her work world became unbearable. If she could not make a difference in the social system, she did not want to stay:

> There are many more small everyday realizations which are beginning to sum up dissatisfaction . . . I really try to be conscientious. But I feel as though I am helping the unit to hold its own without advancing.

KRAMER: Lynn's motivation to make a difference really puts the onus on the organization to create the kind of environment which will enable her to make her contributions. Lynn notes early in her diary that her commitment to this organization was temporary, probably around one year. She reiterates her conditional, temporary commitment here, and I think that it is functional for her. By decreasing her commitment to stay for a long period, she decreases the stress and pressure to conform to a situation that she finds frustrating. Unfortunately though, interpersonal competence is never mastered through flight behavior.

BENNER: Yes, Lynn notes in this section that she is still unsure where she is heading but that her present job is "less a 'job' than another learning experience."

KRAMER: Perhaps more clearly than anyone else has said it, this first job for Lynn is truly an extension of professional socialization.

BENNER: That makes sense. And yet Lynn can't quite talk herself into viewing her first job as just another clinical, since the first job had special meaning to her as a proving ground. Notice when she says:

> It is like an extension of my student clinicals, except that it is my first effort to show myself what I am made of and what I can expect with my future career as a result of it. . . .

KRAMER: Yes, like many other new graduates, she does give considerable weight and importance to her first job.

BENNER: One is struck by the high level of motivation which persists in spite of frustration and fatigue. Lynn shows continued interest in learning and indicates that she misses the teaching aspect of the physicians' socialization.

*January, 1971*

I received a note of suggestions from the night nurse concerning things I have neglected throughout my shift. After the initial resentment at what I felt was admonishment, I looked up the job description for my shift and found how much in error I had been. It was above what she had mentioned. I had read it in the beginning, even took notes so that I wouldn't forget every detail. But as the fog of orientation cleared, so apparently did the memory of what I read. Little things like renewal of narcotics are really important and shouldn't be done by the busier shifts. I talked with her about it briefly. I think she felt uneasy at the time, but I thanked her for it and haven't missed the extras lately. I'm not very routine oriented—it's something which always takes thought for me. So after four months I'm still not completely "settled" in the job as one of the girls. I find it much easier as I go along to converse with and socialize with the RN's and less so with the LPN's. This is in contrast to the original rapport which I established with the staff when I first began working. Also, I find that if I have a suggestion or if criticism is passed my way I am much more able to handle it with the RN's. My leadership qualities are almost nil with the aides. I really become irate with myself for not being able to give even the most minor directions. The reason I see for this right now is the defensiveness I still have. The aides are older and more set in their ways and thoughts. My rapport is slipping with them I think. I have worked with more of them lately so that my subjectivity is somewhat abandoned. . . . The energy consumed in worrying about staff rapport points to decreasing chances of looking for administrative positions of any sort in the future.

Although I'm tired and absolutely everything seems to be getting worse in the way I handle life and the job, I am settling into the realization that I do like nursing. Now to figure where I fit in. I mentioned previously my frustration with nursing as a "nowhere profession." But it sure allows for flexibility—to excel somewhere of one's choice. Hospital staff nursing is not a fertile place for me to find job satisfaction. The proportional frustrations outweigh the satisfactions.

Frustrations:
1. Lack of medical knowledge
2. Lack of responsibility
3. Too little time to accomplish patient care to meet personal standards
4. Lousy hours (worked Christmas, New Year, Thanksgiving)
5. Employee of an institution (completely expendable)

Satisfactions:
1. Patient satisfaction
2. Satisfaction with care given and rapport established with patients

I hate to keep belaboring my fatigue, but it

really does play a top role in this girl's career goals. I expect within the next couple of years to become pregnant again; and the teacher at my daughter's school tells me that my daughter is becoming increasingly anxious, less able to concentrate and louder than usual. So, Mama better tend to a bit of motherhood also. My next job will have to involve either better hours or less of them. I am seriously looking around for another job—one in which I hope I can get more satisfaction. I have applied to some of the local nursing schools for teaching positions. Maybe if I can't find satisfaction in nursing, I'll find it in teaching....

*One week later*

I haven't actually initiated any teaching session with the patients about their cardiac pathology, which was one of my goals. I usually explain the importance of deep breathing, etc. Also it took quite awhile for me to say "heart attack" around the patients. The "injury to heart muscle" skirted the issue a bit. The men didn't collapse with the mention of an attack, and did show interest when I began to explain a little about the nature of an attack (in the heart itself). I haven't spent as much time as I'd like to yet, but I think patient teaching is a good way to perhaps establish a rapport of mutual exchange—patient returns with questions, clarification and more voluntary information about past medical history (clues one in on extent of understanding by patient about his health and its maintenance). Anyway, I'll see. It would be great for the patients and would provide me more nursing satisfaction.

I am gradually learning how to follow a routine. I don't "think routine." Therefore I forget the details, as the note from the nurse indicates. Also my reports are less organized than previously because my apprehension about giving report is lower and I don't have time to completely rewrite what I want to say as I hurried to do before. Again I forget. So to be logical I've run off a bunch of itemized report sheets which I can fill in as I go and put it into my routine. As I finish charting I can jot down information in the appropriate spot.

Job satisfaction has been at a low ebb. Perhaps because of two to three months without very much sleep. *I don't feel like I'm a very good nurse,* as far as nurses go. Efficiency is energy-consuming, and to complete a day's work well I can't read. I haven't done any for awhile, and this really bugs me. Not only am I not particularly confident with my nursing abilities, but my theoretical base isn't building. Drugs—I'm behind on those. I know what

it is: I'm not contributing to the betterment of the unit like I'd like to, or something.

Now that I've had some rest, though, my attitude is changing—not quite as fatalistic, giving more time to what satisfied me in the job. It's the concentrated personal contact. I really like to build a rapport with the men; more aptly, a trust in me as their nurse.

*Several days later*

I've been fussing around long enough trying to establish a social rapport with the staff members on my ward. It has, as you must realize, already thwarted what I might be doing for my own self-improvement on the ward, and unnaturalness comes through as stilted for me. I have guarded myself against competing with anyone; and can you imagine the upshot of this fiasco has been a show of lack of confidence in me as clinically competent and socially as a flop. Yesterday the head nurse asked to talk to me "in the back room." Have you ever gotten that pit in your stomach when you know that someone is going to tell you that you just don't add up? The first part of the admonishment session was devoted to the fact that I had come into work one night with liquor on my breath. Granted this is serious if someone has been drinking. Well, I was completely sober after some beers at a big Italian dinner at the Spaghetti Factory.... My whole family was up from San Francisco and I had four days off. The liquor on my breath from dinner may have been there, but the complaint was unfounded. Also one of the aides with whom I've never worked started complaining about the milk I drink while on duty. She reported the fact to the head nurse, who told me that the kitchen was complaining. It hadn't.

The head nurse continued to say that the staff members thought something was the matter with me, that I was too nervous for them and that she wanted me to come onto days. I am aware of the fact that if I come on days I'd be daily transferred out onto the ward. I couldn't make the shift anyway because of home situations. I felt throughout the conversation that I was a chronic irritant to the girls, and the head nurse goes in spurts in being friendly and uneasy around me. It can't always be me on that score. The whole thing again really hurt. I try so hard to do things just right. In addition I'm always the first to be nice to people, ask them how they are and compliment them. If I didn't give a damn it would be a different matter because I feel that I try harder than some of these girls and have come over as an agitant. The girl who works evenings won't talk to me since the night I had "liquor on my breath."

At the conference with the head nurse, I defended myself only slightly by my complete surprise at being put down for drinking. Then, like a really complete idiot, I began to help her tear myself apart. I solicited from her what she was really concerned about. Was it my inability to socialize with the girls or something? I continued to say that I realized it might be hard to like a person who is very intense and talks fast, etc. She wouldn't say, just that most liked me, and then hesitated. So, I've screwed my first job. After the initial depression I felt like the nurses had opened up for me whatever had been barring me from being myself. I had failed on their terms as I saw them set, and so perhaps me as me won't be any the worse for it. I am *not* going to compete with the staff but with *myself.*

I've revised the little report form that is enclosed to include activity and weight and diagnosis. . . . I think this form will really be a help. . . . I hadn't shown it to the nurses in the printed up form yet so I'm not sure it they'll like the idea. I've hand-done it and revised it a little more as I went. Hopefully it will help at least me, and will not be rejected for the originator but for the idea itself, if it is not valuable to all the others.

This is my day off, so when I go back and feel a bit cooler about this whole thing I'll talk to the head nurse about it. Another thing, I think the idea about the patient teaching is really great as I indicated to you before. It was the head nurse's idea and she said she wanted to include the idea in her next runoff of nursing notes. She didn't, and perhaps will dump the plan. I'd like to help get something specific down and thought I'd find something written on it and do a workup on paper, a preliminary form which we could all work on as we go; get started teaching and pass on by way of this form specific things that are important and should be included. Teaching is so important in this area. The men often are fearful of procedures that they shouldn't be, like the frequency of blood pressures, EKG's, and so forth. Also the doctors come in in packs and leave the patient to huddle outside his door. This would scare anyone and a little forewarning would help.

Funny, just before the head nurse approached me I was beginning to feel more comfortable with everything. My LPN and I have worked together long enough that she and I know what to expect, and things move along smoothly. Also I understand her more now and appreciate her for her clinical competence. Before, you may remember the upsets I experienced when she promptly woke everyone up at five. Now she doesn't do it quite

so much. She takes their temps when they are awake or turns out the lights after she is done so they can go to sleep again. And also I was writing down all the different things from the job description, and extras like the number of charts I want to make up in advance, certain things to stock, points I want to remember about the patients—getting their social histories and so forth. I am not regime oriented so that I have to have reminders for all the red tape. And I chart extensively, which requires a lot of patient contact. So I was feeling better. Then this. Rise to it, Lynn, and show yourself you've got what it takes too! Are any of the others writing these having so much trouble or am I some kind of nut?

Having read what I just wrote, I can see that I am skirting the issue. I can't solve my current problems by innovating projects. But right now I can't see through it all. So until next time. . . .

### COMMENTARY

BENNER: Lynn seems to be beginning to pick up on work values in this series of entries.

KRAMER: Yes, one of the things I particularly noticed was a beginning acknowledgment and perhaps a realization that there might be something to organizational values. This is very difficult for Lynn and other young graduates who find the organizational values and stress on things like replacement of supplies and routines very hard to tolerate.

> Little things like renewal of narcotics are really important. . . . I am gradually learning how to follow a routine. I don't "think routine." Therefore I forget the details. . . .

BENNER: Did you notice, though, that Lynn found it necessary to translate the reminder about the things she had neglected doing into her own school-bred value system before acquiescing? She says: "After the initial resentment at what I felt was admonishment, I looked up the job description . . . and found how much in error I had been." Lynn isn't accepting bureaucratic authority, rather she is handling this situation by looking things up for herself. I would agree with you though that, on the whole, Lynn is becoming more open and tolerant to some of the subcultural values of the work system.

Where do you think Lynn is in the socialization cycle now, Marlene?

KRAMER: Well, she's definitely moved out of the skill mastery state—I don't believe she's mentioned any of that for quite awhile. She's still consciously trying to master routines though, but it seems to be on an acceptance rather than a rejection level. There is still definitely shock and moral outrage. Perhaps the best example of this is Lynn's words during and after the conference with the head nurse. She was "completely surprised." She thought she had been doing well. She was beginning to feel more comfortable and felt her IPR with staff was going along more smoothly. And then this! It's quite possible that Lynn was so busy trying to get across the things she believed in that she was literally unable to hear or perceive messages that others were sending her. On the other hand, the staff did not appear to be very aware of this new graduate's plight. It probably never occurred to them that a young woman of today would not consider it amoral or nonprofessional to have a light alcoholic beverage with dinner and go on duty at 11:00 PM.

There is also considerable data that Lynn is still experiencing fatigue as a result of her reality shock.

> I hate to keep belaboring my fatigue. . . . I'm tired and absolutely everything seems to be getting worse. . . .

Part of Lynn's fatigue, no doubt, is due to her night-shift work and her high level of activity during the day. But part is also the personal toll and energy required in making the many adjustments and feeling the discomfort and rejection in her new environment.

BENNER: It seems to me that one of the major symptoms of reality shock that Lynn is manifesting at this point is the sense of total defeat and failure.

> I don't feel like I'm a very good nurse, as far as nurses go. Efficiency is energy-consuming, and to complete a day's work well I can't read. I haven't done any for awhile, and this really bugs me. Not only am I not particularly confident with my nursing abilities, but my theoretical base isn't building.
>
> So, I've screwed my first job. After the initial depression I felt like the nurses had opened up for me whatever had been barring me from being myself. I had failed on their terms as I saw them set, and so perhaps me as me won't be any the worse for it.
>
> There are many more small everyday realizations which are beginning to sum up dissatisfaction. I don't feel that I am doing a very good job. I'm carrying out all the activities that the job description requires. . . . I really try to be conscientious. But I feel as though I am helping the unit to hold its own without advancing.
>
> I am consciously critical of my failings as a leader, innovator, and with interpersonal staff relations. . . . Within the clinical situation, I have felt closed in

for many reasons. One of these is the authoritarian structure I must function in.

KRAMER: That's interesting. I would agree with you that Lynn's sense of failure does seem quite general and pervasive; she really verbalizes it quite often in her diary entries. I had thought though that her sense of failure was more particularlistic and goal-related. And, as such, it is probably much more a manifestation of recognized interpersonal incompetency rather than the pervasive, nebulous frustration and defeat associated with reality shock.

BENNER: I see your point and I agree that, just as with the euphoria of the honeymoon phase, the feelings of failure associated with the reality shock phenomenon are pervasive and diffuse rather than particularlistic. But don't you think her statement: "I am consciously critical of my failings as a leader, innovator, and with interpersonal staff relations" is quite general? There really isn't too much left of a nurse role, is there?

KRAMER: I guess you're right. There's no doubt, I think, Lynn is sensing and expressing a feeling of failure. And it is true that one is struck with the one-sided criticism Lynn is subjecting herself to. One can imagine that Lynn was making progress, was making contributions that she could value and appreciate if she were not caught up in rejecting her environment. And you're right, it is this one-sided derogatory critisism that is so characteristic of the rejection phase of reality shock.

BENNER: Do you see any signs of recovery yet?

KRAMER: Yes, I see two in fact. One is healthy, and that I referred to a few minutes ago. Lynn is beginning to reach out and become more bicultural. She is beginning to see some worth, logical meaning, and rationale to some of the work values and bureaucratic red tape. Did you notice the section where she is talking about getting better organized in giving reports? Now, that's very much a work system value—the emphasis on organization. In beginning to comply with this value, Lynn says:

> So to be logical I've run off a bunch of itemized report sheets which I can fill in as I go and put it into my routine.

BENNER: Complying with a work value, but doing it in her own individualistic style?

KRAMER: Right. I've noticed many new graduates doing this sort of thing. They take some kind of organizational form or routine and adhere to it in principle but modify it so that it is somewhat closer to their value system. The other example of adaptation is, I'm afraid, less growth-producing than the above. I think you mentioned it in your previous commentary, and it also comes up again later on.

> I am seriously looking around for another job—one in which I hope I can get more satisfaction. I have applied to some of the local nursing schools for teaching positions. Maybe if I can't find satisfaction in nursing, I'll find it in teaching. . . .
>
> I'll be leaving here soon—running into teaching before I'm ready for it. But maybe I can teach others to succeed where I have failed.

This flight-into-teaching coping pattern is similar to that used by foreigners suffering from culture shock. By congregating into homogenous groups who purport values similar to one's own, "little America" or "little Italy" is formed.

BENNER: You think maybe schools of nursing are "islands of idealistic professional nursing?"

KRAMER: Well, I would say that they are good candidates. But I'm not ready to give up on Lynn yet. Judging by the insight she has displayed so far in her diary, I'd be willing to bet that she sees through this flight behavior as a non–growth-producing coping strategy for herself.

BENNER: I think that Lynn is showing quite a bit of growth-oriented recovery in her perceptive entries indicating that she is perceiving differences between her value system and that of the staff.

> I had failed on their terms as I saw them set, and so perhaps me as me won't be any the worse for it. I am *not* going to compete with the staff, but with *myself*.

KRAMER: In a sense, she is saying that she's going to try the loner coping strategy—going off to do her own thing. You'll remember, right in the beginning of the diary Lynn says that this is one of the reasons why she chose CCU and nights. But all along she seems to be in quite a bit of conflict between wanting to compete and win respect from the staff as part of her quest for proving herself and wanting to be able to do her own thing all by herself.

BENNER: It seems as though within a few short weeks we are seeing a variety of coping strategies and also some of recovery from reality shock. There is evidence that she's thinking of flight into teaching; she also says she's going to go it alone. But then at the same time there looks as though there is come evidence of the recovery phase. She is beginning to identify different value systems; she's acknowledging some of the worth of work-related values; and particu-

larly in her description of her interactions with the LVN she was having difficulty with there are signs of empathy and ability to predict the behavior and reactions of others.

> My LPN and I have worked together long enough that she and I know what to expect and things move along smoothly. Also I understand her more now and appreciate her for her clinical competence.

And then too, even earlier, we saw that apparently keeping this diary helped Lynn get in touch with her lack of objectivity to the point where she developed considerably more empathy for the LVN.

> By doing this I finally could figure out that this LPN had no idea in the world what I am upset about, if she is even aware of that. . . . Some people I guess find their security in performing on a schedule that which they are assigned to do and without question or deviation in style. When I could see this, my anger cooled down a lot . . . And I think it is curious that she was perhaps unaware of the majority of the turmoil that I have been experiencing.

That's really quite considerable growth and insight into a conflict situation, and one that certainly indicates that Lynn is making a positive adaptation. We'll just have to wait and see what happens in the next entries.

KRAMER: Yes, but before moving on, there's one other point I'd like to make. In this section we haven't commented on the extent to which Lynn is or is not making progress in the second phase of the socialization process, establishing workable IPR with staff. A couple of Lynn's sentences give us some insight into her attitudinal perspective regarding this goal.

> I've been fussing around long enough trying to establish a social rapport with the staff members on my ward. It has, as you must realize, already thwarted what I might be doing for my own self-improvement on the ward. . . .

It seems quite reasonable to deduce from this comment that Lynn is still seeing the human side of the organization, is still seeing the necessity of working out staff relationships as a necessary evil rather than as an avenue to interpersonal competency and source of influence.

BENNER: Yes, and also she hasn't learned yet that in order to be influential she must get into the backstage reality. She doesn't seem to be aware of the fact that in that conference with the head nurse she was being judged and evaluated on back-region criteria.

KRAMER: It's no wonder that the conference was

a surprise to her. Do you remember earlier that when the LPN tried to clue her in Lynn rejected it? The sense of failure that Lynn experienced in this conference is undoubtedly related to some missed perceptual cues from the back-region reality.

[Oh, and by the way, Lynn, rest assured that you aren't some kind of nut. Most of the other girls are having problems very similar to yours. You are not alone. Your diary was chosen because you express yourself so well and have a better than average insight into what is going on about you.]

*Late February, 1971*

It's been quite a while since I've written . . .I've sort of lost a lot of the hyper attitude about the job, also a lot of my enthusiasm, and sort of just sat back to let things cool down.

It would be so easy just to relax and let the job flow around me. Maybe I should stop fighting and join the others in the deep chasm that is the rut around here. Sometimes I get so discouraged. . . .

I'm extremely paranoid, I think, and really need to be as objective as possible. Also I'm pretty ambitious and impatient with the job, my seemingly slow adaptation to it. A person can make just as big a mess of things by trying too hard as by not trying at all. So I have been trying to relax with it. Everything is going along fine. I'm gradually able to squeeze in some additions to the nursing care plans. The nurses are still negative to the nursing histories. Little additions are the only palatable form of change accepted and even those not with any zest. I've been mostly adjusting things to suit my job needs. For instance, that report form that I showed you has really been a help to me. I began using it and gradually offered it to the nurses who came on days. It was politely tolerated for a few times, and they they said it was confusing and quit using it. Another little thing I've set up for myself and anyone who would like to use it is an IV kit. Whenever an IV needs to be restarted there are umteen things to jam together: tapes, bandages, intercaths, lidocaine, swabs, neosporin, etc., etc. I inevitably forget one thing in a rush, so I put together a little set in a square disposable emesis (cardboard) basin. It doubles as the receptacle for everything and will always be a sanitary carryall. On nights I play around with these things, but this has been another real help for me especially with admissions. There is always rushing and confusion at that time, and I don't have to take the time or thought to assemble the IV equipment. It paid off the other night—

in time. I was pleasantly surprised with myself. I have told the other girls about it and if they wanted to use it that I would keep one made up for them on the IV cart. Someone put it out of reach in the back of the cart, so I haven't said anything more about it. I like it, though, and will keep using it. I can see patterns forming in the way that I do things; for instance, I've found myself writing a small summary on the patients at 12:00 AM when I first check them. Gives me a feeling of thoroughness and keeps clear in my mind those things I should observe for. If they are stable or something, I don't say much. Also my initial enthusiasm for cardiac auscultation, lung sounds, etc., is sort of settling into part of the routine. Nights are somewhat boring, and time is precious to me, so I've talked with the nurse on the ward just outside the unit about trading places for a week or two to get some additional clinical experience. I mean, I haven't irrigated a catheter (Foley) since I was a sophomore. I know the routine but can't do it with any ease. The other night I felt embarrassed in front of a doctor because I couldn't do it snap, snap. Still uptight about these things. The supervisor liked the idea that I get more practical experience. She feels that the practical nurses are worth much more than the university girls. She has had poor luck with their length of stay, ability to work hard, and the amount of time it apparently takes her to train one to be a "nurse." She also feels that total patient care has been in use since nursing began—that we've not progressed one inch as a profession and that we are not a profession but technicians. Further, the night supervisor feels that care plans are a farce and that time put into patient care doesn't require much more than physical management. When asked if she would like to reserve the psychosocial, etc., to a clinical specialist who could tie the patient's needs together, her response was that: "They cost too much and don't do anything." She returned to the university for her degree a few years back and felt it was a big waste of her time—as she knew more nursing than the instructors did. After quite a talk, where I mostly listened and sought her opinions, she concluded that this hospital is backwards: the care isn't up to today's standards. She is especially critical of the medical staff—interns, residents, etc. The time spent in giving her opinion in this recording is that it reflects my views and also what I feel is a generalized opinion here, especially among the older staff. I won't work here beyond the point of learning for me. I'd like to get some ward experience in concentration after a couple of months—

perhaps switch to their postsurgical ward–recovery room area. And I'm definitely pursuing a teaching position. I don't want to be a teacher who is one step (clinically) ahead of the kids, and hopefully by spreading out I'll understand the nursing work-aday world before I go back to the ivory towers. I really do enjoy the fast pace of the hospital intensive care units. I enjoy medicine—the disease process, what's done about [it], and the clinical return to equilibrium. Perhaps I really am heading for the nurse practitioner role? Clinical specialist? It all remains to be seen.

Interstaff relations have been better simply because I control myself. I am trying to relax, keep my private life behind the scenes, etc., and try to maintain a pleasant how's-the-weather rapport. This way I can't be too much of an irritant and allow room for social discord. . . .

*Early April, 1971*

During the diaries written to you before, I was really wrapped up in my own niche in the CCU and not really paying too much attention to the rest of the hospital and the system. Since then I've expanded a lot with my interests and have discovered how really sick this place really is. The incentive to work here is strictly money and fringe benefits. Any patient care incentive is frowned upon at best. If one wants to change the size of the IV bottle used in the unit, it must go through several administrative channels. The night supervisor told me that in order to fit in with the system one must become passive or suffer brain damage from beating one's head. The system's inadequacies are all too clear, even to the population that reads the *Reader's Digest* (March or April issue). I'm glad I've been here so that I can approach any other job with hope. Also it is beginning to be profitable for me in learning the hard cruel paths of administrative bureaucracy. The ironic part of the conclusion of this job will be that I am becoming more idealistic all the time. I refuse to lose it, and am learning where best to place it now. For instance, I had no orientation to the unit; the materials available for comprehensive instruction (especially drugs) were sparse. I've continued the drug data collection system I started, and in addition just completed the start of a pretty nice library of all the most current and classic articles on (1) arrhythmias, (2) clinical aspects of myocardial infarction, (3) pacemakers, (4) electrocardiography. I'm really enthusiastic about it and doubled all the copies so that I have a separate library at home for myself. Then also, I have teamed up with my aide who is quite enthusiastic

in learning how to read EKG's. We spend nights together now going over the strips taken the day before. I've written up in duplicate the principles behind the particular topic we discuss, which she has added to her home collection. . . .

I'm going on days next week. I am afraid that, when seeking another job, night duty will be somewhat of a handicap. I understand that I will become an instant aide. Neither the head nurse nor Sue will bathe a patient or empty a urinal. I will be interested to see how they pull that off. Joan, one of the other RN's, says that she often doesn't get to draw the bloods, pass the meds, etc., when working with these two. Needless to say, she is unhappy about the situation. She won't say anything for fear of turning the friendly tides in this neat tight little group. I'm there to learn as much as work, so that I have no real idea yet what I'll do.

I'll be leaving here soon—running into teaching before I'm ready for it. But maybe I can teach others to succeed where I have failed.

I've sort of ruled out a job at the university for this year. . . . I plan to look for a clinically oriented job: in-service, specialized clinic area, or maybe something out of nursing—in a lab or something.

I've been real glad I could be included in your studies. You may be completely unaware of their impact, but they have been really instrumental in helping me maintain a quasi-analytical attitude toward my job from the very beginning when I started the first project on the psychological impact of the MI on the patient. It is still back there in a lot of writing somewhere. . . . I collect everything from the job and could probably put it to use some day. Occasionally, if you like to get mail, I'd like to continue some of these accounts. It will still give me a chance to vent some views and perhaps you will see some sort of progression beyond these first months. . . .

*May, 1971*

After nine months on the job, I'm ready to step out into an area where I will fit, function better, and be happier. These months have been spent learning about my bent in this profession. The next job will hopefully satisfy it. I've been riding with the firemen on their mobile CCU called Medic I, and I've attended lectures which prepare these firemen to handle cardiac emergencies. For having no background in anatomy and physiology, these lectures are quite sophisticated. They spend quite a lot of time on the treatment and technical skills required in each anatomical site covered. This emphasis on treatment is somewhat new and fascinating. The lectures so far have provided quite a lot of new information, very useful to nursing observations. I can't help but love to get to the poor patient and evaluate what we learned the night before. The oscilloscope is not my bag unless it can be directly applied to what I see happening. Often their heart conduction system snaps along with some irritability while the other systems are really showing significant findings. Also, the heart is more interesting at the bedside. When in the unit, my responsibility is to "man the scopes." I often fail to keep as close a watch as the others and drift into the patient rooms. If I catch some form of irritability on the scope it excites me less than if I catch rales, a gallop in the heart, or can feel the degree of liver enlargement; and, lastly, I enjoy the autonomy of being in a position where my opinions and suggestions have weight. Secretarial jobs in nursing really are effective in pulling one away from that distended neck vein one would like to recheck. It's gradually like adding one and one to find out where I'm heading—clinical specialist? Or out of nursing completely? I'm actively seeking employment elsewhere; I've begun calling some of the various hospitals to inquire about opportunities that might be coming up—in-service jobs, speciality area, etc. . . . Right now it must include continued clinical experience that I still don't have. Perhaps a position in a combination CCU and surgical ICU would do it. I'd like to be assistant head nurse in this area to pick up some administrative experience. . . .

The Medic I doctors are planning a new program where the fireman will be trained to perform treatment in several other needed emergency areas. The bill is in the state congress now. Its implications should be even more far-reaching than the heart team. I'm "antsy" to get involved in the movement. Emergency community medicine is wide open and new! It just may be what keeps me in nursing!

*June and July, 1971*

My attitude about this job has taken a complete turnabout from what it has been for the last several months. As I told you, I had decided it was time for me to meet and talk with the DNS. I had a scheduled appointment with her on the 2nd of last month. The session was quickly turned into a counseling hour. I have apparently been backing myself up into a corner. A lot of the backing up involved backing down from what I believed in about nursing and what I should be doing in my job. I was really frustrated in not being able to do these things, and most days went to work with a pit in my stomach. It's not as though I wasn't

thinking about what was going on, but the focus was narrowed quite a bit and interpersonal relations with staff and doctors magnified way too much. My feelings about usurping the head nurse's leadership role forced me into a passive-aggressive role which wasn't an honest one for myself and probably not pleasant for the rest of the girls. Also the approach wasn't successful in accomplishing anything really worthwhile. In addition my anxieties about the supposed diagnostic end of the nursing role in a CCU were terribly out of proportion when one considers what I was forfeiting— the humanistic side of nursing—to learn them. And that includes a campaign for increasing the continuity of care and the whole-patient bit. The nursing care activities in the CCU are unique in that many of them closely approach a physician's duties: EKG interpretation, individual judgment in treating certain arrhythmias, quasi-responsibility for catching early signs of certain clinical complications, etc. An aggressive nurse (alias, me) tends to compete somewhat, abandoning the *care* role for the diagnostic activities. Having satisfied myself in this situational tragedy, I began to look back again to nursing. I felt safer coming back to it after having proven myself as a CCU nurse—the concept of this as it is known and understood by the nurses on this unit. There has *got* to be much more to nursing than the CCU role as it is practiced here. I don't think I was facing up to what I had to do next. Quitting an institution like this would be passing up one of the most fertile areas for effecting change that I can think of. Also, when considering the autonomy that I enjoy, what better place to do one's own thing! The upshot of the talk I had with Mrs. [X] was that she very politely demonstrated to me (from what I told her) how I was backing down, that there were no utopias (which I was of course aware), and that this hospital is in particular need of leaders who will make their ideas viable to the staff. She felt that a leader should stick out like a sore thumb for her qualities, not necessarily assuming the head nurse's *position* but the functional leadership in terms of progress (right, right, right!) She also felt that this could be effected in whatever position the nurse held—staff nurse in particular, as this is where one must inevitably prove herself anyway.

I went home feeling both elated and guilty that this had to be pointed out to me. Just think, almost a whole year later I would hopefully begin to function as I should have all along. I had been developing a teaching plan for the cardiac patients, which sat home because I didn't want to upset things anymore. I was really feeling the sense of destructive competition that I was very much helping to foster. I assembled two plans (an alternative if needed) and presented the idea about a need for planned teaching to those RN's that my particular shift permitted contact with. Our hit-and-miss (mostly miss) explanation to the patients just doesn't approach teaching. A teaching plan is one step in the door for nursing conferences and regular care plans (*very* badly needed). The approval is there; but saying yes to an idea or plan means nothing. So I began to talk about its implementation with the two alternatives I spoke about. The head nurse hasn't bought it in any enthusiastic fashion and simply wanted to go home while I talked with her about it. With my new courage in hand, I decided not to wait for three months for her approval but to start at least presenting it to each nurse and eliciting her ideas and agreement about the need for nursing conferences. In the ward communication book, I pasted a sample of the teaching form which another private hospital has found useful, and left spaces for ideas about how we might adapt it to fit our particular needs. I left an explanation of what I hoped they would say or how they would like to help implement the teaching. Nothing—no one has contributed at all. That's where I am with it: being on the bandwagon for something which more appropriately fits my nursing role and with something I can accomplish which is much more satisfying, and I don't *have* to leave here or leave nursing!

I'm not sure what's happened, but my perspective about hospital nursing is changing. I no longer feel that it is the second-rate area where one obtains necessary experience and steps out. There is a hell of a lot to do here and it can be a challenge for any of us, I guess. I had a particularly hard time adjusting to the staff role, I feel, basically because of my notions about interstaff relations, my role as a staff nurse, my ambitions for more responsibility and the different changes I wanted to make. I really failed to understand how I might perform openly as an underdog to no one, that I didn't have to "keep in my place." There is certainly a lot of backtracking to do. I feel badly that you've been a witness to my behavior in this respect. My desire of course would have been to impress you, utilizing what my education had offered in a creative way. Fear not. I feel as though I'm just getting started. The termination of this particular job won't be with the frustration that I've spoken to you about before. Take any area that one works in, the staff turnover may be complete in two to four years. However, if one effects some positive changes in the care of patients which persist through these turnovers, then the original resistance to the changes counts for zero. The totality of it all is becoming clearer now.

It's also 4:30 AM—I'm on nights and may shortly lose coherency. This year riddled with mistakes was really a learning experience, and hopefully the same pitfalls won't be stumbled into again. The greatest feeling, though, is that I don't have to stop working here and get another job to start over or reemphasize what I should have. I don't feel like it is backing out or down in the least. As far as staff relations go, they really are quite fun to watch. They are all right now—the complete reversal of what they were originally. The aides and myself get along well. They enjoy my efforts to include them in on teaching of the arrhythmias, etc., and I think they respect me for the effort and care I give to the patients. The RN's are hostile and somewhat tense around me. This I see as reversible. It will take time, but I intend to start.

1. My demeanor must be calmer and with more personal conviction.
2. Any challenges presented to them must be approached so that I elicit their involvement and personal investment of ideas; it will bind the idea into a joint effort not so readily dropped, I hope.
3. Others are beginning to add to the educational library—sort of following what I started—and, would you believe, are listening to chest sounds and cardiac sounds! This brings them closer to the patient and away from the darn scopes. Also I initiated IV daily care where the site is completely cleaned and redressed. The catheter is again secured and antibiotic reapplied. Others are beginning to do the same, and incidence of puffy infiltrated arms and red phlebitic lines all the way up the arm are disappearing.

So the personal business has to step aside somewhat if the idea is good enough.

### COMMENTARY

BENNER: In contrast to the other sections of the diary, this section covers a rather long period—about five months. In it we see the culmination of some aspects of Lynn's becoming and the continuation and beginning of others.

I think one of the most interesting entries is her remarks relative to her view of the bureaucratic organization. Consistent with her earlier entries, she still sees the organization with limited commitment; "I won't work here beyond the point of learning for me." But there's also some evidence of some change and growth in this area. It seems as though she can now relax enough to take off her blinders and see more of the organization than just the CCU.

I was really wrapped up in my own niche in the CCU and not really paying too much attention to the rest of the hospital and the system. Since then I've expanded a lot with my interests and have discovered how really sick this place really is.

KRAMER: Yes, I noticed that too, and I would agree that that is a sign of growth, but doesn't it sort of sound to you like she might possibly encounter reality shock again on a larger organizational level?

BENNER: I suppose that's possible. The above statement certainly does sound like the wholesale criticism and rejection characteristic of reality shock. Perhaps this is a further extension of the phenomenon that will need looking into. For the time being, though, I think the widening of perception is healthy. And the statement she makes later on also suggests that she's viewing the organization and her association with it in a more favorable light.

> I'm glad I've been here so that I can approach any other job with hope. Also it is beginning to be profitable for me in learning the hard cruel paths of administrative bureaucracy.

KRAMER: Lynn seems to be more perceptive of some of the socialization messages being sent to her now also. Whereas earlier they seemed to surprise her, she now seems to be cognizant of them, although she still doesn't buy them or the value system upon which they are based.

BENNER: I can't say I blame her for that. I was struck with how common and consistent these kinds of socialization messages are. No matter where you work, the same kind of priority system comes through. Direct caring for patients is lowest in status.

> I understand that I will become an instant aide. Neither the head nurse nor Sue will bathe a patient or empty a urinal. . . . I will be interested to see how they pull that off. Joan, one of the other RN's, says that she often doesn't get to draw the bloods, pass meds, etc., when working with these two.

KRAMER: So often this kind of status hierarchy of tasks is explained on the basis that more professional nursing skill is needed to draw bloods and observe monitors than to bathe patients. Lynn and many other new nurses have been taught just the opposite. Drawing bloods and monitoring vital signs are really quite routine tasks with predictable levels of resistance [Chapter I, p. 14], but bathing patients in the CCU can be quite an active task. I suspect the real reason for this very common hierarchical arrangement of nursing tasks is something that Hughes (1958) commented on a long time ago: "Ranking has

something to do with the relative cleanliness of functions performed . . . no one is so lowly in the hospital as those who handle soiled linen."

BENNER: It's been quite a year for Lynn. Where do you think she is now in her process of situational adaptation?

KRAMER: Well first off, you can see in Lynn's opening remarks in this set of diary entries that she is aware that there is another potential path of adaptation open to her other than the ones she's already cited (flight into teaching, leaving nursing altogether, going it alone).

> I've sort of lost a lot of the hyper attitude about the job, also a lot of my enthusiasm. . . . It would be so easy just to relax and let the job flow around me. Maybe I should stop fighting and join the others in the deep chasm that is the rut around here. Sometimes I get so discouraged. . . .

That's the only place I see mention of this attitude, and with the tremendous fight Lynn has been putting up all along I think it's quite doubtful that she would seriously consider this route.

BENNER: I would agree. I see much more evidence of recovery and possible bicultural adaptation. One choice that Lynn has been working on persistently ever since she started her job is that of competence acquisition. And for her this is very closely related to her view of herself as becoming a competent, self-confident individual with a sense of power and payoff—a feeling that what she does is important and meaningful. One can sense some of this desire for power and efficacy in Lynn's patient care goals.

> This is really exciting to me that in a susceptible person we can be alerted to this danger [stroke] and act appropriately when the situation arises. . . .
>
> I would like to introduce the article [on titration of IV fluids] to the girls at work and perhaps we could together prevent these unnecessary fluid disasters. . . .
>
> If I catch some form of irritability on the scope it excites me less than if I catch rales, a gallop in the heart, or can feel the degree of liver enlargement; and, lastly, I enjoy the autonomy of being in a position where my opinions and suggestions have weight.

KRAMER: She doesn't seem to have experienced this same sense of efficacy or power in her relationships with staff and her ability to influence others, though. In fact Lynn has vascillated between wanting to go it alone—having isolated independence—and wanting to influence her co-workers.

> I think this [report] form will really be a help. . . .

I hadn't shown it to the nurses in the printed up form yet so I'm not sure if they'll like the idea. . . . Hopefully it will help at least me, and will not be rejected for the originator but for the idea itself, if it is not valuable to all the others. . . .

I'm extremely paranoid, I think, and really need to be as objective as possible. Also I'm pretty ambitious and impatient with the job, my seemingly slow adaptation to it. A person can make just as big a mess of things by trying too hard as by not trying at all. So I have been trying to relax with it. Everything is going along fine. I'm gradually able to squeeze in some additions to the nursing care plans. The nurses are still negative to the nursing histories. Little additions are the only palatable form of change accepted and even those not with any zest. . . .

I began using it [the report form she developed] and gradually offered it to the nurses who came on days. It was politely tolerated for a few times, and then they said it was confusing and quit using it. . . .

I have told the other girls about it [the IV tray she designed and set up] and if they wanted to use it that I would keep one made up for them on the IV cart. Someone put it out of reach in the back of the cart, so I haven't said anything more about it. I like it, though, and will keep using it.

KRAMER: Yes, the above incidents seem to substantiate her feelings that she was unable to change the unit to help it move forward. Her innovations were rejected, and she was left with feeling ineffective—"helping the unit hold its own without advancing."

BENNER: Lynn was much slower in developing interpersonal competency in respect to influencing staff; she seems to have been much more competent in her influence on patients. Don't you think that maybe this was because this area of interpersonal competency with the staff was never particularly one of Lynn's goals? What I mean is that from the very beginning she saw herself and her primary role as one of nursing patients and building her competence in this area. In fact, initially it seemed as though she wasn't even aware that she would have to get involved in staff relationships and the human side of the organization. It was almost because it was literally forced upon her that she began to become involved and motivated to develop interpersonal competence in this area.

KRAMER: Yes, I think you're right. In fact, I'd almost say that it wasn't 'til after the intervention provided by the director of nursing that Lynn really was strongly motivated to develop interpersonal competency in this area and, fur-

thermore, that she had confidence in her ability to do so.

BENNER: In order to be willing to invest herself in interpersonal relationships with the staff, I think that Lynn had to have some help. I think she needed to feel that her investment and energies in interpersonal relationships were worthwhile and would help her achieve the patient care goals which were so important to her before she could feel motivated to make the necessary investment. It was not until after her counseling session with the director of nursing that Lynn had any feelings of hope that her investment would be worthwhile:

Fear not. I feel as though I'm just getting started. . . . if one effects some positive changes in the care of patients which persist through these turnovers, then the original resistance to the changes counts for zero.

And appropriately at the end of the diary Lynn notes *that she is making a difference.*

KRAMER: Yes, that was really quite a counseling session and a timely and effective intervention on the part of the director of nursing. Through this interaction Lynn developed both insight and hope that allowed her to take up her involvement with the staff again. Lynn leaves the question of work group acceptance and interpersonal competency in this area on a hopeful note.

I don't feel like it is backing out or down in the least. As far as staff relations go . . . they really are quite fun to watch. They are all right now . . . the complete reversal of what they were originally. The aides and myself get along well. . . . They enjoy my efforts to include them in on teaching of the arrhythmias, etc., and I think they respect me for the effort and care I give to the patients. The RN's are hostile and somewhat tense around me. This I see as reversible. It will take time, but I intend to start.

BENNER: Lynn's movement toward biculturalism demonstrates one extremely important point. For Lynn to move into a state of hope and comfort with her ability to adapt and innovate in the CCU took the support and counseling of someone in her social system. For Lynn it was the director of nursing. (And remember at the beginning Lynn reported that other nurses said the DNS was unapproachable.) I wonder how many other young nurses don't have anyone to turn to who can help them gain renewed hope and perspective in respect to their value system and the potential conflicts between the school and work value systems.

KRAMER: Lynn really expresses this recovery of hope and beginning biculturalism beautifully, doesn't she?

> I'm not sure what's happened, but my perspective about hospital nursing is changing. I no longer feel that it is the second-rate area where one obtains necessary experience and steps out. There is a hell of a lot to do here and it can be a challenge for any of us, I guess. I had a particularly hard time adjusting to the staff role, I feel, basically because of my notions about interstaff relations, my role as a staff nurse, my ambitions for more responsibility and the different changes I wanted to make. I really failed to understand how I might perform openly as an underdog to no one, that I didn't have to "keep in my place."

Lynn no longer has the glowing one-sided praise of the honeymoon phase nor the derogatory one-sided criticism of the rejection phase. Nor does she still feel a bit above hospital nursing as she did in her recovery phase. She can now understand the social system and can see her potential for making an impact there. This is no small accomplishment! It is at this point that any descriptive system is inadequate. Who can explain the hope and the energy, the commitment for making a difference, for making a creative contribution? We can only be grateful to Lynn for sharing with us what was at times a painfully honest description of her journey.

## NOTES

1. The comparison and contrast of case histories and case studies is abstracted from Strauss, A., and Glaser, B.: Anguish, Mill Valley, Calif., 1970, The Sociology Press.
2. The reader might be interested in knowing that this particular attitude was verified by the head nurses and supervisors of the graduates during followup interviews. It is important to note that early suggestions of new-comers are apt to be more unrealistic or lacking in consideration of cultural norms and limitations than are later suggestions. The challenge is for the newcomer to hold onto his ideas and enthusiasm until he's gotten a grasp of the backstage reality and some beginning interpersonal competence and influence.
3. This may sound deprecatory to nursing service administration. Such is not the intent. From the point of view of both organizational efficiency and availability, it has undoubtedly been necessary for directors of nursing to look toward nurses with these characteristics for promotion. The fact is that they do get the job done and they maintain the status quo! Furthermore, until fairly recently nursing service administrators have had few professionally and interpersonally competent nurses to choose from in making selections for positions of authority.
4. It must be made clear that not all nurse-teachers are behavioral capitulators, but only those who use this avenue as a method of resolving the conflict between how nursing "should be practiced" and "how it is done" in the service setting. Some nurses choose to go into teaching because they feel that they have made constructive conflict adaptation and are stimulated by the possibility and opportunity of sharing their resolution strategies with nurse aspirants.
5. It is difficult to separate values from role specific behaviors, particularly in the work setting where the status of employee demands behavioral actions from which underlying values are (correctly or incorrectly) inferred. In the status of student, the aspirant nurse is often able to verbalize values and attitudes without demonstrating them in role specific behaviors. It is therefore much easier to separate the two in the school than in the work setting.

## REFERENCES

Blau, P.: A theory of social integration, Am. J. Sociol. **65**(6):545-556, 1960.

Brim, O.: Adult socialization. In Clausen, J. N., and associates, editors: Socialization and society, Boston, 1968, Little, Brown & Co., pp. 184-226.

Cleveland, H., Mangone, G. J., and Adams, J. C.: The overseas Americans, New York, 1960, McGraw-Hill Book Co.

Dornbusch, S. M.: The military academy as an assimilating institution, Social Forces **33**:316-321, 1955.

Gale, C.: The nurse's aide; a study of low role coordination, unpublished doctoral dissertation, 1969, Stanford University, Department of Education.

Goffman, E.: The presentation of self in everyday life, New York, 1959, Doubleday & Co., p. 238.

Graham, L.: Planning for priorities in quality nursing care, J. Nurs. Educ., November, 1969, pp. 9-17.

Hovland, C. I., Lumsdaine, A. A., and Sheffield, F.: Experiments on mass communication, Princeton, 1949, Princeton University Press.

Hovland, C. I., and Weiss, W.: The influence of source credibility on communication effectiveness, Public Opinion Quarterly **15**:635-650, 1959.

Hughes, E.: Men and their work, New York, 1958, The Free Press.

Kelman, H., and Hovland, C. I.: Reinstatement of the communicator in delayed measurement of opinion change, J. Abnorm. Psychol. **48**:327-335, 1953.

Lippitt, R.: Improving the socialization process. In Clausen, J. A., and associates, editors: Socialization and society, Boston, 1968, Little, Brown & Co., pp. 322-374.

Luchins, A. S.: Experimental attempts to minimize the impact of first impression. In Hovland, C. I., and associates: The order of presentation in persuasion, New Haven, 1957, Yale University Press.

Olmsted, A., and Paget, M.: Some theoretical issues in professional socialization, J. Med. Educ. **44**:663-669, August 1969.

Peter, L. J., and Hull, R.: The Peter principle, New York, Bantam Books, Inc., 1969.

Rosow, I.: Forms and functions of adult socialization, Social Forces 44:35-45, September 1956.

Schein, E.: The first job dilemma, Psychology Today, March 1968, pp. 28-38.

Strauss, A., and Glaser, B.: Anguish, Mill Valley, Calif., 1970, The Sociology Press.

Treat, M., and Kramer, M.: The question behind the question, J. Nurs. Administration 11(1):20-27, 1972.

CHAPTER SIX

# REALITY TESTING A REALITY SHOCK PROGRAM

PATRICIA BENNER

For groups, as well as for individuals, life itself means to separate and to be united, to change form and condition, to die and to be reborn. It is to act and to cease, to wait and rest, and then to begin acting again, but in a different way. And there are always new thresholds to cross.

VAN GENNEP

The success of the Anticipatory Socialization program stimulated many questions: Is it possible to alter the process and outcomes of reality shock for the new graduate who has *not* been prepared for the conflict and discontinuity between school and work? Would a program based on the skills of constructive conflict resolution be an effective means of intervening in the work setting so that the new graduate could better manage the reality shock? Would such a program increase effective planned change activity on the part of the new graduate? To study the above questions, a special program specifically for new graduates in their first job was developed. This Reality Shock program was a planned series of six seminars to be given as a regular part of a staff development program. In this chapter the planning and outcomes of this pilot venture will be described. No hypotheses were formulated for testing; this pilot venture was mainly in the nature of a trial effort, with concurrent evaluation and modification. It is hoped that the reporting of this initial study, although it will not completely answer the above questions, will stimulate other trial programs. Such programs should do much to intervene in the cycle of frustration and low tenure of new graduates in their first jobs.

The knowledge and skill components for the Reality Shock program were based on the Anticipatory Socialization program and on the interview and diary data on the first work experiences of new graduates reported in earlier chapters of this book. The opportunity to interview sixteen new graduates who had had a special orientation program provided additional information on conflicts experienced by new graduates.

Although the Reality Shock program evolved from and had many points in common with the Anticipatory Socialization program, there were some important differences. Rather than focusing on anticipatory conflict exposure for students in one nursing program as the Anticipatory Socialization program did, the Reality Shock program focused on the reality shock and conflicts that graduates from a variety of educational backgrounds were presently experiencing in their first jobs. Also, the Anticipatory Socialization program focused mainly on conflicts emanating from the differences between the school way of organizing the nurse's work and the prevalent method of work organization in the work scene. The Reality Shock program covered school-work conflicts, but also other prevalent conflicts such as neophyte nurses of one generation working with (and often supervising) nurses or auxiliary workers of an older genration.

In the first part of this chapter the conflicts that were the basis for choosing the knowledge-skill components of the Reality Shock program will be presented. The planning and implementation of the Reality Shock program itself will be described in the section titled The Seminars Unfold. This section is comprised of a chronological narrative and analysis of the Reality Shock seminars, based on seminar typescripts and field notes. In the concluding section, frameworks useful in viewing and describing the situational adjustment of new graduates will be presented. These frameworks were formulated from the experience gained in the seminars and from follow-up interviews with the nurses in the Reality Shock program.

## ROLE TRANSFORMATION AND ITS CONFLICTS

The Reality Shock program was based upon the assumption that one of the major tasks of the new graduate is role transformation. Role transformation means that the person must mediate conflicting demands, reconsidering previously held values so that he becomes, in fact, a somewhat different person. The new graduates must separate themselves from the expectations that were held for them in school and, concomitantly, they must take on new expectations that arise in the context of their new jobs. The Reality Shock program was based on three ideas:

1. Role transformation is necessary and potentially shocking to the degree that the school environment is different from the work environment.
2. Reality shock is likely to occur to the degree that the student or neophyte is unprepared or uninformed about the differences between school and work.
3. Successful role transformation is dependent upon the degree or extent of accommodating devices possessed by or quickly learned by the new graduate.

For most new graduates, school differs markedly from work, and therefore most new nurses are confronted with the task of role transformation. No longer can the new graduate operate in terms of school prescriptions of what the nurse *should* be. Socialization into a specific work situation requires the new graduate to view both general and specific role prescriptions differently. In school the student nurse based her role identity on the performance of explicit observations and explicit performance standards; at work she must sort out a "specific role" from many incoming stimuli, role demands, and ambiguous situations. The specific role she sorts out must be acceptable to both her and the group she is joining. A satisfactory role transformation requires that the new graduate meet her own role demands, the work group's, and the patient's in the everyday mix of work demands.

Instead of a school-type role message indicating that the nurse should be able to devise and implement a goal-directed nursing care plan for Mr. Peters, an alcoholic with tuberculosis, the neophyte nurse is assigned to oversee the care of "the TB alcoholic in Room 219." In school her rather specific role message carried with it all the previous teaching and explicit learning about what a nursing care plan is and the possible nursing interventions derived from behavioral and medical science principles. Her role message at work is a little less clear and much more complex. According to the job description, the message may have these components: provide for the care, the therapeutic intervention and the safety of Mr. Peters. In other words: *do it.* There are necessarily fewer instructions on *how* to do it. The student was supposedly taught how in school. Immediately the neophyte is confronted with very specific questions: How do I do it in the real world of this hospital? How do I provide a climate of acceptance that might enhance Mr. Peter's self-esteem in the midst of an institutional norm that labels alcoholics as drunks and with a work group who interprets the goal of therapeutic intervention as "hang a yellow IV bottle."

In school the neophyte may have been able to view herself as one who intervenes therapeutically. If she is unable to translate this therapeutic intervention into specific role behaviors in the mix of the institutional reality, she may have to redefine her role as one who does not intervene directly or one who participates in a nontherapeutic intervention, or she may come to define herself as one who sees the need for therapeutic intervention and refers the patient to the appropriate source of intervention. For example, one new graduate noted that her success in transferring a psychiatric patient off her medical-surgical unit was one of her most satisfying work experiences as a new graduate. Frustrated by her inability to intervene with this patient, she felt good about being able to transfer the patient to a floor where he would receive adequate intervention. Thus this new graduate's success depended on whether or not she could recombine the elements of the ideal role taught in school with the constraints, opportunities, and predicaments of the social system at work.

## Common conflicts

It was known from earlier studies and from interviews with the 16 new graduates that there were major areas of shock and conflict common to most new graduates:

1. The difference between systems of work organization (the professional system being the predominant system in school, the bureaucratic being the predominant system of organization at work) and the resulting difference between rewards and sanctions in school and work
2. The difference between the school world of explicit expectations and the work world of implied expectations
3. The difference between the school cosmopolitan view and the work world's localite view

*Professional-bureaucratic role conflict.* The major separation and recombination of role identity was expected to be in the area of differences between the system of work organization taught in school and that predominant in the work world. The nurse is taught in school to organize her work on the basis of a whole-task model. Her work role demands will require that she delegate many tasks and that she function in a network of part-tasks that will meet the needs of large groups of patients. That this is a source of great conflict and anxiety for nurses has been attested to in many studies. The unlearning and relearning required by the differences between the professional and bureaucratic organization of work was frequently expressed in the Reality Shock seminars: "It doesn't occur to me to ask someone else." "I feel bad—guilty—to ask someone else to do something for *my* pa-

tient. . . . " These brief statements convey some of the confusion of new graduates who are trying to navigate both in the professional world of doing the whole job themselves and in the reality world of work, which dictates the necessity of delegating tasks.

The new graduate's difficulty in delegating tasks confronts her with the need for leadership skills and leadership acceptance that often she had not learned in school. There has been much talk about leadership in nursing education in the past ten years, but there is a gap between the professional's view of leadership and the nature of leadership tasks as viewed in the work environment. John Gardner describes the academic view of leadership this way:

The students learn to identify themselves strongly with their calling and its ideals. They acquire a conception of what a good scholar, scientist or professional man is like.

As things stand now, however, that conception leaves little room for leadership in the normal sense; the only kind of leadership which is encouraged is that which follows from the performing of purely professional tasks in a superior manner. Entry into what most of us would regard as the leadership roles in the society at large is discouraged. . . .

As a result the academic world appears to be approaching a point at which everyone will want to educate the technical expert who advises the leader, or the intellectual who stands off and criticizes the leader, but no one will want to educate the leader.°

That the new graduate is sharply confronted with differing leadership expectations from the work environment is demonstrated in the following interview excerpt.

The first time I was team leading I didn't know what to do. We did not do team leading in school. What I think they should do is to help us learn what the role of the team leader is. And I think it would be more helpful if they gave us a general outline of what the functions of the team leader are . . . especially on the first day (NG: AD/2[4]6/71)

---

°Gardner, J. W.: in Rowan, N., editor: No easy victories, New York, 1968, Harper & Row, Publishers, Inc. pp. 128-129.

Another aspect of professional-bureaucratic conflict that presents difficulty for the new graduate is the shift from the school emphasis on adequate and desirable methods for accomplishing a task to the work emphasis on results or work output. The training of a professional worker sensitizes him to a close association between adequacy of means and correctness of conclusions. Good results are viewed as a consequence of careful following of correct procedures. It is little wonder that the new graduate is appalled at having to drop her school-bred professional credo of adequacy of means to meet the immediacy of everyday demands of the job. One new graduate described her surprise this way.

[At work] they were supposed to teach me to start IV's, and I expected a class and expected to learn the physiology behind what I was doing; but no, the head nurse showed you a couple of times and that was it. I was really mad about that. (NG:BS/2[7]6/71)

It was equally disappointing when the adequate means did not produce the results promised in school.

You kind of get the idea that there's a right way to problem solve and a right way to approach change; and if you do it the right way and if you don't win the first time, well, you can always try a different approach. I mean there are just so many approaches you can try before you get utterly frustrated. (NG:BS/2[16]6/71)

Difference between the school and work methods of organization also leads to differences in sanctions and rewards. Upon employment, the neophyte must learn to distinguish between the familiar rewards and sanctions she experienced and expected in school and those operating in the work world. This process can be confusing and frustrating, particularly when she is rewarded for what she does not yet value.

I think I set higher levels for myself than maybe the people I'm working with do, because a couple of times I thought I was doing okay—you know, I was getting the stuff done—but I don't think I was performing as well as I feel I should have been. But the RN I was working with said I was doing a really good job. One day, it was kind of a busy day and I didn't know any of the patients. I didn't get out [with the patients] as much as I wanted to, and I didn't feel like I was helping the team members as much as a team leader should. But without knowing the patients and without being familiar with them, you know, that takes more time. There weren't any difficulties that came up or anything, but she [the RN] said I did a good job. But I just felt that I should have been on the floor more. (NG:BS/2[11]8/71)

The work world estranges and confounds the new graduate when she is punished for omissions she is not yet aware of.

I had been on the floor six weeks; and suddenly one day I was on duty and I was told that a meeting was set up. The girl from in-service and the supervisor and one of the nurses and myself were sitting in on this meeting, and there were charges and accusations made. This really bothered me because that was the first I had heard of it. And as I sat in that meeting I was just sort of amazed and dumbfounded to think that I had been on the floor for six weeks and that no one had bothered to tell me that certain charges were being made—certain things that I was not doing—and I was surprised to find out that the person felt that way. I felt bad because all they had to do was to tell me that I was expected to do certain things (NG:AD/2[9]8/71)

•   •   •

My dissatisfactions which I had been feeling became nothing in comparison to what my evaluation brought forth. Essentially, the evaluation overwhelmingly stated my disorganization and my inability to cope with certain situations. Undoubtedly, much of what they said was true or at least partially true. I was not really aware of these things. However, what was devastating to me was their lack of praise as to what I did do well. My only praise was that, since I had graduated from a university, surely I had the ability to do better if I'd just think about it and work at it. Why in heaven's name did they wait until this moment, a month before I was leaving, to tell me what a rotten job I had been doing? Well, they encouraged me: "You have a month to improve and maybe you'll get a better evaluation." I should point out that my head nurse never really showed an interest in me or my work except when I had done something wrong. (NG:BS/12[742]7/72)

*Explicit versus implied objectives.* The new graduates' incredulity over not being told about their omissions and infractions points up the surprise and discomfort experienced when the new graduate moves from the school world of explicit expectations to the work world of implied, tacit expectations. The lack of well-defined performance standards in the work world is due mainly to the increased number and complexity of task and role expectations at work. This is in sharp contrast with the school world of explicit objectives and evaluation tools such as tests, reports, ratings, and instructor feedback. At work the evaluation tools are often vague, filled out irregularly, and may depend on much indirect evidence rather than direct observations. For example, an absence of complaints from patients and co-workers may qualify the employee for a rating comment such as: Is cooperative and gets along well with others. This rating may be more attributable to an informal code of co-workers not to squeal on others and to patients' low energy levels than on the employee's interpersonal competency. Since the worker's objectives are often not clearly defined, her evaluation tends to be even less definite. Thus the neophyte's predicament: she is less sure of her role than she has ever been, and yet she is receiving less concrete specific feedback than she ever has.

*Cosmopolitan versus local view.* Another important adjustment for the new graduate is that of separating herself from the cosmopolitan world of school and joining the local or specific world at work. Individuals with a cosmopolitan orientation are low on loyalty to the employing organization and are likely to use an outer reference group orientation. Localites have the opposite loyalties and orientations. Cosmopolitanism, by definition, is often at odds with localism. What may be best in principle and in general for patients may not be best when given the specific constraints of a particular work group in a particular setting. Take for example the conflict given in the first chapter: Should the nurse tend to the individual needs of Mrs. Swape, a cardiac patient, or should she tend to the needs of the rest of the patients who need their evening meal? A strong cosmopolitan view of the situation causes conflict; both ob-

jectives are important; yet the situation viewed from the supervisor's local perspective contains only the local norms of serving the other patients' food on time and meeting the needs of the largest number of patients. The supervisor operating according to local norms sees no conflict. (If meeting psychosocial patient needs on an individual basis were a strong local norm, then the localite, too, would experience conflict in this situation.)

The conflict between the cosmopolitan and local views may lead to misunderstanding between the new graduate and the work group. The cosmopolitan neophyte has sensitivities to problems that the localite has never thought of. On the other hand, the localite has insight and wisdom about getting things done in the work situation that the new graduate has little appreciation for. The following excerpt from one of the Reality Shock seminars and the interpretive commentary in parentheses show what might be involved for the new graduate in making the shift from the cosmopolitan view to the local reality.

Yeah, I know that it really helps to have someone else just remind you about the patient's need for privacy. Because when people say to me: "How would you like to be treated that way?" [local view] then all of a sudden I think: "This patient should have her privacy" [cosmopolitan view]. (NG:BS/3[17]12/71) (This sounds as if Janet is beginning to realize that the really global principle—privacy is a right—is not so much the issue as is how do you stay sensitive to privacy needs and how do you provide privacy to patient X under Y circumstances? To stay on the level of outrage at the violation of the cosmopolitan principle is to avoid the more arduous daily issue of putting this principle into practice.)

Even though the new graduate has a cosmopolitan grasp of principles (for example, privacy is a patient right), it may take her awhile to identify where those principles might apply or are being applied in an institutional setting. Whereas educators most often talk in terms of principles and their application, at work people talk about situations and circumstances. At work it is up to the new graduate to find the principle that applies to uniᶜ situations.

## Individualistic conflicts

In addition to the three common conflicts just presented, there are other differences between work and school that were expected to engender conflict of a more individualistic nature, depending on the educational background and work milieu:

1. Clinical uncertainty or ambiguity
2. A competency gap
3. The generation gap
4. The constancy of time and time orientation of work
5. Subcultural differences between institutions
6. Racial conflicts as they affect work performance.

*Clinical uncertainty or ambiguity.* Many new graduates are surprised by the lack of precision and certainty in clinical practice. (The new graduates who escaped this surprise seemed either to have spent a great deal of time in realistic clinical practice or else had had fairly extensive work experience in the health care setting.) In school the student nurse had the opportunity for precision in clinical practice. Such precision is possible through selective assignments made by instructors. Procedures are not done until they have been supervised or at least explored in a skill or practice session. The student is exposed to far less ambiguity than that which she will encounter in the work setting. In school theory precedes practice and the student is led to believe that there is a correct way that things should be done. This engenders certainty. In the work setting precision is not so feasible. Clinical practice by its nature is ambiguous since psychosocial and medical knowledge is incomplete and the variables involved in applying knowledge to clinical situations are numerous and complex. Thus the graduate nurse, as a practicing clinician, is confronted with more ambiguous, unexplored, and unexplained situations than she has ever been confronted with during school.

As I came out then and started working, I became frustrated because I found that it was harder to learn some of these things than I thought it might be. I thought I would just go to somebody and ask them. But you get a lot of different answers, depending on who you go to, and you find out that some nurses don't really know how or why. They're just doing it, a lot of times, just any old way. So it takes longer than I expected it might because of that kind of thing. (NG:BS/2[13]8/71)

Educators tend to make school experiences more concrete than real life in order to break down the learning tasks into simpler components. This is sound educational practice if the learner eventually progresses to the less concrete, real situations and can demonstrate or test out the transfer of her learning. But if the learner is not provided with an opportunity to test out learning in a realistic setting, she will not know whether she has really learned until she starts working.

There is also less opportunity for precision at work because there is often an overload of stimuli or clinical demands coming in at the same time. This potentiates role conflict and ambiguity. Patient care demands are not amenable to sequencing and scheduling, although health care workers make valiant efforts along this line. A nurse confronted with five or ten patient care needs at once is placed in the uncertain role of assigning priorities. She must decide which patient's need is more urgent and whose needs can safely wait or be delegated to someone else. A further drawback is the shortage of staff and the multitude of tasks. Thus the new graduate has fewer resources, and more decisions to make. Faced with less time to ask questions and make certain she has enough data, she is confronted with the necessity to make decisions and to make them rapidly. One new graduate explained that time was her greatest hindrance:

Time is the factor that has most hindered me. Down in pediatrics, it's always rushing. Especially during the day. There are so many things to do. Every minute they just keep us running, and I don't have—we don't have—any time to stop and ask questions. And everybody is busy at the same time and I hate to take time from other people. So sometimes I just get stuck and I just have to find my own way of doing things. I could make lots of mistakes. (NG:AD/2[9]8/71)

Ambiguity and uncertainty are situations ripe for ritual. Rituals help people cope with profound uncertainties. The ritualistic worker is one who abandons the goal or the rationale behind his behavior and focuses almost solely on the means. Ritualism is widespread in nursing, with the system of change-of-shift reports being a major ritual. New graduates were well on their way to developing ritualistic behavior, as evidenced by this frequently heard remark:

I know I should look it up in a book when I don't know something. You plan to look it up at night but never get around to it, and soon you find that you can do it without looking it up. (NG: BS/3[823]9/68)

The questions become: How can the new graduate be prepared to increase her tolerance for ambiguity? Where knowledge is scant and a ritual prevails, how can we prepare the graduate to recognize ritual for its possible temporary value but at the same time value its speedy replacement with solid rationale and knowledge?

*Competency gap.* The neophyte may be shocked at the competency gap of both nurses and doctors. School interactions tend to shield the student from such knowledge. Part of the lack of awareness of competency gaps is due to students often being exposed only to front-stage reality (p. 140) during their student clinical experiences. Staff tend to present their ideal selves and best performances to students. Also, the student is less expert and thus less able to detect incompetency during student days. Upon graduation she is less likely to be shielded from incompetency and is more adept in perceiving it when it occurs.

Changes in my ideals and attitudes? Well, my attitude toward other nurses—that they don't all know what they are doing. This really puts a little more pressure on me now that I am a nurse too. And I know I'm not a good nurse at this point because I've got a lot more to learn still. (NG: BS/2[13]8/71)

On the other hand, the new graduate is also apt to be surprised at the level of competency, expertise, and power among the LVN's and nurse's aides. As one personnel turnover study revealed, LVN's and nurse's aides are usually the most tenured, and the most experienced.

There are quite a few people who are quite a bit older than me working at the LVN level, and some of them really know quite a great deal and I respect their knowledge and everything. But I kind of felt like they hindered me sometimes by maybe asserting that they thought I really didn't know anything since I am just starting out and that they should be the ones to take on this responsibility. I don't know them, and they know a lot more than I did and they are a lot older. (NG:BS/2[1]8/71)

*Generation gap.* It is the young nurse's drive for competency that provokes generational conflict. She pours all her energy into her work, has high expectations of herself, and is eager to prove herself. It is this very eagerness and zeal that often disturbs the equilibrium and stability that the older employee has come to enjoy. Often the conflict between the old and the new can become so great that one of the protagonists decides to flee from the field. It is usually the young worker who withdraws, since she is less established and it is easier for her to find another job.

The following excerpts express some of the frustration involved in the meeting of the old and the new, the experienced and inexperienced.

I think this one LVN . . . well, I think it's just her attitude: that I'm not as fast as she is. I'm sure she'd answer the questions that I have if I asked; but I think she thinks, well, that I'm dumb or something like that. (NG:BS/2[11]8/71)

· · ·

The LVN is very sharp, very critical. When you ask her something, sometimes you feel like you have to walk on eggs with that woman. When you ask her something you know she's going to come back with something very sarcastic or turn it around, and she usually does. She really resents; I know she resents me. She's been on that floor for a long, long time—many, many years—and like she said, she has seen many nurses, RN's come and go. And yet technically I am her supervisor. I am an RN and she's an LVN, and I do supervise her work. I'm very much younger than she is. (NG: Dip/2[16]8/71)

As in most of the work socialization process, much of the pressure and conflict is ill-defined and subtle. Nevertheless, as these graduates intimate, the feelings and the pressures come through on an attitudinal and non-verbal level. The student is confronted with the fact that she no longer belongs to a large group of similar age and status, as was the case during her student days. In the work world, youth is not revered as much; in fact, it may even be a disadvantage.

*Constancy of time.* In school the student nurse was accustomed to flexible schedules that changed frequently, and there was always a school term break in sight. When she enters the world of work she joins the world of time. There is much preoccupation with being on *time*, finishing on *time*, working over*time*, taking the appropriate allotted *times* for lunches and breaks. While the world of school also operates on time schedules, often each day has a different schedule. There are usually mornings when you can sleep later, mornings when you must get up earlier. The penalties for missing a class are not too great. Upon beginning work the new graduate is confronted with a more stable but often more arbitrarily changing schedule.

Weekends and nights are no longer necessarily an inherent right; holidays are usually covered by the least tenured workers. She may rotate to different shifts; at times she may work different shifts in the same week. Sometimes she works set periods of six or seven days. To an oldtimer these may seem like small points, but to the new graduate the change in her time schedule—particularly the change to larger blocks of commited time on a more permanent basis—presents no small adjustment. Frequent questions are: When can I make a doctor's appointment? When can I shop? These and other questions relate to lateral life roles she was accustomed to fitting in to the more flexible school schedule that to a large extent was controlled by her, rather than by outsiders.

*Subcultural differences between institutions.* Students may learn theoretically that all institutions differ in their norms and expectations. They usually will have had brief clinical affiliations in a number of settings. However, unless the nursing instructor takes special pains to point out cultural differences,

the students move through affiliations without perceiving these differences. Upon taking a job, the graduate nurse cannot escape the fact that a Veterans Administration hospital differs in its values, expectations, and idiosyncracies from a medical center hospital, a county general hospital, or a privately owned hospital. For example, in a county general hospital supply-hoarding may be common due to the unpredictability of political budget cuts and allocations; in a private hospital where supply procurement is not a problem, hoarding of supplies will not be expected or understood by co-workers.

The new graduate fills in her lack of knowledge of an institution by giving it inaccurate attributes of institutions she has known previously. She makes many assumptions about the rationale behind the way things are run without checking out these assumptions. This filling in of missing information is a widely experienced phenomenon; it is part of the basis for shock when one moves from one culture to another. (The shock of discovering different assumptions and values among institutions may be postponed for the new graduate if she takes a position in a hospital where she has worked during school.) In the following comment, a new graduate describes some of the confusion and frustration that can result from differing cultural expectations:

Well, you see I'm from back East and I feel that the way things are done in the East is much more progressive than here. I used to do many more things there while in training, like discontinuing IV's and CVP lines, things like that. We also drew our own blood, which we don't do here. Well, it's just like you find yourself in a strange environment and you just try to adjust as quickly as possible. And you just feel like you're not gaining any knowledge or going ahead . . . I really can't say that I've learned much here. (NG:AD/2[8]8/71)

*Racial conflicts as they affect work performance.* New graduates in the Reality Shock program seemed to be particularly susceptible to racial misunderstandings. This may have been due to the location and culture of the particular hospital, or it may be generally true, since the new graduate is particularly vulnerable to many conflicts because she has not yet learned the work role. Also, racial conflicts may be accentuated in some institutions because of their own unique history and racial composition. If racial tensions are high, many of the new graduate's inappropriately zealous demands on her co-workers can be misunderstood or misconstrued to have racial overtones.

I asked one aide to do H.S. care, and she just looked at me and said: "We don't do those kinds of things." I said: "You don't? I'd like to see your job description." I wanted to know what they can do and what they cannot do. I intended to take full advantage of what she could do and what she could not do. This got out in the grapevine and it was as if I was out to get her job, and she was not about to cooperate with me because she thought that I was being racist. There were many sighs in the group and someone said: "Not that again!" It blew up into a real thing, and all I wanted to do was to get her to do H.S. care. (NG:AD/3[18]12/71)

New graduates are not exempt from prejudice or racist attitudes. However, for the purpose of this discussion only the increased susceptibility to racial misunderstanding due to lack of knowledge of her appropriate socially approved work role is considered. It is doubtful that an experienced employee would have asked another employee to see her job description, and if she did it probably would mean that she intended to take some kind of formal action. A more acceptable, expected response on the part of the nurse would have been to handle this incident informally rather than resorting to formal rules and expectations.

## THE SEMINARS UNFOLD

### Planning and implementation

The Reality Shock program consisted of six seminars for recently employed new graduates. The main focus of the seminars was to help these nurses identify and manage the conflicts they were experiencing on their first jobs. It was anticipated that the conflicts discussed would definitely include the three common ones (p. 193) and also some of the individualistic conflicts just presented. The goal of the seminars was to facilitate constructive conflict resolution and thus to increase the

chances for bicultural adjustment of these new graduates on their first jobs. It was anticipated that constructive conflict resolution and bicultural adjustment would increase the new graduate's job satisfaction, productivity, and tenure on the first job.

Implementing and evaluating the Reality Shock program in a medical center would also give some indication whether there was a felt need and interest in such a program by nursing service departments. Was nursing service aware of the adjustment difficulties and conflicts experienced by new graduates? Would they be willing to support an intervention program that would require released time for new graduates and parttime support from one of their staff development instructors? The answer to both of these questions was a resounding "Yes" from the two local medical centers approached. The staff development departments and nursing administrators of both institutions noted several reasons why the Reality Shock program was particularly attractive to them: they recognized the need to salvage and retain new graduates for longer than the average stay of six months; they valued the energy and innovative ideas of the new graduate and wanted more of a return for their heavy investment in orienting and training graduates in their first jobs. They also liked the idea of a program that could be evaluated and incorporated or rejected with a minimum of developmental cost to their institutions. In both medical centers, nursing administration and staff development departments were willing to begin the program with the first available group of recent graduates.

The first Reality Shock program was begun in December 1971. It was decided that the seminars should be taught on a team basis, involving myself and one staff development instructor, so that the evaluation of the program would not be clouded by a halo effect of an outsider coming in to do a special program. To further decrease this possibility, the seminars were introduced as a regular continuation of orientation for the new graduates and I was introduced as someone temporarily helping out in staff development rather than as an outsider who works with new graduates.

Administrative decisions and details that were jointly arrived at included the following:

1. The seminars were scheduled on Wednesdays from 1 PM to 3 PM.
2. Either compensatory time off would be granted to the new graduates coming to the seminars on their time off, or they were to be released from their duties to come to the seminars.
3. Only new graduates who had been working for two or three months would be invited.[1] (Because of the institutional request and restraints, two brand new graduates also were included.)

The reception and enthusiasm for the Reality Shock program by both in-service education and administration made the planning of the program smooth and rapid. The following is a chronological description of the program.

*Seminar 1.* A group of twelve new graduates varying in age from 18 to 38 years gathered in a small conference room. There was evidence that the group already knew one another from their earlier orientation meetings, and many also knew each other from school. Of the fourteen new graduates invited to attend, eleven were junior college graduates, one was from a diploma program, and two had graduated from baccalaureate programs. Before the seminar formally started there was much congenial conversation, both social and work-centered. Two of the new graduates were exclaiming to the group: "We had our first code (cardiopulmonary resuscitation) and we did it right!"

"You mean that the patient made it?"

"No, the patient passed; but we had everything there and it was a good one."

Rapid, cryptic questions were fired at the successful code-blue masters, and equally cryptic, rapid answers were given in return.

The seminars formally began with introductions and an explanation that the goals of the seminars were to help identify and manage conflicts experienced by new graduates in adjusting to their first jobs. The initial questions asked were designed to focus on differences between school and work: Have there been any surprises since you started work? Is it like you thought it would be? After a brief pause the room exploded; vivid descriptions of shocks and surprises encountered since graduating from school filled the air. There were many cries of feeling victimized and helpless.

INSTRUCTOR: I can hear the frustration in your voice.

NEW GRADUATE (HER VOICE TREMBLING WITH EMOTION): Yeah, and that's bad too. I never wanted to look at my job that way, but I am just putting in time for experience. And I was hoping not to feel that way. (NG:AD/3[23] 12/71)

There was much head-nodding and empathy expressed for this new graduate's plight. Others chimed in with their feelings of helplessness, anger, and disappointment over their first work experience. Story after story of incompetency of supervisors and auxiliary workers were told. Feelings of moral outrage ricocheted around the room: "It shouldn't be that way!" "There's no excuse for that kind of incompetence or that kind of behavior!"

Words and phrases of generalized frustration and polarization such as "whole institutionalized attitudes," "we," "they," and "it" were used frequently, and no one, including the instructors, thought to ask: "Who are 'they'?" or "What is 'it'?" and "Can you describe 'the attitude'?" Everyone seemed swept along with the venting of anger against the "all bad" or the generalized praise of the "all good" supervisors, auxiliary workers, or staff nurses.

She does not take care of the problem of orderlies sleeping. I think that's her reason for being there. I know that no one likes to go wake someone up and say: "Hey, Jack, get on with your job," but she knows it's going on. She makes cracks about it, but she never does anything about it and that's her job! (NG:AD/3[26]12/71)

. . .

But there's the attitude a lot of people have who have been here for twenty years, and nothing is going to change. I mean you really feel like you are talking to a dead end street! (NG:AD/3[23] 12/71)

. . .

Mrs. [X] comes up and asks us about all the patients and checks on the IV's, but with Mrs. [Y] you could have ten dead patients up there and she would not know the difference! (NG:AD/3 [26]12/70)

It was quite difficult during this venting of feelings for the two instructors to resort from advice-giving. The interactions became like the games described by Berne:

New graduate: "Ain't it awful?"

Instructor: "Have you tried . . .?"

New graduate: "Yes, but that won't work because . . ."

Seminar excerpts and subsequent field notes record some of these dynamics:

During the seminar I kept coming up with the advice that the new graduates check out their assumptions; I tried to get them to try role reversal and put themselves in the shoes of the head nurse or the auxiliary worker. I now realize that it was too soon for such counsel. Any advice or suggestions for action were met with "Yes, but . . ." or "You don't understand . . ." or "I don't do that!" It was as if the new graduates were convinced of their helpless or victimized state and that any suggestions to the contrary provided too much cognitive dissonance for them. (Field notes, 12/71)

The following seminar excerpt is in response to my suggestion that the new graduates document some of the negligence they were observing in a co-worker.

What the hell, why should I? Why me? Besides, someone might document something that you do. I'm not perfect, I might make a mistake. And then nobody is trusting anybody. [There was much consensus with this view.] (NG:AD/2[20]12/71)

This new graduate's objection to documenting the behavior of other employees was realistic because she did not know the system well enough to follow through with the documentation. Also, she did not yet feel secure enough in her own ability to point up another's inadequacies. Other objections, however, were less realistic. When told of a safe resource person, the response was:

That doesn't always work! Once I just asked another RN about something and the supervisor got upset because I didn't call her. (NG:AD/2 [23]12/71)

These "Yes, but . . ." responses could well indicate that the feelings involved with moral outrage—the feeling of not finding things at work the way one expected them to be and the feeling of being victimized as a result of not being prepared for the way things are—must be dealt with before rational or cognitive strategies for solving problems can be explored. Until the new graduate works through her feelings of outrage and victimization, she is not ready to engage in problem-solving.

The venting and expression of wholesale anger and rejection of the current work scene made it very difficult for the instructors to maintain their objectivity. Indeed, it was important to identify with the new graduates' plight if one was to try to help them resolve their conflicts constructively rather than only encourage them to conform and not maintain their differentness. One helpful strategy for increasing objectivity and planning for the next seminar was to do a content analysis of the tape-recorded seminar. It was possible to come up with strategies for the next seminar by reviewing the content of the messages and identifying the areas of strong feelings. Another important resource was an outside consultant who could listen to the seminar recording more objectively and identify the dynamics involved without getting as caught up in the emotion at the time. Dr. Kramer provided this consultation service. From the discussion of the first seminar, it was decided that the approach for the second seminar would be to point out the large-scale use of the words "we" and "they" and "it" and ask the group to identify the concrete referents intended by the use of these words. Also, the basis for the polarization and differentness exemplified by the use of these words would be clarified by identifying opposing methods of work organization and opposing value systems.

*Seminar 2.* Moral outrage and anger were still predominant in the second seminar. A valiant attempt was made by the instructors and the new graduates to make the referent groups and subjects explicit. Three of the new graduates described very difficult days at work and called them tests or trials by fire. The nature and functions of these trials were discussed. With the help of all the seminar members the discussion became more focused. The topics were less random, and anxiety and anger, while still high, seemed less diffuse than they had been in the first seminar.

The following is a verbatim excerpt of the introduction to the second seminar.

I did a typescript of last week's meeting and was amazed at the number of times we used the words "we" and "they" or "it" without clarifying what we meant. This is probably a sign that all our feelings were rather strong and we thought we knew what we were talking about. But afterwards, I realized that we might all have been in a state of diffuse anxiety and that we really did not have these specifics defined. The goal of this meeting will be to clarify the conflicts so that we are talking about specifics. I chose three incidents which I think were the main concerns of the discussion last week: (1) how to deal with an incompetent supervisor (this supervisor seldom makes rounds and makes inaccurate assessments about staffing needs), (2) inability to locate information and resources, (3) how to deal with orderlies who sleep on the night shift. These were the incidents that we spent the most time on last week, and I would like for us to look at them again this week and figure out what was going on and perhaps come up with some alternative ways of dealing with these problems.

The group accepted the three problems as representative and worthwhile. In retrospect, it would have been interesting to know what three problems the group would have chosen. The sorting out of problems and selection of three to work on might have been an effective way to increase the group's problem-solving ability. However, selecting specific problem areas did help to focus the discussion.

Several strategies and principles emerged from the group discussion. The principle of using silence, inactivity, or nonintervention to provide negative feedback to the system was discussed in relation to the supervisor who was not making rounds or gathering firsthand information. It was pointed out that a nurse is prone to spend much of her time and energy nursing the system, that is, filling gaps and thus covering up for inadequacies

in the system. As long as nurses covered up for the supervisors' inadequacies, these inadequacies would not become visible. Written reports and indirect sources of information to this supervisor were to be cut down to a minimum in order to make firsthand information-gathering necessary or else make her deficiency in information gathering visible. There were less "Yes, but that won't work" responses to the strategies suggested. One of the new graduates made another application of the principle of nonintervention:

Ah . . . I had an example of that this week with a doctor. He had written some orders and twice he had initialed them SMO [slips made out], and I checked both times and neither time had he or anyone else filled the slips out. So I filled them out for him. But if I had just let him suffer the consequences instead of worrying about it myself, then he might get the message and change his behavior. I could have done this, too, since the delayed tests would not have been a problem for the patient. (NG:BS/3[17]12/71)

In each of the problems brought up, an attempt was made to distinguish what was only symbolic of a problem and what was a real sign of a problem. Postman and Weingartner's distinctions between signs and symbols were introduced to the group. For example, much of the reaction to the orderlies' sleeping had to do with the symbolic meaning of sleeping on the job. Until a real sign of a problem was identified, for example, work left undone or patients left unattended, it was impossible to develop approaches and determine causes for the problem. The symbolic meaning of sleeping on the job was making the new graduates so angry that they could not focus on the signs of the real problem: Was there work being left undone? If so, why was it left undone?

The difference between part-task and whole-task work organization was introduced in relation to one of the problems with a supervisor. The supervisor was acting on the basis of a part-task approach to work organization, and the new graduate was operating on a whole-task approach. When confronted with some papers and forms that needed to be filled out, the new graduate sought help from the supervisor. The supervisor was unable to help her and had expected the new graduate to delegate this task to a knowledgeable team member instead of doing the whole thing herself. The differing expectations caused conflict and confusion for the new graduate.

The overall tone of the second seminar was still one of moral outrage at the misbehavior of others. The field notes written after this seminar give some of my reactions to the moral outrage expressed.

I am witnessing a lot of moral outrage. It does not seem to be at a very facilitative level (whatever that might be!). If the moral outrage is too great, like radicalization, then the person is not free to hear and process the incoming information. I think that these new graduates have less energy to perceive the perspective of others because of their anger. So my question is: How much commitment is good? Does commitment always interfere with rationality? If so, this would be an intraprofessional role conflict because the professional is supposed to be both rational and committed. (Field notes, 12/71)

In the consultation session after the second seminar it was decided that the culture shock framework might make some of the new graduates' feelings of rejection and polarization more visible to them. It was hoped that this framework would help them identify bicultural adjustment as an attractive alternative to and a possible outcome for their conflict and feelings of shock and rejection. The intention was also to make the pressures to conform more visible and hopefully less powerful.

*Seminar 3.* As planned, the situational adjustment to the first job was compared to the stages of cultural adjustment. There were uncomfortable moments in this seminar. The descriptions of the rejection and shock phase of cultural adjustment produced silence and finally questions and comments such as: "How long does it take to get out of the rejection phase?" "I am not sure I went through a honeymoon phase . . . maybe only the first two days during orientation." There was laughter and joking about how short the honeymoon state had been.

There was a close identification with the process of cultural adjustment as judged by the questions and comments of the new graduates. This close identification created the danger of dealing with a highly emotional issue on a purely intellectual level, as was pointed up in the field notes written after the seminar.

At times during the seminar I had the uncomfortable feeling that the new graduates were experiencing reality shock on a powerfully emotional level. Also there seemed to be a mixed awareness context.[2] I had identified that many of the seminar members were experiencing culture shock but had not stated this impression openly. Until two members openly identified with the process and joked about having a short honeymoon phase and a long rejection phase, the interactions seemed strained and the silences were longer than usual. (Field notes, 12/71)

The ability to influence and create change in a system was discussed in relation to becoming bicultural.

HELEN: What I don't understand is, if and when you get to the final phase of biculturalism, is the reason you are more effective in changing things . . . because you see things not in too extreme ways? Or is it because you have been around longer and people respect you more? (NG:Dip/3[21]12/71)

INSTRUCTOR: I think both. [Several others in the group agreed that both factors play a part.]

HELEN: What would happen if you stayed angry and you never got past the angry stage, but you had been there [in the work setting] the same amount of time. You don't think that you'd be able to change things?

INSTRUCTOR: I don't, at least not directly or in a planned way. The difference is that you would not be in control and you would not be as objective in your analysis and evaluation of the situation.

At least for Helen the consequences of reality shock were becoming more evident. Several group members identified with the recovery phase and gave examples of situations that they were now able to laugh about.

Toward the end of the seminar there was consensus that the seminars were helpful and that they were worth the effort required to get off the unit in order to come.

These classes . . . I think everybody needs them. I find myself looking forward to Wednesday afternoon. I got really defensive about it this morning. I told my head nurse and the other nurse that I was going today at one o'clock and my head nurse said, under her breath: "What a waste." And I thought: "Forget it, I'm leaving at one." But they don't seem to think that they need refueling. (NG:Dip/3[21]12/71)

There was much nodding of heads and agreement with this statement. The land of "we" and "they" still prevails! (Field notes, 12/71)

*Seminar 4.* The fourth seminar demonstrated the new graduates' abilities to support one another. The group met early in the coffeeshop; thus, discussion was under way when the scheduled seminar began. Most of the interactions in this seminar were new graduate to new graduate, with few instructors to new graduate interactions. There were some success stories. Three of the new graduates who had been working on the same unit had been able to work through a difficult personnel problem, and there had been marked improvement in the employees' performance. One new graduate came for the first time specifically for help and support with a problem. During the seminar only two persons lapsed into a victim stage, which was a marked change from the previous seminars.

My field notes indicate some of the growth and growing pains experienced in this seminar:

In the debriefing conference with Dr. Kramer, I was able to see that I was experiencing some independent and dependency conflict myself. The group had grown! They were more independent. They didn't need me as much anymore! . . . As I read my field notes I notice that I am more objective now. Even though I am still recording my feelings, I am spending more time and energy looking at the actual content and feelings expressed in the new graduates' messages. (Field notes, 1/72)

The fourth seminar demonstrated the resourcefulness and source of support a similar-status group can provide. Empathy and shared understanding were high in the group; when problems were brought up by colleagues, each member could relate similar experiences and problems and share approaches to the problems. One way to clarify roles is to make available social support by others who have similar social status and who are experiencing similar difficulties in coping. This social interaction and support assures the individual that he is not meeting a wholly private problem that must be handled in a unique way, all alone. The following seminar excerpt illustrates this support:

SUE: Well, why do you think I am here? The reason I am here now is that I was beginning to feel secure on the fourth floor. I had even reached the point that I felt secure when I was alone on the floor. I thought I was doing petty things well. The usual petty things were going on, you know, but I was just asked the other day to transfer to Ward 3. [This is the unit that now has three new graduates on it.] And I have heard nothing but bad things about Ward 3. (NG:AD/4[24]1/72)

ALICE: Now it is really going to be groovy. We are going to have all new, young, motivated staff; all the old ones have left. . . . (NG:AD/4[22] 1/72)

SUE: But it's just that it's really hard to go into a new situation. It's just like starting all over again. And it's not a good feeling.

The group was able to empathize with Sue. They came up with some ways she might prevent the transfer and offered her some hope if she could not avoid it. If she could not prevent the transfer, she would be working on the unit with three of the new graduates, and they quickly filled her in on the social system of their unit: the head nurse's style and expectations and what Sue could expect from coworkers. At the end of the very lively, informative discussion, Sue stated that she felt better.

The number of problems quickly brought up and expertly discussed were legion. Quite some time was spent on the evaluation process, both in terms of filling out evaluation forms for co-workers and rights in receiving an evaluation. The current hospital evaluation forms were examined and evaluated by the new graduates. The appropriate committee for getting the evaluation forms revised was identified. Time was spent discussing problems in working with unit secretaries and auxiliary workers. There were two success stories shared about interactions and assignment-planning for two LVN's. There was evidence of increased respect and understanding of the abilities and values of the auxiliary personnel.

The new graduates were asked to bring in written specific, manageable problems for discussion at the next seminar. Global problems, such as working with the civil service system, were to be broken down into specific problems with a specific staff member on their unit.

*Seminar 5.* The selection of focused problems proved to be difficult. Only two of the new graduates brought specific problems that they wanted to work on, but even they found it difficult to talk about the problems they had defined without getting into broad issues such as patient privacy rights or preserving the patient's dignity and integrity. Still evident in the group's discussion of the problems presented was the struggle over the differences between the new graduates' values and the values of their co-workers and patients. The seminar discussion was a further confirmation and demonstration that if value conflicts and clashes are not dealt with on an emotional level first so that the newcomer is no longer shocked and appalled by them, then deliberative problem-solving focused on specific situations and specific interactions will be blocked or not forthcoming.

Scenes in which patient–co-worker interactions were upsetting were described: "She can call the patient crazy or ugly right to his face!" "No one on our unit bothers to close the curtains when they are working with a patient!" Attempts were made to get into the co-workers' or the patient's frameworks, but they were unsuccessful because the value conflict was so great:

When I make special nourishment orders for the patients, I get accused of spoiling the patients. It is as if the patients are in the hospital to be punished! It's incredible, and yet they [the co-workers] wouldn't want to be treated that way. (NG:AD/5[23]1/72)

Why didn't more new graduates bring at least partially defined problems to the seminar? Were they just not motivated to bring in such problems? Were they experiencing problem overload and thus unable to sort out specific problems? The conjecture of problem overload was checked out:

INSTRUCTOR: Perhaps one of the problems of beginning work is that you are inundated with problems and suffer from problem overload. It is very difficult to isolate problems out and assign them various priorities.

JANET (shaking her head in agreement, her face brightening): That really is true; that's how I feel.

INSTRUCTOR: Can you elaborate on that, Janet?

JANET: There are so many things happening at once that I can't seem to choose which problems to work on first. (NG:BS/4[17]1/72)

It was easier to check out the conjecture of problem overload than lack of motivation, though the reasons for lack of motivation may have been important also.

*Seminar 6.* Originally, five seminars were planned, but the new graduates felt that one more session was needed and would be useful for evaluation.

The tone of the last seminar was one of reminiscing. Some of the initiation rites discussed in the earlier seminars were reviewed, and the many changes over the past two months were discussed. A considerable amount of time was also spent in group discussion of a complex patient problem that one of the new graduates had encountered. Again there was much shared understanding and suggestions for dealing with this patient problem. The appreciation for the shared understanding that had developed in the seminars was illustrated by one of the participant's comments: "Just knowing that other people are in the same leaky boat has been very helpful." The consensus was that the seminars had been very helpful and that they would be strongly recommended for all groups of new graduates.

There were some constructive suggestions given in this seminar. The following excerpt indicates that some anticipatory guidance might be of great value to the new graduate on her first job and that a reality shock program could be a source for this guidance.

LINDA: I have wondered that if during the first orientation procedure, when new graduates first arrive, if you wouldn't consider it good to discuss the conflicts and the culture shock the new graduate will experience.

INSTRUCTOR: Are you talking about giving some warnings?

LINDA: Yes, since some of these problems are known. They are a fact, I've found out, and since new graduates don't know about them it would be helpful to tell them. If new graduates are made aware that these kinds of things are going to happen it might make the transition easier somehow. Or at least knowing in advance that there is going to be a seminar for new graduates and knowing the reason for it, at least the new graduate would know what to expect at work, and then it wouldn't be half as bad. (NG:AD/4[18]1/72)

The new graduates also pointed out that discussing outside conflicts was not as helpful to them as discussing their own conflicts. This points up one of the marked differences between the Anticipatory Socialization program and the Reality Shock program. The undergraduates in the Anticipatory Socialization program had few real work setting conflicts to bring to the seminars, and could be more removed from those they did have by accentuating their temporary status. For example, they were nurse's aides for the summer only; or they were in the work setting as students for one or three days a week for a limited number of weeks, and as student nurses they were often presented only the frontstage or ideal version of reality. This is not true for the new graduate. Sooner or later she is confronted with real problems and conflicts and usually with backstage reality. She is also confronted with a sense of permanance; it is more difficult for her to remove herself from the work scene. The level of commitment and possibility of change is decreased when a person sees himself as temporarily in a situation. The more long term an individual views himself the greater the possibility for personal change. If the new graduate considers herself to be in a long-awaited proving ground, ego involvement and the threat to self-esteem is apt to be much higher than the undergraduate who might give herself more room for error and imperfection as a student.

## Some conclusions

The first Reality Shock program revealed much about how the new graduate views her first job. These perspectives provide a base for planning a more complete program for other new graduates. During this first trial Reality Shock program, the knowledge-skill components such as workings of a bureaucratic system, skills of role negotiation, and knowledge of the socialization process were introduced. It was soon recognized that knowledge about these processes was not the same as being able to *use* the knowledge to resolve conflict. The new graduates in this first Reality Shock program showed that they had to deal with the emotional responses to the conflicts they were experiencing before they could begin rational problem-solving.

Dealing with emotional responses is a highly personal task, but it can be facilitated through group learning and peer support. It is the new graduate herself who must decide when she is open to pursuing some knowledge and skill areas that would help her to deal effectively with her work situation. It was decided that for future Reality Shock programs individualized, self-paced learning would be offered in conjunction with the seminars. Portable multimedia modules would be designed to provide varied learning experiences related to the identified knowledge-skill area. The new graduate would be able to pursue and pace her learning according to her own readiness and learning style. This two-pronged approach—group learning and self-paced, individualized learning—would allow the instructors to provide learning environments that are most effective for achieving a particular learning goal. The adjustment and reactions to enculturation, conflict resolution and creative problem-solving would continue to be explored in the seminars. Information about the differences between the bureaucratic and professional work systems and practical leadership skill would be available in the individualized learning laboratory.

## THREE VANTAGE POINTS

Three ways in which the new graduate experiences her first job will be described in this section.

1. The first job is a proving ground. The new graduate views her first job as a test to determine whether she has really become a nurse or not and to determine the kind of nurse she is going to be.
2. She is susceptible to feeling victimized and remaining in a victim role.
3. Her first job is experienced as an enculturation process. She experiences reality shock.

Before the new graduate can begin problem-solving, she must deal with some of the anxiety involved in proving herself, some of the feelings of being victimized that she experiences with role conflict, and some of the denial and hypercriticalness she experiences with reality shock. Even though these frameworks have been discussed or alluded to in Chapter 5, they are presented again here in the context of the Reality Shock program. They offer further validation of the emerging theory of occupational socialization of the nurse.

## The proving ground

The new graduates in the first Reality Shock program viewed their first job as a time of testing, a proving ground. The tests were constructed and administered by others, but by themselves too. They seemed never to be quite sure whether they were taking a self-constructed test or one constructed by others. It seemed equally important that they answer for themselves questions that others seemed to be asking, such as: Had they really become nurses? Were they the kind of nurses they wanted to be? Did the staff see them as nurses?

JEANNETTE: But I was really frustrated. I thought that maybe I should be able to handle this load. [The night supervisor had refused to send her additional staff and told her that she should be able to handle the unit by herself with just one aide.] (NG:AD/4[23]12/71)
INSTRUCTOR: That's the problem with being new. You don't know the parameters, therefore it's hard to know when to trust your own judgment.
CYNTHIA: The trouble is that you want to prove yourself. To prove to them that you can get the work done.
JANET: Who are "they?"
CYNTHIA: I guess that I was one of the ones saying

all the "theys." But it's hard, and sometimes it's so unfair. Like when they—the nurses—were testing Linda. You wonder if you really can do it, if you really have what it takes. (NG:AD/3[26]1/72)

In this dialogue the new graduates expressed their uncertainty as to who was constructing the test. By viewing her first job as a test or proving ground, the new graduate opens herself to all the distortions and questions of a test situation: Is the test valid? Should I be able to do X, given Y circumstances? Is the test fair? Is it reasonable, or are "they" just checking me out to see how far they can push me before I will complain? The question of criteria troubles the new graduate. By what standards does she judge herself successful? By what standards and behaviors do others judge her successful? It is the lack of criterion measures that makes the testing procedure so circular for the new graduate. In the following excerpt one graduate questions the fairness of the test, but also illustrates her own uncertainty in judging the fairness.

You come on as a new graduate and say: "Hey, that's not right!" [the RN taking more patients than the auxiliary staff]. I know *I* cannot handle that much. So you take a smaller load for yourself because you think: "That's all I can handle." And pretty soon it's friction time because you're not working as hard as they are. You're not taking care of as many patients as they are. The assignments are not fair. I really do feel that they take advantage of you. They are walking in late. And you are saying to yourself: "What am I supposed to do about this? How do I handle that?" It's really bad for you because you feel so inadequate to begin with, and here you have people taking advantage of you . . . and here you do not even know how to handle yourself. All these things are trying to increase your own knowledge about patient care and yourself. You end up going round and round. . . . (NG:AD/3[26]1/72)

Why does the new graduate view her first job as a proving ground? Part of the answer may be that the testing is the way in which she validates her identity as a worker—as a nurse. In the past, when much of nursing education was done by hospital staff, the testing or proving of oneself occurred during school;

the student was much more a part of the work group. Man's interaction with the work world is a lifelong developmental process with the stage of acquiring identity as a worker in the occupational structure occurring between the ages of 15 to 25 years. It does not take the new graduate long to discover that acquiring identity as a worker is a combination of how she views herself and how significant others view her.

It was more difficult going from student nurse to RN than I had anticipated because I was still feeling my role as a student nurse and I had a hard time seeing myself as a peer member with the rest of the team. I had to keep reminding myself that I didn't have to be a "Mother, may I" all the time—that I could take a more aggressive role, that I had been taught the skills and knowledge along with it and now all I had to do was use it. And it was really hard at first because I was constantly feeling that I had to go ask, you know, is it okay to do this? (NG:Dip/2[5]6/71)

. . .

I think you are a bit more sensitive at the beginning. As you gain more self-confidence, they [the staff] are giving you the same treatment, but it doesn't upset you the way it did because you have more self-confidence now. (NG:AD/3[23]1/72)

The power of how significant others viewed them in terms of acquiring their identity was also expressed frequently in the Reality Shock seminars. In the following excerpts, the new graduate views her performance of little importance if the other RN's did not acknowledge her performance and thus acknowledge her nurse citizenship:

What exasperated us is that we were looked on as students still, and we got this: "Come with me and do this and do that!" And we thought: "Hey, lady, can you see the RN on this name pin?" No, really, they treated us like we were students for the longest time, and the nurse is saying: (Sigh) "I am so tired of orienting you." Our response is: "Well, honey, you don't have to; you can stop!" [This new graduate was speaking for the group. It seemed they had discussed this problem before and were nodding in agreement with her statement.] (NG:AD/3[20]1/72)

. . .

She came in about two weeks ago, and I had worked the night before, alone. It was on a Saturday and she came in. I said: "OK, I am ready to give you report." And she said: "Who else is here?" I said: "Me." She said: "No, I mean what other nurses?" [laughter] You know, see the RN on my name pin? I said: "Look, honey, I work here." And when she realized that I was going to give her report, she said: "You all by yourself?" I said: "Yes, Carol, I was." I felt like, goddamn it, it was the third night, you know [laughter and sympathy with her plight]. (NG:AD/4[20]1/72)

The new graduate's emphasis on the importance of how significant others view them supports the findings of another study. Simpson noted that when student nurses began clinical training their main interest was in technical skills. As they practiced the nurse role on work teams that included hospital nurses and doctors, their interest shifted toward seeking acceptance as professional colleagues. It was as though the student were saying to herself: "Now I am definitely more than an aide, but am I fully a nurse?" The answer seems to be: "You are not a nurse—not until significant others in the work milieu give evidence that they think so."

Gaining membership or identity as a nurse-citizen is often facilitated by initiation rites. It is possible that the hazing of the initiate in an occupation may have a definite function in occupational socialization; the hazing or difficult task creates a sense of belonging. Painful experiences shared with others create a sort of fellowship of suffering. Difficult tasks are also often ritualized and thereby take on meaning and significance beyond their face value.

The new graduates' statements give credence to the possible function of the fellowship of suffering and ritualized difficult tasks in nurse work socialization.

Well, it's like you have to prove yourself. Like all the other nurses are saying that I trained at Cook County or that I worked at Cook County on a 300-bed unit and gave medicines to 125 patients in an hour, and all this. And if you are worth your salt you can do this sort of thing. (NG:Dip/3[21]1/72)

An example that the fellowship of suffering frequently operates in gaining nurse citizenship was also corroborated by the experiences of two senior nursing students who attempted to gain membership in an emergency room.

I think Ann resented that we could wear pants-suits and have so much fun. She and Jenny were always telling horror stories about their nursing school experience—delivering three babies at the same time and all our fun cheapened their RN image and they didn't like that. (Seminar stu.: BS[3]5/71)

. . .

You know, Jenny and Ann were always talking about how things have changed. They told their student stories with such relish, even though they were complaining. They would talk about how awful it was to wear the horrible outfits—crinolines and starch—but they said it as if it were a wonderful recollection! They would talk about delivering a baby at 2;30 A.M. or being on a huge ward all by themselves. (Seminar stu.: BS[4]5/71)

The insight that wearing pants-suits and having fun questioned the value and importance of the older nurses' hardships was probably accurate. What was difficult and once looked upon as necessary is no longer viewed as such and is not even valued by newcomers. Does this mean that a new test for citizenship will have to be developed that is acceptable to both the newcomer and the oldtimer? The following initiation rite described by a new graduate in the first Reality Shock program has a difficult task theme; it may be an example of an initiation rite now being used by both the newcomer and the oldtimer.

In the beginning of my second month I was asked to work on the weekend by myself. I do not know why I was asked; there were plenty of nurses at that time. And I do not know why I accepted; I guess I just thought that I should make myself appear more self-confident. We all talked about my being alone Saturday. In fact we were over at one of the nurses' house the night before for a drink, and we were laughing and talking about it. A couple of nurses said that they would call me the next day to see how I was doing. I had two orderlies and an LVN scheduled to work with me. And everyone said, "Wait til you meet this LVN." I had never worked with her before, but she had a reputation for being impossible to work with. That day started off badly. I was panicked. The report even started out bad because I was so

scared, and I told the LVN off before the report was finished. The ward was really busy that day. I remember that we had one active G.I. bleeder, and there was a man who was hallucinating and who was constantly getting out of bed. When I was pouring my meds this man came up and tried to strangle me! Several doctors were standing around and they pulled him away. After that I called the nursing office, and they sent up an orderlie just to watch this one patient. Then the 'phone kept ringing. Two of the nurses called and asked me how I was doing. I really didn't have time to talk so I just said that I was busy and that I had to go . . ."goodbye." It was just a horrible day and I just kept thinking: "Only two or three more hours . . . if I can just make it through." Towards the end of the shift the man who was hallucinating disconnected the blood tubing on the patient's bed next to him. And when I went to change the tubing I ended up spilling the blood all over my uniform. That just finished up the day for me! I don't know if the nurses treated me differently nonverbally or whether they acted differently, but I felt braver afterwards. That's what changed. I figured that after I had lived through that day I could live through anything. I felt braver. (NG:Dip/3[21]1/72)

Only one of the other new graduates described a similar initiation. However, all of the new graduates indicated that they viewed their first job as a proving ground, a time of testing both by themselves and others. They remained unsure whether they were more prominent in designing the tests or whether the tests were primarily constructed by fellow workers. Whether or not an actual initiation rite occurred, the new graduates were conscious of a "supernurse" ideal, often originating at some renowned place like Cook County. The mythical supernurse was said to be able to handle all emergencies in addition to being in charge of medicating and treating forty to sixty patients. The new graduates talked extensively about wanting to change the quantity trial to a test of quality.

If performance of difficult tasks is, as Moore suggests, an important socializing function for those occupations that are particularly concerned with standards of competence and with identification with the occupation as a collectivity, then there is danger of these tasks becoming arbitrary rituals. The question becomes: How can the difficult tasks be changed to more meaningful goal-related tasks? If initiation rites are important to attaining privileges within a group, how can the initiation be made more symbolic so as not to endanger the lives of patients or threaten the tentative self-confidence of the new graduate? How can this initiation rite be more meaningfully related to the helping role rather than to the taskmaster role?

Even if fellow nurses do not design a day of trial as an initiation, the new graduate awaits a time of real testing. Perhaps it is a time that proves to her that she has become a nurse.

What happens when you have an emergency in the delivery room? That's the only thing that really bothers me—will I be able to react properly? Because I've never been in any sort of an emergency, believe it or not! After all my nursing training, I never have! So I don't know how I'll react. I've got all the background behind me. It's just the question: "Now, can I use it when the time comes without losing my head?" I think that until I've really been tested . . . I don't think that I have really been tested in anything I've had to do. I've learned it and I've done it, but I don't think I've ever really been put to a tough test. So I think I kind of have to wait for that . . . for that day *to see if I am worth my salt.* (NG:BS/2[12]8/71)

### The victim role

A number of different types of role conflict—professional-bureaucratic, doctor-nurse, generational—have been described. All of these types were evident in the Reality Shock seminars; however, one kind of conflict was depicted so dramatically that it deserves special attention here.

New graduates often adopted the role of victim in relation to other staff nurses or auxiliary and supervisory personnel, thus assigning the role of persecutor to the other workers. Why did the new graduate adopt the role of victim so readily? Spiegel's description of *allocative discrepancy* as a source of role conflict offers one plausible explanation. An allocative discrepancy occurs when either role partner enacts a role that is considered inappropriate or not identifiable by the other. In any social situation there are

accepted procedural understandings that indicate to the people involved whether or not the role they are enacting is acceptable. These procedural or cultural understandings can be called allocative principles. There are several important allocative principles. One is that some roles are ascribed, for example, age roles. There is little leeway in the ascribed role. If a child enacts an adult role, he violates this allocative principle by not enacting his ascribed role of child. Another allocative principle is that some roles have prerequisites. They are achieved by meeting certain requirements and receiving certain ceremonial recognition. Completion of nursing school and receiving licensure entitles a person to enact the role of RN; to enact this role without the prerequisites is to violate this allocative principle. Other allocative principles involve more informal roles. For example, some roles are adopted. Since an adopted role is informal, no one must ask permission to adopt it. The example of a new graduate adopting the role of victim and assigning the role of persecutor to other personnel demonstrates this allocative principle. Spiegel points out that adoption of a victim role often occurs when a situation that has been masked or misunderstood suddenly becomes unmasked or understood. The more the backstage reality of the work world has been masked or hidden from the new graduate during the formative stages of her role identity, the greater will be her disequilibrium and conflict upon having the real roles unmasked. The consequences of being given misleading cues about the role behavior of supervisors, graduate nurses, and auxiliary workers during school is that at the point the situation becomes unmasked and discrepancies are revealed (usually upon beginning work), disequilibrium ensues. The disequilibrium caused by the realization of the real role behaviors is characterized by the vocabulary of victimization: disillusionment ("You deceived me."), ("You have no right to do what you did!"), and alarm: ("I've been robbed!"). Such cries were frequent in the first Reality Shock seminars.

The assignments are not fair! I really do feel that

they [the orderlies] take advantage of you. They walk in late and you say to yourself: "What am I supposed to do about this?" And it's really bad for you because you feel so inadequate to begin with, and here you have people taking advantage of you.... It's not fair! It really shouldn't be! You're mad at yourself because you are doing it, and yet you don't have enough guts to stand up to them and say: "This is how it's going to be, regardless." (NG:AD/2[26]12/71)

. . .

You end up doing it yourself just to avoid the hassle with the orderlies! (NG:AD/2[25]12/71)

. . .

You call the night supervisor [to find out what you're supposed to do in this situation]. First of all, she's not in her office; and you page her and she doesn't answer. Then she calls in about an hour and tells you that you should have already sent the patient downstairs! (NG:AD/5[20]1/72)

In addition to the disillusionment, protest, and alarm that come upon discovery of previously masked role behaviors, the new graduate is subject to reading in of intentions based on her role expectations.

Well, I can't say that I have things under control . . . I can't stand having to tell someone to do their job. They know their job. If I have time, I'll do it; and if I don't, well it just won't get done. But I'm not the kind of person who can stand to ride people. After all, this is being tolerated not just by me but by the head nurse on down. I don't feel that it's right, but I just don't know where you go with it. You go home angry and frustrated a lot of the times. But I can't envision myself going to my head nurse and saying "Hey, what's going on?" I really can't. I haven't had any kind of communication about what this person is thinking. But I think that she is aware of it and that she has accepted it that way. And she herself hasn't found a way to deal with it. So I don't think my going to her and giving her my experience is going to change the situation any. (NG:AD/5[23]1/72)

In this instance the new graduate is reading in that the head nurse is aware of the orderlies' not doing their job at night but that she cannot deal with this behavior. Her reading in may be accurate or inaccurate; that is not the point. The point is that it

does not occur to the person who is reading in intentions to validate her information.

Misleading or mainly frontstage cues about nurse role behavior are what student nurses usually see in the school setting. Their assignments and clinical placements generally expose them to the more ideal situations. Students may graduate with misleading interpretations of nurse behavior.

I think a lot of the problem is that while you are in school you're given two patients to take care of. Sure, if it's really busy you're given three patients and you give three whole bed baths. That's like really nothing. And you walk in here —bam! you're a team leader. You are brand new, right out of school, and you go out there and you make assignments for LVN's and aides who have been working here for three and four or five years and you give them three patients. And they say: "Three patients!" And here you are team-leading plus taking three patients yourself, and finally you think: "Hey, maybe something is wrong here." (NG:AD/5[20]1/72)

Kahn and associates found that persons reporting role conflict stated that their trust in the persons who were perceived as having caused this pressure was decreased. They liked them less, held them in lower esteem, communicated less with them, and found that their own effectiveness was decreased. This seemed to be also the experience of these new graduates. It was easy for them to assign the role of persecutor to those imposing pressure and role conflict on them, be they former instructors, supervisors, other RN's, or auxiliary workers.

### Enculturation, a cyclical process

The work world is a new culture for the entrant. The newcomer discovers that there are unfamiliar cues, norms, and expectations. The stages of culture shock and their translation into the reality shock phenomenon have been presented in Chapters 2 and 5. That the reality shock phenomenon and process do occur, and in much the same way as does culture shock, was validated many times by the nurses in the seminars. Use of the framework proposed in Chapter 5 does much to explain the common reactions of new graduates on their first job.

The honeymoon phase of situational adjustment is characterized by almost unbounded enthusiasm. Everything is exciting, wonderful and challenging. The appraisal has a superficial glow. Problems are not recognized. A new graduate in response to an interviewer's request to "describe a dissatisfying experience" responded this way:

I can't think of anything, really. I guess it seems like I'm trying to be difficult, but I'm not. I can't think of anything that's been really frustrating. I guess the only one was that one sick patient we had. She had pre-eclampsia; and it wasn't dissatisfying, it was just frustrating. I've been very contented up in the delivery room. (NG:BS/2[12]6/71)

The honeymoon phase lasts for varying lengths of time, depending on the individual, the institution, and the length of the orientation program. The first Reality Shock program was begun two to three months after the new graduates began work. Only one new graduate in this group expressed any of the wholesale excitement and approval characteristic of the honeymoon phase; most of the new graduates were in the height of reality shock at the beginning of the seminars.

In contrast to the honeymoon phase, the reality shock phase is characterized by wholesale rejection. Reality shock occurs when the new graduate begins to bump up against many blocks to her goals and expectations. In this phase criticism is not realistic, but one-sided. People or things tend to be either all good or all bad, as described in the early Reality Shock seminars. The new graduate became hypercritical, and her world became phrased in terms of "we" and "they."

I don't like the way *they* [referring to auxiliary staff] talk to the patients. *They* just go in and do the job like they were dealing with a herd of cattle or something. (NG:AD/3[26]1/72)

· · ·

In the past it has really been hard to motivate people to do anything because *they* have just been there so long. And I know that new graduates . . . it's not hard to motivate them to do things. In the past when you would tell the night nurse about something that should be done you

would just get this long line of defenses. You would just feel like you were talking to a brick wall. But somehow I don't feel that way when I talk to a recent graduate. At least she will listen to me. *They* don't have those hard shells built up yet. (NG:Dip/4[21]12/71)

The rejection phase also is filled with "should's" and ideals.

And one of the RN's, if *they* get an aide to do anything it's by saying: "I have to go do a treatment; would you go and do such and such?" And I don't think that's the way it *should* be. She *shouldn't* have to be defensive and say that she is doing something first. The orderlies *should* do their job! (NG:AD/3[26]1/72)

The anxiety of the rejection phase takes its toll in symptoms of fatigue and apathy.

When you go home, all you want to do is sleep so you can get up and go to work the next day. Pretty soon all you are doing is sleeping and working. (NG:AD/2[29]1/72)

· · ·

I talked with Anne the other day. I told her that I was in a slump. I felt my first slump! I had never been in such a slump before in my life. You know, I had apathy. I didn't care about any of this junk . . . . (NG:Dip/5[21]1/72)

Often the past is idealized or future escapes are dreamed of. During this phase new graduates often dream of going into public health, teaching, or some other setting that would not be so problematical for them. If new graduates do not flee the scene they may move out of the rejection phase and recover. The recovery phase is pivotal. To "recover" means: (1) to become bicultural and thus integrate past values with the realities and demands of the present situation, (2) to reject past values and opt for all the values of the work world, (3) to cling to school values and leave nursing practice.

One of the first signs of recovery is the return of a sense of humor. There is an ability to laugh at a situation or predicament, but the laughter has a ring of superiority.

I think you really do have to get rid of the emotional thing. You can't just go around horrified all the time. As a nurse, there are so many horrifying things that you have to deal with, it would interfere with your job if you reacted to everything. (NG:Dip/5[21]1/72)

. . .

I have adjusted to my horror of cockroaches. I can laugh about them. One night I was assisting a doctor with a Pap smear, and a cockroach crawled right across the slide! The doctor wanted to know how to get this urine specimen down real fast and asked: "What's the fastest mode of transportation?" And I answered: "Well, you could strap it on the back of a cockroach." [There was much laughter and everyone began sharing cockroach stories.] (NG:AD/5[23]1/72)

During the recovery phase the new graduate is more open to the demands of her new setting. This phase allows her to decide her directions. If she chooses biculturalism, she will choose some of the useful work values, reject nonuseful ones, and retain and integrate some of the school-bred values. Such individuals are highly adaptive and can become effective change agents in their work situation. From this vantage point, the new graduate could see both sides of the coin. Her criticism was more realistic and therefore her conflict more constructive. It was the goal of the Reality Shock program to nurture this kind of integration.

Yeah, it's not all good to work with all your friends. I mean, it's really groovy to come on and see your friends but it's not so great to have to say: "Why in hell didn't you take those orders off in the daytime?" That's really hard to say. Plus its both good and bad to have all new grads, too. I don't know how to say it, but the unit is really crazy and the new grads are not sure of themselves. It's not just all that good to have all new grads. (NG:AD/5[20]1/72)

This was in contrast to an earlier statement that it was good to work with new graduates, while it was problematic to work with oldtimers.

Bicultural adjustment enables the nurse to increase her interpersonal competency, that is, her ability to accomplish her goals in the work setting. In the following excerpt the new graduate demonstrates interpersonal competency by being able to accurately interpret her actions from the LVN's perspective

and thereby gain approval for her approach to patient care.

The duties of the RN, the LVN, and orderlies are really defined. The orderlies take care of the urine. It is almost to the point of being ridiculous. When I started doing some of these things, Mrs. Smith [the LVN] really got offended because she thought I was doing these things because I thought that she wasn't doing her job. The other night she got angry because I was out changing the patient. She doesn't say anything when she is angry . . . she gets very silent when she gets angry, and I knew that she was angry. When she came back into the nurses' station I said: "Mrs. Smith, I wasn't doing that because I didn't think that you wouldn't do it, but I just happened to be out there and it seemed stupid for me to come in and call you when I was there and I could do it in the time it would take me to walk to the desk and ask you to do it." [How did she respond to this?] She responded quite favorably. (NG: AD/5[23]1/72)

This ability to assess without moral outrage—without cries of "But it shouldn't be that way!"—frees the new graduate to interpret her behavior to the LVN and thus to favorably influence her. She is now on the way to becoming a change agent. She neither accepts nor rejects *all* the work values; she can evaluate and choose the best of both worlds.

Unfortunately, reality shock is not always resolved in an orderly progression through the four stages outlined. A new situation with a new set of problems can start the cycle all over again. (Lynn also demonstrated this in her diary.) However, once the new graduate begins to see the perspectives of others while maintaining some of her own perspectives, she has the potential of coming through the recovery phase a more integrative and effective influence for change in her work situation.

## SUMMARY

James Baldwin said: "Not everything that is faced can be changed; but nothing can be changed until it is faced." Conflicts must be made visible before a program for new graduates can be designed that will promote creative conflict resolution. The new graduate must be able to move from the point of discerning conflict to defining it. The new nurse is caught up in the task of role transformation: she must mediate the conflicting demands of school-bred norms and ideals and the situational demands of her first job. Some of the common major conflicts discussed in this chapter were (1) the differences between systems of work organization, and (2) the differences between the school's explicit expectations and the work world's implicit expectations, and (3) the differences between local and cosmopolitan views. Other individualistic conflicts were presented, including clinical uncertainty, a competency gap, the generation gap, constancy of time and the time orientation of work, subcultural differences among institutions, and racial conflicts as they affect work performance.

The evolution of the first Reality Shock program was described in hopes of passing on to the reader the experiential lessons learned. Three vantage points were suggested as an explanation of how the new graduate experiences her first job. If the first job is viewed as a test, events are likely to be interpreted in terms of questions such as: What are the test criteria? Who is giving the test? When will it be finished? Role conflict, too, brings its perceptual distortions. The new nurse who adopts the role of victim assigns others the role of persecutor. Such a view of one's co-workers markedly changes the nature of one's interactions.

The way in which the new graduate elects to resolve reality shock will influence not only how she views her first experience as a nurse but also how she will view her entire career in nursing. Becoming bicultural, integrating two opposing systems and coming up with a unique new configuration, is the hope and creative venture for the new graduate. Innovative solutions and commitment without conformity and absorption is the goal. It is believed that a program for new graduates which fosters creative conflict resolution increases the possibility of commitment without conformity. Even so, it is only a beginning and not a utopian solution to the new graduate's dilemma. Perhaps the new graduate will take heart in the wise therapist's counsel in *I Never Promised You a Rose Garden*.

Look here, Furii said, I never promised you a rose garden. I never promised you perfect justice . . . and I never promised you peace or happiness. My help is so that you can be free to fight for all of these things. The only reality I offer is challenge, and being well is being free to accept it or not at whatever you are capable. I never promise lies, and the rose-garden world of perfection is a lie . . . and a bore, too!°

Hopefully, nursing educators will not hold up an idealistic rose-garden view of nursing but will provide opportunities for the student nurse to discover and be challenged by the conflicts and complex problems that predominate in the real world of nursing.

### NOTES

1. This was essentially a hunch based on the chronological data from Kramer's dissertation sample: disenchantment seemed to set in after the three-month period. It was thought that the new graduates would not be receptive to dealing with role conflict and role transformation until they had experienced some conflict and feelings of need to deal with it. From staff development interviews at the university it was noted that after two months some new graduates were still in the honeymoon phase; therefore, three months on the job was considered a good time to begin the program.

2. In this seminar I believed the new graduates to be in a state of culture shock or reality shock; however, I did not openly state my belief. It later became evident that several of the new graduates believed themselves to be in various stages of culture shock and suspected that I too believed this to be the case. The context remained mixed for some of the group members: there was some closed awareness, some suspected, some mutual pretense, and some open awareness.

### REFERENCES

Becker, H.: Personal change in adult life, Sociometry, March 27, 1964, pp. 40-53.

Benne, K. and Bennis, W.: Role confusion and conflict within nursing, A. J. Nurs. 59(2):196-198, 1959, part one; 59(3):380-383, 1959, part two.

Berne, E.: Games people play, New York, 1964, Grove Press, Inc., pp. 110-122.

Corwin, R. G.: Role conception and career aspirations; a study of identity in nursing, The Sociological Quarterly, April 1961, pp. 69-86.

Corwin, R. G., and Taves, M.: Some concomitants of bureaucratic and professional conceptions of the nurse role, Nurs. Res. 11:223-225, Fall 1962.

°Green, H.: I never promised you a rose garden, New York, 1964, Holt, Rinehart and Winston, Inc., Publishers.

Gardner, J. W.: Leadership. In Rowan, H., editor: No easy victories, New York, 1968, Harper & Row, Publishers, p. 129.

Gouldner, A. W.: Cosmopolitans and locals; toward an analysis of latent social roles, Administrative Science Quarterly 2:281-306, 1957; 2:444-480, 1958.

Green, H.: I never promised you a rose garden, New York, 1964, Holt, Rinehart & Winston, Inc.

Havighurst, R. J.: Youth in exploration and man emergent. In Borow, H., editor: Man in a world of work, Boston, 1964, Houghton Mifflin Co., pp. 215-236.

Kahn, R. L., Wolfe, D. M., Quinn, R. P., Snoek, J. D., and Rosenthal, R.: Organizational stress, New York, 1964, John Wiley & Sons, Inc.

Kramer, M.: Some effects of exposure to employing bureaucracies on the role conceptions and role deprivation of neophyte collegiate nurses, unpublished doctoral dissertation, 1966, Stanford University, Department of Education.

Kramer, M.: Collegiate graduate nurses in medical center hospitals; mutual challenge or duel, Nurs. Res. 18(3):196-210, 1969.

Kramer, M. and Baker, C.: The exodus; can nursing afford it?, J. Nurs. Administration 1(3):15-30, 1971.

Lethi, Y.: The conflict of generations in nursing, Int. Nurs. Rev. 6(2):185, 1961.

Merton, R. K.: Social theory and social structure, New York, 1968, The Free Press, pp. 203-207.

Moore, W. E.: Occupational socialization. In Goslin, D. A., editor: Handbook of socialization, theory and research, Chicago, 1969, Rand McNally & Co., pp. 861-883.

Oberg, K.: Cultural shock adjustment to new cultural environments, Practical Anthropology, July-August 1960, pp. 177-182.

Olmsted, A., and Paget, M.: Theoretical issues in professional socialization, J. Med. Educ. 44:669, 1963.

Postman, N., and Weingartner, C.: The soft revolution, New York, 1971, Dell Publishing Co., Inc., pp. 51-62.

Scott, W. R.: Professionals in bureaucracies; areas of conflict. In Vollmer, H., and Mills, D., editors: Professionalization, Englewood Cliffs, N. J., 1966, Prentice-Hall, Inc., pp. 265-273.

Simpson, I. H.: Patterns of socialization into professions; the case of student nurses, Sociological Inquiry 37(1): 47-53, Winter 1967.

Spiegel, J. P.: The resolution of role conflict within the family, Psychiatry 20:1-16, 1957.

Van Gennep, A.: The rites of passage, translated by Monika B. Vizedom and Gabrielle L. Caffee, Chicago, 1960, University of Chicago Press, pp. 10-11.

Walker, V. H.: Nursing and ritualistic practice, New York, 1967, The Macmillan Co.

## CHAPTER SEVEN

# THE END OF THE JOURNEY—OR THE BEGINNING?

If only dreams and reality were not so far apart.

CERVANTES

## SUMMARY OF FINDINGS

Something can be done about the reality shock experienced by nurses on their first job. Some of our best nurses do not have to flee from nursing or from nursing practice. The nurses of tomorrow can constructively manage the inevitable conflict between work and school values and make the contributions to improved patient care that is expected and hoped for from them. These are some of the messages that can be drawn from the results of the study reported in this book.

A description and analysis of the reality shock phenomenon as it was observed and studied in nurses all over the country has been presented, as much as possible in the nurses' own words through observation, diary data, a case history, and verbatim excerpts from tape-recorded interviews. Utilizing information and insights gained through extensive study and observation of a group of 220 nurses working in medical center hospitals, the Anticipatory Socialization program was designed to help nurses confront and constructively manage school-work value conflicts. This special program was taught to two classes of student nurses during their three years in a school of nursing. It was determined that these two classes of students had characteristics highly similar to a third class of students in the same school who were not exposed to the program. By keeping all other aspects of the educational program—faculty, curriculum, and so on—as similar as possible, I was able to assess the effectiveness of the Anticipatory Socialization program on several variables by comparing the class that

did not have the program with the classes that did.

Since the purpose of the whole project was to reduce exodus from nursing practice and job hopping and increase retention of happy, effective nurses in hospital nursing practice, these factors constituted one set of variables studied. Other variables examined were maintenance of a professional belief system, reduction in reported role deprivation, development of behaviors representing a constructive mix of professional and bureaucratic loyalties, and operationalization of professional role behaviors.

A variety of techniques were used to analyze the data and to test the hypotheses, and a number of conclusions were drawn. First, the Anticipatory Socialization program was effective *during* the school program as evidenced by an increase in both bureaucratic role conception and total role deprivation scores. The increases in these scores did not seem to hurt these young student nurses. Those who had the Anticipatory Socialization program acquired as much loyalty to the nursing profession (as evidenced by professional role conception scores) as did the nurses in the class that did not have the program. Although the nurses who had the program had a mean cumulative grade point average upon graduation lower than that of the class that did not have the program, all classes did equally as well on state board examinations. The pattern of withdrawal from the school of nursing was different for the two groups of nurses, however, but actually a smaller percentage of the classes who had the Anticipatory Socialization program withdrew than those who did not.

Evidence indicated that the program was also effective in producing the desired effect *after* graduation. The role deprivation scores, which were considered in this study to be the closest single indicator of reality shock, of the classes that had the program did not show as sharp a rise upon employment as did the scores of the nurses in the class that did not have the program. This permits the inference that the latter received much more of a reality shock than did the former group. This reality shock, and role transformation made in an uncontrolled fashion was considered to be highly detrimental and promotive of exodus and job hopping.

Markedly different patterns of exodus and job turnover variables emerged for the nurses who had the Anticipatory Socialization program as compared with those who did not. Although virtually the same percentage of nurses from each class started out in hospital nursing there were marked differences thereafter.•The classes of nurses who had the Anticipatory Socialization program remained in their initial jobs longer, did significantly less job hopping, remained in hospital nursing practice longer, and none of them had exited from nursing at the two-year postgraduation followup. In contrast, the class that did not have the program showed the same job-hopping patterns as did the larger medical center sample. This class also tended to evidence flight from hospital nursing and from nursing in general, with 6 of 45 nurses having left nursing by the time of the two-year postgraduation followup.

It is desirable that nurses not undertake extensive job hopping or leave nursing. But is this desirable at the expense of producing nurses who are conformists to the system—nurses who are not visionary and grounded in the professional idealism that will hopefully make for a better health care system in the future? If it is assumed that the response to this question is negative, then it becomes necessary to look at the comparative commitment to professional ideals of the nurses who had the program and those who did not.

It was expected that the latter group would show a drop in loyalty to professional ideals upon employment because of the discomfiture occasioned by the required increase in loyalty to the bureaucratic work system, as had been found in earlier studies. The longer one is employed, the less his loyalty to the professional system of work. This was not borne out by this study. At least within the first two years of employment, neither the nurses who had had the Anticipatory Socialization program nor those who had not, showed significant decreases in professional role conception scores. Perhaps the nurses who did not have the Anticipatory Socialization program and who were expected to show this decrease assuaged their conflict and were able to hold onto their professional ideals by frequent job hopping, by simply not working, or by leaving nursing. Perhaps a longer-term followup would show the expected drop.

If one is to effectively and constructively solve conflict between school and work values, it was considered indicative that, when presented with a conflict situation, the nurse would elect an action that was a compromise between professional and bureaucratic modes of organizing work. This kind of action choice was measured by the Integrative Role Behavior scales. The nurses who had had the Anticipatory Socialization program were much more bicultural in their preferred action choices. They chose significantly more compromise behaviors than did the nurses who did not have the Anticipatory Socialization program.

It is one thing to hold onto one's values; it is another to put them into operation. This was one of the most difficult variables in the study to measure because there are no ready-made programs available for doing this. Operationalization of professional values was assessed in four ways. The Index of Professional Behavior provided a numerical score of the extent to which an individual engaged in professional reading, purchased professional books, subscribed to professional journals, wrote articles, engaged in activities of the professional organization, and so forth. The nurses who had the Anticipatory Socialization program had significantly higher scores on this Index than did the nurses who did not have the program.

The Effectiveness of Change score was a measure of the degree to which changes initiated by the nurses were perceived by co-workers as being effective. Use of this variable as a measure of operationalization of professional values was based on the premise that change agent activity is a strongly promulgated value of professional schools of nursing and the ability to create change in a social system indicates a degree of biculturalism. The nurses in the classes that had the Anticipatory Socialization program reported significantly more change agent activities than did the nurses in the other class. This fact may simply indicate that these nurses had more confidence in themselves. What is important, however, is the fact that the head nurses or co-workers of the nurses who had the Anticipatory Socialization program perceived and reported significantly more changes initiated by these nurses as being effective than did the co-workers of the nurses who did not have the program.

A third, but somewhat indirect, way of looking at the differential effectiveness in operationalizing professional values was based on the idea that to effectively influence someone else (so as to bring about improvements in patient care) one must be able to define a situation as the other person sees it. This is what is meant by empathy. Those nurses in the classes that had had the Anticipatory Socialization program, and who arranged for interviews with either their head nurse or co-worker, were significantly more empathetic than those nurses in the class that had not had the Anticipatory Socialization program. Given more empathy, it follows logically but not necessarily that it will be possible for a person to influence others in the direction he desires. That this was so seems to be indicated by the increase in effective change activities by those nurses who had had the Anticipatory Socialization program.

A fourth and final way of attempting to assess the degree to which the two groups

of nurses were operationalizing professional values was also indirect. Based on the reasoning that if a person saw himself as successful, in tune both with school-bred beliefs and with the system in which he was working (bicultural, to use the phrase introduced in this book), then he would be more self-actualized than if he were in constant, more or less unresolved conflict. Utilizing the time competence and inner-directed scores of Shostrom's Personal Orientation Inventory, no significant difference was found between the nurses who had the Anticipatory Socialization program and those who did not have it, although the former group was more self-actualized than the latter. Both groups of nurses had higher Tc and I scores than what has usually been reported for nurses in the literature. Perhaps this lack of discrimination was because of the relatively high self-actualizing scores of all the nurses, or maybe it was because two years after graduation (which is when the POI was administered) was not sufficiently long enough to produce this kind of change in attitude.

. In summary then, the Anticipatory Socialization program was quite effective. The nurses who had the program seemed to experience less reality shock. They seemed happier and more content in their jobs. They definitely remained in their initial jobs longer, did less job hopping, remained in hospital nursing longer, and at the time of the two-year postgraduation followup none had left nursing. They retained their professional beliefs and reported bicultural action choices to conflict situations. On the variables measured, there was evidence to support the inference that they were operationalizing professional beliefs to a greater degree than were the nurses who had not had the program.

A pilot reality shock program was devised from the knowledge and experiences gained from the Anticipatory Socialization program, and was submitted to a field test. In contrast to the Anticipatory Socialization program, the Reality Shock program was remedial rather than preventative. It was designed to encompass a variety of conflict situations rather than to focus almost solely on school-work value (professional-bureaucratic) conflicts. Although formalized evaluation tools were not used in this initial trial of the Reality Shock program, it did appear that it was effective in helping new graduates struggle through the moral outrage phase of reality shock. The program was quite useful in both generating additional knowledge and theory relative to the process of role transformation and postgraduation socialization and in testing out some of the ideas that had been formed from the study of the medical center nurses. It also demonstrated quite clearly that it was not only the baccalaureate nurse graduate who was prone to reality shock. Associate arts and diploma graduates are also susceptible; the reality shock experienced differs in degree rather than kind. It also appears that the more educationally-oriented diploma education becomes, the more it is separated from the service agency supporting it, and the more professionally oriented the product, the more vulnerable are its graduates to reality shock.

## GENERAL IMPLICATIONS OF THE STUDY

In ferreting out and presenting the implications of a study, considerably more leeway is allowed than in the presentation of the tests of the hypotheses. In the latter, the investigator is bound by the rules of scientific inquiry to be precise, accurate, and to present carefully collected data to support the conclusions made. Implications, on the other hand, are drawn from the results of a study through the interplay of past experiences and current perceptions. As such, they represent the uniqueness and individuality that a person brings to the interpretation. I will describe and discuss some of the implications of this study as seen through my eyes; the reader is invited and challenged to do the same.

In a review of the entire study as a preliminary to the process of abstracting meaning and drawing implications, a plethora of ideas emerged. To bring order and logic to this material so that it could be meaningfully discussed, it was finally decided to present five main implications abstracted from the evolving theory of postgraduation socialization presented in Chapter 5. These will be followed by more specific questions and potential implications for the various nurse populations for whom this book was written.

### Effect of reality shock on patient care

A nurse's whole reason for being is to improve the health of patients entrusted to her care. Ultimately all activity must be measured against this criterion, whether the nursing activity takes place in hospital, clinic, home, or community. The effect of reality shock on patients must be discussed on two levels: the individual patient and the unit or health care system.

Is the nursing care given by a nurse who is in the throes of moral outrage, rejection, disillusionment, hostility, and despair less effective than the care given by a bicultural nurse—a nurse who has managed the school-work conflict in a growth-producing way? Most assuredly the care will be different and also less effective if it is agreed that the climate and milieu that surrounds the patient (the nurse being part of that climate) is instrumental to his health maintenance and recovery process. The affect of nurses is easily perceived by patients: "That nurse looks so unhappy and upset; she says she's always being pulled in several directions at once." A nurse who is severely at conflict and unhappy will experience difficulty in effecting the climate and relationship with her client that is most conducive to his well-being.

On a unit or health care system level, a nurse who is unable to come to grips with the conflict experienced between her value system and the predominant value system in the work world will be gravely handicapped in creating lasting and meaningful changes in the work situation. There are several possible ineffective ways to deal with the conflict. These promote the status quo and prevent the nurse from making the desired impact on the health care system. One alternative is to drop idealistic school-bred values and take up the work values. This is a very appealing solution. Conflict produces tension, and tension is painful. Quick and eager adoption of work values will usually bring about positive reward and regard by others, and a nurse who does this probably becomes more effective more rapidly than a nurse who adopts any of the other kinds of solutions. But on both the individual patient and unit level, such a nurse will tend to maintain the status quo level of nursing practice because she has chosen to disregard the futuristic ideals of what "could be"—of what better nursing care could consist of. Without these ideals constantly in sight — without reaching and working toward them—repetition of "what is" becomes the alternative by default.

Another ineffective way of dealing with conflict, which also serves to maintain the status quo, is refusal to take up any or too few work values and holding firm allegiance to the school values. Such an individual will probably continue to be in conflict because all around her are reminders and demands for at least minimal acquiescence to work values. The tension and conflict may become so painful that she feels she must leave the work scene, either completely or by fleeing nursing practice for teaching. One can fully appreciate the feelings of powerlessness and frustration that motivate a nurse to do this, but in terms of the analysis here this type of conflict resolution does not improve patient care either individually or on a unit level. Nurses who are no longer working within the system can do little to effect needed change. Furthermore, nurse-teachers with unresolved conflict will probably perpetuate not only the conflict but may also be perceived by their students as models for the best way of managing the conflict, thus tending to maintain the status quo in the educational system.

"Plague on both your houses" is another route the shocked and outraged nurse might take to reduce the conflict she feels: "If you can't get along and agree, I don't want anything to do with either of you." This is very understandable. Use of withdrawal techniques for relatively short periods of time often helps us to regroup and mobilize our resources. This is very evident in the grief process and is considered to be healthy and advantageous to the process of handling sudden shocks and losses. In the same vein, a temporary withdrawal might be a precursor to constructive conflict management; it is when the temporary "plague" becomes the adaptive pattern that the impact on patient care is noticeable. As a more or less permanent pattern, the nurse who adopts this position tends to view nursing as just a job. She works hard and does her job, but her minimal involvement and commitment takes its toll in the quality of the care she provides to individual patients. She will probably not make that extra effort to find out what's really bothering a patient that a bicultural, interpersonally competent nurse would make. It is also likely that nurses who select this option of conflict reduction will not become involved or committed to any kind of joint effort to improve the care of patients in an agency or on a unit, nor will they be motivated to initiate needed improvements. The results once again will be a tendency for individual patient care and health system care to remain at the same level as before this nurse entered it.

What about nurses who solve the conflict and frustration experienced in the work situation by job hopping? This is a very tempting solution and one that has understandable logic and rationale behind it: "There's just no point staying here if I'm miserable and unhappy, if I can't give patients the kind of care they should get, and I can't convince others about the way it should be done." It may very well be that this is the most viable resolution for the individual at the time, and as a temporary means of managing the tension from conflict it might well be advantageous. But when frequent job changes because of dissatisfaction become a patterned means of conflict resolution, there are bound to be negative consequences on patient care. Effecting improvements in patient care requires that an individual know enough about the system to make changes within it, and the system cannot be learned unless one is there for awhile.

An ineffective way of dealing with conflict that is the most understandable and yet the most tragic is the "burn-out." If a nurse experiences marked school-work value conflict and feels powerless to create changes, she may in essence give up, feel apathetic or burned out. This choice is understandable because by nature the burn-out is insidious and made up of a series of decisions like "Oh well, I guess it's not important to have a care plan on the patients; let's forget it" rather than a single major decision such as seen in the decision to change one's job. Because of its insidiousness, it becomes a way of acting and reacting before one is aware that it has become a pattern. The tragedy of this route choice emanates from the fact that underneath all of the "give up" decisions there is a spark of the school-bred idealism that is fighting to be operationalized. (This is what differentiates this solution from the "plague on both your houses" solution.) This spark keeps the slow burn going so that these nurses are not content, happy, or satisfied with the kind of care they are giving or that the patients are getting. They constantly want to improve the care patients are receiving but feel powerless or ineffective in bringing this about. Having met rejection of their ideas so often, they now tend to hold them in. In this state it is virtually impossible for the nurse to become an advocate for the patient or even to effectively hear, process, and interpret his care needs to other health care workers. The contribution these nurses might have made to the improvement of health care is lost, and the status quo is maintained.

There are undoubtedly other patterns and alternatives of ineffective conflict resolution. All of them tend to contribute to the maintenance of the status quo, negatively affect the care given to patients, and interfere with general improvements in the total system of health care delivery. The current health care system is regimented and geared toward the best possible care for the majority. It does present many constraints and contingencies for nurses who have been educated with an idealistic version of comprehensive and individualized patient care. Granted it would be nice to reengineer both systems so that many of the constraints and contingencies

would be removed, and I am willing for this to happen; but it is not going to happen tomorrow or next year. It is not unreasonable or dishonorable for nurses to give up, to become apathetic, or to flee the work scene given the constraints and contingencies of the work system and of their education. But there are still positive aspects in both the school and service systems that could be utilized to bring about constructive conflict resolution. Nurses who care and who dare to change the system by working within it will continue to bring about improvements in both individual and unit or agency nursing care.

### Energy consumed in skill mastery

Nursing educators and nursing service personnel have over the years struggled with the subject of the relative emphasis that should be placed on the learning of manual-technical skills by student nurses. There is some variation in position, but generally nurse educators favor less emphasis than nursing service personnel; the end result is that many fewer skills are taught in preservice programs than are demanded of the neophyte when she begins employment. Skill-learning then becomes one of the initial and primary goals of the new graduate, one that consumes enormous amounts of energy. What effect does this energy diversion have on patient care? What effect does it have on the neophyte's ability to constructively manage the conflicting value systems she encounters? What effect does it have on her ability to develop biculturalism? These are the questions about the area of skills that must be asked and answered. Is it worth the energy it takes to learn on the job those basic skills and procedures that an individual must know in order to meet the demands of the job for which he is employed?

Energy can be viewed from two dimensions: behavior and attitude. It does require a certain amount of behavioral energy to put one's muscles through the actions of learning unfamiliar skills. Behavioral energy requirements can be pared to a bare minimum, however, if attitudes toward that which is to be learned are congruent and favorable. The real problem with energy expenditure in the area of skills is the tremendous attitudinal energy cost. This attitudinal energy expenditure consists of the following mixture: (1) lack of confidence in one's ability to learn skills, (2) fear of not being able to learn all that one needs to learn, (3) guilt or embarrassment that one knows less than others expect, (4) the feeling that skills are not really important and are readily learned when needed. If it is this extra attitudinal baggage that so markedly increases the energy expenditure and interferes with the behavioral skill-learning of the new graduate on her first job, then perhaps at least part of the solution is to lessen or reverse it so that neophytes will be predisposed to learn skills more rapidly and with less overall energy expenditure.

Although nursing is changing and will continue to change, there will probably always be some manual-technical component to the act of helping people get well and stay well. Nurses are now and will continue to be faced with a skill-demanding public: physicians, patients, and hospital administrators. Both patients and physicians tend to describe nurses primarily in terms of manual activities. They will probably continue to do so until they've experienced the kind of care that focuses on the patient as a person and consists of assessments, plans, and actions that will make a difference in the patient's progress and well-being.

But part of preparing nurses to give this kind of nursing care does mean that they must be knowledgeable and competent in the performance of basic manual-technical nursing skills. There is probably little disagreement that all nurses should enter their first jobs armed with a basic repetoire of interpersonal relationship skills. Why should the same not prevail for some of the more manual aspects of nursing? Perhaps some of the energy that is now spent debating the issue of whether nurses should be taught manual skills in school or not could be better spent by coming to terms with what constitutes the basic compendium of manual-technical skills needed by all nurses who are going to care for people in the hospital,

home, or community. (It must be mentioned that such a list of basic skills would need to be restudied and possibly revised every five years or so because of the tremendous technological advances.) Educators could then be sure to teach at least these skills, employers would expect all nurses to be competent in them, and everyone could then divert the unexpended energy into creating conditions for an opportunity to give total and meaningful nursing care to people.

### Students who work for pay while in school

Students frequently work for pay either as nurse's aides or in some other kind of classification while they are enrolled in the school of nursing. This may be during the school year when they have time off or during summers or vacation periods. There is little doubt that students perceive these kinds of work experiences as helpful in learning skills and in gaining self-confidence. Some nurse educators are doubtful of the wisdom of this kind of experience, fearing that students will learn how to become good nurse's aides rather than good nurses. Nursing administrators generally favor this kind of experience for students, feeling that it produces more skillful nurses who adjust more rapidly to the work situation.

Since self-confidence, skill practice, and ease of adjustment can all be viewed as positive outcomes, it is more meaningful to look at the potential negative outcome. Does working for pay as a student produce a nurse who functions at a level different from what her professional training is preparing her for? There may be some tendency in this direction. Data from the study reported in this book suggest that nurses who have had extensive work experience as students may have a tendency to capitulate school-bred values more readily than do nurses who have had limited or no work experience as students.

It is not difficult to understand why this might occur. When a student works as a nurse's aide she attacks the learning of skills with zest. She receives commendation and praise from her co-workers for mastering these skills; such rewards become the stimulus for further learning. A vision of the nurse as taskmaster can easily grow along side of or replace the vision of the nurse as an independent decision-maker who possesses knowledge and uses that knowledge autonomously and discriminately to aid her client. Since the work experiences are usually of relatively short or infrequent durations, the opportunity for boredom or the realization of the meaninglessness of enacting segmented routine tasks does not stifle the student's feelings of success and helpfulness. These successes in turn tend to promote loyalty to the part-task work system and make it easier for the student to give only enough acquiescence to the whole-task system to get her through school or to capitulate school-bred values upon full-time employment.

If the work experiences have potential advantages as well as disadvantages, can anything be done to better ensure positive outcomes? Since it is likely that students will continue to work for pay as long as jobs are open to them, perhaps nurse educators would be well advised to think about establishing summer school courses or work-study programs along the lines outlined in Chapter 3 of this book. Such experiences would have as their goal production of cognitive confrontation so that the student could begin the very necessary process of role transformation early. Students could be encouraged and stimulated to learn and explore the bureaucratic part-task system from several perspectives. What areas does this system work most effectively in? In what areas are patient care needs sacrificed to system maintenance? What alternatives could be proposed? The opportunity for guided instruction concomitant with a full-time work experience would also enable the student to begin exploration into defining situations as other members of the health care team see them. By becoming more aware of her own subcultural values (and blinders) and ways in which these differ from the people she is working with, the student lays the basis for development of interpersonal competency. By becoming more interpersonally competent within the work system, the student might well be able to

have a greater impact on patient care and improvement in the delivery of health care.

Obtaining faculty who have developed sufficient biculturalism to be able to teach a class such as that outlined above might be a problem in some schools of nursing. This leads directly to the suggestion formulated in the next section.

### Resocialization of the socialization agents

There has been little prior note in the nursing literature of the fact that nurse faculty are often in conflict or are in the position they are in because of conflict. Tenbrink however, does make this point, and the interview data from the medical center nurses consistently confirm it. Conversations with nurses in graduate programs also substantiate the fact that a number of nurse faculty are teaching because they dislike nursing practice or find it impossible to practice nursing the way they believe it should be practiced. How large is this group of faculty? Perhaps each person can assess this for herself. What has been your average length of stay in each of the jobs you have held? What was your real reason for leaving each job? Were you successful in making changes and in influencing others to give better patient care in any job you held after your first six months of employment? Are you a competent clinical practitioner? Are you equally as cognizant and competent in working with the human side of the organization? Can you give good nursing care within the real work scene or only when you have one patient to care for and considerable time in which to do it? Based on your answers to the above questions, you should get some idea as to whether or not you are one of the nurses who may profit from resocialization.

Resocialization of the socialization agents cannot be done on a "guest in the house" basis. It is difficult to accomplish constructive conflict resolution unless one places oneself in a situation wherein conflict is experienced along with all of the situational constraints that make resolution so difficult. It is probably necessary to have experience as an employee to really develop interper-

competence wherein one is functional and effective in both cultures. The process of developing biculturalism is very similar for the socialization agent and the new graduate, but it probably will be more difficult. The faculty member has already experienced some degree of tension reduction through the previous flight behavior, and the tendency to resort to that solution once again will probably be very strong. It will be worth the discomfiture in the long run, though, as faculty has the position and power to really make a significant change in the socialization process of the nurses of tomorrow.

The comments of one of the nursing students who reviewed this manuscript for me are very germane to the above implication.

A number of our instructors could not function as nurses per se, so therefore they went to graduate school and then into teaching. The problem is, students can *see* this—they know it's so, but they can't do anything about it. We can learn the facts out of the books, but it's how to get what we learn is good nursing care into practice —not just our own practice, but the practice of others we work with . . .. That the faculty don't teach us because they can't really nurse themselves. Some of our faculty don't know how to nurse at all; others can only take care of a single patient when they have lots of time.

### Working together to provide role models

A last area of general implications concerns the necessity of nursing service and nursing education working together to provide viable role models for students. The necessity of doing this has been noted so often that it is almost a truism, but one that is woefully short of being operationalized. In the context of the study reported in this book, modeling of individual nurse-patient interaction is not the issue. Many faculty members are excellent role models of this aspect of clinical nursing. It is the ability to give quality nursing care, *given the resources and constraints of the work situation*, that is the major concern. It is the ability to *influence others to give quality nursing care* that is seldom modeled for neophytes. It is my judgment that it is all but impossible for nurse faculty, even if they have resolved their work-school

subculture conflicts, to do this given *any* of the kinds of organization of faculties or services that we have today. (By this is meant whether there is the traditional separation of service and school or whether nurse faculty are responsible for both service and education.) To effect the kind of role modeling behavior referred to above, the role model must be an *integral* part of the work team, present on a more or less constant and permanent basis and at a level where she is approachable (not higher than the head nurse level, for example). Dual appointments usually result in a much higher status level, making it impossible for an individual to have *interpersonal influence* over his co-workers such as fellow staff nurses, aides, and orderlies. In high positions the status and authority influence supplant the interpersonal influence. To be the kind of role model that is needed by new graduates one must be able to model effective influence postures and techniques from a relatively low status position, since that is the position the neophyte nurse will be in. (Although dual appointments are not seen as viable for modeling the kind of behavior of concern here, this kind of organization may be desirous and effective for other reasons.)

A specific suggestion that is offered to bring about the role modeling conditions described was tried out as part of the Anticipatory Socialization program described in Chapter 3. In one particular hospital where the third-year students in the experimental classes were having a senior leadership experience, the nurse instructors and head nurses on the units met together and drew up a list of staff nurse role behaviors that were judged to represent good clinical practice and effective influence behavior. These included specifics such as:

1. Plans the nursing care plan *with the patient.*
2. Gives evidence in her nursing practice and in verbal comments made in staff meetings that she is reading current professional journals or books.
3. Is able to influence aides, orderlies, and other nurses for whom she is re-

sponsible to give a higher level of care than they would ordinarily give.

4. Plans comprehensive patient care as evidenced by notations made on the nursing care plan and followup referrals.
5. Is frequently seen to approach physicians and other members of the health care team to communicate or develop joint plans of care with them.

On the basis of such behaviors (that were communicated to all staff nurses in the hospital), a role model nurse was chosen for each student nurse. (Only one student was assigned to each ward.) The role model nurse and her student worked together in a buddy fashion. At first the student worked as a team member and the model as the team leader. Later the roles were reversed when both student and model determined the student was ready. The role model was responsible for the student and worked when she did. Students worked three days per week, but could schedule themselves for almost any day or shift that they wished. Most of them chose to work some evenings, nights, and weekends, but of course much fewer than would ordinarily fall to the staff nurse role model during her usual rotation. While a nurse acted as a role model she worked a full 40-hour week but was excused from the usual rotation pattern. Therefore this assignment had built-in rewards and was sought after by many of the staff nurses. The system also had the very desirable side effect of markedly raising the quality of care on the whole unit as well as the main effect of providing for students role models who were putting professional ideals into practice in the reality work setting.

Although this plan was developed for student nurses, there is no reason why it would not work equally as well for the orientation of new staff nurses, particularly new graduate nurses in their first job. The only problem in setting it up is finding role models. In the above described program it was necessary to settle for fewer of the desired behaviors in the beginning, but then gradually increasing the expectations of the role models. Eleven of the senior student nurses who had had this experience remained at the same

hospital after graduation and ultimately became role models for other student nurses and new graduates, benefiting both the role model system and the hospital.

## SPECIFIC IMPLICATIONS AND RECOMMENDATIONS

As noted in the overview, this book was written with specific nurse populations in mind: in-service and preservice educators, nursing service personnel, undergraduate and graduate students, and new graduates. The implications of this study will now be considered for each of these populations.

### Nurse educators in preservice programs

The faculty of schools of nursing have a primary role in determining the later role transformation experiences of the new nurse. Charged with the responsibility of preparing the nurses of tomorrow, the future of the profession is in a sense in their hands. Faculty can continue to send out nurses who are ignorant of many of the realities of the work world and the behavioral strategies needed to cope with omnipresent conflict—nurses who have their professional values protected in germ-free glass jars. This will be a real deterrent to bringing about long sought improvements in health care practice. One of the primary interventions needed immediately is for nurse faculty to model growth-producing conflict resolution behavior for their students. To do this, they themselves must have had nursing practice experience in which they faced the challenge of the conflict and worked it out in a constructive way.

Many nurse education programs are in a state of constant change and revision. Sometimes it appears that inordinate amounts of faculty time are spent in meetings concerned with curriculum development and revision. Most nurse education programs cannot be faulted for failure to self-study and consider changes in curricula. Quite the opposite often prevails; that is, programs and curricula are changed too rapidly without adequate and specific evaluation programs or without sufficient evaluative input from the graduates of the program or from their employers. The

Anticipatory Socialization program described in this book has had just such an extensive evaluative study and was found to be effective for the purposes for which it was designed. The questions for nurse educators to consider now are: Is an Anticipatory Socialization program needed in your nursing curricula? Do all students need it? How can the need for such a program be determined? What skills and abilities are nurses going to need to function both in the present and in the health care adhocracy of the future? How can faculty be prepared to teach such a program?

To get answers to the above questions, it is strongly recommended that faculty in schools of nursing take periodic tappings of the products of their programs and specifically ask them: "Did you encounter any surprises when you started working?" "Were there any things for which you felt unprepared? If so, what were they?" "How do you handle difficult situations?" "What kinds of things have you been able to influence others to do to improve patient care?" Responses to questions such as these should provide information and insight into the degree to which the graduates are encountering reality shock and what they do about it. It will also tell something of the role transformation difficulties they are experiencing and the extent to which they are interpersonally competent in the work world. Armed with this information, nurse educators are then in a position to decide whether their students need an Anticipatory Socialization program and what specific elements need to be included in it.

The above kind of followup of graduates can also provide much useful information as to the prevailing normative climate of the institutions in which the nurses are working and the extent to which the differences between work and school values persist. It must be remembered that organizational systems change over time; the bureaucratic systems of today are not the same as Weber described half a century ago. The skills and abilities needed to function in a bureaucracy are not the same as those needed in an adhocracy.

Beckhard, for example, places acquisition of interpersonal competence at the very head of the list of strategies and abilities needed by people to function in organizational development structures. Educators must keep a continual tap on the work scene to keep abreast of the types of organizations that are evolving and the abilities and skills needed by nurses to function within them. Levinson particularly makes the point that the essential evaluative question that educators must ask themselves is: What personal-professional characteristics has the student developed in school that will influence her later competencies and limitations as a nurse working within a larger professional and societal framework? Any socialization system must try to prepare its members for future roles in new sociocultural contexts. It must take into account the character of the future roles in assessing the effects of socialization. From this perspective, study of the graduates of a socializing system is a necessary complement to study of the socialization process.

Another factor that preservice educators might wish to consider is informing and discussing with nursing students the reality shock process they are likely to encounter upon graduation. Even if it is decided that the complete Anticipatory Socialization program is not needed in a particular program, this aspect probably has universal relevance. Knowing in advance what is likely to happen and that there is a high probability that it will happen to everyone, that "it's not just me who's crazy, mixed up, and frustrated," does much to help the neophyte cope with reality shock conflict.

Some students may begin to encounter some shock and moral outrage while still in school. It would be desirable to help them begin role transformation early. Faculty can do this by creating opportunities for students to face the reality scene unbuffered, even if it is painful. Buffering the student from reality, or attempting to deal with moral outrage with placating statements, such as "That's not the way it's supposed to be done" or "There's no excuse for poor or sloppy nursing care," tends to add more "shoulds" to a bag that is already too full. By encouraging the student to accept the fact that this is the way it is *now*, energy and attention can be freed for the larger goal of helping the student develop some specific influence behaviors that will be useful in bringing the reality situation closer to the shoulds. Faculty would do well to help the student work on marginal values first, to work on discrete problems of manageable size before taking on the universe of problems. Students need to learn how to define the situation as other persons in the work setting see it and then within the other person's definition of the situation to map out potential lines of action to exert the influence desired.

It is strongly recommended to preservice educators that the issues around manual-technical skills be discussed openly and honestly with students. This whole issue needs to be placed in proper perspective; manual skills are a basic resource needed by nurses. The necessity and demand for nurses to have beginning competence in basic manual-technical skills is a reality and will undoubtedly remain so. To give continuous and comprehensive patient care—whether it be to a patient in a hospital bed, in a clinic, or in a home—demands that the nurse be a whole nurse, equipped not only with interpersonal communication and interpretive skills but also with action skills. Granted that the former are more theoretically based, allow for more judgment and autonomy in their execution, and take longer to acquire, manual skills do not lose their relevance or importance because of lack of some of these features. Failure to recognize their importance as one essential component of the nurse's armamentarium tends to saddle new graduates with attitudinal baggage that markedly impairs their ability to learn skills and raises the energy requirements for doing so.

*Graduate students and graduate nurse educators.* Increasingly, graduate nurse programs fit the appellation preservice education programs because of the nonexistence or dearth of experience that graduate students have between baccalaureate graduation and entrance into a Master's degree program. Perhaps it is time for graduate nurse educators to rethink the decision made several years ago to drop the experience requirement for students who enter graduate programs. It is generally understood that this was done because of the tremendous lack of nurses prepared at the Master's level who could fill the many vacancies both in schools of nursing and in departments of nursing service. But the question must be asked: Are we improving the situation by staffing schools of nursing with faculty who have had little or no work experience—faculty who have not constructively managed the conflict between school-work values and who in turn teach the nurses of tomorrow maladaptive ways of dealing with the conflict they are bound to encounter? It is not the quantity of experience but the amount of interpersonal competence that was developed and used during the work experience that is germane to the issue here. The question must also be posed as to whether or not the faculty staffing graduate programs in nursing have themselves developed sufficient biculturalism to enable them to motivate, guide, and direct the young, inexperienced, frustrated graduate students who increasingly constitute the enrollment in graduate programs.

### Educators in in-service settings

Educators in the in-service setting are the formal socializing agents of the work scene; they are usually the first representatives of the work system that the neophyte encounters. To them is entrusted the responsibility of explaining and interpreting the system—not only in terms of orienting new nurses to the various departments and how the equipment works but, more important, in helping the neophyte develop effective interpersonal strategies so that she can nurse within the system and be a positive influence for betterment of patient care. To do this it is necessary for in-service educators to be able to define the bureaucratic system in a context that the new graduate will understand. The in-service educator must be able to define the situation not only as it is viewed by the administration, but also as the head nurse and older staff members view it and also through the very different eyes of the new graduate. She herself must be very highly interpersonally competent. Her change goal is not to make patient care changes for herself, but to influence, motivate, and help others to initiate changes that will improve care.

For some time to come, in-service educators may have to take over and familiarize the new graduate with information she perhaps should have learned in school. (It will take awhile for the assessment of the need for implementation of Anticipatory Socialization programs into the curricula of nursing schools; the curricula of in-service departments are usually more quickly responsive to current needs and development than are the more formalized preservice curricula.) A staff development program focused upon the phases and process of new graduate socialization, as detailed in Chapter 5, should be of inestimable value to both the new graduates and experienced nurses. Such a program might include the following objectives:

1. Acquaint all new graduate nurses with the socialization cycle and the underlying theoretical perspectives.
2. Help them to establish clear-cut socialization goals for themselves.
3. Utilize socialization methods that are appropriate to achieving socialization goals.
4. Develop an awareness and sensitivity to the blind spots and distorted perceptions likely to occur during the moral outrage phase. Learn ways of helping the neophyte deal with her feelings of victimization so that she can move from this closed, threatened position into an open, growing stance.
5. Upgrade the quality of role performance of the socialization agents. Develop role models who portray growth-producing conflict resolution behavior.
6. Develop skills of reactive compromise and the attitudinal perspective that adjustment does not mean enforced abdication of prior values.

In-service educators and head nurses, the two primary formal socialization agents of the work setting, need to work together on the problem of reality shock and its effect on nurses. There are two specific areas in which the in-service educator might well take the initiative to develop assessment and planning programs. First, the head nurse has her own needs. She needs to become knowledgeable of the postgraduation socialization process, the signs and symptoms of the various stages of reality shock. Most important, she needs to learn her own reactions to the conflict experienced by young graduates and ways in which she might constructively manage her feelings and the situation. Since many young nurses in the throes of moral outrage and rejection are not particularly attractive, reaction of the staff to them might be much the same as many nurses' reactions to the dying patient—ignore them. Many head nurses have expressed to me that they are literally stymied by the reactions and behaviors of recent graduates: "They're a whole new breed of cats!" "It's been so long since I was a new graduate that I have no idea of what they're going through and how to help them." "I know I feel defensive, and I don't really understand why." In statements such as these, head nurses are asking for help; they are expressing their willingness to listen and to try and understand at least some of the value system that most new graduates bring with them to the job.

A second area in which it is vital that in-service educators and head nurses work together is in the development of a program of action to help all staff nurses manage conflict in the most constructive and growth-producing way they can. Although the study and this book have focused almost exclusively on new graduates, there are many other nurses who are still in the throes of reality shock or who have elected a less than constructive mode of conflict resolution. It is a real challenge to help nurses who have already settled upon some mode of conflict resolution that is maladaptive for self or the system, for example, the job-hopper or the nurse who has decided to go native. The latter has chosen to give up rather than fight—to do that which is most highly valued by the organization. Intervening with her at this point is extremely difficult; there has already been some reinforcement and corresponding tension reduction for the instituted behavior: "She's a great nurse; you can count on her to get the job done. When Sue's on duty, you know that all the treatments will get done." But difficult does not mean impossible. What in-service educators and head nurses must realize is that often going native or getting into a rut as a way of resolving conflict in values leaves covert and buried a considerable amount of tension, anxiety, and resentment. The problems do not stay solved; there is always a newcomer who painfully reminds the nurse that there is more to nursing than dusting and polishing patients and passing medications. This is the vulnerable spot for the "natives" and the "rutters." A wise socialization agent can help nurses like these rethink their conflict resolution by reawakening and challenging them to make their professional values operative. This group has strength in that they generally know the system well and are thoroughly acquainted with the work subculture: "Help us think this through, Martha; you know the routines and hospital policies well. How do you think we could manage things so that patients can really participate in making out their own care plans so that if they prefer to be bathed in the evening before they go to sleep this can be done?"

It can be seen that the in-service educator is really in a pivotal position in respect to abatement of reality shock and design of programs to help ensure more constructive conflict resolution. In addition to the suggestions made above, one final and important goal is the inception of planned action to help both head nurses and new graduates identify the front- and backstage realities of the work scene. The backstage values are really the predominant ones. The newcomer must be aided and motivated to identify these so that she can interpret her goals within the new value context. Head nurses would gain from an understanding of the predominant school-bred values that most new graduates bring with them so that they can assist the newcomers in operationalizing some of these values. In this way in-service educators will be highly instrumental and will gain tremendous job satisfaction in seeing all nurses on a unit being able to make positive and constructive improvements in the total health care delivery system of the unit.

## Students and new graduate nurses

It would be well for new graduates to come to the work scene as well equipped as a *whole* nurse as they possibly can be with beginning competence in interpersonal, organizational, and manual-technical skills. It is important to view oneself as being prepared for both the Positive Now and the Relative When. The time to start this preparation is during school. Students and new graduates alike must be active and selective in making self-socialization efforts and in taking the self-socialization initiative. By availing herself of every possible opportunity and creating opportunities for herself to learn what she needs to know, the neophyte stands a much better chance of making a satisfactory role transformation than the student who just tries to get through. One new graduate I interviewed reported to me that she managed to get through school while avoiding as much as possible all physical care of patients or the care of more than one patient at a time. She had chosen psychiatric settings for all of her electives and stated that she firmly believed her instructors when they said that "professional nurses do not need to know physical skills" and "you'll learn what skills you need to know after you graduate." This young nurse spent nine months working in a psychiatric hospital and was dismayed when she found that she was expected to give physical care to patients there. Subsequently, she decided that perhaps public health nursing was her niche, but was chagrinned to find that the agency that employed her also gave home health care. In absolute disgust and frustration, she dropped out of nursing nineteen months (with a total of five jobs) after graduation.

Awareness is half of the battle. Making an attempt to learn what the process of post-graduation socialization is likely to be, what some of the feelings and experiences are that new graduates are likely to have, and the reactions that might occur will not lessen the need for role transformation, but it will allow the neophyte to view this difficult transition period from a much less distorted perspective.

It would be well for students and new graduates to learn to accept emotionally the reality of the organization's human side. Many neophytes find that not only are their rational ideals upset but they are also becoming emotionally involved in a way that they did not anticipate. The new nurse soon learns that coming up with a rational, technical solution to a problem is not enough. One business school graduate, experiencing the same kind of reality shock that is prevalent in nurses, put it this way: "I thought I could sell people with logic and was amazed at the hidden agendas people have—irrational objections; really bright people will come up with stupid excuses . . . they have their own little empires to worry about." Many new graduates attempt to handle this situation, not by working in and around the human organization but by attempting to ignore or make the human side of the organization go away. By resisting at an emotional level the legitimacy and reality of the human aspects of the organization, the new graduate is expressing a strong wish to exist in a world that by her definition is totally rational. This is simply not the case, and ignoring the problem will not dissolve it. The degree to which the graduate is able to accept the human organization at the emotional level will be directly related to his potential success and happiness in it. Those who resist accepting this reality tend to use up their energy in denial and complaint rather than in problem-solving.

One of the primary requisites for making a relatively smooth transition from the school to the work setting is self-confidence in one's ability to learn and in one's resources. This does not mean overconfidence, bragging, or a know-it-all attitude, but faith in oneself and in one's ability to think things through under pressure of time, such faith being grounded on at least some experience. New graduates should not be expected to know everything, but it is realistic that they should come to the work scene schooled and practiced in basic interpersonal, organizational, manual, and communication skills. This will not guarantee a smooth transition but, if along with these fundamental learnings the new graduate also has a reasonable self-confidence and the necessary wisdom to seek out support and help at crucial junctures, there is a good chance the road will be smoother.

One of the best suggestions for constructive conflict management comes from the literature on culture shock. If a newcomer is going to relate meaningfully to people with whom he works, he must understand their feelings about things. Instead of brushing off the cultural jolts and turning away, the neophyte would do well to view the work subculture not through his background but in full context of the local life. In the process of receiving and managing the expected cultural jolts, the new graduate will probably need to learn how to withhold strong negative criticism for a time until he is able to see things in perspective. This is somewhat difficult because in many ways it is contrary to the former school teaching or to the norms of today's youth culture, which dictates: "Tell it as it is." "Let it all hang out." Early impressions and snap judgments are often not how it is. Restraint in the beginning will frequently pay off as dividends later on when the nurse attempts to exert influence.

Typically, work socialization agents such as head nurses, staff nurses, and in-service educators get very little feedback from young graduates as to the relative success of their socialization efforts. For the most part, these socialization agents lack standards and criteria upon which to judge the effectiveness of their efforts. By providing them with concurrent feedback, new graduates can do much to help them in developing viable criteria and standards.

### Head nurses and staff nurses

We tend to think that only the new graduate has an adjustment problem, but the receiving subculture—the employed nursing staff—is often faced with almost insurmountable difficulties as a result of these new cultural contacts. There are several major factors that people in the receiving subculture have in their favor, however: they are on home ground, they hold the power, and they have the support of their countrymen. They can much better afford to be generous, to reach out, to take risks, and to help the newcomer make a satisfactory bicultural adjustment.

The nurses in the receiving subculture would do well to learn to recognize the process and symptoms of reality shock. In this way they can plan their interventions so that they are appropriate and timely. For example, during the moral outrage phase the new graduate is most in need of the influence of more experienced staff members. Unfortunately, she is not particularly pliable, receptive, or vulnerable to influence at this time. She is often too evangelistic, angry, and busy emitting her own message to listen to others. Her self-esteem is already threatened, so the influence during this high priority intervention time must be low geared and nonthreatening. Support is necessary and beneficial to some degree, but if given in excess it is often perceived as patronizing. Perhaps one of the kindest and most helpful interventions is to structure opportunities for the neophyte to discharge her moral outrage without creating havoc to be repaired later or without exposing her vulnerability and defense mechanisms to those with whom she later must work.

Although the nurses in the receiving subculture tend to be much more secure, they should recognize one very critical fact. Without the constant input and contamination of the work subculture with the avant-garde ideas and values of the newcomer, any nurse in the work subculture who has attained a bicultural stance is in grave danger of losing it. A bicultural perspective cannot be maintained without constant stimulation from the school value system. If conflict is welcomed and cherished as an avenue for growth, improvements in patient care and in staff morale and competence cannot help but result. Perhaps it would be well for each staff and head nurse to attempt to implement at least one suggestion for improvement in patient care for each new graduate being trained. By asking oneself questions such as "Are all these routines and procedures really necessary?" "Is it not possible for different nurses to do things differ-

ently?" "Must all patients receive care on the same schedule?" it might be possible to set a climate wherein deviance and risk-taking are not only permitted but encouraged. Often nurses will hesitate to innovate new types of practices because they assume that their deviance will be negatively evaluated by their peers.

It is helpful to realize that persons suffering from reality shock feel weak in the face of conditions that appear insuperable.

. . . it is natural for them to try to lean heavily on their compatriots. They may be irritating to the long-term resident but he should be patient, sympathetic, and understanding. Although talking does not remove pain . . . a great deal is gained by having the source of pain explained, some of the steps towards a cure indicated, and the assurance given that time, the great healer, will soon set things right.[*]

### Supervisors and nursing administrators

The results of this study provide many relevant questions about the climate in the institution and the potential effect this climate has on nurses and their nursing care. How long do new graduates usually stay? Are lateral transfers available for the new graduate who has had a particularly difficult adjustment period and who has alienated her co-workers? What are the incidents, procedures, policies, and personal interactions that tend to cause moral outrage and anger? These should provide clues as to the areas of greatest deviance between school and work values. Once these are recognized it is possible to either change them or to make a rational and deliberative decision that the status quo is better for patient care. In the latter event, the helpful activity is to anticipate the need to explain these kinds of policies or procedures to new graduates before they raise cries of protest and moral outrage.

Other questions raised are: Are there some goals that the new graduate brings with her that would be well to foster and nurture?

---

[*]Oberg, K.: Cultural shock adjustment to new cultural environments, Practical Anthropology 7(4):177-182, 1960.

Does the formal sanction and reward system of the organization reward professional clinical performance, or does it reward primarily system maintenance and adherence to established policies and procedures? Are there ways of providing feedback for problem-oriented, goal-oriented patient care? Attention to these kinds of questions, as well as to the highly personal question—What kind of questions do you most often ask those who are accountable to you?—will do much to acquaint nursing administrators with the dominant goals, values, and reward system of the organization as well as of the individual.

There are a number of questions that could be used to focus a series of self-study projects that would be highly instrumental in promoting both the growth and health of the organization as well as the retention and effectiveness of the nurses working within it. Are there some units in the organization that have higher new graduate turnover than others? If so, what factors appear to be related to this? Are new graduates still enthusiastic about nursing after one year of service in your institution? What kind of an impact are they making on patient care? If they are not making an impact, why not? What are the identifiable system constraints and contingencies? Can some of these be removed so that the new graduate can operationalize her values within the institution? What are the compromises that staff nurses in your organization have to make in delivering patient care that they feel bad about?

Systematic investigation of questions such as the above should do much to abate the problems of unhappiness and exodus occasioned by maladaptive solutions to the conflict between school and work values. In the end, nursing administrators who have the heavy responsibility of providing adequate numbers of qualified nurses to provide the care that patients need will not only have sufficient numbers to work with, but also will have stimulated, challenged, and motivated nurses who are able to give top quality nursing care because the climate and conditions that are so necessary have been created.

## Future research

In-depth study of the three- to six-month socialization period, longitudinal studies of nurses representing each of the four subgroups described in Chapter 3, and study of the relationship between length of nursing practice and development of interpersonal competence are a few suggestions for future research study in the area of reality shock that have been mentioned. There is one other research area that needs to be elaborated here. Through the use of instruments such as the Professional Index that was developed in this study some on-going repeated measure of the relative professional health of nursing could be obtained. By a comparison of representative cohorts of nurses on a yearly or biyearly basis on behaviors such as activity in professional organizations, regular professional reading, speeches, articles written, and so forth, it should be possible to make a fairly accurate assessment of the degree of movement of the nursing profession toward self-actualization as a professional group. At present, a comparison of current scores of nurses on some of the above variables with other professional groups indicates that nurses do not behave as though they have loyalty to a discipline that transcends a particular location or employing organization. Perhaps periodic assessment of progress toward this goal would be an additional external stimulus to some nurses to do something about this behavior.

Scott and Scott note that "Just because an individual is used as a source of data is no reason that the data must describe his own characteristics rather than the characteristics of some external system to which he is responding." By periodically asking nurses to provide data about themselves, the characteristics of the external system in which nursing is enmeshed and to which nurses respond could also be inferred.

## SUMMARY

A number of implications and recommendations, both general and specific to particular groups of nurses, have been discussed. It is hoped that they will be understood, welcomed, and acted upon by nurses so that the one goal that unifies us all—improvement both in individual patient care and in the health care delivery system—might be achieved. Reality shock is real. It will not go away by ignoring it. It will continue to take its toll, both in terms of personal loss and in the loss that nurses who leave might have made toward achievement of our common goal. Reality shock has not been extensively studied before nor studied in an organized manner. Second-culture learning is not something that can be accomplished in school, although the school can do much to begin the role transformation and to motivate the student to develop the tools useful in adapting to and learning new subcultures. The fundamental obstacle in adapting to a new subculture is failure to see any purpose in doing so. Faculty can do much to clarify this. Both preservice and in-service educators can aid the new graduate considerably by becoming bicultural themselves. In this way students will have viable role models who demonstrate both interpersonal competence and constructive conflict resolution. Then perhaps the nurses of tomorrow will be able to make the fundamental improvements in patient care that have long been expected of them. Most of all, to the new graduates and the nursing students of today goes this message: Reality shock "is not to be valued for its own sake. Its value lies in the liberation and understanding that can come from such an experience."°

## REFERENCES

Beckhard, R.: Organization development; strategies and models, Menlo Park, Calif., 1969, Addison-Wesley Publishing Co., Inc.

Bock, P. K., editor: Culture shock, New York, 1970, Alfred A. Knopf, Inc.

Hogan, C.: Registered nurses' completion of a Bachelor of Science degree in nursing; its effects on their attitude toward the nursing profession, unpublished doctoral dissertation, St. Louis, 1972, St. Louis University.

Kramer, M.: Some effects of exposure to employing Bureaucracies on the role conceptions and role deprivation of neophyte collegiate nurses, unpublished doctoral dissertation, 1966, Stanford University.

Kramer, M., McDonnell, C., and Reed, J. L.: Self-actualization and role adaptation of baccalaureate degree nurses, Nurs. Research **21**(2):111-123, 1972.

Levinson, D.: Medical education and the theory of adult socialization, J. Health Soc. Behav. **8:**253-265, December 1967.

Oberg, K.: Cultural shock adjustment to new cultural environments, Practical Anthropology **7**(4):177-182, 1960.

Schein, E. H.: The first job dilemma, Psychology Today, March 1968, pp. 28-38.

Scott, W. and Scott, R.: Values and organizations, Chicago, 1965, Rand McNally & Co., p. 130.

Tenbrink, C. L.: The process of socialization into a new role; the professional nurse, Nurs. Forum **7**(2):146-160, 1968.

---

°Bock, P. K., editor: Culture shock; a reader in modern cultural anthropology, 1970, © Alfred A. Knopf, Inc., p. xi.

# SUMMARY OF ROLE VALUE ORIENTATIONS

| Source and date | A Tradition, service- and patient-centered humanitarian | B Abstraction and synthesis of A and C | C Technique-oriented, problem-solving, scientifically based | D Disillusioned with nursing per se, oriented to employing organization |
|---|---|---|---|---|
| Habenstein and Christ[1] (1955) | *Traditionalizer:* Dedicated to ideal; focuses on nursing skills of patient-healing. Does not like to delegate tasks to auxiliaries. Values "tough tasks," higher estimation of "dirty work" than other kinds. Satisfactions come from perception of patient's improved health and expression of gratitude. The old is preferable on basis of past experience. | | *Professionalizer:* Focuses on the things that must be done to more adequately and intelligently heal the patient. Emphasis is on knowledge and application of rational faculties to experience and use of judgment. Creates appropriate therapeutic situations. Delegates freely. Satisfaction from a job well done technically. | *Utilizer:* Relatively indifferent to work tasks. Little ego or self-involvement except to meet short-run needs. Nursing does not occupy a central role in life. Accepts change for practical reasons. |
| Bressler and Kephart[2] (1955) | *High-morale group:* Wanted their daughters to follow in nursing. Inclined to be complacent and uncritical. | | *Limited-morale group:* Would prefer to see daughter in some other occupation. Inclined to find fault and make changes. | *Low-morale group:* Answered no or were undecided about going into nursing again. Disposed to find fault. |
| Reissman[3] and Rohrer (1957) | *Dedicated:* Entered nursing for positive reasons and expected to stay in it. Patient care is *the* great reward. Nothing in nursing is unsatisfying. Obeys the rules and believes they are made by people who know what they are doing. | *Converted:* Patient care is the outstanding satisfaction but it was a joy discovered after entering. Entered nursing on negative grounds but aspires to continue. Tends to blame self rather than others when things go wrong. Takes a middle course in adherence to rules. | | *Migrant:* Came into nursing for negative reasons and plans to leave. Work is just a job. Blames the institution and everyone in it when something goes wrong. Makes her way by suiting the rules to meet her own needs. *Disenchanted:* Came into nursing for positive reasons but does not wish to remain. Finds fault with other people and the institution when things go wrong. Undertakes no more responsibility for making judgments than is necessary to arrange own work schedule. |

| Source and date | A Tradition, service- and patient-centered humanitarian | B Abstraction and synthesis of A and C | C Technique-oriented, problem-solving scientifically based | D Disillusioned with nursing per se, oriented to employing organization |
|---|---|---|---|---|
| Meyer[4] (1959) | *Ministering angel:* Places highest value on undivided relationship with patient. | *Modern nurse:* Prefers to share patient with colleague but also likes individual patient care. Shows concern with psychological aspect of illness. Applies scientific as well as intuitive method to the problems of supportive emotional care and patient education. | *Efficient professional:* Efficient, disciplined professional who most values her work relationships with colleagues. Is oriented toward technical and administrative functions. | |
| Corwin[5] (1960) | *Service-oriented:* Interested in direct, humanitarian service to patients. Traditional approach. | | *Professionally oriented:* Goal-oriented. Service is marked by capacity to solve problems. Concerned with the vast and expanding body of technical knowledge. | *Bureaucratically oriented:* A servant of the organization. Hired to carry out rules and procedures. Specializes in and rewarded for skill in administration. |
| Holliday[6] (1962) | Idealistic image of nurse embodies these *expressive* traits: Tender touch, sympathetic, anticipative, empathic, cooperative, Happy, supportive. | *Ideal qualifications:* Well-trained, empathic, efficient, anticipative. | Idealistic image of nurse embodies these *functional* traits: Well-trained, punctual, instructive, efficient, neat appearance, nonspecialized, communicative, well-educated. | |

[1]Habenstein, R. W., and Christ, E. A.: Professionalizer, traditionalizer and utilizer, Columbia, Mo., 1955, University of Missouri.
[2]Bressler, M., and Kephart, W. M.: Career dynamics, Philadelphia, 1955, Pennsylvania Nurses' Association.
[3]Reissman, L., and Rohrer, J. H.: Change and dilemma in the nursing profession, New York, 1957, G. P. Putnam's Sons.
[4]Meyer, G.: Conflict and harmony in nursing values, Nurs. Outlook 7:389-399, July 1959. Meyer's transition type is not included, as it was numerically very small; if included, it would fall between the modern nurse and the efficient professional.
[5]Corwin, Role conception and mobility aspiration, op. cit.
[6]Holliday, J.: Ideal traits of the professional nurse described by graduate students in education and in nursing, J. Educational research 57:245-249, January 1964.

# COMPARISON OF VARIOUS GROUPS OF NURSES ON CORWIN ROLE CONCEPTION AND ROLE DEPRIVATION SCALES

| | Bureaucratic role conception | | Professional role conception | | Service role conception | | Total role deprivation | | Date of administration | No. |
|---|---|---|---|---|---|---|---|---|---|---|
| | X | SD | X | SD | X | SD | X | SD | | |
| Diploma nurses | 21.63 | 3.29 | 26.71 | 5.80 | 26.74 | 3.83 | 9.94 | 3.23 | 1968 | 147 |
| Diploma students | 21.88 | 3.04 | 28.44 | 3.82 | 28.30 | 1.03 | 9.86 | 2.99 | 1960 | 48 |
| Degree nurses | 21.09 | 2.78 | 28.08 | 5.65 | 25.35 | 11.89 | 14.92 | 3.90 | 1960 | 22 |
| Degree students | 19.63 | 3.51 | 27.21 | 1.20 | 28.42 | 3.97 | 11.57 | 3.93 | 1960 | 19 |
| Degree nurses at graduation | 17.94 | 2.02 | 31.18 | 3.06 | 27.96 | 2.95 | 26.00 | 6.99 | 1965 | 50 |
| Degree nurses 3 months after starting work | 20.60 | 2.14 | 31.06 | 3.05 | 28.68 | 2.55 | 28.76 | 10.11 | 1965 | 50 |
| Degree nurses 6 months after starting work | 21.04 | 1.95 | 30.28 | 3.27 | 27.85 | 3.33 | 24.69 | 12.13 | 1965 | 47 |
| "Highly successful" degree nurses ($T_1$) | 18.76 | 2.21 | 30.75 | 3.05 | 24.47 | 2.88 | 20.94 | 7.65 | 1968 | 74 |
| "Average successful" degree nurses ($T_1$) | 18.64 | 2.64 | 28.03 | 2.60 | 26.57 | 3.40 | 18.71 | 7.40 | 1968 | 74 |
| "Less successful" degree nurses ($T_1$) | 16.24 | 3.62 | 30.69 | 3.82 | 27.85 | 3.68 | 27.74 | 9.77 | 1968 | 72 |
| Total medical center nurses ($T_1$) | 17.93 | 3.09 | 29.78 | 3.41 | 27.31 | 3.33 | 21.42 | 8.65 | 1968 | 220 |
| Nursing supervisors (from one Midwest center) | 23.60 | 1.77 | 24.75 | 4.28 | 29.05 | 5.07 | 26.10 | 5.26 | 1965 | 20 |
| Collegiate nurse faculty | 14.55 | 2.50 | 34.65 | 3.81 | 25.45 | 4.10 | 40.55 | 15.99 | 1965 | 20 |
| Master's students during first week of program | 14.30 | 2.45 | 30.98 | 3.15 | 29.16 | 2.99 | 30.32 | 11.55 | 1969 | 53 |

| | Bureaucratic role conception | | Professional role conception | | Service role conception | | Total role deprivation | | Date of administration | No. |
|---|---|---|---|---|---|---|---|---|---|---|
| | X | SD | X | SD | X | SD | X | SD | | |
| Master's students during first week of program | 14.23 | 2.41 | 31.05 | 3.19 | 29.23 | 3.03 | 30.58 | 11.68 | 1970 | 51 |
| Nursing supervisors (from medical center hospitals) | 19.30 | 2.57 | 27.63 | 2.66 | 25.83 | 3.31 | 18.00 | 8.46 | 1968-1969 | 66 |
| DNS (from medical center hospitals) | 15.26 | 2.84 | 30.32 | 3.58 | 28.42 | 2.83 | 21.95 | 9.36 | 1968-1969 | 38 |
| HB-HP degree nurses $(T_3)$ | 19.85 | 1.42 | 32.61 | 1.97 | 28.34 | 2.64 | 31.36 | 11.11 | 1970 | 41 |
| HB-LP degree nurses $(T_3)$ | 20.37 | 1.78 | 26.65 | 2.67 | 26.08 | 3.13 | 17.49 | 6.09 | 1970 | 75 |
| LB-HP degree nurses $(T_3)$ | 15.05 | 2.06 | 32.95 | 2.02 | 29.10 | 2.81 | 31.58 | 8.36 | 1970 | 41 |
| LB-LP degree nurses $(T_3)$ | 15.69 | 1.74 | 26.94 | 1.96 | 27.52 | 3.13 | 18.65 | 5.39 | 1970 | 52 |
| "Highly successful" degree nurses two years later $(T_3)$ | 18.94 | 2.46 | 29.91 | 3.76 | 27.57 | 3.08 | 23.54 | 10.04 | 1970 | 92 |
| "Average successful" degree nurses two years later $(T_3)$ | 18.25 | 3.05 | 28.17 | 3.26 | 27.30 | 3.35 | 21.51 | 9.02 | 1970 | 76 |
| "Less successful" degree nurses two years later $(T_3)$ | 15.73 | 2.68 | 29.14 | 3.94 | 27.56 | 3.12 | 25.90 | 11.49 | 1970 | 41 |
| Total medical center nurses $(T_3)$ | 18.06 | 2.97 | 29.12 | 3.69 | 27.47 | 3.18 | 23.26 | 10.07 | 1970 | 209 |

# DATA ANALYSIS TABLES

**Table C-1.** Significance of difference in means on stated variables at entrance into program for Classes of 1968, 1969, and 1970

| Qualifying variables | Class of 1968 | | Class of 1969 | | Class of 1970 | | (F) | Scheffé |
|---|---|---|---|---|---|---|---|---|
| | X | SD | X | SD | X | SD | | |
| SCAT | | | | | | | | |
|   Verbal | 48.07 | 5.94 | 48.79 | 5.97 | 47.56 | 7.41 | .52 | |
|   Quantitative | 41.47 | 5.23 | 42.14 | 4.92 | 40.10 | 5.19 | 2.40 | |
|   Total | 90.87 | 13.44 | 90.93 | 8.18 | 87.66 | 10.07 | 1.76 | |
| BPS Scores | | | | | | | | |
|   Bureaucratic | 19.07 | 2.37 | 19.42 | 2.86 | 18.93 | 3.08 | .46 | |
|   Professional | 27.24 | 3.05 | 25.88 | 4.08 | 26.54 | 4.18 | 1.59 | |
|   Service | 28.07 | 2.95 | 27.37 | 3.00 | 24.98 | 4.36 | 11.26° | 2.734 ± .98 |
| GPA | 2.76 | .39 | 2.83 | .37 | 2.75 | .37 | .73 | |
| Number of semester units at entrance | 67.73 | 10.35 | 68.84 | 11.76 | 69.32 | 13.61 | .22 | |

°Significant at .01 level for df 2,150.

**Table C-2.** Significance of differences in interclass comparisons on mean role conceptions and role deprivation scores at stated time intervals

| Scales | Class of 1967 (N = 50) | | Class of 1968 (N = 45) | | Class of 1969 (N = 57) | | Class of 1970 (N = 59) | | Class of 1971 (N = 63) | | Scheffé |
|---|---|---|---|---|---|---|---|---|---|---|---|
| | X | SD | X | SD | X | SD | X | SD | X | SD | |
| Entrance ($T_1$) | | | | | | | | | | | |
| BRC | | | 19.07 | 2.37 | 19.42 | 2.86 | 18.93 | 3.08 | | | |
| PRC | | | 27.24 | 3.05 | 25.88 | 4.08 | 26.54 | 4.18 | | | |
| SRC | | | 28.07 | 2.95 | 27.37 | 3.00 | 24.98 | 4.36 | | | ° |
| Midway ($T_3$) | | | | | | | | | | | |
| BRC | | | 16.20 | 3.28 | 17.19 | 2.99 | 17.70 | 3.06 | | | |
| PRC | | | 30.24 | 3.94 | 30.32 | 3.59 | 30.24 | 3.46 | | | |
| SRC | | | 28.04 | 3.15 | 27.54 | 2.87 | 27.54 | 2.70 | | | |
| BRD | | | 5.67 | 2.42 | 6.77 | 3.83 | 6.90 | 2.74 | | | |
| PRD | | | 9.09 | 2.89 | 10.40 | 3.99 | 9.68 | 3.26 | | | |
| SRD | | | 7.93 | 3.60 | 9.47 | 4.98 | 9.66 | 4.00 | | | |
| TRD | | | 22.69 | 5.92 | 26.65 | 10.52 | 26.22 | 7.91 | | | † |
| Graduation ($T_4$) | | | | | | | | | | | |
| BRC | 15.44 | 2.50 | 15.93 | 2.60 | 17.79 | 4.71 | 17.39 | 2.95 | 14.06 | 3.04 | ‡ |
| PRC | 30.03 | 4.30 | 30.29 | 3.57 | 30.11 | 3.17 | 31.13 | 3.72 | 29.77 | 3.64 | |
| SRC | 28.18 | 2.85 | 28.53 | 2.55 | 28.48 | 2.49 | 29.12 | 2.88 | 28.81 | 2.63 | |
| BRD | 6.29 | 3.61 | 5.84 | 2.94 | 6.53 | 3.48 | 7.30 | 3.59 | 7.85 | 3.64 | |
| PRD | 10.40 | 4.85 | 9.18 | 2.90 | 10.11 | 4.71 | 11.85 | 4.69 | 8.02 | 3.88 | ‡ |
| SRD | 8.62 | 4.72 | 8.58 | 4.10 | 9.65 | 4.81 | 10.03 | 4.42 | 7.53 | 3.80 | |
| TRD | 25.33 | 11.05 | 23.65 | 7.00 | 26.28 | 10.86 | 29.03 | 10.13 | 23.40 | 6.72 | ‡ |

Interclass comparisons: F ratios significant at greater than .05 level were obtained as follows: $T_1$ SRC = 11.26; $T_3$ TRD = 3.19; $T_4$ BRC = 3.60; PRD = 5.33; TRD = 4.02. Degrees of freedom for significance of F ratio is 2,160 for three-class comparison, 4,273 for five classes. Confidence level for the Scheffé was set at the .05 level.

°Scheffé based on comparing mean of Class of 1970 with combined means of Class of 1968 and Class of 1969 was significant.

†Scheffé based on comparing mean of Class of 1968 with combined means of Class of 1969 and Class of 1970 was significant.

‡Scheffé based on comparing combined means of Classes 1969 and 1970 with Classes of 1967, 1968, and 1971 was significant. Other interclass comparisons were also significant.

**Table C-3.** Significance of differences among faculty teaching the classes of 1968, 1969, and 1970

|  | Sum of squares | df | Mean square | F ratio |
|---|---|---|---|---|
| Bureaucratic role conception |  |  |  |  |
| Between groups | 7.5603 | 2 | 3.7801 | 0.4845 |
| Among groups | 717.7439 | 92 | 7.8016 |  |
| Total | 725.3040 | 94 |  |  |
| Professional role conception |  |  |  |  |
| Between groups | 4.4286 | 2 | 2.2143 | 0.2837 |
| Among groups | 718.0964 | 92 | 7.8054 |  |
| Total | 722.5249 | 94 |  |  |
| Service role conception |  |  |  |  |
| Between groups | 2.2047 | 2 | 1.1023 | 0.1922 |
| Among groups | 527.5840 | 92 | 5.7346 |  |
| Total | 529.7886 | 94 |  |  |
| Total role deprivation |  |  |  |  |
| Between groups | 17.4358 | 2 | 8.7179 | 0.1575 |
| Among groups | 5091.3516 | 92 | 55.3408 |  |
| Total | 5108.7852 | 94 |  |  |

**Table C-4.** Significance of differences in graduation GPA and state board scores for nurses in the Classes of 1968, 1969, and 1970

| Sources of variability | Sum of square | df | Mean square | F ratio | Scheffé |
|---|---|---|---|---|---|
| Medical state board exam |  |  |  |  |  |
| Between groups | 36570.39 | 2 | 18285.20 | 2.8029 |  |
| Within groups | 1024230.38 | 157° | 6523.76 |  |  |
| Total | 1060800.77 | 159 |  |  |  |
| Surgical state board exam |  |  |  |  |  |
| Between groups | 2796.53 | 2 | 1398.27 | 0.2412 |  |
| Within groups | 910232.00 | 157 | 5797.65 |  |  |
| Total | 913028.53 | 159 |  |  |  |
| Psychiatric state board exam |  |  |  |  |  |
| Between groups | 20906.56 | 2 | 10453.28 | 2.4049 |  |
| Within groups | 682434.50 | 157 | 4346.71 |  |  |
| Total | 703341.06 | 159 |  |  |  |
| Pediatrics state board exam |  |  |  |  |  |
| Between groups | 7861.69 | 2 | 3930.85 | 0.6568 |  |
| Within groups | 939568.13 | 157 | 5984.51 |  |  |
| Total | 947429.82 | 159 |  |  |  |
| Obstetrics state board exam |  |  |  |  |  |
| Between groups | 19414.14 | 2 | 9797.07 | 1.6826 |  |
| Within groups | 905752.81 | 157 | 5769.13 |  |  |
| Total | 925166.95 | 159 |  |  |  |
| Cumulative GPA at graduation |  |  |  |  |  |
| Between groups | 5836.33 | 2 | 2918.16 | 3.0924† | 15.36 ± .6414 |
| Within groups | 149096.56 | 158 | 943.65 |  |  |
| Total | 154932.88 | 160 |  |  |  |

°State board scores were not available for one student.
†Significant at greater than .05.

**Table C-5.** Significance of differences in mean role conception and role deprivation scores of students in Classes of 1968, 1969, and 1970 at entrance and at graduation: paired t tests°

| | Class of 1968 (N = 45) | | | Class of 1969 (N = 53) | | | Class of 1970 (N = 56) | | |
|---|---|---|---|---|---|---|---|---|---|
| | $M_D$ | $\sigma_{M_D}$ | t | $M_D$ | $\sigma_{M_D}$ | t | $M_D$ | $\sigma_{M_D}$ | t |
| BRC | 3.14 | .3574 | 8.78† | 1.63 | .3966 | 4.10† | 1.54 | .4156 | 3.70† |
| PRC | −3.05 | .4600 | 6.63† | −4.23 | .5658 | 7.47† | −4.59 | .5641 | 8.13† |
| SRC | −.46 | .4449 | 1.03 | −1.11 | .4160 | 2.66† | −4.14 | .5883 | 7.03† |

°Formula for paired t test: $\dfrac{M_D}{\sigma_{M_D}}$ where est $\sigma_{M_D} = \dfrac{SD}{\sqrt{N-1}}$

†Significant at .01 level.

**Table C-6.** Analysis of variance in role conception and role deprivation scores at graduation $(T_4)$ for students having varying amounts of Anticipatory Socialization program°

| | Sum of squares | df | Mean square | F ratio |
|---|---|---|---|---|
| Bureaucratic role conception | | | | |
| Between groups | 33.3050 | 2 | 16.6525 | 1.0948 |
| Within groups | 1718.8284 | | 15.2109 | |
| Professional role conception | | | | |
| Between groups | 83.1300 | 2 | 41.5650 | 3.5801† |
| Within groups | 1311.9272 | 113 | 11.6100 | |
| Service role conception | | | | |
| Between groups | 29.7328 | 2 | 14.8664 | 2.0773 |
| Within groups | 808.7034 | 113 | 7.1567 | |
| Total role deprivation | | | | |
| Between groups | 905.3872 | 2 | 452.6936 | 4.3111† |
| Within groups | 11865.7891 | 113 | 105.0070 | |

°The 116 students in the Classes of 1969 and 1970 were regrouped as follows: Group I had the curriculum only (N = 35); Group II had curriculum plus summer (N = 36); Group III had entire program (N = 45).

†Significant at .05 for df 2,150.

**Table C-7.** Number of transfers in initial job according to number of months of tenure in initial job for all classes°

| Number of months | Class of 1968 | | Class of 1969 | | Class of 1970 | | Total | |
|---|---|---|---|---|---|---|---|---|
| | NO. | PERCENT | NO. | PERCENT | NO. | PERCENT | NO. | PERCENT |
| 1-5 | 1 | 3.70 | 0 | 0.0 | 0 | 0.0 | 1 | 3.70 |
| 6-11 | 0 | 0.0 | 0 | 0.0 | 0 | 0.0 | 0 | 0.0 |
| 12-18 | 1 | 3.70 | 2 | 7.40 | 4 | 14.82 | 7 | 25.93 |
| 19-23 | 0 | 0.0 | 0 | 0.0 | 1 | 3.70 | 1 | 3.70 |
| 24 or over | 1 | 3.71 | 7 | 25.93 | 10 | 37.04 | 18 | 66.67 |
| Total | 3 | 11.11 | 9† | 33.33 | 15 | 55.56 | 27 | 100.00 |

°Class numbers used in $\chi^2$ computation were 43, 55, 59. Those nurses who had never worked were excluded. $\chi^2 = 5.97$ (p = .05, df 2, $\chi^2 = 5.99$).

†Two nurses in the Class of 1969 had two job transfers, but only the first one is entered in the table.

**Table C-8.** Significance of differences in mean integrative role behavior scores for control and experimental classes two years after graduation: ANOVA

| Integrative role behavior | SS | df | MS | F |
|---|---|---|---|---|
| Between groups | 249.1311 | 2 | 124.2656 | 8.2375° |
| Within groups | 2192.6670 | 145. | 15.1218 | |
| Total | 2441.7981 | 147 | | |

°Significant at greater than .05 level.

**Table C-9.** Number and percent of graduates of all classes according to time of return for graduate education in nursing

| Time of return for graduate education | Class of 1968 (N = 45) | | Class of 1969 (N = 57) | | Class of 1970 (N = 59) | | Total | |
|---|---|---|---|---|---|---|---|---|
| | NO. | PERCENT | NO. | PERCENT | NO. | PERCENT | NO. | PERCENT |
| Immediately—1 to 3 months' work experience | 3 | 6.66 | 8 | 14.04 | 4 | 6.78 | 15 | 27.48 |
| One year after graduation—9 to 12 months' work experience | 2 | 4.44 | 4 | 7.02 | 3 | 5.08 | 9 | 16.54 |
| Two years after graduation—18 to 24 months' work experience | 1 | 2.22 | 3 | 5.26 | 2 | 3.39 | 6 | 10.87 |
| Total | 6 | 13.33 | 15 | 26.32 | 9 | 15.25 | 30 | 54.90 |

$\chi^2$ analysis not meaningful because of small expected frequencies.

**Table C-10.** Significance of difference in Tc and I Scores for control and experimental classes two years after graduation: ANOVA

| | SS | df | MS | F |
|---|---|---|---|---|
| Time competence | | | | |
| Between groups | 472.28 | 2 | 236.14 | 2.6909° |
| Within groups | 12461.17 | 142 | 87.75 | |
| Inner directedness | | | | |
| Between groups | 1.12 | 2 | 0.56 | 0.1042° |
| Within groups | 763.81 | 142 | 5.38 | |

°Not significant.

**Table C-11.** Number and percent of nurses ill or absent from work during the past year or since employment if less than one year, by class

| Number of days | Class of 1968 (N = 39) | | Class of 1969 (N = 52) | | Class of 1970 (N = 53) | | All Classes (N = 144) | |
|---|---|---|---|---|---|---|---|---|
| | NO. | PERCENT | NO. | PERCENT | NO. | PERCENT | NO. | PERCENT |
| Very few | — | — | 5 | 9.6 | 5 | 9.4 | 10 | 6.95 |
| None | 8 | 20.6 | 1 | 1.9 | 12 | 22.6 | 21 | 14.58 |
| 1 | 4 | 10.3 | 1 | 1.9 | 3 | 5.7 | 8 | 5.56 |
| 2 | 2 | 5.1 | 4 | 7.6 | 6 | 11.3 | 12 | 8.33 |
| 3 | 3 | 7.7 | 5 | 9.6 | 5 | 9.4 | 13 | 9.03 |
| 4 | 1 | 2.6 | 7 | 13.3 | 1 | 1.9 | 9 | 6.25 |
| 5 | 4 | 10.3 | 4 | 7.6 | 2 | 3.8 | 10 | 6.95 |
| 6 | — | — | — | — | 2 | 3.8 | 2 | 1.39 |
| 7 | — | — | 3 | 5.7 | 1 | 1.9 | 4 | 2.78 |
| 8 | 2 | 5.1 | 5 | 9.6 | 1 | 1.9 | 8 | 5.56 |
| 9 | 3 | 7.7 | 3 | 5.7 | 2 | 3.8 | 8 | 5.56 |
| 10 | 1 | 2.6 | — | — | — | — | 1 | .69 |
| 11 | — | — | 1 | 1.9 | — | — | 1 | .69 |
| 12 | — | — | 2 | 3.8 | 2 | 3.8 | 4 | 2.78 |
| 13 | 1 | 2.6 | 1 | 1.9 | — | — | 2 | 1.39 |
| 14 | 1 | 2.6 | 1 | 1.9 | — | — | 2 | 1.39 |
| 16 | 2 | 5.1 | — | — | 2 | 3.8 | 4 | 2.78 |
| 17 | — | — | — | — | 1 | 1.9 | 1 | .69 |
| 19 | 1 | 2.6 | — | — | — | — | 1 | .69 |
| 21 | — | — | 1 | 1.9 | — | — | 1 | .69 |
| 36 | 1 | 2.6 | — | — | — | — | 1 | .69 |
| 41 | — | — | — | — | 1 | 1.9 | 1 | .69 |
| No answer | 5 | 12.8 | 8 | 15.2 | 7 | 13.2 | 20 | 13.88 |

**Table C-12.** Number and percent of graduates of classes of 1968, 1969, 1970 according to loyalties as perceived by immediate supervisor

| | 1968 (N = 39) | | 1969 (N = 52) | | 1970 (N = 53) | | Total | |
|---|---|---|---|---|---|---|---|---|
| | NO. | PERCENT | NO. | PERCENT | NO. | PERCENT | NO. | PERCENT |
| Primary loyalty | | | | | | | | |
| Self | 27 | 69.2 | 34 | 65.3 | 36 | 67.9 | 97 | 67.3 |
| Employing agent | 1 | 2.5 | — | — | — | — | 1 | .6 |
| Co-workers | 1 | 2.5 | 6 | 11.5 | — | — | 7 | 4.8 |
| Patients | 7 | 17.9 | 12 | 23.0 | 14 | 26.4 | 33 | 22.9 |
| Head nurse or supervisor | 1 | 2.5 | — | — | 1 | 1.8 | 2 | 1.3 |
| Physician | 1 | 2.5 | — | — | 1 | 1.8 | 2 | 1.3 |
| Former teacher | 1 | 2.5 | — | — | 1 | 1.8 | 2 | 1.3 |
| Secondary loyalty | | | | | | | | |
| Self | 3 | 7.6 | 11 | 21.1 | 10 | 18.8 | 24 | 16.6 |
| Employing agent | 3 | 7.6 | — | — | 4 | 7.5 | 7 | 4.8 |
| Co-workers | 5 | 12.8 | 10 | 19.2 | 4 | 7.5 | 19 | 13.1 |
| Patients | 19 | 48.7 | 23 | 44.2 | 21 | 39.6 | 63 | 43.7 |
| Head nurse or supervisor | 2 | 5.1 | 1 | 1.9 | 4 | 7.5 | 7 | 4.8 |
| Physician | 2 | 5.1 | 2 | 3.8 | 7 | 13.2 | 11 | 7.6 |
| Former teacher | 2 | 5.1 | 1 | 1.9 | 1 | 1.8 | 4 | 2.7 |
| Third, fourth, and fifth loyalties | | | | | | | | |
| Self | 5 | 12.8 | 3 | 5.7 | 6 | 11.3 | 14 | 9.7 |
| Employing agent | 22 | 56.4 | 32 | 61.5 | 26 | 49.0 | 80 | 55.5 |
| Co-workers | 28 | 71.7 | 31 | 59.6 | 44 | 83.0 | 103 | 71.5 |
| Patients | 9 | 23.0 | 14 | 26.9 | 15 | 28.3 | 38 | 26.3 |
| Head nurse or supervisor | 25 | 64.1 | 34 | 65.3 | 30 | 56.6 | 89 | 61.8 |
| Physician | 13 | 33.3 | 19 | 36.5 | 30 | 56.6 | 62 | 43.0 |
| Former teacher | 10 | 25.6 | 4 | 7.6 | 9 | 16.9 | 23 | 15.9 |
| Sixth and seventh loyalties | | | | | | | | |
| Self | 3 | 7.6 | — | — | 1 | 1.8 | 4 | 2.7 |
| Employing agent | 12 | 30.7 | 17 | 32.6 | 23 | 43.3 | 52 | 36.1 |
| Co-workers | 4 | 10.2 | 3 | 5.7 | 5 | 9.4 | 12 | 8.3 |
| Patients | 3 | 7.6 | 1 | 1.9 | 3 | 5.6 | 7 | 4.8 |
| Head nurse or supervisor | 7 | 17.9 | 14 | 26.9 | 17 | 32.0 | 38 | 26.3 |
| Physician | 19 | 48.7 | 29 | 55.7 | 15 | 28.3 | 63 | 43.7 |
| Former teacher | 22 | 56.4 | 39 | 75.0 | 40 | 75.4 | 101 | 70.1 |

In some categories there were no answers.

**Table C-13.** Number and percent of graduates of classes of 1968, 1969, and 1970 according to employer's perception of importance placed upon their work as nurses

| | 1968 (N = 39) | | 1969 (N = 52) | | 1970 (N = 53) | | Total | |
|---|---|---|---|---|---|---|---|---|
| | NO. | PERCENT | NO. | PERCENT | NO. | PERCENT | NO. | PERCENT |
| Nurses place primary importance on opinion of | | | | | | | | |
| Physicians | 5 | 12.8 | 6 | 3.8 | 9 | 16.9 | 20 | 13.8 |
| Co-workers | 7 | 17.9 | 16 | 30.7 | 7 | 13.2 | 30 | 20.8 |
| Head nurses | 2 | 5.1 | 4 | 7.6 | 12 | 22.6 | 18 | 12.5 |
| Patients | 19 | 48.7 | 23 | 44.2 | 21 | 39.6 | 63 | 43.7 |
| Patients' relatives | 1 | 2.5 | — | — | 2 | 3.7 | 3 | 2.0 |
| Former teachers | 2 | 5.1 | 3 | 5.7 | 2 | 3.7 | 7 | 4.8 |
| Secondary importance | | | | | | | | |
| Physicians | 6 | 15.3 | 6 | 11.5 | 14 | 26.4 | 26 | 18.0 |
| Co-workers | 11 | 28.2 | 9 | 17.3 | 9 | 16.9 | 29 | 20.1 |
| Head nurses | 10 | 25.6 | 8 | 15.3 | 10 | 18.8 | 28 | 19.4 |
| Patients | 4 | 10.2 | 10 | 19.2 | 9 | 16.9 | 23 | 15.9 |
| Patients' relatives | 5 | 12.8 | 14 | 26.9 | 8 | 15.0 | 27 | 18.7 |
| Former teachers | — | — | 5 | 9.6 | 3 | 5.6 | 8 | 5.5 |
| Third and fourth importance | | | | | | | | |
| Physicians | 16 | 41.0 | 17 | 32.6 | 12 | 22.6 | 45 | 31.2 |
| Co-workers | 14 | 35.8 | 21 | 40.3 | 24 | 45.2 | 59 | 40.9 |
| Head nurses | 20 | 51.2 | 22 | 42.3 | 24 | 45.2 | 66 | 45.8 |
| Patients | 10 | 25.6 | 10 | 19.2 | 17 | 32.0 | 37 | 25.6 |
| Patients' relatives | 7 | 17.9 | 12 | 23.0 | 19 | 35.8 | 38 | 26.3 |
| Former teachers | 5 | 12.8 | 8 | 15.3 | 6 | 11.3 | 11 | 13.1 |
| Least importance | | | | | | | | |
| Physicians | 9 | 23.0 | 18 | 34.6 | 18 | 33.9 | 45 | 31.2 |
| Co-workers | 5 | 12.8 | 4 | 7.6 | 13 | 24.5 | 22 | 15.2 |
| Head nurses | 4 | 10.2 | 16 | 30.7 | 7 | 13.2 | 27 | 18.7 |
| Patients | 3 | 7.6 | 7 | 13.4 | 4 | 7.5 | 14 | 9.7 |
| Patients' relatives | 22 | 56.4 | 24 | 46.1 | 22 | 41.5 | 68 | 47.2 |
| Former teachers | 29 | 74.3 | 35 | 67.3 | 38 | 71.6 | 102 | 70.8 |

In some categories there were no answers.

**Table C-14.** Analysis of variance by ranks of classes on job functions: Kruskal Wallis

| Function | Class of 1968 (N = 39) Rank sum | Class of 1969 (N = 52) Rank sum | Class of 1970 (N = 53) Rank sum | H | Sig. |
|---|---|---|---|---|---|
| Professional | 2341.5 | 3676.5 | 4422.0 | 7.249 | .027 |
| Baseline | 2628.5 | 3559.5 | 4252.0 | 2.921 | .232 |
| Technical | 2638.0 | 3523.5 | 4278.5 | 3.302 | .192 |

**Table C-15.** Significance of differences between classes on professional job functions: Mann Whitney U

| Classes | Rank sum | U | Prob |
|---|---|---|---|
| 1968-1969 | 1663.0 | 883.0 | .1462 |
| 1968-1970 | 1458.5 | 678.5 | .0025 |
| 1969-1970 | 2531.5 | 1153.5 | .0746 |

# MULTIVARIATE ANALYSIS ON OPERATIONALIZATION OF PROFESSIONAL BEHAVIOR

In the description of the data analysis of the nurses in the three classes on the variables selected to represent the construct, "operationalization of professional behavior," the data were collected at different times and under different conditions. Fox example, information needed to construct the Index of Professionalism was obtained mostly by questionnaire and was available for almost the entire sample. Empathy scores, on the other hand, required that the nurse's head nurse or co-worker be interviewed; these data were available for only about three fifths of the group.° This makes regression analysis on the whole group of variables less meaningful. Such multivariate analysis was also complicated by the fact that the data on some of the variables were not interval in nature and did not completely meet the assumption of normality of distribution. However, with the above reserva-

tions in mind and applying normalizing operations where necessary, a stepwise discriminant analysis (BMDO7M) was made, based on the following variables: change agent effectiveness,† Professional Index, the Tc and I scores from the POI, Professional role behavior, Professional role conception, and empathy. Only those subgroups of nurses on which there was complete data on all of the above variables were included in the analysis; this therefore means that the sample was restricted to those 92 (out of a possible 161) nurses whose head nurse or co-worker had been interviewed. The purpose of doing the discriminant analysis was to ascertain which of the above variables best discriminated between the control and experimental groups; in other words, which variable was the best predictor of the placement of an individual into the proper group. At each step in the analysis the variable was entered that conditioned on the variables already entered, had the largest F ratio for testing equality between groups. The order in which the variables entered into the analysis (which can be taken as an order of the importance of the variable in discriminating between groups) and the percent of correct prediction were as follows:

| Variable | Percent of correct prediction |
|---|---|
| Professional index | 64.13 |
| Empathy | 66.30 |
| I score of POI | 72.83 |
| Change agent effectiveness | 69.57 |
| Professional role conception | 67.39 |
| Professional role behavior | 68.48 |
| Tc score of POI | 69.57 |

It is evident from this analysis that the Professional Index was the single best indicator but that the combination of the Professional Index, empathy score, and inner-directedness on the POI yielded the highest possible correct prediction rate. This means that if you

---

°Change agent effectiveness scores were obtained by multiplying each change activity reported by someone other than the subject (that is, either head nurse or co-worker or random selection if both were available) by the following factors: very effective change was multiplied by 3; some adherents or effective but reversed was multiplied by 2; tried but not effective was multiplied by 1.
†It was unfortunate that all nurses could not arrange for interviews with head nurses or co-workers, making it possible to gather complete sets of data on these variables. However, analysis of the variance on the variables where it was possible to compare the two groups indicated no significant difference. Means and standard deviations of the two groups on each of the five variables is as follows:

Comparison of scores of nurses who arranged for interviews with head nurse or co-worker (N = 92) and those who did not (N = 69)

| | Those who did | | Those who did not | |
|---|---|---|---|---|
| Variable | X | SD | X | SD |
| Tc on POI | 18.97 | 2.29 | 18.95 | 2.37 |
| I on POI | 91.66 | 9.69 | 91.61 | 9.26 |
| Professional index | 6.58 | 4.49 | 6.24 | 4.21 |
| Professional role behavior | 44.58 | 4.87 | 44.52 | 4.21 |
| Professional role conception | 30.42 | 3.57 | 29.72 | 3.24 |

know an individual's scores on these three variables, you probably can correctly place him into either the group that had had the Anticipatory Socialization program or a group that had not. The other variables tended to confirm the correct placement but did not help the accuracy of prediction. In terms of operationalization of professional values; therefore, it would seem that Professional Index, empathy, and inner-directedness scores are the best discriminators.

# INDEX

**A**

"Adhocracy," 12, 226
American Medical Association, 48
American Nurses' Association, 84, 116
Anticipatory socialization program, 34, 36-38, 41, 47, 50, 51, 53, 57, 61, 67-102, 216, 217, 218, 226, 228
  attitudinal components, 78-79
  attrition rate, 96-98
    time differential, 97
  "awareness" model, 74
  change agent model, 74
  cost-reward model, 74
  effectiveness, 96-102
  effects of, 104-135
    employer evaluation, 126-134
      behavior and preferences, 131
      function evaluation, 132-133
      performance comparison, 129
    integrative role behavior junction, 105, 113-114
    job turnover and exodus junction, 104, 108-113
      initial job tenure, 109
    professional loyalty and behavior junction, 105, 114-125
    role deprivation school junction, 104, 105-106
      role conception-deprivation scores, 106, 114
    role deprivation work junction, 104, 107-108
      BPS scores, 107
  Hawthorne effects, 101
  knowledge components, 75-78
  phases, 69-75
  reference groups, 79-96
    Bicultural Troublemakers, 91-96
    comparison of, 93
    Lateral Arabesquers, 87-91
    Organization Women, 84-87
    Rutters, 80-84
  role configurations, 79
  social influence theory, 76
  value changes, 99-100
Argyris, C., 33
Asch, S. E., 77
Asch experiments, 77

**B**

Beckhard, R., 226
Benne, K., 22

Benner, Patricia, 167-188, 191-215
Bennis, W. G., 12, 22, 74
Bicultural Troublemakers, 91-96
Biculturalism, 161-163, 218, 227
Blau, P. M., 17
Brim, O. G., 40
Business school graduates, and professional-bureaucratic work conflict, 18

**C**

California State College, 22, 24, 115
Change agent activity, 55-56, 74, 117-123, 121
  effectiveness, 120, 122
  recipient, 120-121
Christ, E., 117
Cleveland, H., 161
Clinical ambiguity, 196-197
Competency gap, 196, 197
Compliance, 34
Conflict, work, professional-bureaucratic; *see* Professional-bureaucratic work conflict
Corwin, R. G., 17-24, 33, 37, 47, 48, 49, 53, 56, 57, 81, 114
Corwin Professional Value Scale, 56
Corwin Role Conception Scale, 37, 49, 53, 56, 57, 81, 114
Corwin Role Deprivation Scale, 47, 49, 53
Cottrell, L. S., Jr., 28
Culture assimilator programs, 10-11
Culture shock, 10-11, 76
  examples, 7
  and reality shock
    differences, 8-10
    similarities, 4-8

**D**

Davis, F., 104
Deutsch, M., 33
Dornbusch, S. M., 148
Dymond, R. F., 123

**E**

Effectiveness of Change Scale, 218
Empathy, 218
  testing, 123-125, 124
Employer evaluation, 126-134
  behavior and preferences, 131

Employer evaluation—cont'd
   function evaluation, 132-133
   performance comparison, 129
Enculturation, 211-213
Etzioni, Amitai, 72

**F**
Foote, N., 28
Foster, G., 76

**G**
Gardner, John, 193
Generation gap, 196, 197-198
Glaser, R., 74
Goffman, E., 140
Goldstein, K., 124
Graduate nurse
   attrition rate, 29
   ineffectiveness, 28-32
   professional-bureaucratic work conflict; *see* Professional-bureaucratic work conflict
   role transformation from student, 137-139
   socialization; *see* Postgraduate nurse socialization
Graham, L., 153
Guthrie, G. M., 10

**H**
Habenstein, R., 117
Heckmat, H., 124
High school teachers, and professional-bureaucratic work conflict, 17-18
Hogan, C., 23, 24, 115
*Hospitals*, 48
Hovland, C. I., 43, 144
Hughes, E., 17

**I**
Identification, 34
Industrialization, effects, 11-13
Integrative role behavior, 54-55, 105, 113-114
   scales, 217
Internalization, 34
Interpersonal competence, 30

**J**
Job turnover, 104, 108-113
   initial job tenure, 109
Johnson, N., 11

**K**
Kahn, R., 77
Katz, D., 77
Kelly, H., 74
Kelman, H., 34, 145
Kraegel, J. M., 45
Kramer, M., 33, 167-189
Kramer Behavior Strategy Scale, 56
Kramer Role Behavior Scale, 57

**L**
Lateral Arabesquers, 87-91, 159-160
Lippitt, R., 163
Luchins, A. S., 145

**M**
McGuire, W., 42, 43, 44, 50, 69
Maslow, A. H., 124, 125

Mauksch, H. O., 28
Merton, R. K., 34, 36, 50
*Modern Organizations*, 72
Moffitt Hospital, 108
Moore, W. E., 209

**N**
National League for Nurses, 48, 84, 116
Nostrand, H., 4
Nurse graduate; *see* Graduate nurse
Nurse educators, 225-227
Nurse's aides, as socialization agents, 139-141
Nursing school, socialization, 40

**O**
Olesen, V. L., 40, 44, 104
Olmsted, A. G., 40, 41
Organization Women, 84-87

**P**
Paget, M. A., 40, 41
Papageorgis, D., 43, 44
Patient care, reality shock effects, 219-221
Patients, as socialization agents, 142
Paynich, M. L., 31
Perls, F., 125
Personal Orientation Inventory, 57, 81, 218
Peter, L. J., 160
Physicians, as socialization agents, 141-142
Postgraduate nurse socialization, 137-189
   agents, 138, 139-144
      formal socializers, 142
      nurse's aides, 139-140
      other socializers, 143
      patients, 142
      perception of, 144
      physicians, 141
      resocialization of, 223-224
   case history, 166-189
   cyclical nature, 154-155
   experience content of, 149-154
      behavioral, 153-154
      normative, 150-153
   methods, 144-149
      exposition, 147-148
      formal, 147
      informal, 148-149
   objectives, 228
   process, 155-164
      conflict resolution, 159-164
      moral outrage, 158-159
      skill and routine mastery, 155-157
      social integration, 157-158
   role transformation, 137-139
Professional-bureaucratic work conflict, 3
   of business school graduates, 18
   development, 11-18
   graduate nurse's dilemma, 27-28
   of high school teachers, 17-18
   of nurses, 19-24
   resolution of, 32-33
      anticipatory socialization in; *see* Anticipatory socialization program
      reality shock program in; *see* Reality shock program
      social influence theory in; *see* Social influence theory
      sociological immunization in, 42-45

Professional–bureaucratic work conflict—cont'd
  social workers, 16-17
Professionalism, Index of, 56-57, 116, 217

**R**

Racial conflict, 196, 198-199
Reality shock, 68
  and culture shock
    differences, 8-10
    similarities, 4-8
  defined, 3-4
  effects on patient care, 219-221
  examples, 7
  implications, 219-232
  summary of findings, 216-219
Reality shock program, 53, 191-214
  enculturation, 211-213
  graduate vantage points, 206-213
  role transformation conflicts, 192-199
    cosmopolitan versus local view, 195
    explicit versus implied objectives, 194-195
    professional-bureaucratic, 193-194
  seminars, 199-206
Reinkemeyer, A., 28
Risk-taking, 163
Ritualism, 197
Rogers, E. M., 56
Role adaptation, 34
Role behavior, 52
  integrative, 54-55, 105, 113-114
Role conception, 52, 54
Role configuration, 34, 52, 79
Role conflict, allocative discrepancy as source of, 210
Role deprivation, 53, 54, 216, 217
  school junction, 104, 105-106
  work junction, 104, 107-108
Role negotiation, 76
Role transformation, 217
  conflicts, 192-199
  from student to graduate nurse, 137-139
Rosow, I., 159
Rutters, 80-84

**S**

Schein, E., 18, 148
School and College Ability Tests (SCAT), 58
Scott, W. R., 13, 16, 17
Self-actualization, 124
Self-confidence, 29-32
Shock; see also Culture shock; Reality shock
  versus stress, 10
Shostrom, E. L., 57, 81, 125, 218
Shostrom Personal Orientation Inventory, 57, 81, 218

Simms, L., 117
Social influence theory, 34-36, 76
Social workers, and professional-bureaucratic work conflict, 16-17
Socialization, 27-32
  anticipatory; see Anticipatory socialization program congruent
    attitudes and values versus behavior, 39-40
  nursing school, 40
  postgraduate; see Postgraduate nurse socialization
  principles, 42
  professional, 38-42
  punishment-centered theory, 39
Socialization program; see Anticipatory socialization program
Sociological immunization, 42-45, 47
Spiegel, J. P., 210
Strauss, A., 74
Stress versus shock, 10

**T**

Theiss, M., 124
Thibaut, J., 74
Thomas, L., 28
Time Competence Scale, 81

**U**

University of California School of Nursing, 61, 108

**V**

Value capitulation, 160
Veterans Administration, 198

**W**

Waters, V., 28
Watson, G., 74
Weinstein, E., 30
Weiss, W., 145
Whittaker, E. W., 40, 44
Williams, M., 40
Williams, T., 40
Work conflict, professional-bureaucratic; see Professional-bureaucratic work conflict
Work organization systems
  active and inert tasks, 14
  evolution of, 11-16
    effects of industrialization, 11-12
    human relations approach, 12
    patrimonial, 11
  examples, 14-16
  part-task, 13
  whole-task, 13-14